Mother Tongue

Mother Tongue

How Humans Create Language

by Joel Davis

A Birch Lane Press Book
Published by Carol Publishing Group

A Birch Lane Press Book
Published by Carol Publishing Group
Birch Lane Press is a registered trademark of Carol Communications, Inc.
Editorial Offices: 600 Madison Avenue, New York, N.Y. 10022
Sales and Distribution Offices: 120 Enterprise Avenue, Secaucus, N.J. 07094
In Canada: Canadian Manda Group, P.O. Box 920, Station U, Toronto, Ontario M8Z 5P9
Queries regarding rights and permissions should be addressed to
Carol Publishing Group, 600 Madison Avenue, New York, N.Y. 10022

Carol Publishing Group books are available at special discounts for bulk purchases, for sales promotion, fund-raising, or educational purposes. Special editions can be created to specifications. For details, contact: Special Sales Department, Carol Publishing Group, 120 Enterprise Avenue, Secaucus, N.J. 07094

Manufactured in the United States of America
10 9 8 7 6 5 4 3 2 1

Library of Congress Cataloging-in-Publication Data

Davis, Joel, 1948-
Mother tongue : how humans create language / by Joel Davis.
p. cm.
"A Birch Lane Press book."
ISBN 1-55972-206-1
1. Language and languages. I. Title.
P106.D295 1993
400—dc20 93-11341
CIP

For Ryan Patrick Nash

Contents

PREFACE

THE MYSTERY OF OUR MOTHER TONGUE

Is language a uniquely human ability, one that distinguishes humans from other animals on Earth? That may well be true. However, it is certainly not the popular belief today. Many of us are convinced that other animals possess language; chimpanzees, whales, and dolphins usually stand at the top of the list. The hard scientific evidence for language use in other species, though, is scant at best. But we need not invoke the image of chimps speaking to invest language with a sense of awe. Human language, all by itself, remains one of our most fascinating and mysterious abilities.

We humans have been creating and using language for tens of thousands of years, at the very least. We have thought about it and studied it in one way or another for more than three thousand years, and we have examined it with the tools of the scientific method for more than a century. Yet we still come up hard against some fundamental questions:

- What is language? How did it come to be?

- What do the things that so many languages have in common say about language, about human communication, and about being human?

And perhaps the most fascinating and mysterious questions of all:

- How do we learn language? How is it stored in the brain?

Mother Tongue: How Humans Create Language tries to answer these questions. It presents some of the most recent research conducted by linguists, biologists, neurosurgeons, psychologists, and other scientists around the world. A few of them are well known, such as the world-famous linguist Noam Chomsky. Most, though, are not; few of us have yet heard of Antonio Damasio, or Janet Werker. But all these explorers of the brain and mind are changing the way we think about our ability to communicate. I hope that this journey into the multileveled universe of human language will lead you to a radically new understanding of how human infants learn language, and how the human brain stores, retrieves—and sometimes loses—language.

Mother Tongue is divided into three main parts: *Language, Yesterday and Today; Language and the Brain*; and *The Birth of Language*.

The opening chapters in Part I, *Language, Yesterday and Today*, set the stage for the rest of the book. They present suggested answers to the question: What is language? These first chapters also provide background information about the biological mechanisms that allow us to speak; they look at the kind of sounds we humans can make and actually use in language, and they summarize the development of linguistics as a science. With this information in hand and mind, we can then begin to explore two of the paramount questions facing linguistics today: How do infants learn language? How do their brains store it?

The next two parts of the book, *Language and the Brain* and *The Birth of Language*, are the meat and potatoes of *Mother Tongue*. Here we begin examining the core questions. These chapters focus on several researchers who have made major breakthroughs in our understanding of how the brain stores languages, and how infants actually acquire and come to use language. In the chapters of Part II, for example, we will meet George Ojemann of the University of Washington and Antonio and Hanna Damasio at the University of Iowa. In Part III, we will encounter Janet Werkman of the University of British

Columbia and Laura Ann Petitto at McGill University in Montreal. We will also meet the famous and controversial linguist Noam Chomsky, baby-babbling expert D. Kimbrough Oller of the University of Miami, infant-language expert Elizabeth Bates of the University of California at San Diego, and other pioneers of contemporary linguistics and psychology.

Mother Tongue follows these researchers as they continue to work in their areas. We will learn about their findings, often in their own words. And we will learn some intriguing and remarkable facts about language, infants, and the human brain:

- Despite what many experts hitherto believed, Broca's area, a region in the brain's left hemisphere about the size of a chicken egg, is not the only place in the brain where language is stored.
- The human brain acts like a parallel computer with many different parts interconnected, or a piece of highly sophisticated software, processing language in time rather than in space.
- The brain may contain special microscopic regions of nerve cells that handle different parts of language, such as verbs and grammar.
- Infant babbling is much more than random noises, and even deaf children can babble—on their hands instead of with their lips.
- From birth until age two, an infant's brain is capable of learning any language, with any combination of sounds.
- Victims of strokes and head injuries can teach us a lot about how the brain learns, loses, and relearns language.

This book could not have been completed without the help of many people. In particular, I want to thank my agent, Joshua Bilmes of Scott Meredith Literary Agency, Inc., for his constant encouragement and helpful feedback; Dr. Antonio Damasio, Dr. George Ojemann, Dr. D. Kimbrough Oller, Dr. Laura Ann Petitto, and Dr. Janet Werker, for the gifts of their time and knowledge; Dr. John Cramer, for explaining neural networks; Frank Catalano, for explaining HyperCard software; and Hillel Black at Birch Lane Press for approaching me in the first place with his enthusiasm for a book on language and the brain.

Most of the recent research about how we create language and languages has never before appeared in popular book form. The reports by linguists, psychologists, brain surgeons, and other scientists on the cutting edge of language study have mostly been published either in scientific journals or in highly technical books. Several researchers, including the Damasios and Drs. Ojemann, Oller, Petitto, and Werker, were kind enough to send me copies of their articles and reports. I wish to acknowledge their help in this regard. The librarians at Eastern Washington University, Gonzaga University's Foley Library, Cowles Library at Whitworth College, and the Spokane County and City library systems all helped me greatly by finding the many books and articles I needed to research this book. In addition, several of our best popular science writers have written about recent advances in language research. They include William F. Allman in *U.S. News and World Report*, Sandra Blakeslee in the *New York Times*, Bruce Bower in *Science News*, John Horgan in *Scientific American*, and Roger Lewin and Virginia Morrell in *Science*. Their articles and news reports proved a valuable source of information and helped lead me to the scientific researchers themselves. Their works are fully cited in the bibliography.

Finally, I wish to especially thank my wife, Judy Davis, for her continuing support and cheerful patience with my weird writer's ways.

I hope you find *Mother Tongue* to be more than a dry scientific tome about a subject most of us have never heard of. We all use language; we swim in it, like fish in a sea of words and sentences. We are never outside of language. Most of the time, we don't think about the miracle we perform each time we open our mouths to speak or lift our hands to sign.

But for those of us who have children or grandchildren, language is a miracle. We see it unfolding before our eyes. My own grandson, Ryan Patrick Nash, even now is making the journey from cries and gurgles into babbling, sound imitation, and—soon, perhaps—his first words. None of us can recall what it was like to travel from no-language to language. The experience is apparently lost to us all, forever locked away in some inaccessible part of our brain. But when we watch the Ryan Nashes in our lives begin their journey, we get a glimpse of the one each of us took, so many years ago.

How does he do it? How did *we* do it?

We are beginning to learn some of the answers. And the process of learning them feels a bit like putting together a jigsaw puzzle. The pieces have been widely scattered throughout different rooms of our house. Many come from the linguistics room, but not all. Some of the pieces we have found in biology, others in neuroscience. Still more came from psychology, and some from medicine. We have even found a few in a new addition to the house, the room called computer science. We have slowly, painstakingly searched for and found them. Now we are putting them together. It is a wondrous picture that begins to emerge.

Meanwhile, oblivious to our puzzle solving, a young child named Ryan Nash—who may someday be a linguist, or a brain surgeon, or a hacker, or a lunar colonist, or who knows what—is busy learning to say *Mama!* And learning what that means.

He is learning his father's and mother's language. He is learning his mother tongue.

PART ONE

LANGUAGE, YESTERDAY AND TODAY

CHAPTER 1

DEFINING LANGUAGE

Ryan Patrick Nash was about five weeks old when he began smiling at me. And despite the fact that I "knew better," that moment felt magical. I knew intellectually that Ryan did not know who I was—not even the way he could identify his mother, my stepdaughter Kirsten. I realized that he could not recognize me as a specific individual whom he felt genuinely happy to see. And I understood intellectually that Ryan was smiling (1) because a smile is a primate facial expression that means "I'm harmless," and (2) because a smile brings to the smiler pro-survival responses from the one smiled upon, such as food, protection, and touches, and (3) that smiling has therefore become a reflex genetically hardwired into primates. All of this I knew, and it didn't matter one bit. Ryan smiled, and I turned to butter.

A week later, Ryan started adding interesting noises—*modulated* noises. I heard no meaning in the sounds; but the sounds themselves had a pattern. Ryan sounded as if he were talking, or trying to talk without the requisite vocabulary. Babbling with no meaning, my grandson was less than two months out of the womb and already taking the first firm step toward language.

In doing so, Ryan Patrick Nash did what untold billions of human infants before him have done. Firmly and unequivocally, he identified himself as one of us. As human. He is the latest creator and user of language in a line that may well reach back some two hundred thousand years.

Since the early 1970s, a far-flung cadre of scientists has created an explosion of new knowledge about *infant language acquisition*, how human infants create and learn their mother tongues. At the same time, these and other researchers have begun uncovering new and at times controversial nuggets of information about the role played by the human brain in language acquisition and use. Both areas of scientific endeavor have achieved a crucial position in the development of a new and still-emerging field called *cognitive science*. Cognitive science is the science of *cognition*, the systematic study of how we know, perceive, and thus think. Larger in its purview than psychology, a scientific discipline with which it has great affinity, cognitive science also embraces neurology, linguistics, computer intelligence, and even the mathematics of chaos. It is a scientific discipline filled with promise and excitement, and also with plenty of pitfalls.

This is not surprising, of course. Science is a human activity and therefore fraught with all the potential and actual shortcomings of humans. We humans may pride ourselves on our rationality, but we are often less than rational. Scientists may insist that they are always objective, but no human is ever truly objective, and that includes scientists. We all have our own sets of prejudices, preconceptions, and personal priorities. So cognitive science and scientists make mistakes and stumble over assumptions. Then they pick themselves up and go on, hopefully learning from their missteps. All fields of science go through this process, particularly new and developing fields.

Another point to keep in mind is this: science—if it is truly science—must offer theories and hypotheses that are *falsifiable*. If a hypothesis cannot be proven wrong, then it is not scientific. For example, "creationism" or "creation science" is a theological argument, not a scientific theory of the origin of species. Creationism is based on the assumption of the inherent and unalterable truth of a particular set of religious and spiritual writings known collectively as the Bible. If the stories in the Bible are assumed to be true, and cannot be false, then there is no point in testing them against the evidence of our senses, of nature, of reason. Science insists that all speculations, hypotheses, and theories be testable. They must be offered up to the bright glare of reason, compared to the wordless but shouted stories of nature, tested by the testimony of our eyes and ears and fingers. Because theological belief systems cannot or will not submit to this process, they cannot be falsifiable. They cannot call themselves scientific, and be truthful. They may contain truth—"There are more things in heaven and earth ... Than are dreamt of in your philosophy," Shakespeare wrote in *Hamlet* nearly four hundred years ago—but they are not science.

Unfalsifiable hypotheses and theories that crop up in some scientific discipline are not science, either. Cognitive science has had more than its share of intriguing speculations masquerading as scientific hypotheses. So has the science of language, over the decades of its existence. But cognitive science will begin to mature as its practitioners sharpen their intellectual and rational prowess, and as they call into play an increasingly powerful and accurate collection of tools. The same maturing process has already occurred in the science of language. Nowhere has this been more evident than in our increasing understanding of the interrelationship of language, infants, and the brain.

THE SCIENCE OF LANGUAGE

Linguistics is the science that studies language and languages. In order to study language, linguists use language. This makes linguistics unique among sciences, for linguists must use the subject of their science as the means of discussing the subject of their science. It is a linguistic Ouroboros in which linguists take part, tail and mouth and body.

Biological linguistics is the study of the biological conditions for language development and use in humans. This field includes not only the biological aspects of infant development but also the evolutionary aspects of the origin of language in the human species. This particular area of study is the subject matter of only a handful of linguists, most of them in Russia. Perhaps it is better named as *paleolinguistics*, in a parallel with paleontology, or *evolutionary linguistics*.

Another subfield of linguistics is *neurolinguistics*, the study of the neurological basis of language development and use in humans. Neurolinguistics is particularly concerned with the role of the brain in infant language acquisition. *Psycholinguistics* deals with the relationship between language and the psychological processes that underlie it, including memory. In recent years several researchers have begun forging intriguing links between neurolinguistics and psycholinguistics. For if memory is, as mounting evidence indicates, a biologically based phenomenon in the brain, then deep and powerful connections must exist between memory and language. And those connections must begin developing from day one of a baby's life.

It has been said that *Homo sapiens* is the animal that talks. The implication, often stated outright, is that the possession and use of language distinguishes us from all other living creatures on this planet. It is self-evident that we do possess and use languages, thousands of them, in fact. It may not be true that we are the only creatures on Earth possessing language. Indeed, the time may not be far off when a whole new order of beings—nonbiological beings, namely computers or sophisticated computer programs—will create and use their own language. And in a galaxy with more than two hundred billion stars and who knows how many other self-aware sentient species, not even the possession of language will make us unique.

For that matter, we cannot even settle on a universally accepted definition of "language." This is a somewhat embarrassing situation for linguistics and linguists. English is a language. So are Amharic, Danish, Goajiro, ikiGusii, Mon, Ojibway, Tagalog, Uigur, Yiddish, and Zyrien. So is Latin, although no society, nation, or tribe uses it today as a native tongue. Is American Sign Language (ASL, sometimes just called "Sign") a real language? Is it a language when humans use it? What about when chimpanzees use it? Do dolphins and whales possess language? What about the dances of bees?

The American writer Charles Dudley Warner once wrote, "Everybody talks about the weather, but nobody does anything about it." Something similar might be said of language. Everybody uses language, but nobody knows quite how to define it. Some of the world's most renowned linguists have taken a stab at it, with the following results:

- Edward Sapir, 1921: "Language is a purely human and non-instinctive method of communicating ideas, emotions, and desires by means of voluntarily produced symbols."
- G. Trager, 1949: "A language is a system of arbitrary vocal symbols by means of which the members of a society interact in terms of their total culture."
- Noam Chomsky, 1957: A language is "a set (finite or infinite) of sentences, each finite in length and constructed out of a finite set of elements."
- Robert A. Hall, 1964: Language is "the institution whereby humans communicate and interact with each other by means of habitually used oral-auditory arbitrary symbols."

Still another definition describes language as a structural system of vocal symbols by which a social group communicates. Linguists long considered this definition acceptable. It made common sense. However, some animal species—such as porpoises and several primates—live in social groupings and communicate using vocal sounds. Are the sounds symbols? Are the animals using language? By the 1960s this definition seemed untenable, and another arose: language is a system of rules that relate sound sequences to meanings. Although this definition does not exclude animal languages, it does sidestep the previous definition's difficulties. "Okay," linguists seemed to be saying, "if you can prove that the sound sequences made by these animals relate to specific meanings, then we'll consider the possibility that they're using language."

This definition, however, has its own inherent difficulty. It elminates from the category "language" any *nonverbal* communication of meaning. For example, American Sign Language cannot be considered a language under this definition. Perhaps we need a modification of this latter definition, substituting "communicative" for "sound." This would include American Sign Language, and other sign languages, as a legitimate language. It would also open the door for exploring other sensory modalities of communication—touch, for example, or scent. We know that many animals communicate using the chemical senses of taste and smell; even humans send nonverbal messages via the chemicals (called pheromones) in sweat.

A set of inclusive and meaningful definitions can be found in a good standard dictionary (*Webster's Ninth New Collegiate Dictionary*, 1988):

- **lan·guage** . . . [ME, fr. OF, fr. *langue* tongue, language, fr. L *lingua* . . .](13c) **1 a** : the words, their pronunciation, and the methods of combining them used and understood by a considerable community **b** (1) : audible, articulate, meaningful sound as produced by the action of the vocal organs (2) : a systematic means of communicating ideas or feelings by the use of conventionalized signs, sounds, gestures, or marks having understood meanings (3) : the suggestion by objects, actions, or conditions of associated ideas or feelings . . . (4) : the means by which animals communicate (5) : a formal system of signs and symbols (as FORTRAN or a calculus in logic) including rules for the formation and transformation of admissible expressions . . . **2 a** : form or manner of verbal expression; *specif* : STYLE **b** : the vocabulary and phraseology belonging to an art or a department of knowledge . . .

The formulations in 1b (1) and (2) stand out as simple but inclusive definitions of what most of us understand language to be. Most language uses sound produced by human vocal cords. The sounds must be "audible, articulate," and "meaningful" to constitute language. The sounds must also have "understood meanings." We combine those sounds in various ways, following a set of rules peculiar to our particular society or community (or both), and thus create a "systematic means of communicating ideas [and] emotions."

However, language is not limited to sounds. We also recognize the importance of gesture in communication. Indeed, considerable evidence exists that we communicate as much or more by our "body language" as we do by our "verbal language." Our facial expressions as we talk with another person, for example, play a powerful role in our communication. If I should tell young Ryan Patrick that I love him, but scowl angrily as I do so, he is liable to get a rather confusing and upsetting message. When I smile happily as I tell him that, however, my facial expression reinforces my verbal communication. In fact, we now know that signs and gestures alone can be used to create real, fully functional language. ASL and other sign languages are now known to be true languages. They have extensive vocabularies, complex grammar and syntactic structures, and even their own dialects and slang. Sign languages are part of what we know as language.

Noam Chomsky is probably the most famous—indeed, the *only* famous—linguist of our times. We will encounter Chomsky again in our journey into the realms of language, babies, and brains. He occupies a central place in the development of modern linguistics, and much recent brain research appears to confirm theories he first proposed in the late 1950s. It is Chomsky's contention that language's essential property is its ability to provide us with a vehicle for expressing "indefinitely many thoughts and for reacting appropriately in an indefinite range of new situations."

Hockett's Criteria

Most linguists avoid the problem of defining language by choosing a comparative approach. They try to identify the characteristics common to all human languages, and thus what is "most important" or essential to any human language. To this end linguists have followed two main paths. The first leads to the identification of universal structural properties. The other compares human language with nonhuman and nonlinguistic human methods of communication. It is this latter path that leads us to at least an approximation of a definition of language.

In following the paths of comparison, linguists are like taxonomists, biologists who identify and catalog the different species of life. Taxonomy may seem more like cataloging than science. However, most of today's sciences started off by observing nature and cataloging what was seen. Science is by its very nature a way of understanding the universe by mentally breaking it apart into small, easily examined pieces. Without the efforts of the taxonomists and other catalogers, science cannot do what it does so well. Language as a subject of scientific study may never be able to lend itself to the process of repeatable experimentation. But lest we forget, astronomy, astrophysics, and cosmology are preeminently observational and not experimental sciences. But they are nonetheless three of the best known, most exciting sciences of our time.

Probably the most effective and widely used comparative approach to defining language comes from American linguist Charles Hockett.

Hockett identfied thirteen "design features" shared by all spoken language:

1. *Auditory-vocal channel:* Sound is the method of communication, and communication goes from mouth to ear. This design feature, by the way, excludes information transmission by means of visually perceived hand movements. Perhaps we could include "or hand movement–visual channel" in this design feature.
2. *Broadcast transmission and directional reception:* Anyone anywhere within earshot can hear the signal, and can identify the source of the transmission because of the directional ability of the human ear. In the case of Sign, anyone within visual range can see the signals and thus visually identify the transmission source.
3. *Rapid fading:* Unlike writing, verbal (and hand) signals are transient and fade quickly.
4. *Interchangeability:* People can reproduce any linguistic message they can understand, no matter who (or what, such as male or female) they are.
5. *Total feedback:* The person creating the communication can hear or see what he or she is creating. This is different from some visual mating displays used by animals, which the displayer cannot see.
6. *Specialization:* There is no biological or other function to the sounds made in verbal language other than the transmission of information. When a dog pants, for example, it is not making language or saying, "I'm hot." Panting is simply a biological function.
7. *Semanticity:* The parts of the signal have stable associations with the real world and real-world events. This allows them to convey meaning. In English, for example, the verbal signal *tree* means a specific type of plant. Its association with that real-world entity is a stable one. I don't have to worry about waking up tomorrow morning and finding that *tree* suddenly means what *computer keyboard* meant yesterday.
8. *Arbitrariness:* "Association," however, is not the same as "dependence." The elements of the linguistic signal are not linked in any *substantive* fashion to the nature of the reality whose

meaning they convey. The speed of bee dancing is directly related to the distance of the nectar from the hive. But the sounds or structure of the word *tree* or of the phrase "The leaves of the tree are falling" has no such connection to trees, leaves, or the force of gravity.

9. *Discreteness:* A small set of elements clearly different from one another make up the basic repertoire of the communication system. This is why emotional sounds do not qualify as language. Growls, moans, and cries vary continuously in strength; they are not made of discrete contrasting elements.
10. *Displacement:* The communication system binds time or space. That is, it can be used to convey information about events remote in space or time from the now. By contrast, the vocalizations and cries of most animals are responses to immediate stimuli.
11. *Productivity:* Old elements can be combined in new ways to express and respond to novel ideas and environmental stimuli. German often does this by linking elements together into new and very long words. English often does it by combining old words into new phrases (*acid rain* or *greenhouse effect*, for example), or by combining prefixes, suffixes, or other word-fragments into new words (*astronaut*).
12. *Traditional transmission:* The communication system is not passed on to new generations genetically, but rather by the process of teaching and learning. The verbal sounds that express certain emotions, such as crying or laughing, are almost certainly encoded in our genetic makeup. But we must *learn* the *words* we use to express our thoughts and feelings.
13. *Duality of patterning:* Though the sounds of language themselves have no intrinsic meaning, they combine to create basic elements that do. By contrast, chimpanzee cries *do* have intrinsic meanings that are genetically passed on through the species; these verbalizations thus fail to meet this particular criterion of Hockett for true language.

Other communication methods have some of these features, but not all. The following table, based on one in *The Cambridge Encyclopedia of Language*, compares five communication systems—including human language—employing Hockett's thirteen criteria.

Communication Systems and Hockett's Criteria

	Human language	*Gibbon calls*	*Western meadowlark song*	*Bee dancing*
Vocal-auditory channel	yes	yes	yes	no
Broadcast transmission, directional reception	yes	yes	yes	yes
Rapid fading	yes	yes, repeated	yes	unknown
Interchangeability	yes	yes	unknown	limited
Total feedback	yes	yes	yes	unknown
Specialization	yes	yes	possibly yes	unknown
Semanticity	yes	yes	partly, perhaps	yes
Arbitrariness	yes	yes	yes, if semantic	no
Discreteness	yes	yes	unknown	no
Displacement	often yes	no	unknown	yes (always)
Productivity	yes	no	unknown	yes
Traditional transmission	yes	unknown	unknown	no
Duality of patterning	yes	no	unknown	no

Hockett's work is an example of linguists' attempts to find *language universals*, features that all languages have in common. Another example of this search is Noam Chomsky's pioneering work. Chomsky's preeminent gift to linguistics has been a "generative theory" of language. He proposes that a single set of "rules" can and does generate all the possible grammatical sentences of a language. Grammar does this with what we could call linguistic "equations." Mathematicians use equations to present specific mathematical truths in an elegant and economical package. In the same way, grammar must resort to some sort of economically packaged set of general principles to generate every possible grammatical sentence. (Chomsky is not considering the *meaning* contained in a sentence, only whether or not it is grammatical. *Sudden green doves blanched furiously* makes little sense, but it is grammatically correct.)

Chomsky is talking about a set of grammatical principles that are language universals. They are true across the board, in every language at every time. Chomsky's position is that linguistics' job is to move beyond the study of *individual languages* to the study of *language*, to uncover these language universals and devise a "universal grammar." In their book *Universals in Linguistic Theory*, Emmon Bach and Robert Harms assert that the purpose of linguistic theory is "to discover what is common to all languages, what is essential in the notion 'natural language,' [and] what are the limits within which languages vary."

In other words, linguistics must comport itself *as a science*. Science looks for "universals." Biology looks for the basic laws that govern the functions of life; physics strives to uncover the basic laws of the universe; mathematics seeks to find the fundamental equations underlying existence. Linguistics ultimately seeks to uncover the origins of language in our species, the origins of languages in each individual's brain, the common ground from which all the trees in the linguistic forest spring, the common sounds and signs and rules that all mother tongues share.

Misconceptions About Language

We all have our own set of preconceptions and prejudices about other people, other cultures, and even the nature of the universe. Some are innocuous, others deadly. Racism, sexism, and religious bigotry are behaviors that are extremely offensive and downright dangerous to others. Millions of people died during World War II because of those kinds of prejudices. "Holocaust" is a completely appropriate term for what happened to Europe's Jews, Gypsies, and homosexuals. Linguistic misconceptions are somewhat less harmful, but they are still walls that separate us from truth.

Two of the most common misconceptions about language have to do with our own mother tongues. Many people feel certain that there is one correct way to speak their language. This attitude of *prescriptivism* is depressingly common, not only in English but in many other languages as well. The assumption is that one version or dialect of our mother tongue is somehow "better" than another. A Boston accent is better than a Southern drawl. Parisian French has it all over a Marseilles accent. BBC English is better than cockney. In fact, in 1993 the BBC issued a set of guidelines for its broadcasters that decries many American English usages as "improper."

As early as the sixteenth century this prescriptive attitude led to the creation of language academies. The first one, the Academia della Crusca, appeared in Italy in 1582. Cardinal Richeleu founded the Académie Français (the French Academy) in 1635. The Spanish Academy was founded in 1713, the Hungarian Academy in 1830, and the Hebrew Language Academy in 1953. All had and have as their purpose the purification of the mother tongue.

The English writers Daniel Defoe and John Dryden urged the creation of an English Academy in the seventeenth century, and in 1712 the Irish writer Jonathan Swift added his voice to the call. However, Dr. Samuel Johnson, creator of English's first dictionary, opposed the whole idea of an English Academy as contrary to the spirit of a living language. The idea keeps surfacing from time to time, but the English language has never been saddled with such an official arbiter (with the possible exception of the BBC!) of this prescriptive idea.

The truth is, of course, that no language or dialect is better or worse than any other. People speak the way they speak; they communicate with one another quite well. Each language is much like a collection of living beings, a "linguistic ecology," as it were. Not everyone accepts the same set of "linguistic values." But the various dialects of a particular language continue to grow and evolve and cross-fertilize.

Just as many are convinced that there is only one way to properly pronounce their language, so others are sure that it is wrong for their language to change over time. "All this slang!" people complain. "It's polluting the language." Or, "You know it's all going to hell in a handbasket when people start using *facilitate* and turn *task* into a verb!" This is a variation of the "things-were-better-in-the-old-days" attitude about life. "English used to be a better, cleaner, purer language when I was a kid back in [fill in the blank]." Who is to blame? Usually either (a) the schools or (b) the news media.

In fact, change in language is just as much a constant as it is in the biological world. Everything changes. Stars condense from interstellar clouds, begin burning with thermonuclear fire, grow old and either blow up as supernovas or shrink into white dwarfs. The Earth's surface changes continually as the crustal plates slide and rotate, crash and crumble. Under the relentless pressure of environmental changes and the presence of other life, a species changes—usually slowly, sometimes in a relative blink of an eye—into something new that fills an ecological niche. In the same way, languages change. New words enter a language; new technologies generate new vocabularies; social or economic changes generate new patterns of discourse; sounds shift about. Today's teenage slang will probably disappear. I used to say *Far out*! a lot in the late 1960s; no one does now. *Cool* is still around; but will *gnarly* make it into the language? Will another sound shift, like the one that changed the texture of English in the fourteenth century, happen again? It could, and English would find itself evolving into a new form.

Other misconceptions have less to do with languages and more to do with language. One of the most common is the idea that other people express their thoughts in the same way we do. The majority of us are *monolingual*, speaking only our mother tongue. We unconsciously assume that everyone else on the face of the earth "thinks" the same way we do when we speak. When a Spaniard says *Tengo hambre* he must be thinking the same thing I am when I say *I'm hungry*. It's not true. The Spaniard is saying something that's more like, "I have hunger." I may say *I feel sorry for you*. A Japanese would not say that at all. She would say *O kinodoku desu*, which is closer to "It's a poison for your soul." I can say *How are you*? Someone speaking Burmese cannot, for such an expression simply does not exist in Burmese. Even more telling is the difficulty in translating literary works from one language to another. Some essential part always seems to get lost "in the translation."

All Languages Are Created Equal

Related to these misconceptions is the idea that some languages are inherently superior or inferior to others. This is an extension of the prescriptive fallacy, as well as an offshoot of the idea that "everyone thinks the way I do." This particular misconception comes with a huge collection of folklore and popular beliefs. The French like to say that "what is not clear, is not French." Germans are convinced that their language has mystical powers of clarity of expression. Italians can go on for hours about the music of their language, not to mention its honored age. Charles V of Spain once said that English was the language for conversing with merchants, German with soldiers, French with women, Italian with friends, and Spanish with God. Hebrew was once considered the perfect language, because it was "obviously" the language that God spoke. For more than a thousand years Latin held a position of honor in Europe as the language of religion and learning. Latin was the true mother tongue; everyone knew that.

At the other end of this fallacy is the idea that some languages are "primitive." The ancient Greeks felt that any language but Greek was nothing more than babbling, the literal meaning of the word *barbaroi*, "barbarian." During the nineteenth-century heyday of the British Empire, upon which the sun never set, the English felt the same way about their language. Americans have always felt this way about American English; British English is "snobbish," and every other language is inferior. The languages of the American Indians were "clearly" primitive. The sooner they learned American English, in a government or church school, of course, the better. In the process, of course, many Indian cultures spiraled into oblivion.

However, there are no "primitive" languages, any more than there are any "superior" ones. No "stone age" languages exist, not even among supposedly "stone age" peoples in South America or Africa or Australia. Every language ever studied, from Dakota to !Xi, proves to be as sophisticated and complex as any other. !Xi is as complex in its own way as English, and Warlpiri is as sophisticated as French. I may not be able to discuss astrophysics in Romani the way I can in English; Romani lacks that vocabulary. But I can certainly do a better job of communicating snow conditions in Aleut than I can in Italian.

Languages, then, are like the individual humans that speak them: different in many ways, but equal in the ways that count.

Dialects and Slang

We all know that not everyone speaks our mother tongue in the same way, with the same pronunciation, grammar, and vocabulary. In fact, no two individuals speak their shared language exactly alike, even those who grew up in the same family and community. If nothing else, the unique shape of each person's vocal apparatus will put a stamp of individuality on his or her speech patterns. For the most part, though, those who live in the same town or region, or who belong to the same social class, will tend to speak their mother tongue in a nearly identical fashion. A *dialect*, then, is a regional or class variety of a language. An *accent* is a way of speaking that reveals the speaker's dialect, thus indicating the speaker's social class or geographic origin. Certain accents are thus associated with certain dialects. Some linguists therefore treat accents as part of dialects, but others consider them as separate subjects of study. Though dialects differ from the *standard language* in various ways, including vocabulary and pronunciation, all contain enough linguistic features in common with it to make them understandable to speakers of other dialects. Together, this complex of dialects comprises the language itself. Thus the different dialects used by English speakers throughout the United States make up what we call American English.

In the development of most languages, a particular dialect gains in prestige or common use, often by becoming the predominant written form. Social prestige becomes attached to this particular dialect, and it becomes the preferred usage in literature, economic life, and politics. This process culminates in the development of a standard language. The basic dialect of a country's standard language is often the dialect originally used in its capital. The London dialect of the seventeenth and eighteenth centuries eventually became the standard language of British English. The same happened for the Parisian dialect of French, and the Muscovite dialect of Russian. In Italy the Italian dialect of Florence, a strong cultural center, eventually became the standard language.

In the United States the rise of the movie industry in the 1920s and 1930s put a powerful stamp on American English. The English spoken by Hollywood actors and actresses, influenced by the dialect of southern California and the American Southwest, began to exert its power over other dialects. With the dominance of television as a medium for news and entertainment, a standard American English language has emerged. It is clearly not the dialect of New England or the Deep South, but rather includes the flat tones of the American Midwest and Southwest.

The characteristic of dialects that makes them understandable to others, called *intercomprehensibility*, is really a continuum or a scale. Some dialects we can easily understand. I speak a dialect of American English specific to the Southwest, particularly southern California, where I was born and raised, and that particular dialect sounds "normal" to my ears. I can easily understand someone who speaks with a northern Minnesota accent, a high-class British accent, or even a Southern American accent. Some Southern accents I do have trouble with, though, and I often find the Australian English dialect rather difficult to understand. But I do understand it. The language is still clearly English. At some point a dialect may move so far down the continuum that it is no longer comprehensible to other speakers. At that point, one that is nearly impossible to quantify, the dialect has become a separate language.

Languages contain many different dialects because, quite simply, languages change. They are like living creatures, which grow and change from infancy to adulthood. Perhaps more specifically, a language is like a biological species. A species of animals or plants changes over geological time in a process called evolution. The pressures of environmental changes, the competition for ecological niches among different species, and other factors all combine to force a species to evolve. It changes both its physical form and its social and individual behaviors to survive and best fit into its ecological niche. A species does not consciously initiate or follow through on an evolutionary change. Evolutionary changes are the result of an accumulation of many small but random changes, called mutations, in the genetic codes of the individual members of the species. Harmful changes get weeded out, since the individuals with these "anti-survival" modifications tend to die before they can breed. Changes that improve an individual's ability to survive tend to be passed on to the next generation. They eventually become part of the species' characteristic form or behavior, or both. "Neutral" mutations may also be passed on, and they could end up being "pro-survival" ten thousand years from now.

When a species can no longer adapt fast or effectively enough to changing environmental conditions, when it cannot keep a sufficient number of its individual members alive long enough to reproduce, the species becomes extinct. So do languages. But those that continue to live continue to change. Every living language constantly undergoes linguistic change. A species of animal or plant is an extremely complex system; different circumstances will cause it to evolve into different forms and patterns of behavior. That is one reason why so many different types of flowering plants, for example, exist today.

And that is why so many different languages, and dialects within languages, also exist. Languages, like species, are extremely complex systems. Different communities of English speakers, for example, living in different localities or at different levels of income or class, will inevitably develop slightly different ways of speaking their mother tongue. Most of these changes in pronunciation or grammar are random. No one deliberately set out to create a Southern American dialect of English or the Smolensk dialect of Russian. These dialects simply developed over time, as speakers in a particular area came to speak their mother tongues in a particular fashion. Linguistic changes are slight at first, but they accumulate the way genetic mutations do in a species. That is why the English spoken by George Bernard Shaw was quite different from that spoken by William Shakespeare.

Several different types of dialect exist, including geographic or regional, social, and prestige dialects. A regional dialect is a dialect characteristic of a specific geographic area. This is the kind of dialect with which most Americans are familiar: for example, the New England dialect, the Southern American dialect, and the Southwest dialect. These large regional dialects in turn contain within them smaller, more distinct regional variations. South Carolina English, for example, is included in Southern American English; the Delaware Valley dialect is part of the larger New England dialect. Then there are local dialects, which are part of a larger regional dialect. The Boston dialect and the Yankee English dialect of Cape Cod, for example, are local variations on the New England dialect.

In many places dialect differences are associated with social class or educational levels. Social dialects certainly occur in American English; people with higher levels of education tend to speak dialects closer to the standard language than do people with limited education. Social variations in speech are particularly likely to develop in large cities, among concentrations of poor people, blue-collar workers, the white middle class, and so on. But we are probably most familiar with the social dialects of British English. There is a big difference between cockney and London English, or between a Midlands dialect and the British English spoken by someone who has graduated from Cambridge. Prestige dialects, a form of social dialects, are dialects that are preferred over others for reasons of status.

Linguists who study dialects often speak of *focal areas, relic areas*, and *transition areas*. A focal area is a geographic region in which the linguistic forms of a language are undergoing vigorous changes, and from which those changes are spreading. It is often a major cultural or economic center. Relic areas, by contrast, are regions in which speech forms or dialects are not developing. They are the places toward which linguistic changes are headed. For example, Boston is a focal area, while Cape Cod, Nantucket Island, and rural Maine and New Hampshire are relic areas. A transition area is a geographical region that lies on the border between different regional dialects. The language variation spoken in a transition area tends to have features of both its neighboring dialects.

There is a difference between dialect and *slang*. A dialect is a variation upon a standard language that develops naturally. It comes into existence through the action of typical language use and transmission. No one individual or group deliberately sets out to create a dialect. (Though we will encounter in Chapter 2 at least one famous American who tried to do exactly that, and actually had some success.) We can push our biological metaphor a bit further and think of the development of a dialect as resembling the natural evolution of one species into another.

However, consciously created language variations do exist. Each society contains within it different groups that place a very high value on group identity or group consciousness. They include labor unions, tradespeople, members of political parties, criminal underworld organizations, students at specific colleges or universities, and—of course—teenagers. These groups often develop their own special variations on the mother tongue, variously called *jargons* or *argots*. *Pig Latin* has often been a popular argot among students. *Loucherbeme* is a trade argot used in Paris. Scientific discourse is chock-full of technical jargon, and the jargon of computer science differs considerably from that of astrophysics.

Often these subgroups use established words in new ways or coin new ones, and the words filter out into the language at large. When this happens, the new usage—deliberately created—is on the way to becoming slang. The word *slang*, which first appeared in the eighteenth century and may come from *sling*, refers to these continually changing agglomerations of colloquial words or phrases. Slang is the result of deliberate, conscious attempts to create new words or phrases for particular purposes. In this way, slang is a bit like genetic engineering, the conscious creation of "mutations" or changes in an individual creature's genetic code. To be more precise, it can be compared to science-fictional manipulations of a *genome*, the genetic code of an entire species. No one has tried such a thing, yet; but it could someday happen.

In language it happens all the time. The metaphor breaks down at this point, however. Slang, by definition, is ephemeral. Back in the 1960s I was happily saying *Boss!* and *Bitchin'!* to express great satisfaction or delight. Both expressions were forms of surfer slang. While I was never successful at standing on a surfboard, much less actually surfing, I was a genuine blond teenage boy who loved to hang out on the Ventura County beaches during the summer. I eagerly adopted the prevailing jargon when it became an accepted form of slang expression. Today, though, I would never think of saying *Boss!* or *Bitchin'*. I'm not even sure the surfers today use the expressions. Slang comes into style and then fades away.

When it does not fall into disuse but becomes a part of the accepted language, slang stops being slang and becomes "acceptable." *Fizzle, jazz, hit the spot*, and *funky* were all slang words that became respectable parts of the English lexicon. *Jeopardy*, once a slang term used in gambling, is now the title of a television game show as well as a common English word. Just a few years ago *ghetto blaster* was a slang phrase for a large portable stereo radio/tape player. Now it is part of general usage. *Bouse*, now spelled *booze*, was slang for *liquor* in the thirteenth century, and *pooped* was slang for *exhausted* in the sixteenth. Both words are now commonly used in informal contexts and are no longer considered slang. Some words, though, have defied the odds and remained slang for centuries. *Bones* was slang for dice ("Gonna roll them bones!") as far back as the fourteenth century, and still is. Shakespeare used the phrase *beat it* to mean "run away" in the early fifteenth century; it was slang then and it is now, even though Michael Jackson has used it as the title of a song.

Slang words come into existence through the deliberate actions of individuals, but the specific methods people use to create slang are quite varied. Like many other new words, slang often enters a language's vocabulary through a process of recycling older words or parts of words. *Affixation*, the adding of prefixes or suffixes to words, plays a major role. Consider slang words like *megabucks* and *megawork*, created using prefixes. *Acidhead* and *homeboy* are examples of slang created by compounding one new word from two older ones. In American English, many new slang words are created by adding a particle like *off, on*, or *out:* for example, *blow off, blow out, blimp out, hit on, rock on*. Shortening or even abbreviating words or phrases creates slang terms; examples include *def (definitely)* and *VJ/Vee-Jay* (video jockey). The latter term is also an example of a parallel construction; it imitates an earlier slang term, *DJ*, that is now in general informal use.

American English has often borrowed words from African-American usage and turned them into slang: witness, for example, *dude, schiz out*, and *Yo! Rock 'n' roll* was an African-American American English phrase that in the 1950s became slang for a new African-American-influenced popular music form. Then it stopped being slang and became even more respectable than the music form it denotes. The slang phrase *one for the book* came into the language from sportswriters, who in turn stole it in the 1920s from then-legal bookmakers. *Trip, acid, horse, magic mushrooms*, and *freak-out* are slang words that migrated from various drug subcultures.

For all the differences between slang and dialect, though, there is at least one interesting similarity. Like many dialects, much of slang today is becoming socially tolerable. It is an acceptable form of rebellious expression for teenagers, an important tool of satirists, humorists, and newspaper reporters, and for many people a way of adding an exciting and descriptive edge to their daily language. This is especially the case with derogatory slang. Let's face it: no "acceptable" words in the standard language quite express what we want to say with slang words such as *sucker, jerk, creep, wimp*, and *wuss*.

Tower of Babel, Tower of Song

The biblical story of the Tower of Babel is one culture's attempt to explain the origins of languages. The story is clearly mythological, not true or false in some scientific sense. It is a story that tries to explain a mystery. It does so by tapping into deep psychological truths about all humans: we communicate with one another using language. We meet other people who do not understand our language, nor we theirs. We long to *know* them, to speak with them, to connect with them and be united with them. We feel the separateness, and we want to banish it. Shared language ties us together, connects us to our families, lovers, friends, neighbors, even enemies. It erases—for a time, anyway—the existential loneliness of our lives. Why can we not speak with these others, who clearly have language but not ours? The Babel myth offers a divine explanation.

In the seventeenth century a Swedish linguist claimed that in the Garden of Eden the serpent spoke French, Adam spoke Danish, and God spoke, of course, Swedish. Biblical scholars long insisted that the *ur-language*, the original proto-language of all humans, was Hebrew. It made theological sense, but no other kind. Many linguists, trying to be more scientific, probably had the Eden story in mind when they asserted that human language arose from our deep desire to name things.

Other theories for the origin of human language are equally conjectural. Some have pointed to onomatopoeia as the possible origin of human languages: some words do indeed sound like the entities they name; ergo, language arose from the attempt to imitate the sounds of those entities. In the *Cratylus*, the Greek philosopher Plato has Socrates make this argument. Charles Darwin suggested that language is a form of verbal pantomime. Early humans, he said, perhaps found themselves making mouth motions that attempted to imitate hand gestures. Then there is the "bow-wow" theory. According to German academic Max Mueller, language began as an attempt by humans to imiatate the sounds of nature. This is more than simply onomatopoeia; Mueller suggested that dogs became known as "bow-wows" because that is the sound they make, and that the first humans called roosters "cock-a-doodle-doos." The problem with this theory is that language reality invalidates it: different cultures give different names to the sounds of the same animal.

Some other theories of language origin include these:

- *The Pooh-Pooh theory:* Language arose through people making instinctive sounds caused by emotions or pain.
- *The Ding-Dong theory:* Language originated as "oral gestures" in response to environmental stimuli.
- *The La-La theory:* Language came about because of the human response to the joyful aspects of life, such as play and song.

No evidence exists to support any of these theories, most of which arose in the nineteenth century, when science was less rigorous and more speculative.

The evidence we do have to work with comes mainly from paleoanthropology, the study of the origin of the human species, biology, and anthropology. Brain size may mean little; no correspondence exists between the size of a person's brain and the ability to use language. Brain structure complexity is a different story, though. Brain size may matter only in its relationship to internal complexity. It appears that once a brain possesses sufficient internal neural complexity, it can support language. Later on we will learn more about the brain and the complex networks of nerve cells which comprise it. In general, the smaller the volume of a brain, the less complex is its structure and thus the less capable it is of generating language. But even this relationship between size and language capacity is not straightforward. Even humans with relatively small brains have more capacity for language than chimpanzees, gorillas, elephants, and whales.

Also, some intriguing fossil evidence exists for the general shape and size of the human and prehuman (or hominid, as paleoanthropologists call our ancient ancestors) vocal apparatus. Much of the vocal cavity consists of soft tissues: the tongue, lips, voice box, and so forth. These structures, of course, rot away after death. We have no real idea of their shape in ancient humans and hominids. However, we do have good fossil representations of hominid jaws and oral cavities. And we know for a fact from such apparatus that present-day nonhuman primates, including chimpanzees and gorillas, simply do not have the anatomical equipment to create speech. They do communicate, in part, with sounds, but are unable to create the myriad sounds that go into making our spoken language.

It is also quite certain that our earliest hominid ancestors, *Australopithecus* (literally, "southern ape") and *Homo habilis* ("Handy Man," as in "handy with tools"), could not speak. Their vocal apparatus was very much like that of present-day nonhuman primates. The hominids who roamed the African plains more than two million years ago undoubtedly communicated with one another, and very efficiently at that. So do chimpanzees; but they do not speak. Neither did *Homo habilis*. The evidence is nearly as certain for *Homo erectus* ("Upright Man"), who succeeded *Homo habilis* in Africa about 1.5 million years ago. *Homo erectus* is probably our first direct primate ancestor.

Homo erectus gradually evolved into *Homo sapiens* and its various subspecies. Some of these very early humans (or very evolved members of *Homo erectus*) had a vocal apparatus somewhat resembling ours by as early as two hundred thousand years ago. We do not know if they had a sophisticated nervous system and brain to go along with it. The former would give them the ability to create verbal language, but the latter would be indispensable for it.

Homo neanderthalis, or Neanderthal man, flourished from about 100,000 to 35,000 B.C.E. (the abbreviation for "Before the Current Era," which historians and other scholars now prefer over B.C.). Neanderthals may have been a subspecies of *Homo sapiens* or a separate species of their own; anthropologists still debate the evidence. Fossil evidence reveals that the Neanderthal vocal tract resembles that of a present-day human infant more than that of a chimp. Neanderthals could probably make some vocal sounds, but their repertoire would have been far smaller than even the smallest modern language's. Still,

Neanderthals were certainly capable of creating far more—and more sophisticated—sounds than any of today's primates.

Neanderthals may have evolved into, interbred with, or been wiped out by Cro-Magnon man, who were without doubt members of *Homo sapiens*. They appeared on the scene in Europe about 35,000 B.C.E., and in Africa and the Middle East somewhat earlier. Even more archaic forms of *Homo sapiens* lived in northern and eastern Africa still earlier, as much as two hundred thousand years ago. Cro-Magnons had a skeletal structure that was practically identical to ours. Their vocal apparatus resembled ours. And the "fossils" of their social activities reveal them to be as fully human as we are. Those "fossils" include the astonishing cave paintings found in the Pyrenees mountains and ritually arranged caves in Spain. These and other artifacts, including powerful and sophisticated carvings that probably represent a female deity, date back some thirty thousand years.

Religion and art presuppose highly intricate modes of communication. They exist within and rise out of a complex *gestalt*, a sophisticated paradigm of reality. That communication system could easily have been a form of sign language, or it could have been vocal communication, spoken language.

Certainly, it could well have included spoken language. For that is what we use today.

Still, the questions remain: When did we begin using language, and why? The short answer to both questions is "We don't really know." But we can speculate. Some linguists might consider these suggestions to be scientifically unsupportable, but others think they are at least possible.

One way to try to determine when humans began using language is to date the emergence of different languages or families of languages. As we will see in more detail in the next chapter, English belongs to a large family of languages called Indo-European. Considerable evidence exists that the ancestral language of all Indo-European languages, called Proto-Indo-European, emerged some six to eight thousand years ago in a region of Turkey. Several Russian paleolinguists, linguists who study the very ancient history and origins of language, think they can trace it back further than that. In the late 1950s and early 1960s, Aaron Dolgopolsky and the late Vladislav Illych-Svityich developed a theory that Proto-Indo-European belonged to a more ancient and larger "superfamily" of languages they called Nostratic. After Illych-Svitych's death in 1966, Dolgopolsky continued his work on Nostratic with other researchers, including Vitaly Shevoroshkin, Thomas Gamkrelidze, and V. V. Ivanov. These scholars now believe that Nostratic was spoken about fifteen thousand years ago by people living between the Black and Caspian seas. This was a time before humans had invented agriculture. We were still hunter-gatherers then but possessed a sophisticated culture that produced remarkably beautiful pottery, paintings, and worship objects.

Shevoroshkin and his colleagues come up with these radical "family trees" by first comparing words that many linguists consider to be the most stable parts of a language's vocabulary. They include words for body parts, natural objects such as the sun, moon, or earth, and personal pronouns like *I* and *you*. They compared these words first from different related existing languages, such as English, German, and Latin. Then they used the comparisons to reconstruct the likely forms of the ancestral words in various proto-languages. These reconstructions are, of course, not necessarily accurate. No one really knows their precise construction or pronunciation, and this adds considerable fuzziness to these speculations. But the comparisons are intriguing nonetheless. Reconstructed Nostratic, says Shevoroshkin, has no words for domesticated plants. The putative word for dog, *kuyna*, can actually mean either "dog" or "wolf"; the oldest known bones of domesticated dogs just happen to date to about fourteen thousand years ago. About a thousand words of Nostratic have been reconstructed so far.

These proposed language superfamilies and their ages are somewhat controversial, but not groundbreaking. As we have seen, humans could easily have been using language at least fourteen thousand years ago, and likely more than twice as long ago as that.

Some scientists, though, think they can push the date for the origin of human language back even further. Stanford University geneticist Luigi Cavalli-Sforza has pioneered the development of techniques that trace the evolutionary history of human genes. He has used these methods to try to trace the earliest migrations of humans around the world, and to pinpoint the place where *Homo sapiens* probably began. Cavalli-Sforza believes that his results mesh well with previous work by historical linguists. For example, linguistic evidence points to a family of African languages as being among the oldest in the world. They have particular characteristics, such as clicking noises used in words, that are only distantly related to other languages. Recent anthropological discoveries of archaic *Homo sapiens* remains in the Middle East have been dated to about 90,000 B.C.E. Cavalli-Sforza's genetic markers tend to support the notion that modern humans, like our more distant ancestors, evolved in Africa. Conclusion: humans were speaking some form of language nearly one hundred thousand years ago.

And perhaps even earlier than that. A few years ago a group of researchers at the University of California at Berkeley, including Allan Wilson, Mark Stoneking, and Rebecca Cann, made a remarkable genealogical discovery. They traced the genetic material from women around the world to a tiny population of *Homo sapiens* living in northern Africa nearly two hundred thousand years ago. The news media immediately proclaimed that the researchers had "found Eve."

Why did language evolve? Though the simplest answer is "We don't know," the next-simplest answer is probably "For survival." All animals have some sort of communications system enabling individuals to issue warnings, announce the discovery of food, point out directions, signal an intention to mate, and so on. Our nearest living primate relatives, chimpanzees and gorillas, have very sophisticated communication systems, but there is still considerable doubt that they possess anything with all the characteristics of human language. It is reasonable to assume that *Australopithecus* and *Homo erectus* also had highly sophisticated and flexible methods of communicating. They lived in families and communities, knew how to make and use tools considerably more elaborate than those used by chimps, and moved through an environment that was changing and dangerous. A highly flexible communications system was thus a strongly pro-survival trait. Prehumans that could communicate effectively, in ways that could quickly adapt to suddenly changing conditions, were more likely to live long enough to make more babies. Their social structures would continue to survive, evolve, and improve.

These prehumans also had something their primate cousins did not: a brain that was becoming larger and more complex. As we will discover later, the human brain appears to have some remarkably complex structures associated with language and memory. And this neurological complexity could not exist without a sufficiently large brain. We don't know exactly what their vocal apparatus was like; the soft tissues of the mouth and throat do not fossilize. But we do know that the earliest versions of *Homo sapiens*, and possibly also *Homo neanderthalis*, had large and very complex brains, and also a vocal tract like ours. The combination of complex brain structures, advanced vocal tract, and the evolutionary pressures of a harsh world moving in and out of ice ages may have done the trick.

We evolved language to survive. The rest, as they say, is frosting on the cake.

Today, the world is filled with the sounds of language. Thousands upon thousands of them. Some may perceive it as a Tower of Babel. It is really a Tower of Song. Each day, more human infants begin adding their unique notes to the melody.

CHAPTER 2

Our Linguistic Family Tree

No infant learns language in isolation. We all have a mother tongue, the language of the dominant society or culture into which we were born. Nor does our mother tongue exist in social isolation. Some people still live in tribal communities in South America or New Guinea that have yet to encounter the hypercharged world of the contemporary global society. Yet even their languages are influenced, in one way or another, by the languages of other surrounding peoples. Out here in the electronic village, the influence of language upon language is downright frenetic. English in particular sweeps across the globe at the speed of light, worming its way into nearly every country and society. French and Spanish are not far behind. As our infant daughters and new grandsons begin learning their mother tongues, they are learning languages that have daily connections to many others.

Just as important, they are learning a mother tongue with a history. For no language exists in historical isolation. Every language has a history. Every language has a family tree.

The Languages of the World

Nearly two centuries of scholarship have resulted in today's picture of the world's languages as groups of *families*. Each language family includes dozens and sometimes hundreds of different individual languages. One way linguists graphically envision this complex agglomeration of languages is as a set of trees. Each language family is a tree, with a broad trunk, many main branches, and many more smaller branches and leaves.

Of course, determining how many language families or family trees exist is itself something of a problem. Different scholars come up with different groupings. The controversial schema devised by the Russian linguists discussed in Chapter 1, for example, offers fewer than a dozen superfamilies. Most scholars, though, prefer linguistic taxonomies with a larger number of families. One of the most commonly accepted schemes incorporates the world's languages into twenty-nine different families. Each language family is like a tree, and each of the trees in the forest of languages has sent forth its own set of branches, limbs, and leaves. Each branch is a separate language or subfamily of languages. The following table lists the twenty-nine language families in alphabetical order, grouped by their main geographical regions:

Language Families of the World

Geographical Region	Language Family	Sample Subfamilies/*Languages*
Africa	Afro-Asiatic (also in Asia)	Berber, Chadic, Cushitic, Omotic, Semitic
	Khosian	Khoi-Khoin, San
	Niger-Congo	Adamawa-Eastern, Benue-Congo, Mande, Kwa, Voltaic, West Atlantic
	Nilo-Saharan	Chari-Nile, Koman, Maban, Nilo-Hamitic, Nilotic, Saharan
Asia	Altaic	Manchu-Tungus, Mongolian, Turkic
	Caucasian	Abkhazo-Adjghian, Nakho-Dagestanian, Kartvelian
	Dravidian	*Kannada, Malayalam, Tamil, Telugu*
	Japanese	*Japanese*
	Korean	*Korean*
	Paleosiberbian	Gilyak, Luorawetlan, Yeniseian, Yukaghir
	Sino-Tibetan	Burmic, Miao-Yao, Sinitic, Tibetic,
	Tai	*Lao, Nung, Shan, Thai, Tho, Yuan*
	Uralic (also in Europe)	Finno-Ugric, Samoyedic

Geographical Region	Language Family	Sample Subfamilies/*Languages*
Europe	Indo-European	Albanian, Armenian, Balto-Slavic, Celtic, Germanic (which includes *English*), Greek, Indo-Iranian, Italic
North America	Algonquian	*Arapaho, Blackfoot, Cheyenne, Choctaw, Cree, Fox, Micmac, Mohican, Muskogee, Ojibwa, Potawatomi, Shawnee*
	Aztec-Tanoan	*Aztec, Comanche, Hopi, Paiute, Pima-Papago, Shoshone, Tarahumar*
	Eskimo-Aleut	*Aleut, Eskimo*
	Hokan	*Tlapanec*
	Macro-Siouan	*Cherokee, Crow, Dakota, Mohawk, Pawnee*
	Na-Dené	*Apache, Navaho*
	Oto-Manguean	*Mixtec, Otomí, Zapotec*
Oceania	Australian Aboriginal	*Aranda, Tiwi, Mabuyag, Walmatjari, Warlpiri, Western Desert*
	Austro-Asiatic	*Mon-Khmer, Munda, Nocobarese*
	Austronesian	*Chamorro, Javanese, Rukai*
	Indo-Pacific	*Andamanese, Figian, Gilbertese, Malay, Malagasy, Maori, Motu, Pilipino, Rapanui, Tok Pisin, Samoan, Sundanese, Tahitian, Tasmanian, Tongan*
South America	Andean-Equatorial	*Aymará, Goajiro, Guarani, Quechua*
	Ge-Pano-Carib	Carib, Macro-Panoan
	Macro-Chibchan	*Cuna, Epera, Guaymi, Paez, Waica*
	Penutian	*Araucanian, Cakchiquel, Maya, Quiché*

In 1985 American linguist Joseph Greenberg offered a new, controversial regrouping of the native languages of North and South America. Rather than the eleven or so language families most linguists recognize, Greenberg has proposed just three superfamilies: Amerind, Eskimo-Aleut, and Na-Dené. As in the more conventional classifications, Na-Dené includes languages spoken not only by Native Americans in Canada and Alaska but also by the Navaho in the southwestern United States Greenberg suggests that Eskimo-Aleut is related to a "Euroasiatic" superfamily of languages, which also includes Altaic, Japanese, Korean, and Indo-European. This is a particularly radical interpretation: most linguists think there is little if any conection among the aforementioned language families, and many linguists classify Korean and Japanese as so-called isolate languages, with no connection to any other languages on earth. Finally, Greenberg's Amerind language superfamily incorporates nearly a dozen "conventional" language families and more than two hundred groups of languages.

A few languages have no known relatives. They appear to have no relationship, either structurally or historically, to any other languages on the planet. Linguists call them *isolates*. In effect, they are their own language family. Sometimes researchers know quite a bit about a language but can find no significant points of contact with any other language group or family. Other languages are classified as isolates simply because we know so little about them. Some languages are spoken by small groups of people in out-of-the-way locations. Others, though, are *extinct languages*, mother tongues that died out long ago and left few if any written records with which linguists can work. Other extinct isolates left plenty of written records, but scholars are still unable to place them in any language family.

The most famous isolate language is *Basque*, which is spoken by about half a million people who live in a circumscribed area of northern Spain and southwestern France. Some linguists have tried to find connections between Basque and the Caucasian language family, spoken mostly by people living between the Caspian and Black seas. Other researchers suggest a connection between Basque and various North African languages. Still others think Basque is a remnant of the now-extinct Iberian language once spoken in Spain. None of these or other attempts, however, are really convincing. It is possible, though, that Basque is the last remnant of the language or languages once spoken by humans living in western Europe before the arrival of the Indo-Europeans.

Three of the best-known extinct isolate languages are *Etruscan, Iberian*, and *Sumerian*. They continue to fascinate scholars. Even some of us nonscholars have been mesmerized by the mystery that surrounds these long-lost tongues.

Etruscan is one of the most famous of all extinct isolate languages. The Etruscan people lived in the area of Italy now known as Tuscany, the word itself coming from *Etruscan*. Their country was called Etruria, and their complex and sophisticated civilization reached its height in the sixth century B.C.E. The Etruscan language may have been spoken until about the fourth century C.E. (the "Current Era," which historians now prefer to A.D. A few thousand Etruscan inscriptions exist, all written in an alphabet derived from Greek. However, no one has been able to translate more than a few words. No "Rosetta Stone" for Etruscan has ever been found; the language bears no resemblance whatsoever to Latin, Greek, or anything else; nor does any contemporaneous record exist of Etruscan history. Like present-day Basque, Etruscan is one of the great linguistic mysteries of our time.

Nearly as famous and mysterious as its still-living neighbor Basque, Iberian was the language spoken in parts of southern and eastern Spain before the Romans invaded the Iberian peninsula. A twenty-eight-letter alphabet exists, showing traces of Greek and Phoenician influence. Most of what we know of Iberian today comes from scattered inscriptions on stones and ancient artifacts. Some researchers suggest that Iberian was spoken throughout much of western Europe. Others speculate that it was the mother tongue of the earliest humans in Europe and Spain, the people who created the astonishing artwork in the caves of Lascaux and the outdoor sculptures at Laussel more than sixteen thousand years ago. This is a wonderfully romantic notion, but no evidence exists to support it. Iberian remains as mysterious as Etruscan.

Sumerian is the oldest known language that exists in written form. The oldest Sumerian inscriptions date to about 3100 B.C.E. and are in cuneiform script. When cuneiform was finally deciphered in the nineteenth century, scholars discovered that the language spoken and written in southern Mesopotamia differed from others written in the same script. Numerous written records of Sumerian exist for scholars to study, but controversy still rages over what language family—if any—Sumerian belongs in.

The language family of greatest interest to English speakers and readers is Indo-European. It is the best-known language family in the West because it is the one to which English belongs. It is among the most intensively studied because modern linguistics was invented by Europeans. The parent language of the Indo-European languages, the "grandmother tongue," as it were, is called *Proto-Indo-European*. It was spoken at least five thousand years ago by the people who began migrating into Europe and Turkey from points north, often called the Aryans or Indo-Europeans; archaeologist Marija Gimbutas has referred to them as the "Kurgan culture," from the name for their distinctive burial mounds. Archaeologist Colin Renfrew recently has disputed this accepted origin for Proto-Indo-European. In his controversial book *Archaeology and Language: The Puzzle of Indo-European Origins*, as well as in an article in *Scientific American*, Renfrew argues that Proto-Indo-European and the people who spoke it had their origins in the region of Turkey called Anatolia.

As with so many other aspects of historical linguistics, different researchers offer different versions of the Indo-European family tree.

For example, Victor Stevenson's *Words: The Evolution of Western Languages* has an Indo-European language tree with eleven major branches. *The Cambridge Encyclopedia of Language* offers a more commonly accepted family tree with eight major living branches and two more extinct ones. The family tree suggested by Renfrew differs slightly from both. Of course, those who like to explore their own personal family trees may find this difference of opinion understandable. Genealogical enthusiasts are not always able to pin down every relationship unto the fifteenth generation. The following chart compares these three proposed family trees for Proto-Indo-European. Like other language families, each major branch of the Indo-European language tree has in turn its own collection of smaller limbs, each a language or subfamily of languages. For example, the Germanic family includes not only present-day German but also English. The asterisked listings are languages or language families that either are extinct or are schematic historical reconstructions.

Examples of Proposed Proto-Indo-European Family Trees

Stevenson	*Cambridge Encyclopedia of Language* *Proto-Indo-European *Indo-European	Renfrew
Albanian	Albanian	*Illyrian
	*Anatolian	*Anatolian
Armenian	Armenian	Armenian
Baltic	Balto-Slavic	Baltic
Celtic	Celtic	Celtic
Germanic	Germanic	Germanic
*Hittite		
Indo-Iranian	Indo-Iranian	Indo-Iranian
Italic	Italic	Italic
Mycenean Greek	Greek	Hellenic
Slavonic		Slavonic
*Tocharian	*Tocharian	*Tocharian

The historical stories of these languages are fascinating in their own right. Here are some basic facts about each of the major Indo-European language families (the Appendix includes more details):

- We know very little about the origins of *Albanian*, which today is spoken by about three million people living in the country of Albania, as well as in regions of Greece, Italy, and the former country of Yugoslavia. No written records of the language exist before the fifteenth century. In fact, an official alphabet based on the Roman one most Westerners use did not exist until 1909. The result is that Albanian is a language cloaked in obscurity.

- *Anatolian* is an extinct group of languages once spoken by people living in regions of modern-day Turkey and Syria. It dates back to about 2000 B.C.E., making it one of the oldest known—albeit no longer living—languages. The oldest known Indo-European texts are written in Hittite, an Anatolian language, and date to the seventeenth century B.C.E.
- Like Albanian, the *Armenian* branch of the Indo-European family includes just one language—itself, Armenian. Some five million people speak Armenian. Most of them live in Armenia and parts of eastern Turkey. The older version of Armenian is called *Grabar*. It is the classical form of Armenian, used in older literature and in the religious ceremonies of the contemporary Armenian Church. Spoken Armenian probably dates to around 1000 B.C.E.
- The *Baltic* languages include Old Prussian (now extinct), Latvian, and Lithuanian. Linguists know very little about the origins of these languages. The earliest document in Lithuanian, for example, is less than five hundred years old. Some linguists lump the Baltic and Slavonic languages together in the Balto-Slavic branch because of their several similarities. The earliest written records of Old Church Slavic date to the ninth century C.E. The main Slavic languages today include Belorussian, Bulgarian, Czech, Macedonian, Polish, Russian, Serbo-Croatian, Slovak, Slovene, Sorbinian, and Ukranian.
- *Celtic* languages once were spoken by people living throughout large areas of prehistoric Europe. By the middle of the third century B.C.E., Celtic peoples had migrated across the English Channel to the British Isles and Ireland. Some eight hundred years later, the inhabitants of those islands were almost the only people still speaking Celtic languages. New invaders from Europe eventually pushed them back into Wales, Ireland, and a few other locations. Today the only surviving Celtic languages are Gaelic (or Irish), Welsh, and Scots.
- The branch of Indo-European that is of greatest personal interest to English speakers is *Germanic*. English is a part of this branch.

Linguists subdivide the proto-Germanic tongue itself into three main branches: *North Germanic, East Germanic*, and *West Germanic*. East Germanic languages are all extinct. The only language of this branch we know much about is Gothic, because some manuscripts written in Gothic still survive. As a spoken language, Gothic probably died out near the end of the sixteenth century; a few written inscriptions in Gothic found in the Crimea date from that period. North Germanic gave rise to two Scandinavian subbranches. West Scandinavian includes Norwegian, Faeroese, and Icelandic. (Faeroese is spoken by the inhabitants of the Faeroe Islands, which lie about five hundred kilometers north of Great Britain and about eighteen hundred kilometers northeast of Denmark and are politically a Danish dependency.) East Scandinavian includes Danish and Swedish. North Germanic also includes the now-extinct language known as Old Norse, a literary variety of Old Icelandic that is the language of the ancient Icelandic sagas.

- The *Greek* branch consists of just one language, Greek. But what a language! All of Western civilization ultimately rests on the thoughts of ancient Greeks, thoughts preserved for posterity in this ancient but still-living language. No direct connection exists between Greek and English, but borrowing and coinages based on Greek permeate the scientific and technical branches of modern English. Greek's influence on our mother tongue is profound indeed.
- *Indo-Iranian* consists of two large groups of languages, Indo-Aryan and Iranian. The Iranian languages have roots going back at least three thousand years. They seem to have arisen in what is today called Afghanistan and Iran. Today's Iranian languages include Kurdish, Persian (or Farsi), and Tadzhik. Many hundreds of languages reside in the Indo-Aryan group, including Hindi and Panjabi. Romani, the language of the Rom, commonly called Gypsies, is also an Indo-Aryan language. However, the most famous Indo-Aryan language is one that is no longer in common use: Sanskrit, the sacred language of the Vedas, the holy writings of the Hindu religion.
- Almost everyone has heard of at least one *Italic* language: Latin, which dates to at least the sixth century B.C.E. As the city of Rome grew in power and conquered Italy, Latin displaced other languages on the Italian peninsula. As Latin spread, it spun off its

own "daughter" languages, the so-called *Romance languages*, including French, Italian, and Spanish.

- *Tocharian* is an extinct branch of the Indo-European language tree. No one even knew it existed until the late 1800s. Tocharian was spoken in the northern part of Chinese Turkestan at least through the first few centuries of the Current Era.

A Short History of English

The single most important spoken and written language in the world today is English. Chinese is spoken by more people as a mother tongue, but English plays the preeminent role in politics, economics, and science. English has come a long way from its origins in the northern European coastlands some two thousand years ago.

The language we know as English is part of the Germanic branch of the Indo-European family of languages. Other living languages closely related to it include Danish, Dutch, and German. English has its roots, therefore, in Europe, the continent where the Germanic tongues arose and first flourished.

We can trace its origins to the coastal areas of present-day northwestern Germany and southern Denmark. The Germanic tribes we know as the Angles, Saxons, Jutes, and Frisians lived in this part of northern Europe. The Angles occupied areas on the western shore of the Danish peninsula; the word *English*—which is used to refer to the language, the people, the country, and courses in the literature of the language—comes from the Old English words *englisc* and *œnglisc*, which in turn come from the word *Engle*, "the Angles." The Jutes probably lived on Denmark's northern tip, which is still referred to as Jutland. The Saxons originally occupied areas along the northwest coast of present-day Germany, and the Frisians lived in what we now know as the Netherlands, or Holland. During the fifth century C.E. many families and clans from these tribes began moving west. They crossed the English Channel and invaded the island of Great Britain.

The British Isles were not unpopulated, by any means. The Celts—themselves originally from Europe—had long lived in Great Britain, with their own language and a flourishing culture. Indeed, the Celtic language was itself once a family of languages as great in extent as Germanic and Italic. Celtic tongues had been spoken throughout southern and central Europe and the British Isles as far back as 1500 B.C.E. By about 400 B.C.E., though, their geographic distribution had shrunk to some areas in France and Germany along the Danube River, and to the British Isles. Germanic tongues had come to dominate the continent. The first great blow to the Celts in Britain had come from the Romans, who under Julius Caesar had invaded Great Britain in 55 and 54 B.C.E. Other Roman military legions followed. The Romans stayed in Great Britain—an uneasy occupation at best—for four hundred years.

In 383 C.E. Roman legions began leaving Britain. The final withdrawal took place in 410. The way was open for the Germanic tribes to move in. And they did, with a vengeance, in 449. The Germanic tribes were fierce fighters, but they met with resistance. The most successful opposition came from a Celtic leader known by the Latin name Artorius. He is probably the historical basis for the well-known legends of King Arthur and the knights of the Round Table. Artorius managed to establish an uneasy cease-fire that lasted about a generation, but it eventually failed. In the end, the Angles, Saxons, Jutes, and Frisians were unbeatable. The surviving Celts fell back to the southwestern shores of Great Britain and the islands of Ireland and Man. The Germanic tribes took over England at the point of a bloody sword. They sneeringly referred to the Celtic survivors—the original peoples of the British Isles—as *wealas*, "foreigners." The words *Welsh* and *Wales*, the people and land of the surviving Celts, come from this Saxon slur.

The conquest of England proved so overwhelming that the language of the conquerers absorbed few Celtic words. The Germanic occupiers simply could not be troubled to learn even the most common words of the Celtic people. A few Celtic words still survive here and there. *Avon*, as in the river and town, is a Celtic word meaning "river." The Old Irish word *lond* means "wild." The Romans named one of their settlements *Londinium*, and it eventually became London. The Welsh word *dwefr* means "water." The Romans turned it into *Dufer*, and it eventually became *Dover*. Other Celtic words absorbed into the language of the Germanic conquerers of Britain include *combe* (a deep valley), *crag*, *puca* (an evil spirit), and *tor* (a high peak). *Combe* and *tor* rarely appear in contemporary English. *Crag* is common; and *puca* shows up in Shakespeare's play *A Midsummer Night's Dream* as *Puck*, the crafty imp.

By the beginning of the eighth century C.E., the Saxon occupation of Britain had long become permanent. In the year 730, less than three hundred years after the initial arrival of the Saxons and their kin, the Venerable (now Saint) Bede wrote a book entitled *Historia Ecclesiastica Gentis Anglorum* ("A History of the English Church and People"). The people called themselves Angelcynn ("Angle-kin"), they called their language Englisc, and everyone else called their land Englaland, "the Land of the Angles."

The languages spoken by those first Germanic conquerers of England were the Germanic tongues of the Angles, Saxons, Jutes, and Frisians. For the first century or so after their arrival, the occupiers could easily converse with their relatives back home on the Continent. But separation breeds dialects, which eventually turn into new languages. By the year 1000 the language of the Angelcynn had evolved into something quite different from that spoken by the folks "back home" (which by then wasn't "back home" any more). And the language spoken by English speakers today is quite different from that spoken by the Angelcynn of the ninth and tenth centuries. Languages evolve and change, and English is no exception.

The following six phases cover more than fifteen hundred years of the evolution of the Germanic-based language of Great Britain:

1. *pre–Old English*, from the time of the Germanic invasions to the first appearance of Old English texts, c. 500 C.E.;
2. *Old English*, from c. 500 to c. 1150;
3. *Middle English*, from c. 1150 to c. 1430;
4. *Early Modern English*, from c. 1430 to c. 1700;
5. *Modern English*, from c. 1700 to c. 1945; and
6. *World English*, from c. 1945 to the present.

Depending on how one looks at linguistic change and evolution, Old English is (a) the earliest stage of the continually evolving language we today call English, or (b) the distinct and unique language from which evolved first Middle English and later Modern English, or (c) the common ancestor language of English and Scots, the two national Germanic languages spoken in Great Britain. All of these points of view about Old English are correct.

Old English emerged, as we have seen, from the Germanic dialects of the Angles, Saxons, Jutes, and Frisians who occupied England beginning in the late fifth century. It was actually a continuum of West

Germanic dialects rather than a monolithic language. The oldest surviving Old English inscriptions date from about 450 and are written in the old Celtic runic script. In 597 St. Augustine baptized Æthelberht, the king of Kent, beginning the conversion of the Anglo-Saxon tribes to Christianity. One literary and linguistic result was the gradual adoption of the Latin alphabet.

By the eighth century, four major dialects of Old English, which can be distinguished in surviving manuscripts from those times, existed in England:

- *Kentish:* This Old English dialect was associated with the Jutes and was spoken in the area around present-day Kent (thus the name).
- *Mercian:* The Mercian dialect was spoken by people living in the kingdom of Mercia, which stretched from the Thames to the Humber River.
- *Northumbrian:* This Old English dialect was spoken in Northumbria, the northernmost Anglo-Saxon kingdom, from the Humber to the Forth.
- *West Saxon:* This dialect was found in the southern part of England called Wessex, which eventually became the most powerful Saxon kingdom.

Old English is a language entirely distinct from present-day English. In order to read Old English texts such as *Beowulf* in their original form, a person must learn the language from scratch. It might as well be Cantonese or Kikuyu—or at least French or Frisian. Modern English speakers can struggle through Chaucer's *Canterbury Tales*, but with difficulty; early Middle English has enough resemblance to contemporary English to make that possible. Both Old and Middle English, when spoken, sound different from Modern English. Many English literature students, including this writer, have been entranced and captivated by the sounds of *Beowulf* or *The Pardoner's Tale* read aloud by a college professor.

But while Middle English does have some important resemblances to Modern English, Old English is all but a foreign language. Its speech patterns were similar to those of its North Sea Germanic ancestors, Old Frisian and Old Dutch (both, like Old English, now extinct languages). Old English's stress patterns were different from

Modern English's, and many of its vowels differed greatly in pronunciation from those we use in contemporary English. Its grammar was wildly different. Old English nouns, pronouns, and adjectives had three numbers (not only singular and plural, but also sometimes dual), three genders (masculine, feminine, and neuter), and five cases (nominative, accusative, genitive, dative, and instrumental).

Beginning in the early ninth century, Danish tribes began raiding England from the Continent. In 865 Danes occupied Northumbria, and the Danish influence on Old English began in earnest. It appears clearly in the writings of Alfred, king of Wessex. In 871 he began translating Latin texts into Old English, using the Latin script that had largely replaced the old Celtic runic script. These texts marked the first writing of prose in Old English. Aldhelm, the first known Anglo-Saxon writer of Old English prose was writing around 670 C.E. The earliest manuscript records in Old English date from about 700.

Poetry had long been composed and written in Old English. Caedmon, the earliest known English poet, was composing poetry around 670. Late in the eighth century and early in the ninth, the Anglo-Saxon poet Cynewulf composed several works in Old English, including "Christ," "Elena," "Fates of the Apostles," and "Juliana." In 970 *The Exeter Book*, a collection of Old English poetry, appeared. The oldest known manuscript of the epic Old English poem *Beowulf* dates from about the year 1000.

The climax of Danish influence on Old English came in the early eleventh century. Danish invaders succeeded in conquering all the Saxon kingdoms. Canute and his sons reigned over England from 1016 to 1042.

One of the leading versions of the theory of biological evolution, called *punctuated equilibrium*, proposes that evolution proceeds in a slow and steady fashion that is occasionally broken by sudden and dramatic evolutionary shifts. The same might be said of the evolution of the English language. The single most important such leap took place in 1066. That year, after an initial defeat at Stamford Bridge, an army led by William of Normandy defeated an English army led by King Harold II at the Battle of Hastings. William was crowned William I, the Conqueror, on Christmas Day.

William's invasion was the result of a broken promise. St. Edward the Confessor, king of England from 1042 to 1066, had been so impressed by the French-speaking Norman ambassadors to his English court that in 1051 he decreed that William of Normandy would be his heir. Fifteen years later, as he lay on his deathbed, Edward had a change of heart, doubtless encouraged by his son Harold, and decided that Harold should be king after all. One day after Edward's death Harold II was crowned king.

When William finally got the news, he was not amused. He raised an army and crossed the English Channel to take what he felt was rightly his, the crown of England. (Britain, by the way, has never suffered another invasion in the nearly one thousand years since, despite the intentions of one Adolf Hitler.) As the Angles and Saxons had done more than five hundred years earlier, William the Conqueror wrested control of Britain from its previous inhabitants in fire and blood.

The massive linguistic infusion of Norman French that followed over the next several centuries utterly changed the English language. For the next 250 years French was the "official" language in England. Norman nobles ransacked Saxon lands and mercilessly persecuted those who dared speak English. The French influence on both spoken and written English was pervasive. The language's grammar simplified while French and Latin borrowings increased the complexity of its lexicon. The last known document written in Old English, part of the *Anglo-Saxon Chronicle* written in 1154, shows many features of what we now call Middle English. The transformation—or evolution, if you will—by then was nearly complete.

Historical linguists date the emergence of Middle English to about 1150, when the influence of the Norman invasion was complete. Three major features marked the difference between Middle English and Old English: a greatly reduced system of grammatical inflections; a greatly increased lexicon, flooded with words from Latin and French; and highly varied *orthography*, or methods of writing. There was, in fact, no standardized form of written Middle English; spelling varied from person to person and region to region in England. Some Middle English writings are very easy for present-day people to read; others are nearly as difficult to read as the Old English text of *Beowulf*. As one simple example, consider the Old English word *leaf* (Modern English *leaf*). In Old English it had just that one spelling. In Middle English, though, the word appears as *lief, lieif, leif, lefe, leue, leeue,* and *leaue*.

The sounds of spoken Middle English remained similar to those of Old English. Some changes did occur, though. For example, Old English had a series of distinctive short and long vowel pairs. These changed in Middle English. Instead of the length of the sound being important, the tension of the tongue—whether or not the speaker held his or her tongue in a relaxed or tense state—became paramount in making the right sound. Another change involved the pronunciation of consonants. In Old English the speaker pronounced the first consonant in an initial consonant cluster—the hard *c* in the word *cnāwan*, for example. In Middle English the hard *c* pronunciation continued for several centuries, while the *cn* came to be written as *kn*. However, the pronunciation of that initial consonant eventually disappeared in later Middle English, leaving us today with words spelled *know* and *knight* but pronounced with a silent *k*.

Another pronunciation change involved the consonantal sound found in words like the German *ich* and *ach*. This sound from Old English remained in Middle English for much of its time period, and still exists in modern-day Scots. In later Middle English, though, it disappeared. Like the once-sounded hard *c* in *cn*, this particular *ch* sound became silent. Its silent "fossil" in contemporary English is represented by the *gh* in *dough, thought*, and *night*.

A third change in Middle English from Old English involved consonants lying between vowels. In Middle English these consonants were increasingly *elided*, that is, slurred or omitted. One example is seen in the Old English word *hlāfweard* (pronounced "loaf-ward"). In later Old English and early Middle English it became *hlāford*, and then *laford, louerd* (thirteenth century), and finally *lord* (fifteenth century). The *f* consonant sound had disappeared.

Intense contact with Danish and later French reduced Old English's inflectional system to a much simpler one in Middle English. Verbs got simpler, and so did nouns. The inflectional suffixes used in Old English for the plural and the infinitive began disappearing. A few still existed during Chaucer's time, and appear in his writing, but all were gone soon after. Old English's five case inflections for nouns shrank to two, common and possessive.

Some of the changes clearest to contemporary English speakers took place in the language's vocabulary or lexicon. Many Old English words survived into Middle English—and even to this day. Old English *bricg* became Middle English *bregge* and Modern English *bridge*. Old English *strang* became Middle English *stronge* and Modern English *strong*. However, the profound social and political changes wrought by the Norman occupation also displaced many other Old English words. For example, *nobilite* ("nobility") replaced *eorlscipe* ("earlship"), and *retorn* ("return") replaced *eftsīð*. Finally, Middle English began developing a dual Germanic-Romance (i.e., French) vocabulary that exists to the present day. So we have equivalent pairs of words such as the Anglo-Saxon-based *freedom* and the French *liberty*; *kingly* and *regal*; *lawful* and *legal*; *pig* and *pork*; *cow* and *beef*.

As mentioned earlier, ultimately a large portion of Middle English is still intelligible to the modern speaker or listener. Not only can we understand much of written Middle English, we can comprehend it when when we hear it spoken. This is not the case with Old English. Few of us can understand the meaning of this Old English sentence written in about the year 1000:

Gemiltsa mīnum suna

But it means the same as this Middle English sentence written some 385 years later:

Haue mercy on my sone

Without doubt Geoffrey Chaucer (1343–1400), the author of *The Canterbury Tales*, was one of the greatest writers of the English language. The son of a well-to-do wine merchant, Chaucer probably had the best available schooling that the child of wealthy parents would receive. He was familiar with Latin and several vernacular tongues besides his own. After some youthful adventures, in 1367 he became a member of the King's household. He carried out many diplomatic missions and was awarded with appointments to several important posts. Chaucer's own spoken language was the East Midland dialect of Middle English. During his lifetime he was saluted as a "good translator" of numerous poems and books of philosophy. But it is for his original writing that Chaucer is now honored: *The Book of the Duchess, The Parlemant of Fowls, Troilus and Criseyde*, and the greatest of them all, *The Canterbury Tales*. These would eventually establish his reputation as the greatest writer of Middle English and the founder of the English literary tradition.

However, Middle English was not an archaic form of Modern English. It was a different language, or perhaps we could think of both as radically different "dialects." Several reasons exist for this significant difference between Middle English and Modern English. One of the most important is called the *Great Vowel Shift*.

Starting around 1400, significant changes in pronunciation began taking place in English vowels. These changes are what make many of Chaucer's works so difficult for us to understand today. For one thing, in Chaucer's time people usually pronounced the final *e* in words like *stone, have*, and *love*. Within a century the final *e* in these kinds of words had become silent. We still have them in the words' written forms because the English writing system did not keep pace with the sound changes. The invention of the printing press in particular began a process of "freezing" the spelling of words into single accepted forms. That process was also gradual, ending in the late eighteenth century. But its effect was felt even after Chaucer's time.

Another shift in vowel pronunciation was even more influential, though. Long vowel sounds changed in a fundamental fashion as people formed the sounds differently in their mouths. The process applied specifically to long stressed monophthongs. These are vowels whose qualities are fairly constant, like the vowel sounds in *see, sit, hat, got, cup*, and *fur*. These vowels began changing from sounds similar to those used in Continental languages to the sounds they have today. You can feel the change for yourself: first say the word *spot*, and then the word *spat*. You will discover that you make the vowel sound in *spot* near the back of your mouth. The vowel sound in *spat*, however, you form up near the front and top of your mouth. That is the essence of the Great Vowel Shift in long stressed monophthongs. The *a* in Chaucer's Middle English word *fame* was actually pronounced like the *a* in today's word *father*. But it shifted forward and upward in the mouth, and *fame* eventually came to be prounounced as it is today, with a long *a*. The word *life* is another good example of the Great Vowel Shift. Chaucer pronounced *lyf* (as it was then often spelled) the way we pronounce the word *leaf*. Today we pronounce it with a "long" *i* sound.

Each shifting vowel in turn "pushed" the next one forward. The vowel sound we make in a word like *spat* got pushed further forward into the mouth and became like the vowel sound in *speed*. The sound in *speed* got pushed forward into the sound we make in *spate*. Vowels that were already formed at or near the top of the mouth became diphthongs with *ah* as the first part and the old vowel as the second part.

This monumental change in the way English speakers pronounced these vowels is the single most important influence on spoken English in its history. By 1700 it was complete. The following two tables illustrate the effects of the Great Vowel Shift on English and give some examples of changed words. The first shows what some of the vowels in Chaucer's English sounded like in terms of today's words. The second illustrates the Great Vowel Shift itself with vowels from several words.

Chaucer's English Sounds

In Chaucer's time, the ____ in ____	*actually sounded like the ____ in today's ____*
a in *fame*	*a* in *father*
e in *see*	a in *same*
i in *fine*	ee in *fee*
o in *so*	*aw* in *saw*
o in *to*	oe in *toe*
ou/ow in *crowd*	*u* in *crude*

The Great Vowel Shift, c. 1400–hr c. 1600

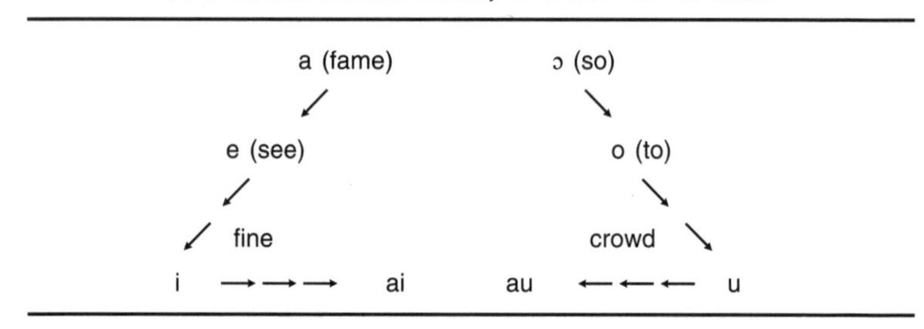

The Great Vowel Shift is probably a rather dramatic example of a process linguists call *drift*. Drift happens all the time. The pronunciation of words constantly changes. Drift is why dialects exist, and one reason why new languages eventually split off from older languages. The differences in pronunciation between American and British English, for example, are in part caused by linguistic drift. The Great Vowel Shift was a gradual change, taking well over two centuries to make its most dramatic changes obvious in the language.

Linguistic drift can even happen on very short timescales. A fellow-writer of Scandinavian ancestry once told me about an elderly Norwegian woman he knew. She had come to America as a very young child and had not spoken with people from her homeland in nearly eighty years. When she finally did, her visitors said that they had not heard anyone speak as she did since they had been youngsters.

Pronunciation can change in even shorter timespans, though. My own mother was born in Hungary and came with her family to the United States as a teenager just before World War II. American English then became her primary language; she spoke Hungarian only with her parents, and even then not often. In 1956 other relatives arrived from Hungary after the failed revolution against the then-Communist government. When my mother spoke to them in Hungarian, they remarked that she "sounded funny." In less than twenty years, Hungarian pronunciation had changed from what it had been in my mother's childhood.

But we are still faced with the question of *why* this dramatic change in vowel pronunciation took place. The short answer is that no one really knows. A part of the answer may lie in the geographic separation between England and Europe, the land of origin for the influx of the powerful French influence on English, like the geographic separation between England and North America. The English Channel is "only" about 240 kilometers wide at its widest, and just 34 kilometers across at the Strait of Dover. However, that was quite enough distance to slow significantly the language flow between the Jutes, Angles, and Saxons who had invaded England in the fifth century, and their mainland cousins. That is why Old English began to split away from the continental Germanic tongues. The same forces of separation contributed to the linguistic drift that caused the slow but inexorable Great Vowel Shift of the fifteenth to eighteenth centuries.

Moreover, the period of the Great Vowel Shift coincides with a very tumultous period in English and French history. The Hundred Years War between the two countries climaxed with the English defeat of the French at Agincourt in 1415. By 1430 England controlled a large section of northern France. Then fortunes reversed, as St. Joan of Arc led French troops to victory. Despite her capture and execution, France continued to prevail. By 1453 the English had been thrown out of France (with the exception of Calais, which they held until 1558).

From 1455 to 1485 the domestic Wars of the Roses occupied England, as vicious battles for the throne raged between the houses of Lancaster and York. They climaxed with the victories of Lancastrian champion Henry Tudor, who eventually became Henry VII and reigned from 1485 to 1509. His son Henry VIII followed, reigning from 1509 to 1547. His removal of the English Christian church from Rome's leadership was dramatic and bloody, and it increased English patriotic fervor. Following the death of Edward VI in 1553, Henry VIII's daughters Mary and Elizabeth fought another fierce civil war over the throne. Elizabeth won. By the end of her reign in 1603, as Shakespeare began writing some of his greatest plays, the Great Vowel Shift was in full swing.

Then there was the effect of disease. England suffered serious outbreaks of the plague on more than half a dozen occasions during the years of the Great Vowel Shift. More than twenty thousand people died in London from an outbreak in 1563. Another fifteen thousand Londoners died of the disease in 1592. The Great Plague of 1665 killed more than sixty-eight thousand people in London alone. All of these dramatic and often bloody events in English life may well have added to the isolation of Middle English from European influences to give linguistic drift plenty of room to operate on English pronunciation.

Much of the history of Middle English is a history of the written form of the language. But truth to tell, written Middle English was, despite Chaucer, a poor cousin in its own land. It never had the prestige of written Latin or French, which were widely used in England throughout the Middle English period from 1150 to 1430 or so. Most English writers of the time were multilingual, writing mainly in French or Latin. The basic reason for this state of affairs was simple: English—Middle English—was the language of a conquered people. It had all the status of the language of a conquered people, that is, none. However, Middle English was the common spoken language, the vernacular, of nearly everyone in England. The only exceptions were the Norman rulers.

Even these rulers had begun using English by the middle of the fifteenth century. By then the descendants of the Norman and French invaders had finally become assimilated into a culture and society—and language—they had themselves helped create: England's. This, too, is an important factor in the Great Vowel Shift. English culture and society had become distinct and separate from its earlier French influences. And the language of the former Norman conquerers and occupiers was no longer Middle English, much less Norman French. It had become Early Modern English.

Once again, one's point of view determines how one defines Early Modern English. We can think of it as the third stage in the continuing evolution of English from its Germanic roots to its present form, or as the first stage of a new language, different from both Old English and Middle English.

Certainly by about 1450 spoken and written English had changed sufficiently from its Middle English roots so as to be demonstrably different. The Great Vowel Shift was largely responsible for this. Two other major influences on the rise of Early Modern English were the development of a "standard" literary and administrative form of the language and the spread of English throughout England and Ireland. The English language traveled outward, carried by the expansionist actions of the Crown. Other languages in the British Isles went into decline, including the Celtic languages of Cornwall, Ireland, the Isle of Man, Scotland, and Wales. But the spread of English was not limited to its home islands. Explorers and colonists carried the English tongue to North America, the Caribbean islands, Africa, and Asia.

The grammar and pronunciation of Early Modern English continued to simplify, but this process was not a steady one. In fact, the evolution of Early Modern English is marked mostly by its great variability, particularly in its written forms. Spelling, especially, was quite unsettled.

Meanwhile, the English lexicon exploded in size. Travelers and scholars brought huge numbers of new words into the language. They came from Latin and Greek for scholarly and scientific purposes, and from Italian for literary uses. Borrowings came from Spanish and Portuguese as well.

The period of Early Modern English also saw a flowering of written literature in the language. Much of the "classic" English literature we all read in high school or college was written not in Modern English but in Early Modern English. *Everyman*, the morality play, appeared first in 1510. Thomas More's *Utopia* first appeared in an English translation from the Latin original in 1551. Christopher Marlowe wrote *Tamburlaine* in 1587 and *Doctor Faustus* in 1588. In 1590 the first three books of Edmund Spenser's epic poem *The Faerie Queene* were published. Thomas Kyd's *The Spanish Tragedy* was first performed in 1592. William Shakespeare's plays (including *A Midsummer Night's Dream*, with its *puca* named Puck) were all written in Early Modern English. John Milton began writing *Paradise Lost* in 1667.

Modern English did not begin appearing in anything like its current form until the beginning of the eighteenth century. By then the English colonies in America had successfully revolted against the Crown, and Marlowe, Spenser, Shakespeare, Ben Jonson, Sir Philip Sidney, and John Milton were all long dead. It is not surprising that much of this classic English literature is difficult to read. It is also hard to understand when spoken aloud, which is the best way to experience poetry or drama. The language in which it was written—while demonstrably English—was still quite different from our contemporary English, but it was well on the way to becoming Modern English.

By the nineteenth century English had spread well beyond the island first overrun by Jutes and Frisians fourteen centuries earlier. The British were busy conquering India and occupying Australia, where they did unto the aborigines what their own ancestors had done unto the Celts. And American English was becoming a dialect distinct from British English. By the end of World War II, Modern English was transforming into World English, with American English leading the way.

THE LANGUAGE OF SCIENCE AND LITERATURE

Despite being a "dead language," Latin remains very much alive in English today. As we briefly noted earlier, Latin as a language has existed in Italy from at least the sixth century B.C.E. The armies of Rome later carried vernacular Latin to the far corners of the Roman Empire. Latin totally replaced the Celtic tongues spoken in present-day Italy, France (then known as Gaul), Romania, and Spain and influenced the languages of those living in England. From these beginnings sprang the Romance languages of French, Italian, Spanish, and Romanian.

Italian eventually replaced Latin as the common language of the average person. But a classical form of Latin continued to be used by the Christian church in its rituals and prayers. During the Middle Ages, Latin was the "universal language" of scholarship throughout Europe. You might be from England, Germany, or Spain, but if you could speak or write in Latin, you could spread your ideas. Though it finally fell from grace as a common scholarly language after the Renaissance, Latin continued to exert a strong influence on its daughter languages. This is certainly the case with English. Church Latin contributed vocabulary to English for centuries. But as we have seen, a huge influx of Latin words and Latin-inspired words enriched the English vocabulary from about the fifteenth century onward. Middle English was evolving into Early Modern English, and part of that evolution was an enrichment of vocabulary.

Today, English is stuffed with Latin-derived words. For example, take one sentence from two paragraphs earlier: "The armies of Rome later carried vernacular Latin to the far corners of the Roman Empire." Look at the words in that sentence with Latin roots:

- *Armies* comes from *armare*, "to arm."
- *Carried* derives from *currere*, "to run."
- *Empire* has its origin in the Latin word *imperium*, "absolute authority."
- *Latin* comes from *Latium*, the ancient name for Italy.
- *Roman* derives from *Romulus*, the legendary founder of the city.
- *Vernacular* has its origin in *vernaculus*, "common."

Nowhere, though, has Latin's influence on English vocabulary been more obvious than in the sciences. Many scientific words and terms have Latin roots. Astronomy (*astronomia*), genus (*genus*), geology (*geologia*), refraction (*refractus*), and tissue (*texere*) are just a very few examples of scientific or technical words with Latin origins. The realms of science, medicine, and technology are rife with them. The reason goes back to the Middle Ages and the Renaissance, when Latin was the language of every educated person. In that tradition scientists have diligently used Latin as a principal source for the specialized words of their jargon.

There was once a time when that tradition of a Latin education still existed. Even in the supposedly classless United States, an "educated person" would have some academic knowledge of Latin, perhaps studying it for a year or two in high school or college. Many of us over the age of forty or so have had some exposure to the language of the classics. My own experience with Latin was somewhat out of the ordinary. I took nearly five years of Latin classes, four in high school and a semester in college. That was because, at the time, I was in a Roman Catholic seminary studying to be a priest.

Today, though, few young people know anything about this important language. Latin is definitely not "hip." Hardly any high schools or colleges offers classes in Latin. And that is, in my opinion, a shame. To know Latin, even in a cursory sense from just a semester class, means having a deeper appreciation for English. Ours is a wonderfully rich language, and Latin has helped make it so. Though I never became a Catholic priest, I now find myself grateful for that exposure to Latin. Unfamiliar words are not as incomprehensible as they might otherwise be. I can often puzzle out the basic meaning of a word by seeking its Latin origins. And even if the word is one I do know, discovering its Latin derivation gives me a more enjoyable understanding of the word's history. English has roots, and they include Latin. We can all use some more "rooting" these days. Perhaps our language's roots would be a good place to start.

THE LANGUAGES OF THE BIBLE

Two other languages that have had an influence on English do not belong to the Indo-European family. They are Hebrew and Aramaic, among the oldest living tongues on the planet.

Both are members of the Afro-Asiatic family of languages. More than two hundred major languages spoken by well over two hundred million people belong to this family, which covers North Africa, much of the Middle East, and southwest Asia. The parent or proto-language to all the Afro-Asiatic tongues probably arose and was spoken some eight to ten thousand years ago in the present-day Sahara region of North Africa. The family has six major branches. Five of them are fairly minor: the Berber, Chadic, Cushitic, Egyptian, and Omotic branches. The Chadic group includes about a hundred tongues spoken by perhaps twenty-five million people. The Egyptian branch had one language, Egyptian, which is now extinct. It was the language of the ancient Egyptian civilization and evolved into Coptic. Today Coptic is extinct except as a religious language used by the Monophysite Christians of Egypt.

The sixth and most important branch of the Afro-Asiatic family is the Semitic group of languages. This major group of languages stretches from the Atlantic coast of North Africa to the shores of the Persian Gulf and into southwest Asia. The oldest Semitic languages are all extinct; they include Akkadian, Moabite, and Phoenician, and date to about 3000 B.C.E. The most important Semitic language today, in terms of contemporary influence and number of speakers, is Arabic. For more than 150 million people Arabic is their mother tongue, and several million more use it as a second language. Other contemporary Semitic tongues include Amharic, the official language of Ethiopia, and Tigrina. However, neither Arabic nor these other Semitic languages have had the impact on English that the Semitic tongues known as Hebrew and Aramaic have had.

Until it was displaced by Arabic in the seventh century C.E., Aramaic was the most widely spoken language in western Asia and the Middle East. Scholars have documented the use of Aramaic as far back as the seventh century B.C.E. Aramaic's biggest claim to fame is biblical. Several sections of the Jewish scriptures, most of which are part of the Christian Bible's Old Testament, were originally written in Aramaic, including the Books of Ezra and Daniel. Aramaic was the vernacular for most of the people living in the biblical lands of Galilee and Judea at the beginning of the Current Era. Jesus therefore almost certainly spoke Aramaic. Most of the Talmud and many important works of Jewish mysticism are written in Aramaic dialects. Many Yiddish words originated as Aramaic.

Several Aramaic words from the Jewish and Christian Bibles have entered the English language. Though not commonly used, they are nonetheless familiar to many in a literary sense. One is *maranatha*, which appears in St. Paul's first letter to the Corinthians (16:22). Another is the famous phrase *mene, mene, tekel, upharsin*, the writing that mysteriously appears on the wall of King Nebuchadnezzar's palace in the Old Testament Book of Daniel (5:25–31). This story, by the way, is also the origin of the phrase "the writing on the wall," as in "President Nixon saw the writing on the wall and resigned."

Around the fifth century C.E., the Aramaic dialect spoken around the Turkish city of Urfa, then known as Edessa, evolved into another language called Syriac. Until the spread of Islam across the Middle East and western Asia in the eighth and ninth centuries, Syriac and Aramaic continued to be spoken by a great many people. Afterwards it entered a decline, replacing Hebrew as the vernacular in Palestine but in turn being dominated by Arabic as the major spoken language of the region. Aramaic is today considered by many to be an extinct language. However, several Aramaic dialects continue to be spoken by small communities in Syria, Lebanon, Iraq, Iran, and parts of the former Soviet Union.

Aramaic's influence on English is primarily indirect, as the language of portions of the Jewish scriptures, the Talmud, and many Jewish religious rituals. Hebrew has had a considerably larger influence. One of the world's oldest languages, Hebrew is still spoken in much the same way as it was more than two thousand years ago. It is closely related to Aramaic and ancient Phoenician and also has linguistic connections to Arabic. Most of us know it best as the language of the Jewish Bible.

Historical linguists divide the history of the Hebrew tongue into four parts. *Biblical Hebrew* was the form of the language spoken from about the twelfth century B.C.E. to about 70 C.E. It was the language of the Jewish patriarchs, prophets, and kings. This phase came to an end in 70 C.E. with the destruction of Jerusalem by the Romans. *Mishnaic Hebrew* was spoken from about that time until the beginning of the fifth century. It was followed by *Medieval Hebrew*, spoken until about the thirteenth century. During these periods Hebrew was gradually replaced by Aramaic and its dialects as the vernacular of the people. It continued to be used as a liturgical or religious language, though, in Jewish rituals and prayers.

The most recent phase in the history of Hebrew, called *Modern Hebrew*, began in the late nineteenth century through the efforts of one man. The Jewish scholar Eliezer ben Yehuda was born in Lithuania in 1858 and settled in Palestine in 1881. He made it his life's work to revive Hebrew as a living language. Ben Yehuda compiled the sixteen-volume *Dictionary of Ancient and Modern Hebrew*. He not only reintroduced the classic forms and vocabulary of Hebrew to the modern world but also incorporated thousands of contemporary words into the language. This revised form, known also today as *ivrit* or *Israeli Hebrew*, gradually became the language of Jewish settlers of Palestine. When Israel became a state in 1948, it adopted this form of Hebrew as one of its two official languages. The other is Arabic, spoken as their mother tongue by the nearly half-million Arab citizens of Israel.

Hebrew influence on English, like that of French or Latin, has been through vocabulary. That effect has been both direct and indirect. The direct influence comes from English translations of the Bible. Biblical Hebrew words that now have a place in English include obvious ones like *amen, babel, hallelujah, rabbi, Sabbath, seraph*, and *shibboleth*. Other English words of Hebrew origin may come as surprises: *behemoth*, for example, and *camel*, as well as *cherub, leviathan*, and *Satan*. During the Renaissance a number of Hebrew religious and cultural terms filtered into English, including *Cabbala, mezuzah*, and *Talmud*. A number of Hebrew words have entered English indirectly through

Yiddish, especially since the nineteenth-century influx of Yiddish-speaking Jewish immigrants into the United States from Eastern Europe. They include *chutzpah* (gall, outrageous impudence), *goy* (a non-Jew or gentile), *kosher* (ritually appropriate or approved), *magilla* (a long story), *mazuma* (cash or money), and *shamus* (a detective).

Some recent additions to English from Israeli Hebrew are *kibbutz* (a collective farm community) and *sabra* (a native-born Israeli). These days, though, the linguistic influence tends to run in the opposite direction. British English has had a significant influence on *ivrit* as a result of the lengthy British colonial stewardship over Palestine and the Middle East. However, American English is also exercising considerable lexical influence on Israeli Hebrew. This is due mainly to motion pictures, English-language magazines and newspapers such as the *Jerusalem Post*, the extensive American Jewish immigration to Israel since 1948, and the stormy but still-real political influence of the United States in Israel.

AMERICAN ENGLISH

American English, also called *United States English*, is the version of English spoken by those in the United States. American English speakers outnumber British English speakers by almost four to one, and all speakers of English variants around the world by nearly two to one. Thus American and not British English has come to dominate the global linguistic scene. Historical linguists tend to divide the history of American English into three distinct periods: the *Colonial Period*, from 1607 to 1776; the *National Period*, from 1776 to 1898; and the *International Period*, from 1898 to the present.

On May 14, 1607, a group of colonists sponsored by the London Company established the first permanent settlement on mainland North American by English-speaking people. Jamestown, named for the King, is located in what is today Virginia. This settlement marks the beginning of the Colonial Period of American English. Other settlements soon followed, including the Plymouth Colony in 1620 in present-day Massachusetts and the Maryland Colony in 1664. The 1624 Dutch settlement on Manhattan Island was taken over by the English in 1664. In 1681 William Penn started his colony of Quakers in today's Pennsylvania. Early English-speaking settlers came from many different parts of England. So from the beginning no specific English dialect gained precedence. Rather, the different British English dialects mixed together in the Colonies to produce a fairly uniform version of British English.

The vast geographic separation caused by the Atlantic Ocean, and the accompanying slowness in transportation between England and her colonies, meant that American English quickly began to diverge from its British roots. The colonists continued to use old pronunciations for some words and changed others. They also added new words to their vocabulary, adopting words from Native American languages as well as from French and Dutch. By the time the Revolutionary War began in 1776, American English was well on its way to becoming distinct from British English.

The National Period began with the Revolutionary War and lasted more than a century. As the United States slowly and then more rapidly expanded across the continent, the language of its people picked up still more additions to its vocabulary. An influx of immigrants from throughout Europe added richness and variety to the American lexicon. The Great Potato Famine of 1845 in Ireland eventually resulted in more than a million and a half Irish immigrants coming to America by 1855. In 1848 a failed revolution in Germany started an influx of an equal number of Germans to America. Both nationalities contributed new words and phrases to the fast-changing American English language.

A sense of "Manifest Destiny" and intense nationalism reigned in America for much of the nineteenth century. A linguistic expression of that nationalism appeared in the work of Noah Webster, who put together the first dictionary of what he called Federal English. Webster deliberately set out to promote, and create if necessary, an American English distinct and separate from British English. It was Webster who was responsible for some significant changes in spelling between British and American English. He urged the use of *-or* instead of *-our* in words like *color* and *favor*, as well as *-er* instead of the British *-re* in words like *center*. Webster also established the American practice of using *check* for *cheque* and *jail* for *gaol*. The Civil War disrupted American society and language development, and some scholars feel the National Period ends at the Civil War. Others, though, suggest 1898 as its conclusion.

After the Civil War, Americans began settling the West in greater numbers, and the language grew richer for it. During the period from 1865 to about 1890, American English was strongly influenced by this

Western migration as well as by the growth of the railroads, the explosion of industry, the rise of the labor unions, the development of the telegraph and telephone, the increase in literacy, the aggressive development of newspaper journalism, and a boom in magazine and book publishing.

By the end of the nineteenth century, America had begun running out of domestic frontiers. Its formerly isolationist foreign policy began to change. In 1898 President William McKinley broke with that long isolationist tradition and took America into the world arena. The United States fought Spain in the four-month-long Spanish-American War and won. This marked the end of the Nationalist Period of American English and the beginning of the International Period. The United States annexed Hawaii and took possession of Puerto Rico and the Philippine Islands. America was taking the first bold steps toward becoming an international power. By 1917, when it entered World War I, America had already helped Panama secede from Colombia in order to build the Panama Canal, meddled in other Latin American affairs, bought the Virgin Islands from Denmark, and mediated the Russo-Japanese War.

Now the United States was "exporting" its languages as well as its political policies and economic desires. The returning soldiers brought new words to the language. Hollywood and its movies affected American English, as did the development of jazz. World War II wrought profound changes in American English, of course, bringing new words into its vocabulary from around the world. Americanisms in turn were globally propagated. American science, technology, and industry influenced the language, and the language spread across the planet. Meanwhile, new waves of immigrants brought their languages and accents into contact with American English. African-Americans fought for their civil rights and became a greater force in American politics, and their dialects added texture to American English. By the 1980s the fastest-growing minority in America was Hispanic-Americans, with their own rich cultural traditions and equally rich language.

American vs. British English

Few of us are versed in linguistics, but most of us can tell the difference between English dialects. We can often identify a Bronx accent or recognize that someone is from the Deep South. And almost all of us can distinguish between American and British English. After all, hasn't everyone watched *Monty Python* on television? Or thrilled to Sir Alec Guinness as Obi Wan Kenobi in the *Star Wars* movies?

Of course, that's a bit of an exaggeration. But the truth is that American English has been diverging in pronunciation and vocabulary from its British parent for more than two centuries. Both Americans and Britons have been aware of that for nearly as long. Comparisons and contrasts of the two versions of English have gone on for decades, often within the context of intense nationalistic feelings. Noah Webster, as we have seen, urged the development of a Federal English as a patriotic duty of all Americans. Even today, the attitudes of Americans and Britons towards the others' language are tinged with patriotism and, indeed, a little snobbishness. Most Americans tend to think that a British accent is "highfalutin'." Most British consider an American accent to be crass. However, the differences between American and British English go much deeper, in both the written and spoken forms of the two varieties.

Several differences in spelling stand out. Many are systematic; they cover whole classes of words. The best known include the *color/colour* group of words, the *center/centre* group, the *-ize/-ise* group, and the *-lyze/-lyse* group of words. In general, British spellings tend to be more acceptable in America than American spellings in England.

Many more differences exist between the spoken forms of American and British English. They include not only the obvious differences in pronunciation but also differences in grammar and vocabulary. One good example of a pronunciation difference is the sound symbolized by the written letter *r*. In American English this sound is *rhotic*; it is pronounced in all positions within words, as in words like *rare* and *rarer*. In British English the sound is *nonrhotic*; it is pronounced only when a vowel follows it. A speaker of British English would not pronounce the second *r* in *rare*, unless the word following it began with a vowel: *That's a rather rare article*. The second *r* in *rather* is not pronounced, since it is not followed by a vowel. But the second *r* in *rare* would be, since the word following *rare* (*article*) begins with a vowel.

A more general difference in pronunciation has to do with differences in melody and rhythm. American English, in general, has less variation in pitch than British English.

Many grammatical differences exist between British and American English. The use of *should/would* is a good illustration. Using *should* is much less common in American English. In British usage *should* is often used to indicate advice or to make demands: *I should be more careful, if I were you* or *I insist that he should leave at once!* Some other grammatical differences include the following:

- *Group nouns:* British English will emphasize the individual members of a group noun in a phrase like *The government are divided*, something almost never heard in American English. Both variations of the language, though, will use the collective form *The government is divided.*
- *Give:* The form *Give it me* is British English, while *Give me it*—admittedly bad grammar!—is mainly American English.
- *Enough:* The form *They're rich enough that they can retire* is mainly American English and would almost never be heard in British English usage. Both varieties would use the form *They're rich enough to retire.*
- *Time expressions:* Both American and British varieties share forms like *Monday to Friday inclusive.* More American than British is *Monday through Friday*, while *Monday through to Friday* is much more British than American. A speaker of British English is likely to say *a week on Tuesday*, while an American speaker is more likely to say *a week from Tuesday.*

Just as important as these specific differences is a more general difference in attitude toward grammar. Educated Americans, for the most part, try to "obey the rules of grammar." Equally educated Britons, though, are more inclined to violate them.

There are the multitudinous differences in vocabulary between the two variants of English. Some are exclusive, some nonexclusive. The words *windscreen* and *windshield* illustrate an exclusive vocabulary difference. The former word is used only in British English, the latter only in American. *Boot* versus *trunk* (of a car) is another example, as are the words *chemist* and *pharmacist.* Nonexclusive differences in vocabulary include some words that are shared, along with a variant or synonym that is exclusive. Both British and American English use the word *autumn*, for example, but only American English uses the synonym *fall.* Some shared words have exclusive British and American variants. One example is the word *socket*, as in *electrical socket.* Both British and American English use the word. However, American English has the synonym *outlet*, which does not appear in the British English lexicon; British English uses the synonym *power point*, which you will never hear used in the United States.

Americans and Britons often use prepositions differently. Americans live *on* a street, while Britons live *in* a street. Americans go sailing *on* the weekend, while Britons do it *at* the weekend. Americans are *of* two minds about that nasty political situation, while Britons are *in* two minds about it. They also use articles differently at times; Americans *go to the hospital*, but Britons *go to hospital*. Americans might like to *go on a vacation*, while Britons *go on holiday* (no *a*).

The Top Ten Mother Tongues

Language	*# of Native Speakers*
Chinese	1,000,000,000
English	350,000,000
Spanish	250,000,000
Hindi (India)	200,000,000
Arabic	150,000,000
Bengali (India)	150,000,000
Russian	150,000,000
Portuguese	135,000,000
Japanese	120,000,000
German	100,000,000

Figures from *The Cambridge Encyclopedia of Language*. All numbers are best estimates only and will undoubtedly change over time.

As we approach the end of the twentieth century, English, particularly American English but also British English, is now the preferred language of commerce, science, technology, politics, economics, literature, and education. English literacy has grown slowly but steadily. The boom in book and magazine publishing that began after World War II has not slowed down, despite the arrival of the Electronic Age and the computer screen. At the beginning of the new millenium, English is certainly not the most widely spoken language in the world. That honor goes to Chinese. But English *is* the most important language on the face of the Earth. Of that there is no doubt.

The Saxon raiders of 449 would doubtless be astonished at what their descendants have wrought.

CHAPTER 3

THE SOUNDS OF LANGUAGE

When children speak, the words that come out of their mouths travel across the space between them and their listeners on waves of sound. They are density waves: the air compresses and expands as it moves outward from our mouths. The waves hit the ears of the listeners and are converted into electrochemical impulses that travel along the auditory nerves into the brain. Our children and grandchildren speak; we hear them.

Written language converts those auditory signals, those density waves of air, into marks on paper, or papyrus, or clay, or stone. The marks may stand for entire words or phrases. In English and most other contemporary languages, the marks are letters, and they stand for the distinct vocal parts of spoken words. However, not all written letters are equal in sound. One person's *k* may be another's *c*. My *ph* at the beginning of *phone* may be utterly baffling to you. And the *e* in *let* surely has not the same sound as the *e* in *seam*. For that matter, why do we use *ea* in *seam* to stand for the same sound as the *ee* in *seem*?

One of the important jobs of any science, of course, is to classify the objects of its attention. The same is true of linguistics. So phoneticians, phonologists, and other linguists happily classify the sounds they study.

Babies don't. They don't have to. None of us needed an intellectual grasp of any principles of physics in order to learn to ride a bicycle. We did not need to know the ins and outs of avian taxonomy to learn that a robin is not a bluejay. Nor does my grandson need to know the difference between an unvoiced bilabial plosive and a voiced dental fricative to discern the difference between *pat* and *that*. Somehow, some way, young Ryan is grasping the rules and regulations of English, his mother tongue. He is creating vowels and consonants, vocoids and contoids, diphthongs and triphthongs. Soon he will begin putting them together to make syllables, words, sentences, and finally narratives. He will do it with no formal tutoring in linguistics but with enormous amounts of input from his parents and other adults, and almost certainly with the help of some kind of genetically programmed neurological affinity to create language.

Some infants like Ryan Patrick Nash grow up to become linguists, who proceed to categorize the sounds they once learned almost intuitively. People who as babies couldn't care less about vowels and consonants now puzzle out ways to arrange them in graphs and tables. They use language to study language, completing the circle that began with their first babbles.

As linguistics began to mature as a proper science, its practitioners recognized the necessity of bringing order to *phonetics*, that branch of linguistics that studies the production, transmission, and reception of speech sounds. In 1886 a group of French language teachers started the Phonetic Teachers' Association. They had found the practice of phonetics useful in their own teaching and wanted to popularize it. That same year they began printing a journal entitled *Dhi Fonètik Tîtcer*. The editor was Paul Passy, the French phonetician and language-teaching specialist who had founded the Phonetic Teachers' Association. Eleven years later they changed the name of the group to L'Association Phonétique Internationale, or the International Phonetic Association. Otto Jesperson (1869–1943) first proposed the creation of a *phonetic alphabet* the same year. The Association published the first such alphabet two years later.

Vowels

	Front		Central		Back
Close	i y		i ʉ		ɯ u
		i ʏ		ʊ	
Mid-Close	e ø				ɤ o
			ə ɵ		
Mid-Open	ɛ œ				ʌ ɔ
	æ		ɐ		
Open	a œ				ɑ ɒ

Where symbols appear in pairs, the one to the left represents an unrounded vowel, and the one to the right represents a rounded vowel.

In a phonetic alphabet each symbol represents a specific sound, regardless of the language or languages in which the sound may appear. Jesperson and the Association decided that the alphabet would use Roman alphabet letters to represent as many sounds as possible. They agreed to use new symbols only when needed. (The Roman characters are the letters with which we are all familiar. You are reading them now. All the Germanic and Romance written languages, including English, use the Roman alphabet. Russian uses the Cyrillic alphabet, with some letters differing from those in the Roman alphabet. Arabic letters, on the other hand, are completely unrelated to those of the Roman alphabet.)

More than a century later, the original phonetic alphabet has been revised and modified several times. It is also accepted nearly worldwide. The phonetic symbols you see in a dictionary are essentially taken from it. The two illustrations depict the International Phonetic Alphabet (IPA) in graphic form. Keep in mind that the symbols in the consonant grid and the vowel box *are not letters*. They are phonetic symbols that represent specific sounds. In the Appendix are the formal descriptions of the IPA phonetic symbols, a list of sample pronunciations for the IPA symbols used in English, and a list of the common pronunciation symbols used in dictionaries and examples of words in which they appear.

The IPA is the "written language" of linguistics. These are the symbols linguists use to denote all the possible language sounds and the specific sounds used in specific languages. To understand how the IPA works to represent sounds, and to understand what the symbols mean, we first need to have a basic grasp of just how we make those sounds.

Consonants

	Bilabial	*Labiodental*	*Dental, Alveolar, or Post-Alveolar*	*Retroflex*	*Palatal*	*Velar*	*Uvular*	*Pharyngeal*	*Glottal*
Pulmonic									
Plosive	p b		t d	ʈ ɖ	c ɟ	k g	q ɢ		ʔ
Nasal	m	ɱ	n	ɳ	ɲ	ŋ	ɴ		
Fricative	Φ β	f v	θð ʂz ʃʒ	ʂ ʐ	ç ɨ	χ ɤ	ŋ ʁ	h ʕ	h ɦ
Lateral Fricative			ɬ ɮ						
Approximant		ʋ	ɹ	ɻ	j	ɯ			
Lateral Approximant			ɪ	ɭ	ʎ	ʟ			
Trill	ʙ		r				ʀ		
Flap			ɾ	ɽ					
Non-Pulmonic									
Ejective stop	p’		t’	ʈ’	c’	k’	q’		
Implosive	p ɓ		ɾ d		c ɟ	k g	q ɢ		

Where symbols appear in pairs, the symbol to the left is an unvoiced consonant, and the one to the right is voiced.

A Few Important Words

It is also worth knowing some of the jargon of phonetics. One important term is *phone*—not a telephone, but a basic unit in phonetics. A phone is defined as the smallest perceptible discrete segment of speech sound. In fact, *speech sound* is a formal synonym for phone. Another way to think of a phone is as a sound segment a listener can clearly identify as a vowel or consonant. Of course, no two people say the same word or syllable in exactly the same way, and each of us uses sounds in a slightly different fashion each time we speak. So the number of possible phones used in any language—not to mention all possible languages—is practically infinite. As we will learn later in more detail, each healthy human infant is born with the ability to make all possible linguistic sounds or phones. *All* of them. During the first few months of life a baby does make them, in a sense trying them out and seeing which ones get positive responses from mom and dad. Not all languages use all possible phones. Each language uses a smaller subset of possible speech sounds. A baby soon learns which phones are "acceptable" and which are not. The particular phones used in a particular language are called *phonemes*.

The phoneme is the basic unit of a language's *sound system*. Syllables are formed out of phonemes, which we can think of as the basic building blocks of a language. Words are like houses, and phonemes are the bricks, boards, nails, plaster, and glue we use to build them. We can build many different kinds of houses, and we can use a huge variety of materials to build one. However, all the houses built by any one tend to be similar, using a small subset of the possible building materials available. A phoneme is a unit of language, according to the *Oxford English Dictionary of the English Language*, that "cannot be analysed into smaller linear units and that in any particular language is realized in non-contrastive variants." The word *bin*, for example (which is also a single syllable), consists of the three units or phonemes /b/, /ɪ/, and /n/.* These particular sound-units cannot be broken down into smaller pieces. They are like the electrons or quarks that make up an atom. They are the "fundamental particles" of a particular language.

A more practical definition of *phoneme* is offered by the *Longman*

*Most linguists use the phonetic symbols of the IPA to represent both phones and phonemes. They denote a phone by surrounding the phonetic symbol with brackets: [t] or [k] or [ʍ]. They signify a phoneme in writing by surrounding the phonetic symbol with slashes: /t/ or /e/ or /lʒ/.

Dictionary of Applied Linguistics: "the smallest unit of sound in a language which can distinguish two words." Suppose your husband says to you, "Darling, I put that pin in the bin marked FUSION GENERATOR PARTS." "Thank you, dear," you reply. "I'll finish repairing that generator right after lunch." When we hear *pin* and *bin* spoken, we know they are different words with different meanings. The only difference between the two words /pɪn/ and /bɪn/ are the phonemes /p/ and /b/. In the two words *pan* /pæn/ and *pin* /pɪn/ the only differences are the phonemes /æ/ and /ɪ/.

Phonetics is one branch of linguistics. Another is *phonology*, the study of the sound patterns in languages. Sometimes phonology is considered a subbranch of phonetics, sometimes a separate study. Phonologists study both the phonemes in a language and a language's use of *prosody*, its rhythm and pacing. *Phonemics*, the study of phonemes and phonemic systems, has long been the primary focus of phonology. In the last several decades, though, that has changed, as phonologists have begun looking at the rules that govern the creation of a language's sound patterns.

THE SOUND SYSTEM

When we talk about language we are usually referring to spoken languages, not sign languages, even though sign languages are full-blown, complete languages. So we ought to take a look at the physical mechanism we use to create spoken languages, the *larynx*.

The larynx—commonly referred to as the "voice box"—is a tube made of four sets of cartilage along with connecting membranes and ligaments. Inside the tube are two bands of muscular tissue called the *vocal cords* or *vocal folds*. The larynx is located in the *trachea*, the upper part of the throat. The front part of the larynx, the *thyroid cartilage*, sticks out of the neck and is called the *Adam's apple*. (Anyone remotely familiar with the biblical Book of Genesis and the associated nonbiblical but popular story of Eve and the apple can figure out the origins of the phrase.) Three other sets of cartilage in the larynx help control the way the vocal folds vibrate.

The opening between the vocal folds is called the *glottis*. The glottis in men is between 17 and 24 millimeters wide. In women it ranges from 13 to 17 millimeters in width. Women tend to have higher-pitched voices than do men because the glottis is smaller in women. The reason? Women tend to be smaller overall than men. This difference in body size, by the way, is not a case of nature discriminating against women—the other way around, in fact. Female humans are much tougher than the males of the species. They can endure much more physical punishment and environmental stress. Their smaller bodies contain more fatty padding and can last longer on less food and water. Women live longer than men, all other factors being equal. Nature's bottom line is this: women make babies, and men don't. The more women there are, the more likely the species will continue. So think of high-pitched feminine voices as a sign of Mother Nature's support.

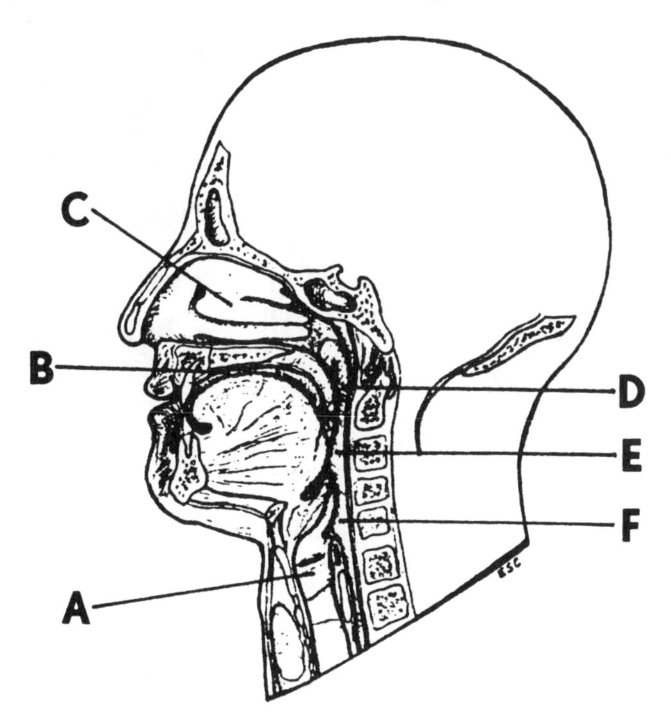

This drawing shows the major parts of the upper respiratory system in an adult human. They include (A) the larynx; (B) the oral cavity or mouth; (C) the right nasal cavity; and three parts of the throat leading from the larynx to the mouth called (D) the nasopharynx, (E) the oropharynx, and (F) the laryngopharynx. All play a part in speech.
Illustration courtesy of Dr. Edmund S. Crelin, from his book *The Human Vocal Tract* (New York: Vantage Press, 1987).

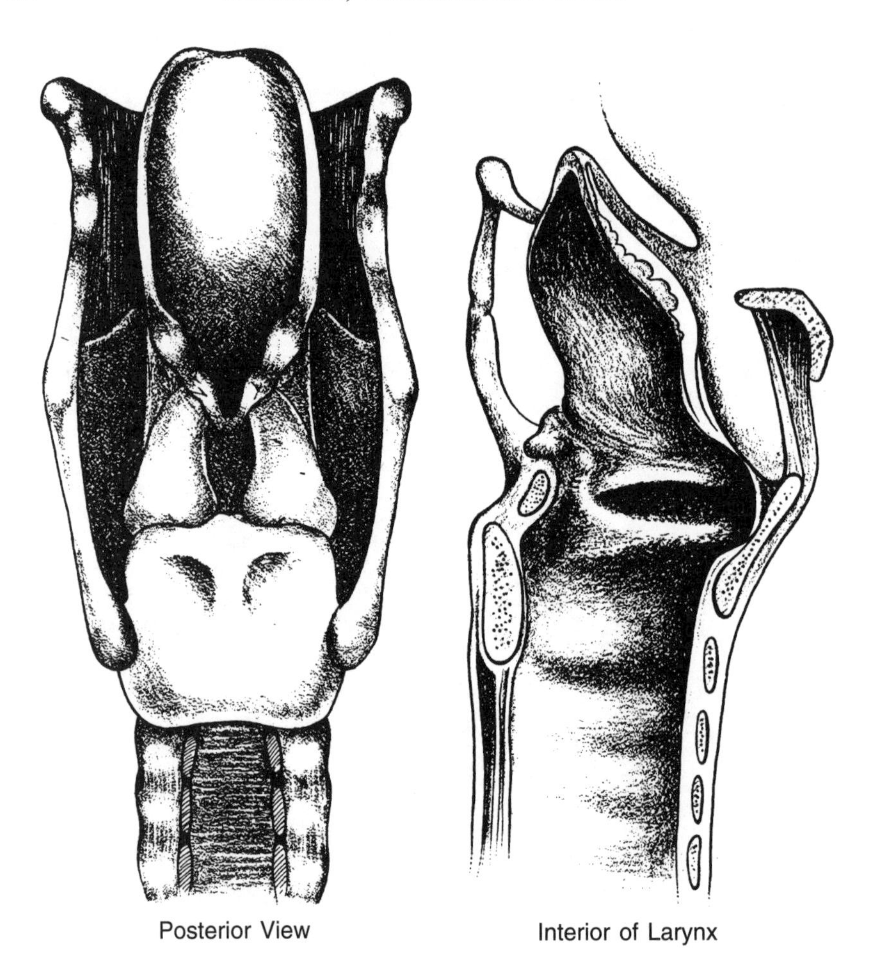

These drawings show a rear view of the human larynx, as well as the larynx's interior.
Illustration courtesy of Dr. John M. Palmer, from *Anatomy for Speech and Hearing* (New York: Harper and Row, 1965). 1st Edition.

The complex interactions of the muscles controlling them, combined with the movements of their three associated cartilages, make the vocal folds extremely adaptable. Their elasticity, height, length, tension, thickness, and width can all change from instant to instant. The result is a wide variety of sounds and auditory effects: *voice* or *phonation, pitch, glottal stops, glottal friction*, and other vocal qualities.

Nearly all the speech sounds we create make use of the vocal quality called voice or phonation. This is the buzzing, vibrating quality that

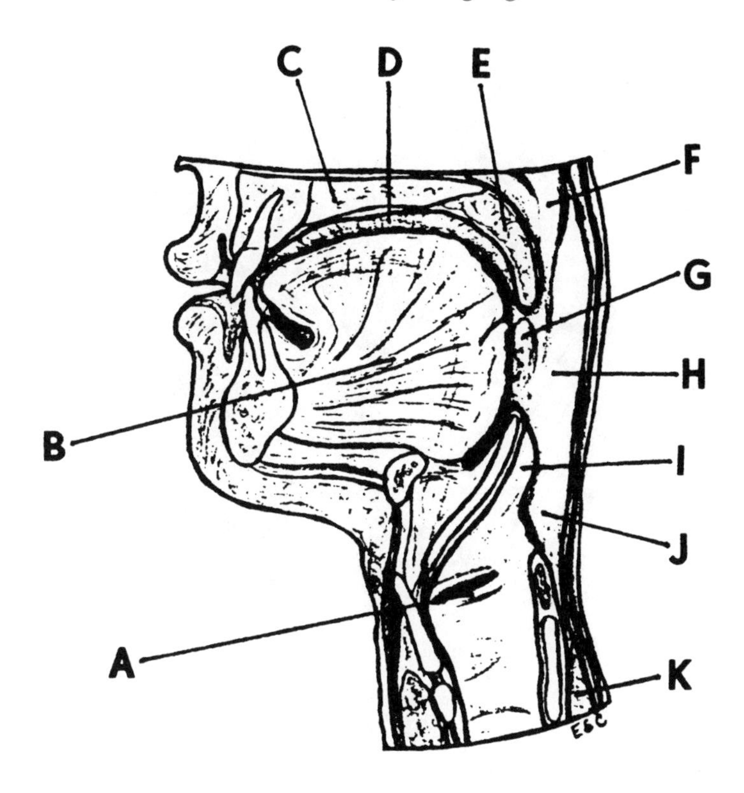

This drawing is a closeup of different parts of the human vocal tract. They include (A) the right vocal chord or fold; (B) the tongue; (C) the hard palate; (D) the oral cavity or mouth; (E) the soft palate; (F) the nasopharynx; (G) a tonsil; (H) the oropharynx; (I) the epiglottis; (J) the laryngopharynx; and (K) the esophagus or throat.
Illustration courtesy of Dr. Edmund S. Crelin, from his book *The Human Vocal Tract* (New York: Vantage Press, 1987).

phones possess. Place your fingers on your Adam's apple and make the sounds [m], [zzz], [d], and [a]. You can not only hear the buzzing sound, you can actually feel the vocal folds vibrate. Each vibratory pulse marks a single opening and closing of the vocal folds. In adult males this happens on the average about 120 times or cycles per second. In adult females, with their smaller vocal cords, it averages about 220 cycles per second, about middle C on the piano. A newborn has a larynx with very short vocal folds, so his cry averages about 400 cycles per second.

Pitch is a function of the vibratory cycles of the vocal folds. The

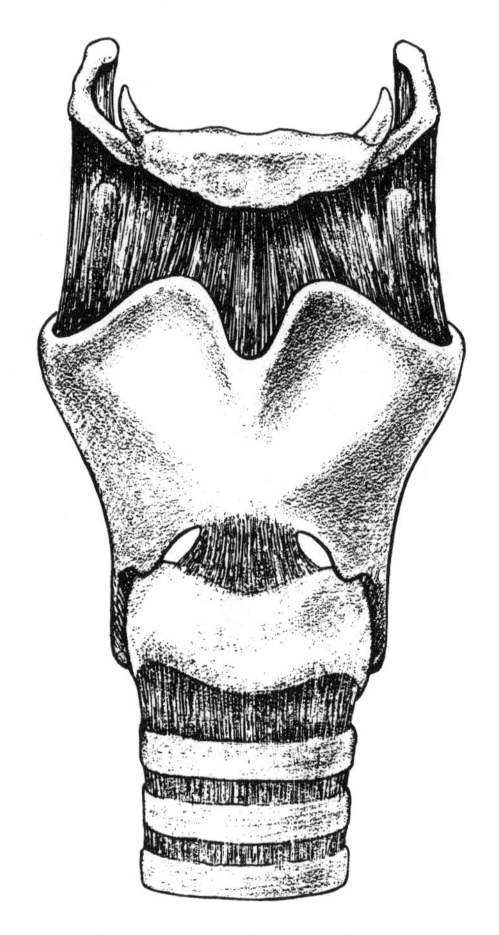

This drawing shows the front view of the adult human larynx or "voice box." Illustration courtesy of Dr. John M. Palmer, from *Anatomy For Speech and Hearing* (New York: Harper and Row, 1965). 1st Edition.

more vibrations per second, the higher the pitch. If you have ever played guitar or violin, you know about pitch. Pluck a guitar string and it vibrates. If you place your finger on the string halfway up the guitar neck and pluck it again, because the string section is shorter it vibrates faster. The sound has a higher pitch. Tightly closing the vocal folds creates an auditory effect called a *glottal stop*. Keeping the vocal folds wide open creates a sound effect called *glottal friction*. A glottal stop is a sound like that at the beginning of a cough. Try it—there, you just made a glottal stop! The IPA symbol for a glottal stop is ʔ, sort of a question mark without the period. If you speak the British English dialect common in London, you probably say *bottle* with the [ʔ] in place of the [t] sound. Glottal friction, by contrast, produces an [h] sound.

Variations in the vocal folds' flexibility and movement can produce other voice qualities. We all know the sound of a whisper. If you've seen one of Marilyn Monroe's movies, you know what a breathy voice sounds like. An elderly person might speak with a creaky tone of voice.

Once the air passes through the larynx, it enters the *vocal tract*. The vocal tract includes the rest of the throat or trachea, the tongue, the soft palate, and the lips. Each of these organs or physical structures can modify the air stream passing by and thus the speech sounds. *Articulation* is the process by which speech sounds are made or modified by these structures.

Passive articulators are immobile structures: the upper teeth; the ridge behind them, called the *alveolar ridge*; and the bony arch behind the alveolar ridge, called the *hard palate*. The upper teeth help form several phones, including the [θ] at the beginning of the word *thin*. The alveolar ridge helps make sounds like [t] and [s]. The hard palate plays an important role in a few sounds, such as the [j] at the beginning of the word *you*.

Active articulators are organs in the vocal tract that the speaker can more or less control. They include the *pharynx*, the *soft palate* or *velum*, the *lips*, the *jaw*, and the *tongue*.

The pharynx is the long muscular tube that provides passage for air from the nose to the larynx, and for food from the mouth to the esophagus. The "frog" or "tickle" in your "throat" is really in your pharynx. The muscles of the pharynx can flex and cause it to constrict or widen. Some consonants can be produced by constricting the pharynx; these appear in several languages, notably Arabic.

The soft palate, or velum, is a broad band of muscular tissue in the upper rear region of the mouth. Its best-known feature is the *uvula*, the wattle-like piece of tissue that hangs down at the back of your mouth. You can easily see it by standing in front of a mirror and opening your mouth wide. The velum normally lowers when you breathe, to allow air to pass from the nose to the pharynx and back again. However, it can take basically three different positions: rising against the upper part of the pharynx to block air from exiting the nose; lowering to allow air to escape through both the nose and mouth; and being lowered with the mouth closed. Each position can affect the quality of speech sounds.

The lips play a very important role in creating speech sounds. The muscle that controls the lips is highly flexible. We can shape our lips into a myriad different subtle positions. By simply closing the lips completely, we make speech sounds like [m] or [p]. The degree to which we open our lips and the shapes we make with them influence the rounding or *spreading* of vowel sounds. It also creates a kind of friction on some consonants, like the *b* in the Spanish word *saber*.

We can also regulate the position of our jaw. This controls the position of the lips and the amount of gap between the upper and lower teeth.

The tongue is the most active of the active articulators. We can maneuver it into a wide range of positions and shapes. It therefore plays a significant role in producing a huge number of speech sounds, including most consonants and all vowels. Moving the tongue upward and backward, for example, helps create the [u] sound. Moving it downward and backward creates [a]. Moving it upward and forward creates [i]. Raising and lowering just the tip (or *apex*) of the tongue affects the sounds we make. So does moving it to the left or right in the mouth. In order to make [s], we have to make a groove in the middle of the tongue.

Talking About Vowels and Consonants

Everyone knows what a vowel or consonant is. We learned about them in grammar school English: vowels are *a, e, i, o, u* and sometimes *y*; consonants are everything else. But those are written letters, used in written language. Phonetics deals with the spoken word. In phonetics, vowels are distinguished from consonants by how they are articulated in the vocal tract. Consonants are sounds made by a closure of the vocal tract. Narrowing the tract causes audible friction as the air escapes. Vowels, by contrast, are sounds made with no such restrictions placed on the air as it escapes the mouth or nose.

Phonology distinguishes vowels from consonants by how they are used *in the structure* of a spoken language. Imagine that a word is like an island or a continent. It has margins and a center or core. In phonology, consonants (let's represent them as *C*) are sound units that either cannot occur on their own or that typically occupy the *margins* of syllables. Vowels (call them *V*) are sound units that either can occur on their own or that usually occupy the core or center of the syllabic continent. Consider the words *pet, cat, see, you*, and *stop*. The following table arranges them in a way that compares their vowels and consonants phonologically and phonetically. Most, but not all, of these words follow the phonological guidelines mentioned above for defining vowels and consonants. But some problems arise. The phonological and phonetic definitions for vowels and consonants do not always produce the same letters.

Word	*pet*	*map*	*stop*	*see*	*you*
Phonetic	/pet/	/map/	/stɒp/	/si/	/juː/
Phonological	CVC	CVC	CCVC	CV	CV

Most of the time, the phonological and phonetic approaches to defining vowels and consonants coincide. They live in peaceful coexistence. Phonetically and phonologically, for example, the phones [f], [m], and [p] are consonants. Phonetically they involve closure or audible friction. They also function phonologically as syllabic margins. We do not find syllables like */mfp/ or */fpm/; /p/ and /f/ do not crop up in the continental cores of syllables. (That *, by the way, signals an *asterisked form*; it means that the "word" or "phrase" that follows it is either ungrammatical or otherwise unacceptable.) The phones [a], [i], and [o] are vowels under both points of view. Phonologically they usually occur at the center or core of syllables, and phonetically they are created without audible friction or any closure.

Now look at the word *see*. It has only two phonemes, /s/ and /i/. It cannot very well have two consonantal margins and a vowel core. However, the general descriptive definitions of consonants and vowels still apply. The /s/ is a sound that cannot stand on its own, but it can form a syllabic margin. It does so in *see*. The /i/ is a sound that can stand on its own, so it is a vowel, even though it forms the "other margin" of *see*.

You, on the other hand, poses a problem. Some phones, like [l], [w], and [j], do not fit both sets of definitions for vowels and consonants. Phonologically units like [l], [ɹ], [w], and [j] occur on the margins of syllables. We find them in words like *wet* /wet/ CVC, *let* /let/ CVC, and *you* /juː/ CVC. So they must be consonants. Phonetically, however, they are vowels. We articulate them without any audible friction or closure of the vocal tract. They also have the same acoustic "signatures" or auditory energy patterns as other vowels. So are they vowels, or consonants? The answer is probably yes. That is, they are a little of both. Some linguists refer to them as semi-vowels or semi-consonants. Others have invented entirely new categories for these kinds of speech sounds; Kenneth Pike has suggested the names *vocoid* and *contoid* for them.

Speech sounds like /w/ and /l/ are the exceptions that act as frames for the larger picture. In general, we can describe vowels and consonants with fairly consistent sets of benchmarks. When phoneticians describe vowels, they basically refer to the following criteria:

- The shape of the lips, how open or rounded they may be;
- Whether the soft palate is raised or lowered;
- Which part of the tongue is raised (the front, the center, or the back); and
- The extent to which the tongue rises toward the palate (the top of the oral cavity). The height of the tongue is variously described as high (or close), mid-high (or mid-close), mid-low (or mid-open), or low (or open).

Each of these criteria affects the vowel's sound. For example, the position of the lips helps determine how *rounded* or *unrounded* the vowel may be. When the soft palate is lowered, air tends to escape through the nose. This lends a nasal quality to vowel sounds, and the process is called *nasalization*. Changes to other active articulators in the vocal tract also affect the qualities of vowels. Pulling the tongue forward and lowering the larynx tends to widen the pharynx. This creates *wide* vowels. In some languages, vowels are articulated with the tip of the tongue raised. This adds an *r-coloring* to the vowel, and the process is called *rhoticization*.

Sometimes the quality of a vowel changes as it is pronounced. This *vowel glide* occurs when the tongue moves as the person articulates the vowel. When only a single tongue movement takes place, the result is a *diphthong*. When more than one movement of the tongue occurs, the glide is a *triphthong*. Both are common in English. Say the word *cow*, or *fine*. You are articulating diphthongs. When you say *sure* or *fire*, you are articulating triphthongs.

The Pieces of a Language

A sound-based language, the kind of language nearly all of us speak, has several main components:

- Phonemes, as we have noted, are the fundamental building blocks of any sound-based language. They are the smallest contrastive units in a language's sound system. *Contrast*, in linguistic terms, is any formal difference allowing us to distinguish meanings. *Pet* means something different than *pot*. So the two vowel sounds in these two words are phonemes.
- Linking together a series of phonemes in a particular order produces *morphemes*. Morphemes are the smallest *meaningful* units of a word.
- *Syntax* (from the Greek word *syntaxis*, meaning "arrangment,") is the way words are combined to produce meaningful relationships in phrases and sentences, or between sentences. Syntax is popularly known as *grammar*.
- The next major component of a sound-based language is its *lexicon*. A *lexicon* is the collection of all the words in a given language—its vocabulary.
- In linguistics the term *semantics* does not have the negative connotions of its popular use, where "That's just semantics" is a way of saying "You're manipulating the meaning" or "You're just quibbling over details." Rather, semantics is the study of meaning in language.
- Vocal intonations can modify the meanings of words and sentences. Such vocal intonations are called *prosody*.
- When we link sentences together to form a narrative, we create a *discourse*.

The Basic Building Blocks

What we commonly call vowels and consonants are phonemes. However, vowel and consonant sounds can be broken down into smaller categories. For example, the IPA categorizes vowels as *rounded* or *unrounded*. Each of these types of vowels can be sounded in the front or back of the mouth.

Another system analyzes and categorizes phonemes by what are called their distinctive features. In this system ten possible pairs of distinctive features exist for each phoneme. They are *consonantal, vocalic, diffuse, compact, grave, flat, voice, continuant, strident,* and *nasal*. Each distinctive feature can be either positive (+) or negative (–). Placing the basic consonant or vowel sound symbols in a horizontal line and the distinctive features in a vertical line creates a matrix to categorize each phoneme. The matrix for English consonants, for example, has twenty-four consonant sounds along the top and the ten distinctive features along the left side. *Phonetics* is the study of how speech sounds are made, transmitted, and received.

But that is *not* what we're talking about here. The study of the principles governing the way sounds are organized in languages, and of how and why variations occur, is the linguistic science of phonology. Phonology studies, among other things, phonemes. As we have already found out, when linguists write or transcribe phonemes, they place them between two slashes //, like /t/ or /e/ or /I/. The number of phonemes varies from language to language—sometimes even dialect to dialect. The number of phonemes used in any specific language or variety of language is called its *phoneme inventory*. The phoneme inventory for British English, for example, includes twenty-four consonants and twenty vowels. By contrast, the phoneme inventory for the Rotokas language includes only six consonants, while that of !Xū has ninety-five, forty-eight of them clicks and forty-seven nonclicks.

Meaningful Morphemes

Morphemes are the smallest meaningful units of a word. Take the word *happiness*. It contains two morphemes, *happi-* and *-ness*. The word *prepotency* ("the quality or state of being prepotent, or having exceptional power") contains three morphemes: *pre-*, *-poten-*, and *-cy*. *Two* is itself a morpheme. Each of the units in these words has some kind of meaning. We know what *happy* is, and what *potent* means. The morpheme *-ness* expresses a state or quality—of being happy, in this case. *Pre-* says something about the temporal characteristic of the word. Like *-ness*, *-cy* means a quality or state of being. They are all morphemes, because they carry some kind of meaning for the people speaking and hearing the words. On the other hand, the constituent sounds in the word *two* have no meaning attached to them. We can analyze the sounds phonologically, but they are not morphemes.

Specific combinations of morphemes, of course, create words. In linguistics, however, identifying words is not always easy. One is tempted to apply many people's definition of art—"I know it when I see it"—to word identification. Like art, words are hard to pin down, at least as a component of a spoken language. They are easy to linguistically identify in written languages, of course. For written languages, words are the basic units of meaning. It is considerably more difficult to identify words as they occur in the river of spoken language. In normal speech we do not usually pause after each word; rather, words flow into one another. And some languages have words that are highly complex structures in and of themselves: in Eskimo *Angyaghllangyugtuq* is one word meaning "he wants to get a big boat." Is it art, or trash? Words may be a major component of a language, but what "words" are depends on the language and on who is studying it.

Another commonplace concept that linguists have difficulty defining is the *sentence*. More than two hundred definitions have been proposed over the years, none of them completely satisfactory. The traditional definition of a sentence has been "the complete expression of a single thought." However, linguists rarely use that definition today, because it is difficult to define "thought." *A planet* is a thought, but no one would identify it as a complete sentence. *I stole the loaf of bread because my brother-in-law was starving* is a complete sentence. It could also be said to contain two separate thoughts.

The definition or explanation familiar to many of us is that a sentence has a *subject*, which is the topic of the sentence, and a *predicate*, what is being said about the topic. For some sentences this definition works well: *The dog was in the house*. The most likely topic here is *the dog*; that is what the sentence is about. But what do we do with *Go! Go!*? It is a sentence—but where is the subject and predicate?

In 1933 the great American linguist Leonard Bloomfield (1887–1949) proposed that a sentence is "an independent linguistic form, not included by virtue of any grammatical construction in any larger linguistic form." In other words, a sentence is the largest linguistic unit to which syntactic rules apply. A more recent and acceptable definition of a sentence is "the largest structural unit that displays stateable grammatical relationships, not dependent on any other structure."

Getting Into Grammar

Noam Chomsky defined grammar as a "device of some sort for producing the sentences of the language under analysis." Nearly all linguists agree that syntax is an essential component of a sound-based language.

It was Chomsky who first suggested that the human brain must contain some innate mechanism—he has often referred to it as "an organ"—for creating syntax. Chomsky noted that all infants everywhere learn their mother tongues almost effortlessly. They do this without benefit of any formal education in the grammar of their native tongue—that comes later (if at all) in school—and with only continual informal coaching and encouragement from parents and bystanders. Yet we all learn our mother tongue. We speak it well enough to communicate with others by the time we are three or four years old, and we have begun to speak it fluently by the time we are seven or eight. He correctly concluded that the human ability to create and use the rules of syntax must be an "inborn" human trait. As we will see, neurosurgeons and experimental psychologists are vindicating Chomsky's hypothesis in rather spectacular fashion.

When linguists speak of grammar they may be talking about any of several different concepts:

- *Traditional grammar* is a term that applies to the historical sweep of approaches to syntactical study before the development of modern-day linguistic science. Many linguists use this term as synonymous with "unscientific grammar."
- *Prescriptive grammar* passes judgment on grammatical usage. It "lays down the law" about socially correct usage. Prescriptive manuals used to be very common and had a powerful influence on people's attitudes toward language from the late eighteenth through the mid-twentieth centuries.
- *Descriptive grammar* describes the grammatical constructions in a sentence without passing any judgments on their correctness.

- A *pedagogical grammar* is a book designed to develop an awareness of the grammatical rules of one's native tongue or to teach a foreign language.
- A *reference grammar* is a comprehensive grammatical description of a language, often a multivolume reference book. During the early twentieth century several grammarians compiled manuals of this type.
- *Theoretical grammar* is a syntactical approach that moves beyond the nitty-gritty study of particular languages to address more universal questions of syntax. As theoretical physics, for example, tries to uncover the basic laws of physics, so theoretical grammar tries to reveal the basic constructs needed to do any kind of grammatical analysis of any language.

Chomsky is the preeminent figure in theoretical grammar today. His work and insights have transformed not only grammar but also much of the rest of contemporary linguistics.

The Meaning of Semantics

Semantics has to do with the meanings that correspond to words and to all possible sentences. The major components of a sound-based language we have discussed so far have not had any connection to meaning. They are like quarks or electrons in the world of nature: essential building blocks. An electron is an electron. A charmed quark is a charmed quark. End of story. Put them together in the right order, though, and we get houses, cars, flowers, water, air, beach sand, even giant chocolate manhole covers—entities that mean something to us. So it is with the language component called semantics. It deals with the meanings of words and sentences, and not just the building blocks or the rules for manipulating them.

For years—indeed, centuries—the big debate in semantics was over the meaning of *meaning*. It began, as did nearly all things philosophical, with the ancient Greeks. Two major points of view emerged from the debate: the *naturalist* view and the *conventionalist* view. The former came largely from Plato, the latter from Aristotle and his disciples. The naturalist view of *meaning* holds that an intrinsic connection exists between sound and sense. The conventionalist view, to the contrary, holds that any connection between sound and sense is utterly arbitrary. Neither point of view is entirely acceptable in the "real world" of language and communication.

Only onomatopoetic words, that is, words that sound like what they represent, really come close to the pure naturalist view of linguistic *meaning*. *Plop, splash*, and *wheeze* may conform to the naturalist position, but what about *tree*? Or *timetable*? Or *mother*? Even onomatopoetic words remain true to this only within a specific language.

The conventionalist view, too, is limited in its explanation of the meaning of *meaning*. It is certainly true that the forms of most words do not bear any specific relation to the entity or "thing" they represent. The connection does seem arbitrary. For this reason, many conventionalists hold that linguistic meaning results from an agreement among people about what words to use. However, there is a subtle yet devastating flaw in this position. Such an agreement among people *presupposes the existence of language to communicate the particulars of the agreement!* The argument is therefore a circular one.

As philosophical as all this is, the debate was long an important one to linguists, and out of it came several conceptions of *meaning*. The first is similar to the naturalist one, with which most of us are familiar:

words → things

This conception of meaning goes back to Plato. Words "refer to" or "name" things. For many words this is true: *Judy Davis*, for example, or *rock* or *mother*. But what "thing" does the word *easy* name? Or *the*, or *different*? Most words in a language's lexicon do not refer to things in any fashion. We know, or at least have a good idea, what *tradition* is, or *fashion*. But neither word refers to some concrete "thing."

Another view of *meaning*, which claims there is no direct link between words and things is:

words → concepts → things

This view suggests that any and all links between words and things occur only in the mind. Each word is associated with a *concept* (another slippery word, there; certainly as hard to pin down as the greased pig called *meaning*). The concept in turn links up to the thing. Of course, the concept of *fashion* is nearly as indefinable as the "thing" to which the word *fashion* refers. Moreover, what I mean by *fashion*—the concept associated with it in my mind—may well not be the same as the concept in your mind.

A third perspective on words and meaning is a behaviorist view, with ties to B. F. Skinner:

stimuli → words → responses

This particular position was championed by Leonard Bloomfield. In his book *Language* Bloomfield suggested that the meaning of words arises from a stimulus-reponse process. Meaning is situational: a stimulus (S) leads a person to respond (r) by speaking. That speech is itself a stimulus (s), which in turn will have another response (R). For example, my friend Frank Catalano is hungry. He smells the scent of freshly baked bread (S, the stimulus) and asks his friend Teri Howe to bring him some "bread, please" (r, his response). Teri hears his request (another stimulus, s) and brings Frank some bread (R, the response). Bloomfield's view of semantics, meaning, and the process of language was essentially mechanistic.

The problem with it is the same as with any behaviorist or mechanistic explanation for complex human behaviors. Behaviorist schemata work fairly well with simple behaviors; they can be easily broken down to a series of stimulus-response patterns, fairly cut and dried, black and white. But much of human behavior is so complex that the trails of stimulus-response get lost in the gray. For example, what if Teri, instead of bringing Frank a slice of bread, comes into his office with a .38 pistol and shoots him dead? We do not know why this reponse takes place. But it could—and certainly things this strange have happened, in more than a few instances. No simple S-R explanation can cover them.

For all its fascination to philosophers and linguists with a philosophical bent, the search for the meaning of *meaning* has been all but abandoned by contemporary linguistics. For better or for worse, modern semantics is not much concerned with following this particular road in the forest called language. Semanticists today look at *meaning* in much the same way physicists consider concepts like *height* or *width*. They have no real existence independent of the entities to which they apply. We cannot point to something and say, "Ah! There is *width*! Pretty ugly, eh?" Or, "Marla, I'd like to introduce you to *meaning*. He's a nice fellow, works at Tony Roma's." No, these concepts have existence only in their application. We can say that Edward has a height of six feet two inches. We can measure that mountain ash outside my window and conclude that its trunk is about two feet wide. We can talk about the meaning of words and sentences. But that is about as far as linguists can go—or want to go—in discussing *meaning*.

Semanticists today study the meaning of language by following the advice of philosopher Ludwig Wittgenstein, who said that "the meaning of a word is its use in the language." Semanticists focus on the "sense" of words. They examine the way people relate words to each other, within the framework of their particular language. They do not deal with the "reference" to the "real world" that words have. Different languages deal with the real world in different ways. By studying the internal relationships of words within a language, semanticists can avoid tripping over the differences that naturally exist among languages.

One easily understood example is the words we use to describe biological relationships. In English we speak of *father, mother, son, daughter, brother, sister, cousin, nephew, niece, aunt, uncle, grandfather,* and *grandmother*. My mother's brother is my *uncle*—but so is my *father's* brother. My father's sister is my *aunt*—and so is my mother's sister. English has no single word that simply means "mother's sister," as opposed to "father's sister." The biological relationships are different. They exist in the real world. English, however, uses the same word for them.

Other languages, such as an Australian language called Pitjanjatjara, use separate words. The Pitjanjatjara word for "mother's sister" is *ngunytju*, while the word for "father's sister" is *kurntili*. Pitjanjatjara also has its complications. The same Pitjanjatjara word for "mother's sister" (*ngunytju*) also means "mother." The Pitjanjatjara word for "father's brother" (*mama*) also means "father." This may seem confusing to English speakers, but then, speakers of Pitjanjatjara are probably confused by the cavalier fashion in which English speakers use *aunt* and *uncle*.

Semantics: Sense, Reference, and the "Real World"

Real World	*Female parent*	*Female parent's biological sister*	*Female parent's biological brother*	*Male parent*	*Male parent's biological brother*	*Male parent's biological sister*
Pitjanjatjara	*ngunytju*	*ngunytju*	*kamuru*	*mama*	*mama*	*kurntili*
English	*mother*	*aunt*	*uncle*	*father*	*uncle*	*aunt*

LANGUAGE'S LEXICONS

We have already seen that linguists are a bit uncomfortable with the idea of *words*. Words are slippery critters, especially when one is dealing with spoken rather than written language. For that reason, linguists—especially semanticists, linguists who specialize in semantics—prefer to speak of *lexemes* instead of words. A lexeme is the smallest contrastive unit in a semantic system. In other words, a word. More or less. A lexeme can be one word, or have several forms, or be composed of several words. The lexeme EAT, for example, can have the forms *eat, eats, eating, eaten*, and so on. GREEN WITH JEALOUSY is a lexeme composed of three words. The listings in a dictionary are typically not really "words" but lexemes.

A lexicon is the vocabulary of a language. The term also refers to a list of a language's lexemes. When lexicographers compile a language's lexicon, each entry includes all morphological and grammatical information. A lexical entry does not, however, include any conceptual knowledge about the word. Most of us are familiar with the variation of a lexicon called a dictionary. Dictionaries list the words of a language and give information about their spelling, phonology, and grammatical status. They also provide information about a word's history, use, and meaning.

Dictionaries list words in alphabetical order, but many ways exist of organizing a language's lexemes. When linguists talk about semantics and lexemes, they often are dealing with the idea of *semantic structure*, the relationships among the semantic units of a language. Lexemes are these units, which is why they are also often called lexical units or lexical items. Semanticists study, among other things, the relationships between and among a language's lexemes. Alphabetical arrangement may be easy to use when you want to find the definition of a particular word, but it cannot portray relationships of meaning. Other lexemic arrangements preserve these "sense relations."

Different languages have differing semantic structures and lexemic relationships. An essential task for any infant learning his or her mother tongue is to acquire an understanding of those particular sense relationships and of the language's semantic structure. Some of these relationships include the following:

- *Antonymy* is the relationship of opposite meanings. *Antonyms*, words with opposite meanings, include *converse terms*, which are two-way contrasts in which one member presupposes the others, such as *parent/child*, *send/receive*, or *talk/listen*; *gradable antonyms*, which permit an expression of degree (*big/small*, *very big/extremely small*); and *nongradable antonyms*, which do not allow any expression of degree (*male/female*).
- *Hyponymy* is a lexemic relationship of inclusion. "A is part of B" and "C is an example of D" are hyponymic relationships. In English, *potato* is a hyponym of *vegetable*, and *hammer* is a hyponym of *tool*. *Potato* and *hammer* in this examples are "subordinate" lexemes, while *vegetable* and *tool* are the "superordinate" terms. This kind of linguistic relationship is similar in some ways to the biological discipline of taxonomy, the study of the theory, practice, and rules for classifying living and extinct beings. In taxonomy a genus is a superordinate classification to which different species belong. In somewhat the same way, a superordinate term like *flower* can have several hyponyms: *daisy, lily, petunia, rose*, and so on. Because hyponymy is a linguistic classification, different languages have different hyponyms. *Potato* is a hyponym of *vegetable* in English, but it is not in German. In Classical Greek, occupations like "carpenter" and "doctor" were hyponyms of *demiourgos*; no such hyponymic relationship exists in English.
- *Synonymy* is a lexemic relationship with which many of us are quite familiar. It is a relationship of "sameness of meaning." There is never really a complete sameness of meaning between two or more lexemes. The context in which the lexeme is used can change its meaning; regional or emotional differences also exist. But we can nevertheless group many lexemes together in this kind

of sense relationship: *infant/baby, youth/kid, grown-up/adult, hot/scorching*, and so on.

These categories of lexemic "sense relationships" are examples of *semantic fields*, a linguistic device for organizing lexemes into groups with some kind of meaning. Other semantic fields might be, for example, "parts of the body" (including lexemes like *arm, foot, head, neck, shoulder, torso*), "tools" (*hammer, saw, chisel, lawnmower, tire iron, tree trimmer* [lexemes made of two words]), "fruits" (*apple, orange, kumquat, persimmon, banana*), and "domestic animals" (*cat, dog, cow, horse, pig*). All of these lexemic relationships can differ from language to language. In some Eskimo languages "snow" is a semantic field, containing dozens of different lexemes. In English it is not—or, at best, it is a semantic field with relatively few lexemes.

Some lexemes have a tendency to "hang out together." Linguists call this *collocation.* Say *bacon* and your listener will probably think *eggs*. *Meow* will inevitably accompany *cat*. *Blonde* collocates with *hair*, *spick* with *span*, and *letter* with *alphabet, spelling,* and *write*. Different languages have different collocations, of course. The Japanese word for *drink* collocates not only with *water* but also with *cigarettes*; that latter collocation is absent in English.

One of the most interesting and intensively studied semantic fields of lexemes is color. In the real world of light and shadow, particle and wave, object and energy, "color" is a function of light's wavelength. The electromagnetic spectrum stretches from extremely-low-frequency radio waves, with wavelengths measured in many kilometers, through high-frequency gamma rays, with wavelengths measured in the range of 3×10^{-14} meters—that's 0.00000000000003 meters! The phenomenon we call "color" is just a small sliver of the electromagnetic spectrum. The color spectrum has no edges in reality; no fences or borders separate the wavelengths.

But when we speak of colors, we speak of *distinct* colors; we use specific lexemes to denote them. And different languages, perhaps reflecting the underlying mental constructs or paradigms of the people who speak them, have different color semantic fields. They group colors in different patterns, using different lexemes for different colors. English has eleven basic color lexemes in the color semantic field:

white, black, gray, brown, yellow, orange, red, blue, green, purple, and pink. A Philippine language called Hanunóo, which has only about six thousand speakers, contains only four basic color lexemes: black, white, green, and red. Russian has two separate terms for blue; Hungarian has two lexemes for red. Navaho has two different "black" lexemes, one lexeme that means both "brown" and "gray," and another that means both "green" and "blue." In Japanese, *awo* can mean "blue," "green," or "pale." It depends on the context.

Linguists like to study color lexemes because color perception is, with relatively few exceptions, universal among humans. As we will discover later in the book, some of the exceptions to this ability, and to the ability to express color lexemes in language, have led directly to new and exciting insights into the way our brains create, store, and use language.

The Nuances of Prosody

Prosody is defined as the linguistic use of *pitch, loudness, tempo,* and *rhythm* to change or modify the meaning of words and sentences. In other words, there is truth in the old saying "It's not what you say, but how you say it." We use vowels and consonants to create syllables and words, and words to create sentences. There is more to language, though, than these purely verbal components. When we *speak* them (or sign them, in the case of languages such as ASL) we add another dimension to the communication stream. Variations in the tone of voice we use will modify the meaning of the words and sentences. For example, there are worlds of different meanings among these three sentences: "They're coming." "They're coming?" "They're coming!"

In written English (or English *orthography*, to use the more scientific terminology; the word *orthography* comes from the Greek words meaning "straight" or "right" (*orthos*) and "writing" (*graphein*)), we designate some of these verbal changes in tone with signs like *?* and *!*. In other cases, we signify them by using appropriate adjectives, adverbs, or other modifiers. We can easily imagine what these exchanges sound like:

- "Did you want this cup of coffee?" asked John. "No," snapped Mary rudely.

- "Did you want this cup of coffee?" asked John. "No," said Mary, grinning slyly.
- "Did you want this cup of coffee?" asked John. "N-n-n-o," Mary answered slowly.

In spoken language, loudness and pitch are the two most important aural properties that modify meaning. Tempo and rhythm can also play a significant role. Loudness, of course, is the auditory sensation that relates to a sound's intensity. Loudness can convey fairly broad changes in meaning, as well as more subtle changes when different words or syllables are stressed. Whispered words of love have a very low sound intensity; when we shout angry words at someone, our voices have a high intensity. There is a big difference in meaning between a whispered "I want you" and a shouted "I want you"; between "*I* want you" and "I want *you*."

Pitch is the auditory sensation of a sound's "height." We speak of some sounds as having a high pitch and others as having a low pitch. British rock singer Kate Bush has a singing voice with a high pitch. Soul and blues singer Lou Rawls has a voice with a very low pitch. Different levels of pitch, called *tones*, can express a huge range of meanings. While different languages use changes in pitch in different ways, one pitch change seems common in all languages. That is the difference between a rising and falling pitch pattern, which is used to express questioning (a rising pitch) and stating (a falling pitch).

Go back to the "they're coming" sentences. The one that is a question ("They're coming?") ends with a rise in pitch. The one that is a statement of fact ("They're coming.") ends with a drop in pitch. The excited statement ("They're coming!") also has a pitch pattern that's different from the more matter-of-fact statement. For that matter, the sentence "*They're* coming!" has still another pitch pattern. The changes in meaning that we create simply with changes in pitch are astonishingly large, as we can determine for ourselves just by taking a few minutes to pay close attention to them.

Tempo is still another way we change the meaning of words or sentences. Tempo is the relative rate of speech—fast, slow, moderate. Speeding up the tempo of speech can convey urgency or excitement. A slow tempo conveys emphasis or importance.

Rhythm, in phonology, is defined as the perceived regularity of prominent units in speech. Loudness, pitch, and tempo all converge to create prosodic rhythm. In ancient Latin the length of a syllable was a crucial feature of its rhythm. Modern French uses a steady production of syllables to create its essential rhythm, while English tends to stress syllables in regular temporal fashion. Pitch height is the central feature of rhythm in many languages, such as Chinese.

We can create other vocal effects that play a role in prosody by using the various cavities that are part of our vocal tract. These effects are often referred to as *timbre* or *voice quality*. Many languages use whispering to convey a secretive or conspiratorial effect. However, most of these vocal effects are far from universal. For example, in English we use a husky or breathy tone to convey sexual interest. When Lauren Bacall tells Humphrey Bogart how to whistle—"Just put your lips together ... and *blow*"—we're all sure we know *exactly* what's going through her character's mind. That husky voice conveys it quite effectively. In Japanese, however, a husky tone of voice has nothing to do with amorous desires but conveys submission or respect. Portuguese, to offer another example, uses nasalized tones to convey a wide range of emotions; English has nothing even remotely resembling this specific kind of prosodic effect.

All these features of prosody—timbre, rhythm, pitch, and so on—combine to give human language a communicative texture that surpasses any other mode of communication. And it is important to remember that sign languages have their own equivalents for prosody. For example, by modulating the temporal aspects of a sign, speakers of Sign modify the meanings of words. The sign for *be sick* changes to *very sick* with a change in its modulation from "uninflected" to "tense modulation."

Even more amazing is this simple fact: all of us, from French infant to American baby to Chinese child, learn the intricate aspects of prosody very early in our lives. The rhythm of language—all languages—is a basic part of an infant's initiation into his or her particular language. Pitch, loudness, and especially tempo play vital roles in infant language acquisition. By the time human infants have begun creating short but complete sentences, they have already incorporated some of the nuances of prosody into their speech. They know how to modulate pitch to ask a question, to express delight, to create emphasis.

When your children says "NO!" they are demonstrating their mastery of prosody. Whether you like it or not.

The Magic of Discourse

In order for language to be a richer, more complex form of communication than those that already exist among other animal species, we must link sentences together into some sort of narrative. This is discourse. Linguists who study the extended structure of written languages use text analysis to examine written "texts," which can mean chapters of books, magazine articles, printed notices, road signs, and advertisements. Linguists who study spoken languages use a technique called *discourse analysis*.

Conversation, the linguistic interaction between two or more people, is the most common form of spoken discourse. Naturally, it is also the most intensively studied form of discourse. The "rules" for conversation are complex, usually unspoken, and rooted deeply in a sociological and psychological gestalt of a specific culture. Yet they are known by nearly all speakers of a language. In any particular culture or group of people using a particular language, everyone usually "knows" how to begin a conversation, when to speak, when to listen, when to be silent, how and where to look, what kinds of body language to use in specific situations, when to offer information, when to hold back, under what circumstances to be deeply involved and when to be aloof, how to change the subject, and—very important!—how to end the conversation.

The rules of discourse, like so many other "rules," vary from language to language, culture to culture. A good example is the role of silence in discourse. In American and British English conversations, often a period of silence longer than a few seconds is excruciatingly awkward, painful, and downright embarrassing. Among the Apache, however, silent periods in conversation are perfectly normal. At the other end of the spectrum, as it were, it is considered "bad manners" in American and British English for several people to talk at once. However, this is perfectly normal among Antiguans.

At some point between his twelfth and fourteenth months, though it could easily be earlier or later, Ryan Nash will speak his first true words. Mom, dad, and grandparents will naturally be delighted. "Ryan can *talk*!" we will cry with joy. And, of course, he will be talking. A little. He will have taken the first full step into language, making the conceptual connection between mom and *mama* and dad and *papa*. Then Ryan will make the connection between the cat and *cat*, a ball and *ball*, and so on. He will already know the difference between [*cat*] and [*car*]. By two years of age Ryan will begin using two-word phrases and short sentences: "Mama come!" "Want cat!" The happy parents will surely call grandma and grandpa with the good news. At this point Ryan will have begun to toddle, linguistically speaking. By age four he will have a large vocabulary and a good command of basic English grammar. He will begin telling stories, linguistically walking. Soon he will go on to a lifetime of running, skipping, and jumping.

CHAPTER 4

THE SCIENCE OF LANGUAGE

In 1859 Charles Darwin published his ground-breaking book on evolution and natural selection, *The Origin of Species*. Twenty-eight years earlier, he had joined the crew of the HMS *Beagle* as the ship's naturalist. His five-year voyage provided him with voluminous raw material for his ponderings on the origins of different life forms. He observed many different forms of life that were clearly related to but more primitive than others. He found fossils, the lithified remains of ancient plants and animals, that appeared to be ancestral to present-day forms of life. All this data allowed Darwin to fashion a plausible hypothesis for the origins of species. Nearly a century and a half of research and discovery by biologists and paleontologists has soundly confirmed the basic schema of Darwin's theory of evolution.

Linguists, however, have no way to engage in a similar process. There is no such thing as a "primitive" language, any more than there is such a thing as a "primitive" culture. Every one of the five thousand or more languages that exist today is a complex structure for communication. No "fossil" languages exist against which linguists can compare current languages. Even the written remains of ancient tongues—"fossils" that go back no more than six or seven thousand years—are of only limited use. Humans today are biologically and neurologically indistinguishable from our ancestors for at least the last forty thousand years. Instead, linguists must work with linguistic "fossils," words from different languages. They draw inferences and conclusions by comparing present-day languages to one another, examining the written records of ancient languages, and studying the structure and linguistic functions of the human brain. Our knowledge of the biological origins of humans, as fragmentary as it still is, nevertheless rests on a solid foundation of bone and stone. Our understanding of the origins of human language, however, remains at best informed speculation.

Linguists are also like modern-day biologists. Biologists work with living animals and plants, studying their shape, their behavior, and their life cycles. From the data they compile, biologists begin to uncover the rules that govern the lives and deaths of living creatures. Some species are endangered, at risk of becoming extinct and lost forever from the face of the earth. Many biologists struggle to learn as much as possible about these species before they are gone. (Others, including biologists, work to prevent extinction from happening, a worthy goal.) The more we learn about living beings—both healthy species and those in danger of extinction—the more we can understand the underlying rules that guide all life on earth. In the same way, linguists today focus on living languages. Some are huge and healthy: English, French, Chinese, Russian. Others are in danger of extinction: Amuesha in Peru, with about four thousand speakers; Nanai in China, with perhaps seven thousand speakers; Tlingit, in Alaska and Canada, with only 2,000 or so. The Appendix includes a list of one hundred of the many thousands of languages still alive today.

All those languages are equal. None is inferior to the other, none is "primitive." Eskimos do not communicate in grunts but in languages with sophisticated grammars, vocabularies, and linguistic structures. French is not—despite the protestations of the French!—a language superior to all others. Nor is American English, despite the propaganda offered by some educators and politicians.

We still fight wars in part over language, for language, like religion, stirs deep emotions. We have still not uncovered the entire history of language and languages; however, we do understand much more than our intellectual ancestors, the ancient Greeks, who considered anyone who didn't speak Greek a barbarian.

Like other sciences, the science of language has a history of its own.

PĀṆINI'S CHILD

The earliest known dictionary is in Chinese and was written sometime between 1500 and 1000 B.C.E. It contains about forty thousand different characters. However, the oldest known document that can legitimately be called a work of linguistics dates back to between the seventh and fifth centuries B.C.E. It is a Sanskrit grammar compiled by an Indian scholar named Pāṇini. His grammar had a religious purpose. Pāṇini wanted to codify and preserve the more ancient language of the sacred Hindu scriptures. The Hindu priests realized that the pronunciation and grammar of their current language differed from that of their scriptures, the Vedas. Their language had changed since the more ancient times when the Vedas had been written. They also believed it was vital that certain religious ceremonies be carried out using the accurate form of the original texts. Linguistic change threatened the spiritual purity of their rituals.

In order to resolve this danger of profanation, they essentially invented several building blocks of linguistics, including phonetics, grammar, and etymology. They set about to establish the basic facts of the old language. Pāṇini's *Aṣṭādhyāyī* ("Eight Books") contained about four thousand aphorisms or *sutras*, a word that literally means "threads." The sutras set out the rules for word formation in the old language of the Hindu scriptures and Sanskrit literature. The *Aṣṭādhyāyī* is, in fact, a remarkable work of linguistics. For example, it contains detailed phonetic descriptions of words.

If the cultures and societies lying west of India had had access to the writings of Pāṇini and his colleagues, linguistics as a science would have had a much earlier and more vigorous start in the West. As it was, though, the linguistic work of the Indians did not reach Europe until the ninth century C.E.

GREEKS, ROMANS, AND LANGUAGE

At about the same time that Pāṇini was compiling the *Aṣṭādhyāyī*, one of the greatest Greek philosophers of all time was putting together his own observations about language. In the *Cratylus*, Plato (c. 427–347 B.C.E.) offered readers two dialogues about the origins of language and the nature of meaning. In one the philosophical conversation is between Socrates, Plato's teacher, and Hermogenes. In the other the debate takes place between Socrates and Cratylus.

In the first dialogue Hermogenes argues that the relationship between words and "things" is an arbitrary one. "Nothing has its name by nature," says Hermogenes, "but only by usage and custom."

In the second dialogue, Cratylus tells Socrates that the opposite is true. Language is not a matter of arbitrary convention, he says, but something that has come into existence naturally. A deep, essential relationship exists between words and the objects they name, says Cratylus. "There is a correctness of name existing by nature for everything," he asserts; words are not arbitrary symbols that people jointly agree upon.

Although Plato offers no firm conclusion to these debates, one senses that his sympathy lies with Cratylus's position. Plato has Cratylus invoke the support of the gods for his position.

The greatest of all the Classical Greek philosophers took the opposing viewpoint. Aristotle (384–322 B.C.E.) does so in his essay *De Interpretatione* ("On Interpretation," the Latin title of the work). "No name exists by nature, but only by becoming a symbol," he wrote. As we have seen, these two sets of positions, those of Plato and of Aristotle, are the foundations for two schools of philosophical thought about language. The *conventionalist* position, basically that of Aristotle, holds that language is a product of convention; the words we use in our mother tongue to refer to some entity "out there" have their meaning purely by the agreement *in toto* of the people who speak the language. No intrinsic connection exists between the sound and the entity it represents. The *naturalist* position, that of Plato, holds the opposite view: words have some inherent connection with the entities they represent. "For everything there is a natural name, and for every natural name there is a thing" might be the motto of this position.

In the third century B.C.E., the Greek Stoic philosophers began organizing a more formal kind of language study, establishing the notions of grammar that have influenced Western thought ever since. They categorized words as different parts of speech, for example, and invented names for them. In about 100 B.C.E., more than five hundred years after Pāṇini's *Aṣṭādhyāyī*, the Greek philosopher Dionysius Thrax wrote the first Greek grammar. His work was addressed as much to Romans as to Greeks.

One major difference between the "linguistics" of the ancient

Greeks and that of today was its focus on the written rather than spoken word. Phonetics was given short shrift, at best. Greeks were interested in *etymology*, which is the study of the origin of words, and grammar. It's worthwhile noting that the original Greek word actually means "the art of *writing*." By contrast, the Indian word for grammar, *vyākaraṇa*, means "analysis." A world of difference existed between these two approaches to grammar. The truth is that the Greeks—like the Romans who supplanted them, for that matter—cared little for learning about their own language, and even less about others.

Though they had conquered most of the known world by the end of the second century B.C.E.—including Greece in 146 B.C.E.—the Romans had not developed any celebrated home-grown philosophers or other thinkers. So they turned to the conquered Greeks, who had plenty of great thinkers, for their "culture." As they did with most things, the Romans borrowed their linguistic philosophy from the Greeks. Eventually they began developing grammars for their own mother tongue, Latin. In his twenty-six-book opus *De Lingua Latina* ("On the Latin Language"), Marcus Terentius Varro (116–24 B.C.E.) codified Latin grammar. In the process he pointed out the differences between Greek and Latin. He arranged his observations under the headings of etymology, morphology, and syntax, an arrangement that prefigured that of modern linguistics. However, he added nothing new to the description of Latin as a language. Like other Roman philosophers to follow, he mostly imitated the work of Dionysius Thrax and other Greek writers.

Nevertheless, Varro's works had great influence on Roman linguistic thought. Other Romans who contributed major works on language included Marcus Tullius Cicero (106–43 B.C.E.), Julius Caesar (100–44 B.C.E), and Marcus Fabius Quintilianus, or Quintilian (c. 35–c. 95). Cicero, probably the greatest Roman orator, wrote influentially on style. Caesar wrote treatises on grammatical regularity. Quintilian was a rhetorician and teacher, whose book *Institutio Oratoria* included his thoughts on public speaking and language usage.

Two other important Latin treatises on grammar appeared in the first several centuries of the Common Era. Aelius Donatus wrote a grammar entitled *Ars Major* that became the standard throughout Europe through the Middle Ages. *Ars Minor* was an edited version for children. *Ars Major*, by the way, was the first grammar book to be printed in wooden type.

In the sixth century Priscianus Caesariensis, known as Priscian (we do not know his birth and death dates), wrote *Institutiones Grammaticae* ("Categories of Grammar"). Priscian lived and worked in Constantinople, the seat of the Eastern Roman Empire after that region's break with Rome in 395. His eighteen-book collection is the most complete grammar of that period that still exists. Like *Ars Major*, it was very popular up through the Middle Ages.

These two books, along with Quintilian's *Institutio Oratoria*, set the pattern for language teaching in Europe through the Renaissance. They became the basis for the so-called traditional approach to grammar that has, for good or ill, influenced language and grammar teaching in English and other modern languages to this day.

THE MIDDLE AGES AND THE RENAISSANCE

From the fall of Rome in 476 to the beginning of the Renaissance in the fourteenth century, little of importance happened in linguistics. The medieval educational curriculum, such as it was, included grammar and dialectics, which dealt with language. The studies mostly involved memorizing Donatus's rules and parroting them back. Only the great Italian writer Dante Alighieri (1265–1321) showed any creative interest in linguistics. Dante, of course, is justly famous for the *Divina Commedia* ("The Divine Comedy"), his three-book, fourteen-thousand-line poem of Hell, Purgatory, and Heaven, composed between 1307 and 1322. In fact, with *The Divine Comedy* Dante established the Tuscan dialect as the literary language of Italy. In a 1304 book entitled *De Vulgari Eloquentia*, Dante showed remarkable prescience in examining the relationship between the Romance languages (French, Italian, and Spanish) and the Latin tongue from which they descended. He also devised a well-thought-out categorization of the various Italian dialects.

In the Arab world the situation was different. The Qur'ran, the Muslim scriptures, was forbidden to be translated from its Arabic original into any other language. So Muslim scholars resorted to the equivalent of linguistic studies to carry out scholarly discussions of the scriptures. Beginning in the eighth century, several Arab grammars and dictionaries appeared, as well as treatises on pronunciation. In

Spain, then under Muslim influence, Jewish scholars produced several important Hebrew grammars.

If this seems a slightly unbelievable situation to us, it is because we tend to view past events through our contemporary prejudices and preconceptions. It is true that several Islamic countries today persecute Jews. However, many Islamic societies during the Middle Ages were quite tolerant of other religions, including Judaism. Islam itself recognizes Abraham, the ur-figure of Judaism, as one of its own most revered spiritual ancestors. Muslims consider Ishmael, the son of Abraham and Hagar the slave girl, to be the ancestor of all Arabs. The Prophet himself supposedly ascended to Heaven from a hill in Jerusalem, the Dome of the Rock, thus making Jerusalem a city sacred to Muslims as well as Jews and Christians. It is thus not surprising that the intellectually enlightened Muslim world of the Middle Ages was a culture of refuge for Jews. Exactly the opposite situation existed for Jews in Christian Europe.

The Renaissance had been ignited in large part by the discovery of the Classical Greek philosophers. Many of these discoveries came about because the Islamic Arab world had kept alive the writings of Aristotle and others. The rise of the Renaissance in Italy and later in the rest of Europe also saw a gradual resurgence of creative interest in language. Dante's work in the early fourteenth century presaged that trend. Around 1495 the Italian architect Leon Battista Alberti published the first known Italian grammar. In the sixteenth century the *risorgimento* picked up speed. Julius Caesar Scalinger of Italy (1484–1558) began exploring the linguistic ins and outs of Latin. His 1540 book *De Causis Linguae Latinae* analyzed the style of Cicero's writing.

In France, Robert Etienne and his son Henri examined Greek and Latin. Henri Etienne also wrote of the superiority of the French language. We might find this rather amusing today: "Ain't that just like the French?!" But Etienne was leading the way to a new appreciation for the so-called vulgar languages of the time. French, Italian, and Spanish had been considered inferior to Latin, the "true" mother tongue, but Henri Etienne and his followers insisted that they were as noble and valuable in their own right as their ancestor. In 1531 Jacques Dubois composed one of the first French grammars. Louis Meigret followed in 1550 with a more scholarly and complete attempt.

This period also saw the rise of the great European explorers and Christian missionaries. Europeans became acquainted with the great Chinese literary and linguistic tradition. They also discovered and nearly destroyed the literary and linguistic traditions of the New World native cultures. Nevertheless, scholars did begin compiling grammars for these exotic new languages. For example, a grammar for Quechua (an Andean-Equatorial language spoken by peoples in what is now Bolivia, Colombia, Ecuador, and Peru) was published in Europe in 1560, just sixty-eight years after Columbus's first voyage of discovery.

In 1582 the Accademia della Crusca was founded in Italy, with the purpose of "purifying" the noble Italian tongue. Cardinal Richelieu established the Académie Française in 1635 to do the same thing for French. Philip IV founded the Spanish Academy in 1713. Other language academies eventually sprang up throughout Europe, Russia, and the Spanish-colonized regions of Central and South America.

Meanwhile, a technological breakthrough had taken place that would have the single most profound effect on language for the next four hundred years. By 1450 a German inventor named Johann Gutenberg (c. 1397–1468) had developed the first European movable type printing press. (An obscure Chinese commoner, Pi Sheng, had invented movable type in the mid-eleventh century, and Chinese books had been printed in movable type by 1060, but the Europeans knew nothing about this.)

In 1453 Gutenberg printed the Masarin Bible; the revolution was about to begin. By 1470 the Sorbonne in Paris had its own printing press; Renaissance academia was going high-tech. Four years later the Englishman William Caxton (c. 1421–1491) printed the first book in English, at Bruges in present-day Belgium. He soon moved his printing presses to England and published the first printed version of Geoffry Chaucer's epic *Canterbury Tales*. The English language would never be the same. By 1563 printing presses were being used in Russia. In 1639 the first printing press in North America began operating in Cambridge, Massachusetts.

The rise of the language academies and the development of the movable-type printing press led to the publication of the first printed dictionaries. In 1598 John Florio (1553–1625) produced *A World of Wordes*, an English-Italian dictionary. *The Interpreter*, a law dictionary compiled by John Cowell, appeared in 1607—and in 1610 a hangman burned a copy of it to protest its enhancement of the King's legal authority. The French Academy's first dictionary appeared in 1694. It was a natural outgrowth of its mission to preserve and purify the French language. Other academies followed suit, publishing dictionaries of their mother tongues throughout the seventeenth and eighteenth centuries. One of the most famous dictionaries of all appeared in 1755: *The Dictionary of the English Language*, compiled by Samuel Johnson (1709–1784).

For all their interest in languages, however, nearly all these writings in grammar and etymology followed the lead of Priscian and Donatus. They assumed that Latin was the "only real and true" language, the exemplar of all languages. The language scholars of the Renaissance all tended to apply the grammatical traits of Latin to other, non-Latin languages. That would all change because of the remarkable scholarship and intuition of a British judge in India.

"SPRUNG FROM SOME COMMON SOURCE . . ."

The era of true linguistics, the scientific study of language, began in 1786. It was the year that Frederick the Great died, Sir Joshua Reynolds painted *The Duchess of Devonshire*, Mozart wrote his opera *The Marriage of Figaro*, the American inventor Ezekiel Reed built a nail-making machine, and the German folklorist Wilhelm Grimm was born. It would be nearly a hundred years before Charles Darwin would write his famous book about biological evolution. But an English judge in India made a remarkable evolutionary discovery of his own, not about the biological origins of our ancestors but about the origins of our languages. Like most Englishmen of the upper classes, Sir William Jones had a formal education that included a firm grounding in Greek and Latin. Unlike many of them, he also had a deep fascination with the Orient and its peoples. That fascination led him to the ancient religious and literary texts of India, which were written in a language called Sanskrit.

Jones set out to learn it. In the process he stumbled upon something quite remarkable, something no European before him had noticed. In the sixteenth century, European explorers and travelers to India had begun noting the similarities between Sanskrit and European languages. They concluded that Sanskrit was the parent to their languages. Jones, though, reached a different and more sophisticated conclusion. First of all, he found a deep resemblance between the grammar and vocabulary of Sanskrit and those of Latin and Greek. The parallels were so striking, so pervasive, that Jones became convinced they were not coincidences.

When Jones first deduced the connections among Greek, Latin, and Sanskrit, he had no idea of the great linguistic exploration he would set in motion. Jones sensed that contemporary human languages are the greenest branches of an ancient tree, but he had no way of knowing just how old. A small group of scholars in the United States and Russia believe they can trace the outline of the tree's trunk down to its roots at the very beginnings of humanity.

Start with words. Words are the basic building blocks of a language. Words are made of sounds, but the sounds that make up words do not carry any meaning. Say *three*. When you say that word, you know what it means. The collection of sounds that is *three* means something specific in English. The sounds that compose it, though, do not have any meaning: *r*, *th*, and *ee* are just sounds. Make the *th* sound, [θ], and I will look at you blankly. Perhaps I will think, "This person is sticking her tongue out at me," or "This guy is trying to give me the raspberry." But the sound itself is meaningless.

The meaning of the word *three* is arbitrary, also. Nothing about the word connects in any way to the concept of the specific number it represents in English. The word carries its meaning because the community of humans who use that language have agreed upon it. In this way, words are like coins. A nickel stands for a specific amount of money (five pennies) only because the community at large agrees it does. The community could also decide that a nickel equals one hundred pennies, or a thousand, or one. Given the right set of historical circumstances and cultural choices, *three* in English could just as easily be the word that represents a cat. The word *cat* means that small furry animal who pounces on mice or catnip balls and likes to sleep on the window ledge. But the word *giraffe* or *book* or *taihun* could have served just as well.

The arbitrariness of word meanings is the key to uncovering the origins of languages. Any combination of sounds (equaling a word) can stand for any particular concept. So when words in different languages have both similar sounds and similar meanings, we can rightly assume a relationship among them. That relationship is likely to be a common ancestral word. It was this similarity in vocabulary and grammar that led Sir William Jones to his conclusions about Latin, Greek, and Sanskrit. In an address to the Bengal Asiatic Society in 1786, Jones enunciated his suspicions:

> The Sanskrit language, whatever be its antiquity, is of a wonderful structure; more perfect than the Greek, more copious than the Latin, and more exquisitely refined than either, yet bearing to both of them a stronger affinity, both in the roots of verbs, and in the forms of grammar, than could possibly have been produced by accident; so strong, indeed, that no philologer could examine them all, without believing them to have sprung from some common source, which, perhaps, no longer exists.

Even before Jones's provocative proposal, lovers of languages knew of the relationships among languages in Europe. French, Italian, Spanish, Romanian, and other so-called Romance languages clearly had their origin in Latin. Latin by now was no longer spoken by people on a daily basis. However, it had been the official language of the Christian church since the third century. Christianity had evolved from a Jewish sect to a distinct religion with its power center in Rome, where they spoke Latin. In the fourth century, St. Jerome translated the Christian Bible into Latin. His translation was called the Vulgate, because Latin was indeed the "vulgar" or common tongue of the Roman Empire. Other important Christian books were written in Latin, including St. Augustine's *City of God*. So even after the fall of Rome as a political power, the Christian church kept Latin as the language of its ceremonies and administration. As a result, Latin also became the language of scholars. It remained so through the seventeenth century. The Roman Catholic church kept Latin as the language of rites and rituals until the 1960s. It is still used as the official administrative language of the Catholic church.

By the end of the eighteenth century, philologists and historical linguists had begun broadening the evidence for common origins beyond the Romance languages. *Philology*, or comparative philology, is the study of the historical relationship between languages. A person who does comparative philology is a philologist. Languages that prove to be historically related or descended from a common ancestor language are called cognate languages. French and Romanian, for example, are cognate languages because they derive from Latin. So are Urdu and Bengali, which derive from Sanskrit.

By the early 1830s it was clear that most if not all of the European languages had deep ancestral connections to Sanskrit. The period from about 1800 to 1870 has been called the "Age of Comparative Philology" in the science of linguistics. Today this field is called comparative linguistics. Its premise is that "genetically related" languages have a common ancestral language. The relationship may be clear, like that of the Romance languages with Latin, which still exists in written form. It may instead be a hidden relationship that must be reconstructed when the original proto-language no longer exists in either verbal or written form. This is the case with Proto-Indo-European. It is important to remember that the reconstruction is not the actual proto-language itself. That is lost forever. Rather, the reconstruction is like a schematic or a drawing of the proto-language, not the real thing but enough of a rendering to make it recognizable.

A fundamental assumption of comparative linguistics is that linguistic change happens continually and in a regular fashion. This assumption has been verified by decades of observation and scholarship. In a given language, during a specific period, a particular change takes place in all forms with the same "linguistic shape." As a theoretical example, during a particular time period and in a specific location all the [θ] sounds (such as the *th* in *thin*) in a language become [ð] (like the *th* in *then*). A real-world example is what occurred with the phone /t/ used in Latin in an intervocalic position, that is, when it lay between two vowels like the /t/ in the English word *atom*. The Latin /t/ in this position mutated into /d/ in Spanish. The Latin word *cantatum*, for example, changed into the Spanish word *cantado*. As far back as the Renaissance the Italian writer Claudio Tolomei (1492–1555) had suggested the possible existence of this kind of etymological regularity. His speculation, though, had been seed falling on rocky ground. Rediscovered by Jones and others, it fell on the fertile soil of the Scientific Revolution. A basic assumption of the then-new way of thinking was that all human behavior, like the behavior of stars, planets, animals, plants, and even the earth itself, follows regular patterns. Language is a human behavior; ergo, regularly patterned. Linguistics began to mature into a science.

Philologists began using the comparative method, systematically comparing languages in order to find historical relationships among them. In 1808 Fredrich von Schlegel (1772–1829) wrote about the language and philosophy of India and developed some morphological classifications of Indo-European languages. In 1816 the German philologist Franz Bopp (1791–1867) published a study entitled *On the Conjugation System of the Sanskrit Language, in Comparison With Those of the Greek, Latin, Persian, and Germanic Languages*. Two years later the Danish linguist Rasmus Rask (1737–1832) demonstrated the relationship of Germanic languages to Latin, Greek, Baltic, and Slavic tongues. He published his findings in the treatise *Investigation on the Origin of the Old Norse or Icelandic Language*. Rask said nothing about Sanskrit. He had not heard of Jones's or Schlegel's work.

Philologists referred to all of these related tongues as Indo-European languages. Plenty of evidence now supported the theory that an ancient language once existed that was the "mother tongue" for many of the languages in Europe, Asia, and India. The researchers called it Proto-Indo-European.

The next breakthrough came from Jacob Grimm (1785–1862). He is best known today for the collection of fairy tales he compiled with his brother Wilhelm. Jacob made an equally enduring mark in the science of language, explaining the relationships of consonants in Sanskrit and various European languages. In 1822 he published his findings, and they have come to be known collectively as Grimm's Law. (Actually, Rasmus Rask had uncovered the existence of this "sound shift" process four years earlier; but few people read Danish, and his discovery went unnoticed). Grimm had noticed that many words in Sanskrit, Greek, or Latin that begin with the consonantal sound *p*, which linguists write as [p], corresponded to words in Germanic languages that began with [f]. One example is English *fish* and Latin *pisces*. Another is English *father*, Old English *fæde*r, and Sanskrit *piter.* Similarly, many Sanskrit, Greek, or Latin words beginning with [t] often had corresponding words in the Germanic languages that began with the *th* sound, which linguists represent with the Greek letter theta [θ]. One good example is English *three*, Old German *thrija*, and Sanskrit *tryas*.

Grimm thus demonstrated that a regular "shifting" of certain consonantal sounds had taken place over thousands of years in the development of both English and German. For example, the consonantal sounds *k*, *t*, and *p* in Sanskrit, Latin, and Greek shifted to *h*, *th*, and *f* in English and *h, d,* and *f* in German. Altogether he found nine sets of correspondences falling into a regular pattern of pronunciation (or phonetic pattern; phonology is the study of the rules for pronunciation). Grimm's consonant shifts are summarized in the following table. Grimm's Law is a larger and more far-reaching example of the same kind of drift or sound shift we encountered earlier with the Great Vowel Shift in the English language.

Grimm's Law

Beginning phonetic type	*Sanskrit/ Greek/ Latin*	*German*	*English*	*Current phonetic type*
voiceless plosives	*p* *t* *k*	*f* *d* *h*	*f* θ *x*	voiced aspirate
voiced plosives (unaspirated)	*b* *d* *g*	*f* *ts* *kh*	*p* *t* *k*	voiceless plosives
voiced aspirates	*bh* *dh* *gh*	*p* *t* *k*	*b* *d* *g*	voiced plosives (unaspirated)

Another powerful influence on historical linguistics was the "family tree" theory, introduced in the mid-nineteenth century by German linguist August Schleicher (1821–1863). Schleicher used a genealogical tree format to represent the growth and evolution of languages. He believed that languages could grow and die as did living creatures. Moreover, Schleicher suggested that the methods of the natural sciences could be used to analyze the growth, death, and relationships of languages.

Linguists and philologists were now happily busy studying correlations, not only among the major European languages such as French, German, and English but also with Lithuanian and the Slavic tongues such as Russian and Czech. In 1837 Bopp began publishing the first parts of the first major Indo-European grammar, *Comparative Grammar of Sanskrit, Zend, Greek, Latin, Lithuanian, Old Slavic, Gothic, and German*. It took nineteen years to complete and eventually included the Albanian and Celtic languages. In 1897 another major grammar appeared, Karl Brugmann's (1849–1919) *Outline of Comparative Indo-European Grammar*. It was not completed until 1916.

In the late 1870s an intellectual offshoot grew out of the comparative linguistic work of Grimm, Schleicher, and others. A group of mostly German philologists called the neogrammarians claimed that the sound laws governing linguistic changes "have no exceptions." This group included Brugmann, August Keskien (1840–1916), and Karl Verner (1846–1896). The neogrammarian position, though modified and weakened by more than a century of new scholarship, remains part of linguistics.

By the beginning of the twentieth century, the actual origins of the Indo-European languages still remained open to debate and controversy, as they are today. Nevertheless, the main outlines for the evolution of the Indo-European languages were in place. The comparative method and Schleicher's family-tree concept proved invaluable.

The significant similarities between many European languages and Sanskrit become clear by comparing the words for the numbers 1 though 10 in several Indo-European languages. The table below, based on one in Colin Renfew's 1989 article in *Scientific American*, shows those comparisons

Words for Numbers, Indo-European Languages

English	*Old German*	*Latin*	*Greek*	*Sanskrit*
one	ains	unus	heis	ekas
two	twai	duo	duo	dva
three	thrija	tres	treis	tryas
four	fidwor	quattuor	tettares	catvaras
five	fimf	quinque	pente	panca
six	saihs	sex	heks	sat
seven	sibum	septem	hepta	sapta
eight	ahtau	octo	okto	asta
nine	niun	novem	ennea	nava
ten	taihum	decem	deka	dasa

This kind of comparative study reveals to linguists the deep relationships among most languages in Europe, India, and Asia. It is also clear that not all languages in Asia belong to the Indo-European family. Compare, for example, the words 1 through 10 in English and Sanskrit with the corresponding words in Japanese:

Indo-European vs. Japanese

English	*Sanskrit*	*Japanese*
one	ekas	hiitotsu
two	dva	futatsu
three	tryas	mittsu
four	catvaras	yottsu
five	panca	itsutsu
six	sat	muttsu
seven	sapta	nantsu
eight	asta	yattsu
nine	nava	kokonotsu
ten	dasa	to

The relationship between English and Sanskrit is clear, especially if we remember Grimm's Law and how it reveals some of the consonant shifts that have taken place over the centuries. For example, the Sanskrit [d] became the English [t]: Sanskrit *dva* turns into *two*. At the same time, it is just as clear that Japanese has no relationship at all with Sanskrit, English, or any other Indo-European language.

The family tree concept also provides a clear demonstration of the relationships among various Indo-European languages. It also shows how historical linguists go about reconstructing words from the Proto-Indo-European ancestral language. One example is the word *father*. Some of the Romance language words are Spanish and Italian *padre*, Catalan *pare*, and French *père*. We already know that the Latin ancestral word for *father* in the Romance languages is *pater*. Latin still exists in both written and spoken form. But even if it did not, linguists could use the present-day words for *father* in the Romance tongues to make a highly accurate reconstruction. Linguists can also compare the words

The *father* Family Tree

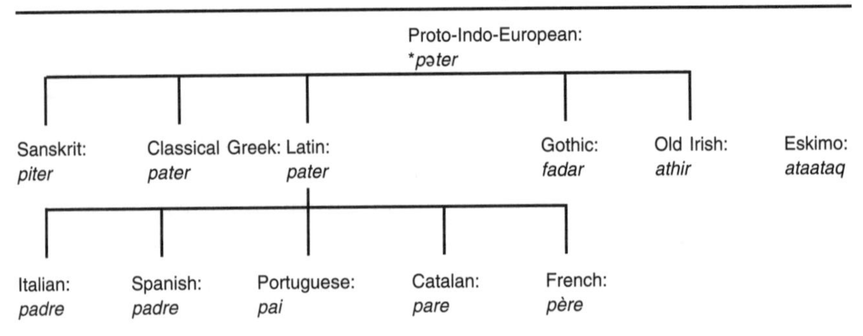

for *father* from several different language families, such as Classical Greek, Sanskrit, or Old Irish. By using the family tree concept to make comparisons, linguists construct a reasonable facsimile of the original Proto-Indo-European word: **pəter*. The asterisk means that the word is a reconstruction, with no confirmation from any written record.

Boas, Bloomfield, and the Behaviorists

At the beginning of the twentieth century, linguistics took a sharp turn in direction. Up to this point linguists had relied heavily on written language records and had emphasized historical analysis. The Swiss linguist Ferdinand de Saussure (1857–1913) helped change that approach. Though he started out as a philologist (someone who studies the historical relationship between languages), Saussure went on to establish a structural study of language. His insights reached a wider audience when his notes from lectures at Geneva University were posthumously published in 1916 in *Cours de Linguistique Generale* ("A Course in General Linguistics"). Saussure introduced the idea of studying the structures of living languages. He emphasized the difference between the act of speaking and the grammatical system that governs speech; the arbitrary nature of the relationship between the sound symbol itself and the entity it signifies; and the separation between descriptive and historical linguistics. These and other insights helped lay the foundation for *structural linguistics*, the study of a language's formal patterns—especially grammar and phonology—as we know it today.

Meanwhile, two American scientists were also taking linguistics in a new direction. Franz Boas (1858–1942) and Edward Sapir (1884–1939) were anthropologists keenly interested in American Indians and their languages. Like some other American linguists, they were concerned about learning as much as possible about native American languages before those languages became extinct. Since these languages had no written counterpart, linguists studying them could not use the European-developed tool of historical analysis. Rather, they had to develop detailed accounts of the speech patterns of these still-living languages. In 1911 Boas published the first volume of his pioneering work *The Handbook of American Indian Languages*. In 1921 Sapir released his equally important and appropriately named book *Language*.

Saussure's work gained much support in Europe and still exerts an influence on linguistics. The linguistic disciplines of semiotics and structuralism rise on largely Saussurean foundations. Meanwhile, American linguists took to heart much of what Boas and Sapir had to say. Their work on linguistic analysis spurred considerable progress in the linguistic disciplines of phonetics, phonology, and syntax. The next truly significant step was taken by Chicago-born linguist Leonard Bloomfield.

Because of the variety of techniques Bloomfield and his followers used to analyze and classify the structures of sentences, the name *structuralism* came to be applied to his brand of linguistics. In his book *Language*, published in 1933, Bloomfield laid out principles that continue to guide much of linguistics:

- The study of language must always center on the spoken (or signed) language, and not on written language.
- Definitions used in the grammar of a language must be based on the forms of the language itself.
- The history of a language form does not explain the form's meaning; for at any given point in its history, a language is a whole and complete system of sounds and forms.

Bloomfield's approach came to be understood as behaviorist. This was especially true, as we have already seen, in his approach to the meaning of *meaning*. Bloomfield always insisted upon an uncompromisingly scientific approach to language study. Linguistics must be, he urged, an empirical science, a science based on observable and observed facts, on real data. "If you want to compare two languages," Bloomfield is said to have remarked, "it helps to know one of them."

Another example of the Bloomfield behaviorist view of language study was an utter refusal to have anything to do with "mind." Followers of American structuralism followed the lead of behaviorist psychologists and insisted that the mind was unobservable. It was not amenable to scientific study. Therefore, linguists must eschew any reference to it. American structuralist linguists tended to ignore semantics and to focus on the smallest units of language, phomenes and morphemes, to the near-exclusion of syntax.

That approach came to a screeching halt in 1957, with the publication of a truly revolutionary work of linguistics by a twenty-nine-year-old scholar from Philadelphia. Noam Chomsky had to go all the way to Holland to find a publisher for his book. In one fell swoop he changed the direction of modern linguistics, put the mind back in language, and indirectly opened the way to the extraordinary work of researchers who are showing that perhaps the mind *is* something that science can study. It will be worth our while to take a closer look at this controversial figure in linguistic science.

Chomsky, Grammar, and the Standard Theory

Born in Philadelphia in 1928, Avram Noam Chomsky was first introduced to the wonders of linguistics (philology, to be precise) by his father, Herbert, a Hebrew scholar. He studied linguistics at the University of Pennsylvania, where his mentor was the famous Zellig Harris. His 1955 Ph.D. dissertation was on "Transformational Analysis." Chomsky went on to teach linguistics and modern languages at MIT. In 1961 he became a full professor, and he received the Ward Professorship of Foreign Languages and Linguistics in 1976.

With his first published book, *Syntactic Structures* (The Hague: Mouton, 1957), Chomsky put the world of linguistics on notice that he was a force to be reckoned with. He took the dramatic and somewhat controversial position of breaking ranks with the long-held mechanistic view of language that had been established by Leonard Bloomfield. Chomsky began laying the groundwork for a new paradigm for linguistics, a framework more "mentalistic" and generative than any seen before. Other books followed: *Aspects of the Theory of Syntax* (1965), *Cartesian Linguistics* (1966), *The Sound Pattern of English* (written with Morris Halle, 1968), *The Logical Structure of Linguistic Thinking* (1975), *Reflections on Language* (1975), *Lectures on Government and Binding* (1981), *Barriers* (1986), and *Language and Problems of Knowledge: The Managua Lectures* (1988). Chomsky also began gaining a reputation as a fierce and uncompromising critic of American foreign and domestic government policy. One of his most famous sociopolitical works was *American Power and the New Mandarins* (1969), and he has continued to speak his mind publicly and frequently on political, social, and economic issues.

In the world of linguistics, though, Noam Chomsky is best known as the creator of transformational and generative grammar. When Chomsky talks about grammar, he is not using the same definitions most of us use. He is primarily interested not in some formal descriptive system but rather in *the linguistic structures and processes at work in the human mind.* It is for this reason that his approach to grammar and syntax is often called "mentalistic." Chomsky wants to know how the human mind creates grammar and what structures the mind and brain use to do this. As we mentioned earlier, Chomsky sees the syntactic process as rooted in some human genetic predisposition to language. It is universal, he says, and therefore must be genetically coded for in some fashion.

Chomsky's name is associated with *transformational grammar, generative grammar*, and *transformational-generative grammar*. He basically borrowed these terms from mathematics. When Chomsky first proposed the idea of transformational rules of grammar in 1957, he meant rules that allowed one kind of sentence to be transformed into another, in the same way one form of ... another. For example, $E = mc^2$ can be transformed into $E/c^2 = m$ with no change in meaning or validity. In an analogous fashion, the active sentence *Local carpenters built the house* can be transformed into the passive sentence *The house was built by local carpenters* with no loss of information.

Transformational rules governed such linguistic transformation processes. All previous forms of grammar, said Chomsky, dealt with what he called "phrase-structure rules." They set forth the rules by which words create phrases, phrases created sentences, and so forth. Previous grammars had not tackled the larger question of the relationships of sentences with different structures. For example, these earlier grammars could not explain why the sentence *Local carpenters built the house* could be transformed into *The house was built by local carpenters*. They did not get down to basic rules. Transformational grammar did. In somewhat the same way, ancient metallurgists could make bronze from copper and tin; they could show others how to do it. But they could not explain *why* specific mixtures of copper and tin produced bronze. That had to wait for the development of the science of chemistry.

Chomsky's development of transformational grammar for linguistics can also be compared to the development of unified field theories in physics. Physics recognizes the existence of four basic forces in the universe: gravity, electromagnetism, the nuclear strong force, and the nuclear weak force. It once assumed that electricity and magnetism were two separate forces, but in 1873 James Clerk Maxwell published his equations showing they were two manifestations of the same force. One could transform into another. In 1967 physicists Steven Weinberg, Sheldon Glashow, and Abdus Salam formulated their "electroweak theory," showing the essential unity of the electromagnetic and nuclear weak forces. Their equations showed how different fundamental forces of physics "transform" into one another under specific conditions, mainly the extreme heat and pressure that prevailed in the first few instants of the Big Bang.

Chomsky's transformational rule accomplishes a similar task in linguistics. As an example, here is a linguistic transformational "equation" to turn *The horse chased the man* into *The man was chased by the horse:*

$$NP_1 + V + NP_2 \rightarrow NP_2 + Aux + \mathit{Ven} + \mathit{by} + NP_1$$

NP_1 is the first noun phrase in the active sentence. It gets placed at the end of the passive sentence. NP_2, the second noun phrase in the active sentence, goes to the beginning of the passive sentence. The verb V changes from past tense to a past participle (*Ven*), and an auxiliary verb (Aux) goes in front of it. A particle (*by*, in this case) gets inserted between the verb and the final noun phrase. This rule, as expressed in the shorthand of the equation above, will always generate all regular transformations of active to passive sentences.

This is more than merely theoretical work. Chomsky has also been deeply interested in the mental processes by which we can generate a near-infinity of possible sentences from a specific set of lexemes, morphemes, and phonemes. He draws a distinction between *competence* and *performance*. Competence, in Chomsky's view, is a person's knowledge of the rules that govern the creation and use of a language. Performance is the actual use of that language in the real world. Chomsky insists that linguistics spend more time looking at competence than it has heretofore.

We create language with our minds, with our brains. Human children are doing this with considerable facility by the time they are five. They are creating meaningful two- and three-word statements by the time they turn three. How is this possible? Competence lies in the mind. So the mind, whatever it turns out to be, is a legitimate object of study for linguistics. More than legitimate: it becomes an *essential* object of study. Because of this innate knowledge of the rules of language, young children can understand sentences they have never heard before. They can also recognize nonsense when they hear it, and learn to spot errors of linguistic performance.

Chomsky believes that the human brain itself is somehow preprogrammed for language. Some "organ," as he calls it, exists in the brain that gives us—and only us—the ability to create and use this incredibly flexible and powerful mode of communication. In a sense, this "linguistic organ" is akin to our immune system. In ways scientists are only now beginning to understand, our immune systems can create antibodies—killer cells and disease fighters—against bacteria, viruses, and environmental pollutants the body has never encountered before. If I go into a laboratory, create a brand-new chemical compound that has never before existed on the face of the earth, and inject it into you, in a matter of hours or days your body's immune system will create the precise antibody needed to neutralize it. In somewhat the same way, our minds and brains hold the rules needed to create a language and to understand the meaning of sentences we have never heard before.

Human infants—our children, my grandson—do it every day.

How is this possible?

Part Two

Language and the Brain

Chapter 5

A Map of the Territory

We create and store language in our brain, that marvelous organ Richard Restak has called "the enlightened machine." In order to understand how that takes place, we need to become familiar with this ball of tissue that sits behind our eyes.

The Playing Field of the Mind

The brain is part of the *central nervous system*, which also includes the spinal cord and its associated nerve ends. Taken together, the central nervous system generates the electrochemical impulses that govern every bodily function and stores information coming in from the body's various internal and external sensory receptors. It is the "playing field" for the "games" we call consciousness, self-awareness, thinking, and the mind. The territory of the brain is vast and mostly unexplored, but it is also crisscrossed by a myriad of roads and trails.

The average human brain weighs between 1,300 and 1,500 grams, roughly the weight of an ordinary dictionary. Its volume (between 1,300 and 1,500 cubic centimeters) is about that of three pints of milk, and it has the consistency of cooked oatmeal. With its many wrinkles and folds, the brain has a much larger surface area than is obviously visible. In fact, if the brain were completely smoothed out on a flat surface, it would cover about 2,100 square centimeters or about 324 square inches. That is about the size of a table napkin 18 inches on a side. Women's brains tend to be slightly smaller than those of men, because women tend to be slightly smaller than men overall. No correlation has ever been found to exist between brain size and intelligence. One of the most brilliant and creative men of all time, the French writer Anatole France, had a brain that weighed "only" 1,017 grams. Conversely, one of the largest human brains on record belonged to a man with severe mental retardation. (For what it's worth, the writers Jonathan Swift and Ivan Turgenev had brains weighing two kilograms, nearly 1.5 times larger than "average.")

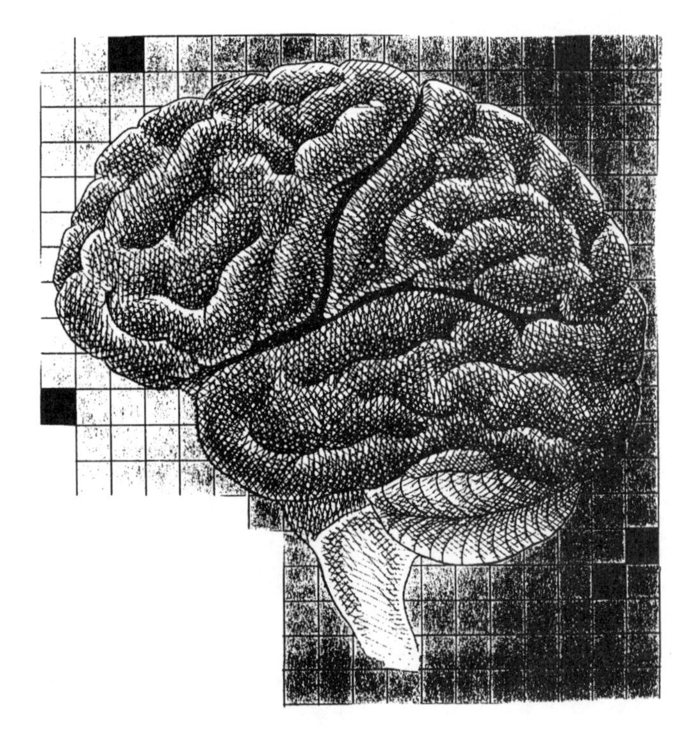

The brain is the seat of consciousness, thought, intelligence, memory, and language.
Illustration courtesy of the Office of Technology Assessment, United States Congress, "New Developments in Neuroscience" series.

The brain is composed of three general types of tissue: *gray matter*, *white matter*, and *neuroglia* cells. The white and gray matter of the brain actually consist of *neurons* or brain cells. Neuroglia cells—also called *glia*; the Latin word means "glue"—are the supporting cells and fibers of the central nervous system. Glia acts as supporting or connective tissue in the spinal cord and brain. Bundles of insulated axons are called *nerve fibers*.

In many respects neurons are like the other cells in the body. What distinguishes them are their *axons* and *dendrites*. *Axon* is derived from a Greek word and literally means "axis." An axon is a long, thin extension of the neuron's cell body that transmits signals to other cells. Some axons may be no more than a few millimeters long. Others, linking the brain to remote areas of the body, are more than a meter in length. An axon is a transmitter, but it transmits its electrical signals without ever touching the next cell or cells.

A nerve impulse consists of many tiny waves of electrical charge. They cascade down the axon from the central cell body like a series of tiny waterfalls pouring down a rock face from a stream above. When it reaches the axon's tip, the nerve impulse causes the release of a highly specialized chemical, a *neurotransmitter*. The neurotransmitter floods into the space between the cells, the *synaptic gap*. The entire region of axon, synaptic gap, and receiving cell wall is a *synapse*. The neurotransmitter travels across the synapse to the next cell. There the neurotransmitter triggers the creation of another electrical signal. That signal in turn passes down the receiving cell, and the process continues.

Neurotransmitters in the brain that create electrical impulses in the neurons with which they interact are *excitatory* neurotransmitters. *Inhibitory* neurotransmitters block the transmission of electrical impulses in the neurons they encounter. A well-known family of inhibitory neurotransmitters is the *endorphins* and *enkephalins*. These chemicals inhibit the action of neurons that transmit pain signals. Endorphins and enkephalins are found in many regions of the brain. Their discovery, beginning in 1975, was a dramatic advance in our understanding of the brain as an electrochemical organ. It has also opened new avenues of inquiry into the mechanisms of pain, acupuncture, mental illness, and drug addiction.

While axons are transmitters, dendrites are receivers. These networks of short nerve fibers branch out from axons or the cell body.

Together with axons from other cells they create the synapses. Dendrites receive the electrical signals being transmitted from other neurons and pass them along to their neuron's cell body and thence down the axon to another synapse. Under a microscope the network of axons and dendrites looks like a hopelessly tangled ball of twine. In fact, it is more like an intricate network of superhighways, freeways, city streets, county roads, and dusty trails. Traveling those pathways are an uncountable number of messengers, carrying information to and from a billion different addresses.

The Brain vs. the Computer

One brain cell may at any moment be receiving many thousands of signals from other neurons, because each cell may have thousands of synaptic connections with other neurons in the brain. Whether that particular neuron in fact fires off a signal down *its* axon depends on how many signals it receives and of what kind, excitatory or inhibitory. So the process of sending a signal through a brain cell is a lot more complicated than it first seems.

In fact, it is enormously more complicated than even the most powerful computer. Most computers process information in a linear fashion. The computer's central processing unit, with its computer chips and operating system, handles data one step at a time. Even when it crunches sixteen or even thirty-two bits of data at once, today's fastest and most sophisticated desktop computers, and most large mainframes as well, have to break a problem down into a series of sequential steps. Newer *parallel processing* computers deal with data in a fashion a bit more like that of the brain. Their chips are wired together in parallel fashion. Each processing unit may be connected to four, eight, sixteen or more other units. The computer is thus able to process several pieces of a problem simultaneously and then combine it all together.

But even the most sophisticated, massive parallel computer pales in comparison with the human brain. The average adult brain contains perhaps a hundred *billion* neurons. And these neurons are not wired together one-to-one. The interconnections among them are intricate beyond belief. Each neuron may have only one axon, but each axon may have many small branches at its end sending signals to many other neurons. And each neuron, with its many dendrites each having many branches, may have dozens, hundreds, or even thousands of different neurons feeding it impulses across synapses. Each of the hundred-billion-plus neurons in your brain is synaptically connected to an *average* of a thousand other neurons. In fact, there are brain cells in at least one part of the brain, the cerebellum, that have connections to as many as a hundred thousand other neurons. The result? Your brain contains *a minimum of a hundred trillion interconnections.* That's a hundred trillion (100,000,000,000,000) yes/no switches in the human brain.

Two neurons connected by one synapse yields a very simple "brain," one that can have one of two mental states or bits of information: on or off. Yes or no. If those two neurons share two synapses, they can exist in four possible mental states: yes and yes, yes and no, no and yes, or no and no. Four is two squared, 2^2. The big 2 represents the two possible states (yes or no; on or off) of a synapse; the exponent represents the number of synapses. The number of cells is irrelevant; the connections are what count. So, for example, three synapses have eight possible states—two cubed, or 2^3: yes, yes, yes; yes, yes, no; yes, no, no; no, yes, yes; yes, no, yes; no, yes, no; no, no, yes; and no, no, no. Four synapses is sixteen states (2^4); five, thirty-two states (2^5), and on and on. If the brain contains a hundred billion neurons, and each neuron has an average of a thousand synapses, then, as we have seen, we are talking about a hundred trillion synapses, $2^{100,000,000,000,000}$ possible mental states for the human brain. There are not that many atoms in the known universe, much less potential smarts in even the most complex computer on earth. It is not too surprising that humans are building computers, and not the other way around.

Onions and Broccoli

The brain grows out of the top of the spinal cord like a head of broccoli flowering from its stalk. We could also compare the brain to an onion. Like an onion, the brain is made of layers.

To see the brain's structure, we start by removing the skin and skull from the top of the head, and then looking in. What we observe first are three membranes: the *dura mater* ("hard mother"), the *arachnoid* ("cobweb"), and the *pia mater* ("soft mother"). The dura is the outermost of the three membranes or *meninges*. It lies just underneath the skull. This hard, fibrous membrane, difficult to cut through, serves to protect the more delicate membranes lying below it. The arachnoid lies across the brain's various folds and crevices. Its delicate structure led early brain researchers to compare it to a spiderweb, thus its name. Underneath the arachnoid is the pia. It follows the hills and valleys of the brain's topography like a second skin.

Flowing between the arachnoid and the pia is the central nervous system's *cerebrospinal fluid*. Although there is not much of it—no more than about 120 milliliters, perhaps enough to fill a small teacup—it fills every nook and cranny of the brain. It is mainly composed of water, with dissolved salts and proteins. Its main purpose is to act like hydraulic fluid, protecting the brain and central nervous system from mechanical injury.

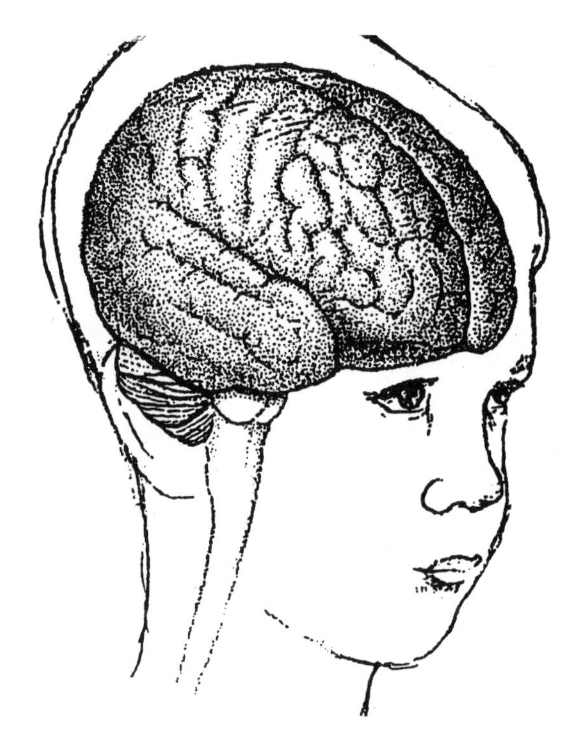

It is in the brain of the young child that language begins, builds, and reaches maturity. Researchers are now uncovering new and exciting information on how the brain creates, stores, and sometimes loses the gift of language.
Illustration Courtesy of U.S. National Institute of Neurological and Communicative Disorders and Stroke.

Once we have penetrated the three outer membranes and peeled them away, we can view the main structural characteristics of the brain. As we can see from the illustrations, the brain looks very wrinkled, and it seems to have two main parts. The many folds and crevices of the brain's outer surface are referred to as *sulci* ("valleys"), or fissures, and *gyri* ("ridges"), or convolutions. Running from front to back along the center of the brain is the *longitudinal fissure*. It divides the brain into two *cerebral hemispheres*. The left and right hemispheres appear to the unaided eye to be identical in size and shape. Closer analysis, though, reveals differences. For example, some of the fissures in the brain's surface differ in length and orientation between the two hemispheres. The cerebral hemispheres are joined together by a thick band of nerve tissue, the *corpus callosum* ("hard body"). The corpus callosum is about ten centimeters long, about the width of your hand. It carries information from one hemisphere to the other. The frequent comments one hears about being "right-brained" or "left-brained" are imprecise at best. We do not, in fact, have two brains inside our skulls, just one with two hemispheres joined firmly together by the corpus callosum. The two hemispheres work closely together.

The "left brain/right brain" idea does have a foundation in fact. Each cerebral hemisphere controls movement and receives sensory data from the opposite side of the body. Thus, the *left* cerebral hemisphere controls the movement of the body's *right* side and receives information from the sensory receptors on that side of the body. The opposite is true of the right cerebral hemisphere. Nerve fibers from the two hemispheres cross one another as they descend into the brain stem and spinal column, where they fan out into the body's weblike nervous system. This bilateralization of functions is not universal. For example, sensory data from each ear goes to both hemispheres, though most travels to the opposite one. In the case of the eyes, the situation is more complex: data from the left half of each visual field of each eye travels to the left hemisphere, and vice versa.

The cerebral hemispheres are the two main divisions of the part of the brain commonly called the *cerebrum*. The corpus callosum lies buried deep within the cerebrum. The cerebrum in turn is a large part of one of the brain's three major divisions, the *forebrain*. The other two main divisions are, not surprisingly, the *midbrain* and the *hindbrain*.

Besides the longitudinal fissure, the brain's outer surface has several other major sulci running through it. Along the outer edge of each hemisphere is the *Sylvian fissure*, also called the *lateral sulcus*. Across the top of the brain, running from left to right and blending into the Sylvian fissure at each end, is the *central sulcus* or the *Rolandic fissure*. Both these valleys in the brain's landscape are important landmarks for those who study language and the brain. Several well-known language areas, as we will discover, lie close to the Sylvian or Rolandic fissures.

Neuroscientists, researchers who study the brain and central nervous system, use these fissures and ridges as boundary lines to divide each cerebral hemisphere into different major territories or *lobes*:

- The *frontal lobe* takes up everything that lies in front of the Rolandic fissure. This part of the brain basically runs from your forehead back to the top of your skull.
- Behind the Rolandic fissure lie the *parietal lobe* and *occipital lobe*. The word *parietal* comes from the Latin word meaning "wall," and *occipital* from the Latin *ob-*, "against," and *caput* or "head." The parietal lobe lies directly behind the central sulcus. The occipital lobe is behind the parietal lobe, lying at the very rear of the brain.
- Everything below the Sylvian fissure is the *temporal lobe* of the brain. The word *temporal* means "time." The temporal lobes lie along the left and right sides of the brain, about where your ears are. They contain regions that play extremely important roles in language and memory.

If we think of the two cerebral hemispheres as continents, then the four lobes—the frontal, parietal, occipital, and temporal—could be considered the major countries of those continents. Like any country, they have different geographical, social, and political regions. Each region has a different purpose.

For example, the *precentral ridge*, lying in the frontal lobe just in front of the Rolandic fissure, governs movement on the opposite side of the body. That is, the left precentral ridge handles movement of the right side of the body, and vice versa. In front of that is the *premotor cortex*, which governs complex motor movements. The word *cortex* comes from a Latin word meaning "bark," like the bark of a tree. The brain's lobes are often referred to as cortexes, as in "occipital cortex."

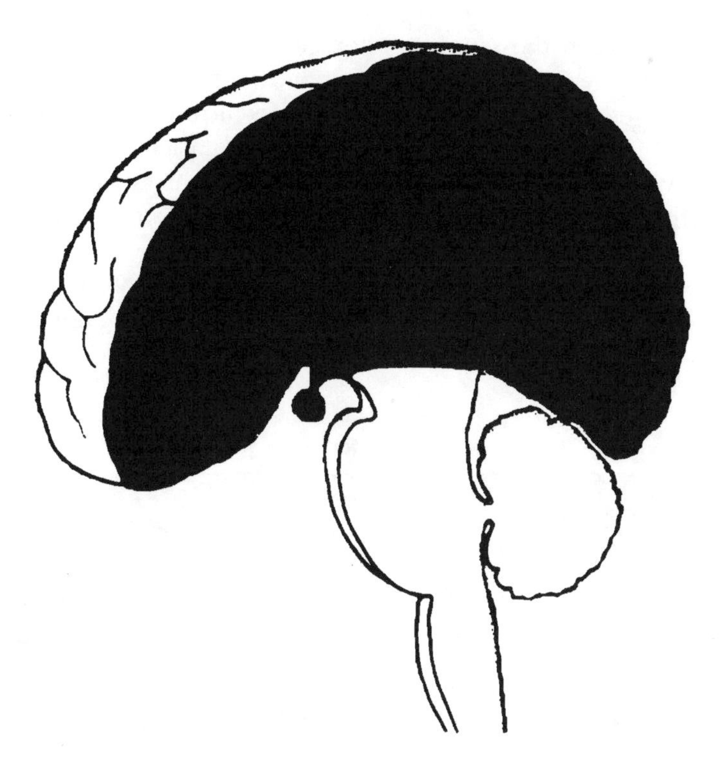

The forebrain is the largest area of the brain and is divided into the left and right hemispheres. This illustration shows the right hemisphere. The two hemispheres are divided into the frontal lobes at the front, the temporal lobes on the sides, the parietal lobes along the top and rear, and the occipital lobe at the very back. The forebrain not only regulates body functions like temperature, blood pressure, and sexual desire, it also is home to regions that control complex mental activities such as language.
Illustration Courtesy of U.S. National Institute of Neurological and Communicative Disorders and Stroke.

Still closer to the front of the brain in the frontal lobe are the *prefrontal fibers*. This area controls what you ought *not* to do, that is, it handles inhibitory commands.

In the *post–central ridge* region of the parietal lobe is the *sensory cortex*. This is the main collection region for sensory data. Information from each of the body's sensory receptors is funnelled into some specific part of the sensory cortex. However, the sensory cortex does not simply provide us with sensory "feelings." Raw sensations such as touch, pain, and pressure are processed in regions lower down in the brainstem. Rather, the sensory cortex gives the person specific information about the "where" of the sensation. If a part of my sensory cortex is damaged, by a stroke, for example, I will respond appropriately if you hit me with a hammer. However, I will not be able to tell you whether you smashed my thumb or my big toe unless I am watching you do this. The "where" of the sensation is processed in the sensory cortex.

Below the Sylvian fissure is the brain's temporal lobe. It is appropriately named. The temporal lobe is involved with the sense of hearing and with memory. When researchers stimulate the temporal lobe

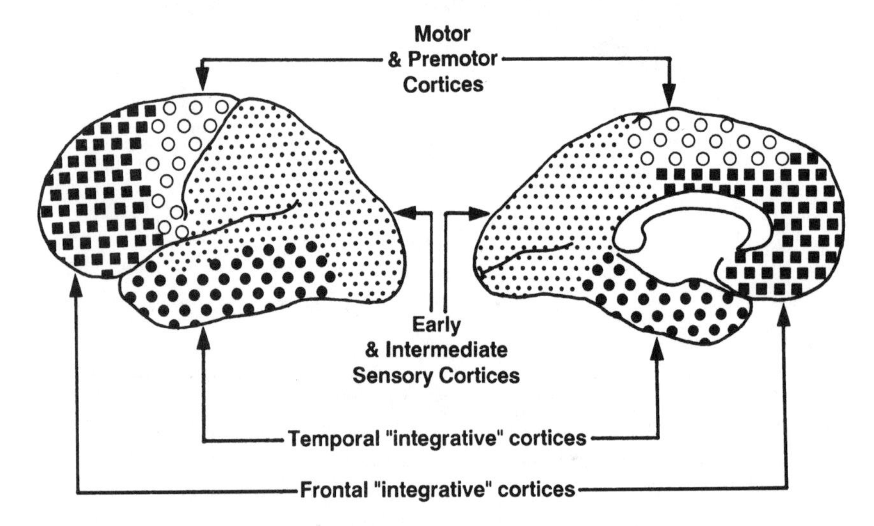

This illustration shows fundamental divisions of the human cerebral cortex, the outer convoluted layer of the brain. At the rear of the brain (small dots) are the early and intermediate sensory regions, including the areas of the brain that process sight, hearing, and the position of the body in space. Along the top of the brain (open dots), just in front of the fissure called the Rolandic fissure, are the motor and premotor regions, which handle the movement of the body's different parts. Near the front of the brain (square black dots) are the frontal "integrative" regions. The temporal lobes along the side of the brain are home to the temporal "integrative" regions. The integrative regions include "convergence zones" that coordinate the meshing of information from the other areas of the brain.

Reprinted from *Neural Computation*, 1: 125 (1989), Antonio Damasio, "The Brain Binds Entities and Events by Multilingual Activation From Convergence Zones." Copyright 1989 Massachusetts Institute of Technology.

with an electrical impulse, for example, the person stimulated may experience a sense of *déjà vu*, the eerily familiar sense of having done this before. Other people, however, sometimes experience a sense of *jamais vu*, the feeling that some familiar person or event is weird or strange. These sensations are connected with memory. The temporal lobe is also connected to other structures deeper in the brain. These connections allow us to experience emotions: sexual desire, fear, anger, rage, despair, hope, joy, and so on.

Behind the parietal lobe is the occipital lobe. This region includes the *visual cortex*. Centuries ago physicians and natural scientists discovered this region's function. People suffering severe wounds in battle to the back of their heads became blind, even though their eyes were unharmed. The visual cortex processes the complex signals coming from the eyes and creates vision. The incredibly complex transformations occurring in the visual cortex are only today being slowly unravelled.

The cerebrum, that part of the forebrain composed of the two cerebral hemispheres and their four lobes, makes up a full 70 percent of the entire central nervous system. The gray matter making up the outer part of the cerebrum, the *cerebral cortex*, is less than five millimeters thick, the height of three quarters stacked on top of each other. But that layer has a rather complex structure. Like the onion we compared the brain to earlier, the cortex has layers—six, to be exact. Within those six layers are some eight billion—*billion*, as in 8,000,000,000—neurons. Those eight billion neurons are woven together by an immensely dense network of neuronal interconnections, a thousand kilometers of fibers per cubic centimeter. Imagine taking a superthin piece of thread that stretches from Boston to Cleveland, almost exactly a thousand kilometers, and then bundling it up tightly enough to fit into a cube smaller than the tip of your little finger. Dense.

Beneath the skin of gray matter cortex lies a thicker layer of white matter containing hundreds of millions of nerve fibers. These fibers make up three different types of neural connections in the cerebrum. *Association fibers* connect different areas within the same cerebral hemisphere. *Projection fibers* rise up from the brainstem and penetrate every part of the cerebrum. The corpus callosum is made of a dense bundle of *commissural* (or "joining") fibers.

Diving Deep Into the Brain

As we move deeper, down past the cerebrum and its hemispheres of gray and white matter, we come upon the other major parts of the forebrain. They are the *limbic system*, the *basal ganglia*, and the structures of the *diencephalon*. The word *diencephalon* comes from the Greek *di-*, "doubled" or "two," and *enkephalon*, "brain." It lies deep in the forebrain, between the cerebral hemispheres and the brainstem. The diencephalon includes the *thalamus*, *hypothalamus*, *pituitary gland*, and *pineal gland*. The thalamus (from the Greek word meaning "chamber") consists of two egg-shaped masses of gray matter sitting atop the brainstem. Each ovoid snuggles up against the concave inner wall of one cerebral hemisphere. The two are connected by a band, or *tract* as neuroscientists call it, of nerve fibers called the *massa intermedia* ("intermediate mass"). The signals from every sensory organ except the nose pass through the thalamus on their way to the cerebral hemispheres. The thalamus is a combination switchboard and processing center. It receives, processes, and associates sensory data arriving from the body via the central nervous system. Different regions in the thalamus's two ovoids handle input from different parts of the body. For example, the medial genticulate body processes data from the ears. The ventrobasal complex handles input arriving from the body through the spinal cord.

Just below the thalamus and above the brainstem is the hypothalamus (literally, "under the thalamus"). It is extremely tiny—no larger than the tip of your thumb and weighing only fourteen grams—but it is a powerhouse. No other brain structure this size does as much as does the hypothalamus. It has four main regions or nuclei: preoptic; anterior, which means "forward"; middle; and posterior, "rear," of course. The hypothalamus is the command center for regulating aggression, appetite, body temperature, fear, sexual behavior, sleep, and thirst. A tiny electrical stimulation of just one part of the hypothalamus will cause an experimental animal such as a cat to fly into a rage. The hypothalamus, however, is not the seat of emotional states. Rather, it regulates the behaviors that accompany them.

Dangling just beneath the hypothalamus is the pituitary gland. It looks like a cherry. The word *pituitary* means "slime." Early neuroscientists thought this gland was the source of nasal secretions. The pituitary gland's two regions, anterior and posterior, do release "secretions," but

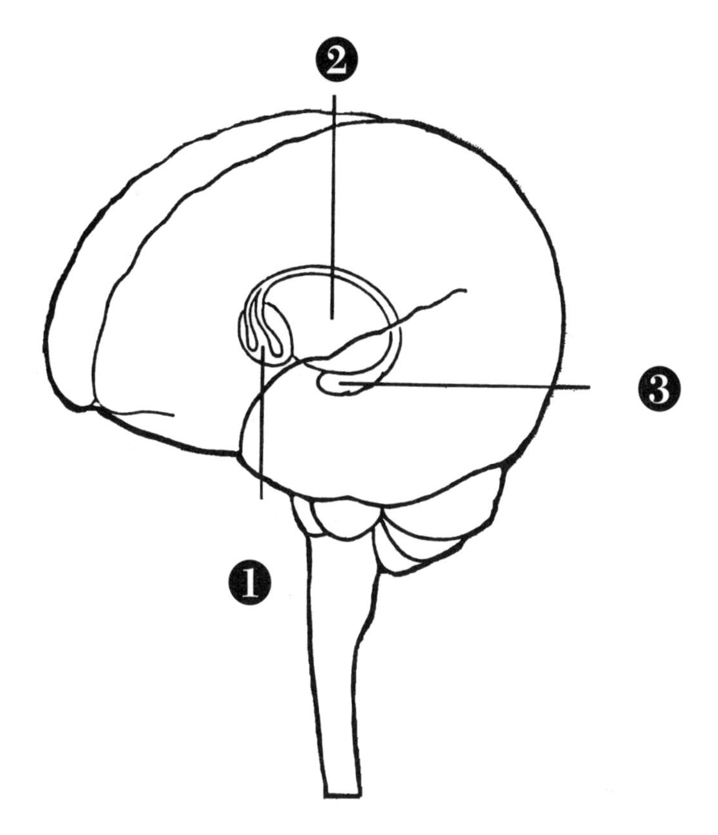

The inner brain lies deep within the forebrain and includes several structures vital to human thought and feeling. They include (1) the *hypothalamus*, the brain's emotional control center; (2) the *thalamus*, a major way station for messages coming from the muscles and sense organs; and (3) the *hippocampus*, which plays a vital role in long-term memory and thus language.
Illustration Courtesy of U.S. National Institute of Neurological and Communicative Disorders and Stroke.

not nasal mucous. The pituitary is the body's "master gland." It is a conductor whose orchestra is the body's intricate set of various hormone-secreting glands, including the adrenal glands, mammary glands, prostate gland, thymus, and thyroid glands. The posterior pituitary stores hormones produced in the hypothalamus that regulate the production of urine. Other hormones from the posterior pituitary affect the muscles in the uterus and the smooth muscles of blood vessels.

The anterior pituitary produces hormones that govern growth, the development of the testes in males and ovulation in females, the thyroid gland's activity, and the secretion of milk in a new mother's mammary glands. The pituitary is also the source of a huge chemical compound called pro-opiomelanocortin or POMC. This is the precursor molecule for the hormone ACTH, which regulates the adrenal glands. It is also the precursor for a chemical compound well known to the general public: *beta-endorphin*, usually called endorphin, a key peptide in the body's pain-regulation system.

Lying behind the hypothalamus and just below the thalamus, near the thick rear portion of the corpus callosum, is the tiny structure known as the pineal body (from the French word meaning "pine cone"). Many popularizers of so-called New Age philosophy have adopted the outmoded scientific suggestion that the pineal is a vestigial third eye. The gland is, in fact, sensitive to light levels, but not in such a straightforward fashion; after all, it is buried deep below the cerebral hemispheres and never sees the light of day or dark of night. Research has now revealed that the pineal body is the body's "master clock," regulating our temporal rhythms and sleep patterns. It does so when the hypothalamus commands it to release a hormone called melatonin. People who suffer from the affliction called Seasonal Affective Disorder have malfunctions of the pineal body. SAD can be alleviated by suppressing melatonin production through the use of high-intensity full-spectrum lights.

Sitting atop the two lobes of the thalamus are a pair of four neuronal clusters that comprise the *basal ganglia* ("bottom nerves"). They include a tiny structure called the *amygdala*, which helps regulate emotions such as rage. The basal ganglia in general help handle physical movements by acting as a relay station, passing information from the cerebral cortex back to the brainstem and other brain structures.

Just above the hypothalamus and interconnected with it is a set of structures called the *limbic* ("rim") *system*. The limbic system itself looks like two wishbones, each bent around one of the thalamic ovoids. There is little difference between this structure in humans and in primitive mammals, and it is often referred to as our "old mammalian brain." The limbic system's wishbones are comprised of several structures that seem to nest inside of one another like a Chinese puzzle box. One of the parts of the limbic system is the *hippocampus* (the word means "seahorse"; apparently early neuroscientists thought it resembled this sea animal).

Like the hypothalamus, the limbic system is intimately involved with emotional states. It also has deep connections to the cerebral cortex's temporal lobes and to a structure in the hindbrain called the cerebellum. Many neuronal fibers run among these structures and help constitute an "emotional circuit." Limbic structures create or modulate emotions ranging from love to hate, joy to sorrow, rage to bliss. The connection between the limbic system and the cerebral cortex is what allows emotions to reach our consciousness, and our consciousness to affect our emotional state. The limbic system is also involved in memory, and this in turn has implications for how we learn and remember language.

The forebrain's structures are by far the largest and most extensive in the brain. The two other main divisions, though, are also important.

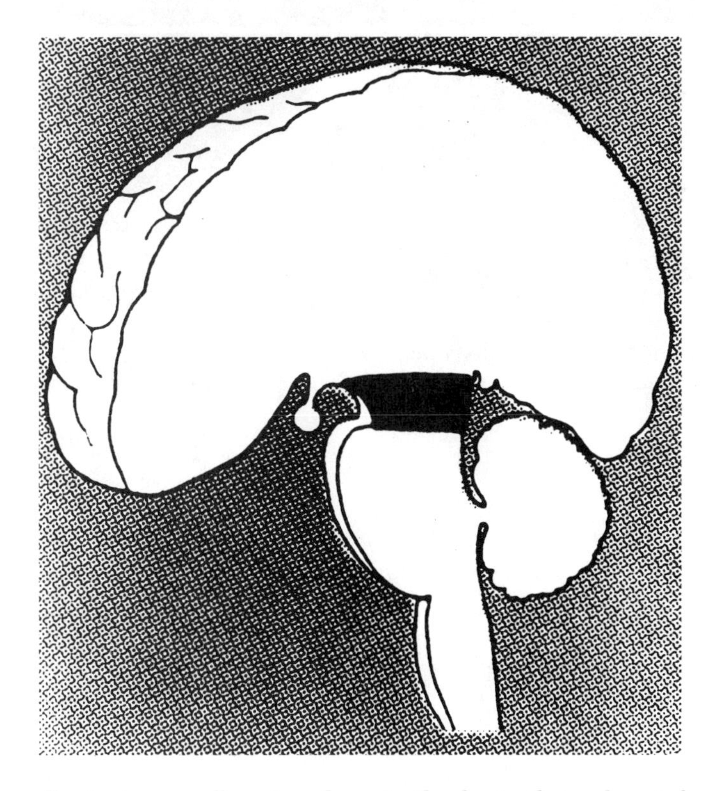

The midbrain is a small region deep in the brain that relays information about sound and sight, as well as almost all other data coming to or from the forebrain.
Illustration Courtesy of U.S. National Institute of Neurological and Communicative Disorders and Stroke.

The hindbrain contains regions that control breathing and heartbeat, as well as the fine muscle control needed for walking or manipulating objects with the hands.
Illustration Courtesy of U.S. National Institute of Neurological and Communicative Disorders and Stroke.

The midbrain is essentially the topmost section of the brainstem, the part of the brain that extends downward and into the spinal cord. It lies just below the pituitary gland. The midbrain is a relay station, transmitting sensory impulses back and forth from the forebrain to the rest of the central nervous system, and vice versa. Four small structures in the midbrain called *colliculi* ("little hills") make possible elementary forms of hearing and sight.

Below and behind the midbrain is the hindbrain. It includes the *pons* ("bridge," as in "pontoons"), the *medulla oblongata* ("moderately long marrow"), and the *cerebellum* ("little brain"). Just below the midbrain, and blending into it, is the pons. As its name implies, the pons is a bridge of nerve fibers connecting the cerebral cortex with the

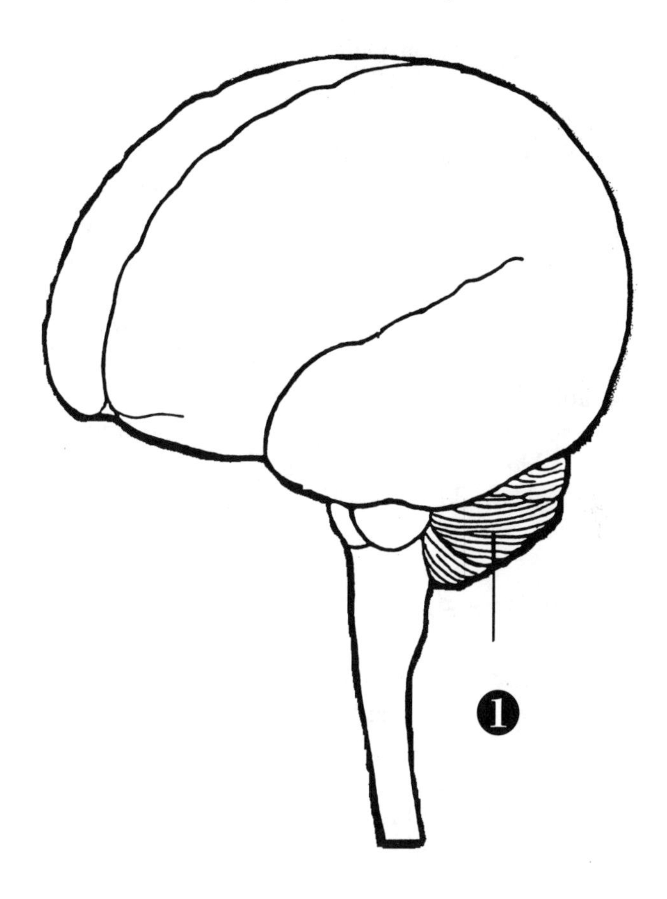

The cerebellum (1) is the best-known part of the hindbrain. It helps coordinate our every movement.
Illustration Courtesy of U.S. National Institute of Neurological and Communicative Disorders and Stroke.

cerebellum behind it. Below the pons is the medulla. Like the pons it is about two centimeters long, less than the length of your little finger. It is here, in this "switchboard" of the central nervous system, that the nerve fibers from the cerebral hemispheres pass down into the spinal cord. It is here that those nerve bundles criss-cross in what brain researchers call the *corticospinal decussation*. It is this crossover in the medulla that causes the right cerebral hemisphere to control the body's left side, and vice versa. The medulla itself is a vital part of the brain. It controls blood pressure, breathing, the heart rate (in part), singing, swallowing, and talking. Destroy the medulla, or cut the brainstem below it, and a person will die within minutes as the heartbeat and breathing come to a sudden halt.

The hindbrain's cerebellum is the brain's choreographer. This remarkable structure contains within its cells a complete "map" of the body's motor and sensory functions. It coordinates the movements of the body, posture, and muscle tone. Damage the cerebellum—through an accident, perhaps, or years of alcohol abuse—and you will walk in a staggering, stumbling gait. If you try to scratch your head, your arm will flail about. You will be unable to draw, write, dance, play baseball, or play the piano: the cerebellum governs eye-hand coordination. You will not be able to sit up straight without assistance. You might not even be able to walk and chew gum at the same time. You certainly would have trouble conversing in Sign.

But at least you would still be able to talk.

THE TALKING BRAIN

Some of the most exciting work in brain research since the 1970s has focused on the areas of the brain involved with language. Much of the excitement has come from the discovery of possible new language regions in the brain. These new discoveries, which we will examine in some detail later, have only served to confirm the linguistic role of several cerebral regions long known to linguists and neurologists. All these previously known language areas sit in the brain's left hemisphere in nearly everyone, and they cluster around the Sylvian and Rolandic fissures.

- Discovered by Pierre-Paul Broca in 1861, *Broca's area* lies in the lower back part of the left frontal lobe along the inner part of the left frontal ridge, the third ridge of brain tissue on the left frontal lobe. The left Sylvian fissure lies just behind it, and the orbital ridge is just beneath it. Broca's area has long been thought to be the brain's center for encoding speech.
- *Heschl's gyri* is named for the Austrian pathologist R. L. Heschl (1824–1881). It lies along the upper part of the brain's temporal lobe, just below the Sylvian fissure. Heschl's gyri is the main region for auditory perception and so must have an important role in verbal language.

- *Exner's center*, lying to the rear of the frontal lobe, may play a role in written language. It sits just above Broca's area. Named for the German neurologist Sigmund Exner (1846–1926), this area may control the movements involved in writing.
- *Wernicke's area*, first discovered by Karl Wernicke in 1874, lies along the upper regions of the left temporal and parietal lobes,

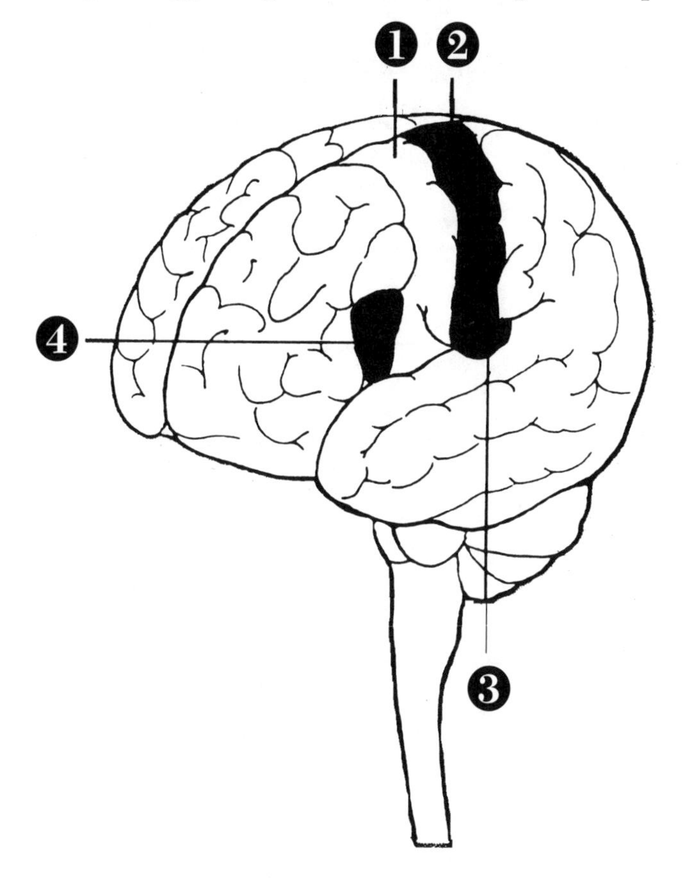

The cerebral cortex is a major part of the forebrain. It includes (1) the *motor cortex*, which controls all voluntary body movements from blinking one's eye to shaking hands; (2) the *sensory cortex*, which receives the flood of information coming from the different senses; (3) the *auditory cortex*, which makes it possible for a person to tell the difference between a Miles Davis trumpet riff and an Eric Clapton guitar lick; and (4) *Broca's area*, which is a vital area for speech and language.
Illustration Courtesy of U.S. National Institute of Neurological and Communicative Disorders and Stroke.

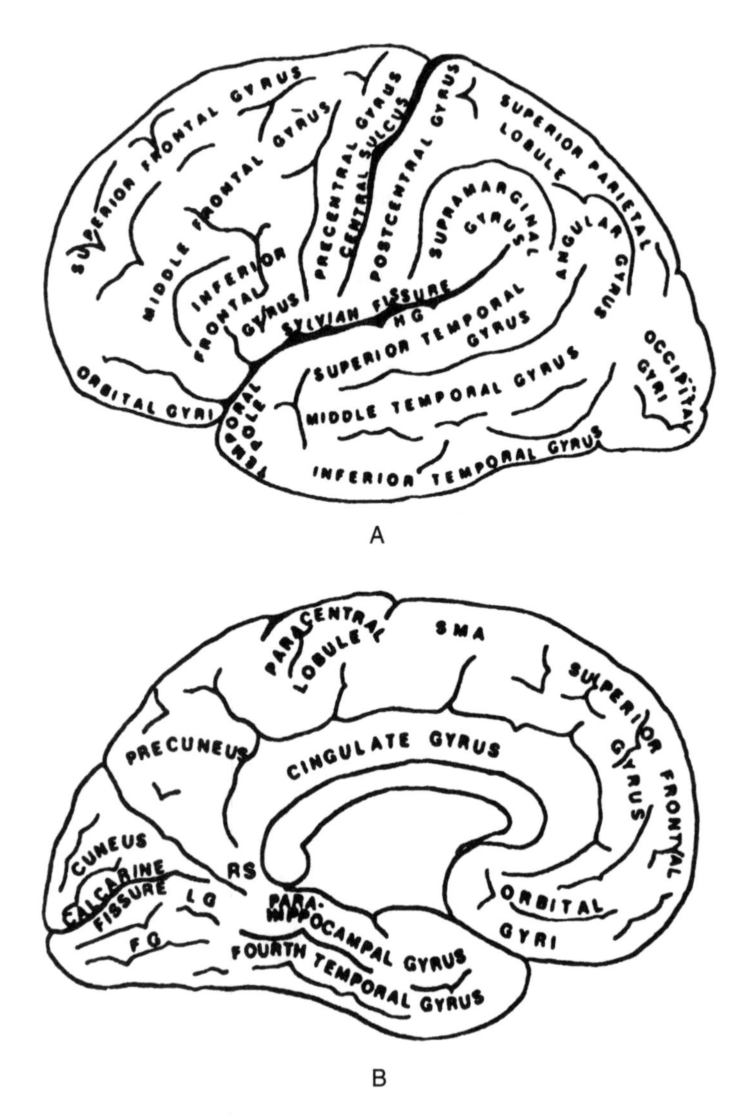

Here are external (A) and internal (B) views of the brain's left hemisphere, with the main ridges (or gyri) and fissures (or sulci) of its surface and outer layers. The central sulcus is also called the Rolandic fissure. The brain's frontal lobe lies in front of it, and the parietal lobe is behind it. The Sylvian fissure marks the boundary of the temporal lobe, which lies below and behind it. At the rear of the brain is the occipital lobe, which includes the occipital gyri. The initials "HG" in (A) note the location of Heschl's Gyri, which play a role in language.
Reprinted by permission of the *New England Journal of Medicine* (326; 533, 1992)

behind the Sylvian fissure and Broca's area. Neuroscientists have long believed that Wernicke's area plays an important role in our ability to comprehend speech. A region lying along the left angular ridge, just below Wernicke's area, is involved in the control of the hand movements of sign language.

- The front region of the parietal lobe along the Rolandic fissure is mainly involved with processing sensory inputs. Researchers believe this area has deep neuronal connections to the brain's speech and hearing regions. Also, the motor processing area lying in front of the Rolandic fissure plays an important role in language. It controls, among other things, the movements of our arms, hands, fingers (relevant to signing), lips, jaw, tongue, and pharynx (essential to vocal language).
- Finally, the *visual cortex*'s visual processing areas play a role in written, signed, and verbal language. The visual cortex is the rearmost part of the brain's occipital lobe, at the very back of the head. These regions process the written symbols that constitute writing, or the gestures used in sign language, then pass that information on to other language areas.

We receive the vast majority of our information about the world through our sense of sight.* So the visual processing area must, and does, contribute mightily to the vast influx of data that contributes to language. Without the visual cortex, we would not have much to talk, write, or sign about.

All of this activity happens in the brain, the seat of our intellect, emotions, perceptions, wishes, dreams, fantasies. The oatmeal-mushy fifteen-hundred-gram ball of tissue behind our eyes is the territory of the mind, the playing field of language.

* For blind people, touch and hearing take center stage.

CHAPTER 6

OUT OF DARKNESS, LIGHT

Some of the most important and provocative discoveries about the brain and how it works have come from tragedies and failures: strokes, accidents, gunshot wounds, mistakes in the surgical theater. The insights come because part of the brain is damaged, causing the person to lose some or all of the cognitive abilities he or she once had. When researchers are able to pinpoint the exact location in the brain of the damaged area, they may also find the location of the now-lost cognitive ability.

THE GERMAN, THE SCOT, AND THE FRENCHMAN

Some of our earliest understanding of how the brain works came from such "natural experiments." Four centuries before the birth of Christ, Hippocrates noticed that a sword wound to the side of a soldier's head caused paralysis on the opposite side of the man's body. More than twenty-two centuries years later, two German surgeons stumbled upon the same finding. Gustav T. Fritsch (1838–1927) in 1864 was treating the head wound of a soldier injured in a battle of the Franco-Prussian War. Fritsch noticed that touching the man's bare cerebral hemisphere caused twitching on the opposite side of the body. Fritsch shared his finding with Berlin physiologist Eduard Hitzig (1838–1907). Hitzig had long been interested in mental illness and insanity, and this in turn led to an interest in the brain. The two men decided to carry out additional experiments on dogs. In 1870 they provided the first scientific evidence for brain localization of specific bodily functions and activities. By electrically stimulating portions of the cerebral cortexes of living dogs, they caused the contraction of specific muscles. The two researchers also showed that damaging those brain areas caused paralysis or weakening of the associated muscles. This in turn made it possible for the two to construct a kind of map, superimposing a drawing of canine body parts on the brain.

The work by Hitzig and Fritsch inspired others to follow their footsteps into the brain. One such researcher was Sir David Ferrier (1843–1928), a Scottish neurologist born in Aberdeen. After he obtained his medical degree in 1868, Ferrier did not go into general practice. He was much more interested in doing research, and followed his desire. Inspired by Hitzig's findings, Ferrier began carrying out his own research on dogs. (One side effect of this was a lawsuit brought against him in 1882 by anti-vivisectionists, who today call themselves animal rights activists, for cruelty to animals. Ferrier successfully defended himself in court, arguing persuasively for the value and necessity of animal experimentation in science.) Ferrier reproduced Hitzig's findings about brain localization in dogs. Then he experimented on other animals, including apes. Ferrier showed that the brain had both motor regions and sensory regions. The former controlled the movements and responses of muscles and other organs, while the latter regions gathered sensory data from the sensory organs, muscles, and other parts of the body. Ferrier constructed highly valuable maps of the brain, showing the locations of these regions.

The discoveries by Hippocrates, and later by Fritsch, Hitzig, and Ferrier, mostly had to do with motor control by the brain. Others had uncovered similar information about the brain's processing of sensory data. For centuries, doctors and others had noticed puzzling cases of blindness among wounded soldiers whose eyes had not been injured.

Rather, they had suffered crushing skull wounds at the back of their heads. In the process, they had also suffered damage to that part of their brains. The physicians treating them realized that this rearmost region of the brain, today named the occipital lobe, was somehow responsible for sight.

Similar kinds of injuries led to the first discoveries of brain areas involved with language. Pierre-Paul Broca (1824–1880) had received his medical degree at the University of Paris in 1849. He then specialized in brain surgery. Broca was also an enthusiastic amateur anthropologist. In 1859, for example, he had founded the Société d'Anthropologie in Paris. This interest in anthropology was not surprising. During Broca's time much of anthropology had to do with measuring skull sizes, a discipline called *craniometry*. As Stephen Jay Gould has noted in his book *The Mismeasure of Man* (1981), craniometry was less a science and more a pseudo-scientific justification for the institutionalized racism of Western society. However, Broca was a man of his times. He was also Europe's premier expert in craniometry. He knew more about skull measurements than anyone else.

For all his fascination with measuring skulls, Broca was first and foremost a superb brain surgeon. It was this talent, and his fascination with a man with a tragic affliction, that led to his best-known discovery. Early in 1861 Broca carried out an autopsy on the brain of a man named Leborgne, whose nickname was "Tan-tan." He had received the appellation because those were the only sounds he could utter, even though he could understand what people said to him and communicate with gestures and facial expressions.

Tan-Tan's affliction was a form of disorder generally called *aphasia*, from the Greek word *phasia*, meaning "speech." Aphasia is the loss or impairment of the ability to use spoken and written words. While sectioning Tan-Tan's brain, Broca discovered a damaged area about the size of an egg in the left frontal lobe. In April of that year Broca displayed Tan-Tan's brain to a meeting of the Société d'Anthropologie. He pointed out the damaged area, arguing that the brain's speech mechanism was located there. Broca carried out several other autopsies on people who had suffered afflictions similar to Tan-tan's. He found the same kind of brain damage in the same region. This area has since been named *Broca's area*.

Though best known for discovering his eponymous brain area,

Pierre-Paul Broca also played a significant role in another important scientific discovery. This one helped redefine the field of his hobby, anthropology. In 1856 a skull had been found in a valley near Düsseldorf called the Neanderthal. Though clearly human, it was considerably more primitive-looking than modern human skulls. It was also quite old—the rock strata in which it had been found made that clear—but just how old? And was this the skull of a "regular" person with some cranial malformation, or the skull of a genuinely primitive form of human? The controversy raged through science and the popular press and only intensified in 1859 when Charles Darwin published *The Origin of Species*. Bolstered by his vast knowledge of the human skull, Broca threw his support on the side of Darwin and evolution. He argued persuasively for the "primitive man" theory of the Neanderthal skull, a position that eventually won out.

His Wife's Epilepsy

Still more breakthroughs came from the keen observation and creativity of a self-taught British neuroscientist named John Hughlings Jackson (1835–1911). Jackson was a physician at the London Hospital from 1859 to 1894, and from 1862 to 1906 at the National Hospital for the Paralyzed and Epileptic. He was one of the first neuroscientists to make a careful and thorough study of epileptic seizures. His studies of epilepsy, speech disorders, and other nervous system defects caused by injury to the spine and brain are still highly useful. In 1864 his investigation of various aphasias allowed him to confirm Broca's hypothesis about localization of language functions in the left cerebral hemisphere.

A year earlier, Jackson had made another significant discovery about the brain and epilepsy. *Epilepsy* is a general term for more than two dozen different disorders of brain function. Most forms of epilepsy may be classified as either *idiopathic* or *focal*. Idiopathic forms of epilepsy are those for which there is no known or evident cause. Focal epilepsies are those associated with certain kinds of brain damage. The most common idiopathic epilepsies are *grand mal* seizures and *petit mal* seizures. In a grand mal seizure the person loses consciousness and suffers muscle spasms and jerking of various parts of the body. A petit mal seizure is characterized by a brief attack of impaired consciousness, accompanied by the flickering of the eyelids and the twitching of the mouth. Focal epilepsies are usually caused by a scar or lesion in some part of the brain. This tiny region of brain damage in turn can be caused by trauma during birth, by cerebral *edema* (swelling caused by a buildup of fluid) in infancy or childhood, or by an accident, a tumor, or even an infection. Focal seizures are often characterized by hallucinations, by sensations of fear, elation, depression, and foul odors, and by impaired consciousness and muscle spasms.

The beginning of an epileptic seizure may be signaled by the perception of an *aura*: a peculiar feeling in the stomach, flashes of light, noises in the ear, or vertigo. The mechanisms that initiate a seizure are not yet understood. During the seizure, neurons in the brain fire simultaneously to a highly unusual degree.

Seizures can be controlled by drugs in many cases. In others, surgery is resorted to. Brain scans are taken to reveal which tissues are malfunctioning, and when those tissues are removed, the seizures stop. This radical method is used much more often on children than on adults, whose brains have diminished powers of recovery. However sometimes brain surgery is the only way to end epilepsy in some people. The unforeseen side effects of this kind of surgery have led to new breakthroughs in our understanding of how the brain stores language.

John Hughlings Jackson's interest in epilepsy had a personal foundation. In 1863 he identified the form of epilepsy now called *Jacksonian epilepsy*. The discovery was easy to make: Jackson's wife suffered from the disorder. Jacksonian epilepsy is marked by a peculiar seizure pattern. The seizures usually begin in the hand, move up through the arm to the face, and then pass down the side of the body to the leg. This puzzled Jackson for years. What kind of connection between the brain and body could cause it? In 1873 his years of work led him to define epilepsy as "a sudden, excessive, and rapid discharge" of brain cells. That definition has been confirmed by contemporary technological methods of recording electrical discharges in the brain.

Two years later, Jackson finally solved the puzzle of Jacksonian epilepsy with a combination of persistent study and a creative leap.

Like Fritsch, Hitzig & Ferrier, who were working at the same time, he imagined the brain to have a kind of *internal geography*. Perhaps, he theorized, the brain is organized into different regions. Each region controls some specific part of the body's motor activity. The seizure discharges causing his wife's epileptic seizures were caused by a lesion or damaged area in a particular part of the cerebral cortex. From there the discharge moved from region to region, triggering off motor malfunctions as it went. In other words, Jackson was suggesting, in the cerebral cortex there exists a region that could be called the *motor cortex*.

Wernicke, the Holists, and the Locationalists

At about the same time, a young German researcher discovered the relationship between a different kind of aphasia and the brain. Karl Wernicke (1848–1905) studied medicine at the University of Breslau and did graduate medical work in Breslau, Berlin, and Vienna. He then returned to Berlin to start his own practice. Wernicke worked with people suffering from various forms of aphasia. One in particular affected its victims' command of syntax. Their mechanical speaking ability was normal, but they could not speak *grammatically*, and they were unable to grasp the meanings of what other people said. When Wernicke autopsied the brains of such people, he found damage to the left temporal and parietal lobes.

In 1874, though he was only twenty-six and far from established, he felt his research had uncovered important new information about the brain. That year he published a small booklet summarizing his work. Wernicke attempted to show connections between the various aphasias he had studied and damage to different parts of the brain. The book included his description of the aphasia affecting syntax and of damage he had found to the temporal and parietal lobes. It was the first time this particular aphasia had been connected to specific brain damage. The region of the brain he pinpointed later came to be known as *Wernicke's area*. Wernicke went on to study the human brain in much more detail. He also published another book: *Lehrbuch der Gehirnkrankheiten* ("Textbook of Brain Disorders," 1881), an attempt to prove that all neurological diseases were caused by damage in different areas of the brain.

With the discoveries by Broca and Wernicke, scientists for the first time had a clue to the *distributed nature* of how the brain creates and stores language. There was, it appeared, no single location in the brain for language. Rather, different parts of the brain controlled different aspects of speech and language. Broca's area, for example, seemed to be the region that controlled speech production. Wernicke's area, on the other hand, dealt with language comprehension and grammar. It did appear, though, that Broca's and Wernicke's discoveries indicated the language centers were located in the brain's left hemisphere.

However, not everyone accepted this suggestion. The battle had long raged in the nineteenth century between the "holists" and the "locationalists." The former faction claimed that the two cerebral hemispheres were mirror images of each other, and that functions in one hemisphere were duplicated in the other. To the contrary, the latter faction insisted that certain brain functions were localized in one or the other hemisphere. The discoveries by Broca and Wernicke seemed to bolster the locationalists' position.

However, Broca's discovery came under attack. In 1906 the French neurologist Pierre Marie re-examined Tan-tan's brain, which Broca had preserved and which was still available to researchers. He claimed to find more damaged areas or lesions in Tan-tan's brain than Broca had reported. Marie asserted that this additional damage proved that Broca's area had no role whatsoever in the creation of language. In the early 1980s a new generation of researchers used a new generation of technology to examine Tan-tan's brain once again. Using the most advanced methods of medical imaging, the researchers found that Marie was at least partly correct: Tan-tan's brain did have many more lesions in it than Broca had found.

Marie was nevertheless wrong in his assertion that Broca's area is not involved in language. Numerous other brain studies have confirmed that it is. However, a steady accumulation of research throughout this century has revealed a picture considerably more complex than either Broca or Wernicke had envisioned.

Researchers became more sophisticated in their analysis of the consequences of damage to the brain from strokes and accidents. They also began to develop methods of probing the living brains of certain patients. These probes involved the electrical stimulation of the exposed brains of conscious patients during neurosurgery. One of the pioneers in this kind of brain research was the American-Canadian neurosurgeon Wilder Penfield (1891–1976).

The Man from Spokane

Born in Spokane, Washington, in 1891, Penfield graduated from Princeton in 1913 and became a Rhodes Scholar at Oxford in Great Britain. It was there that he became interested in the brain through his work under the great British neuroscientist Sir Charles Sherrington. After finishing at Oxford, Penfield returned to the United States and received his medical degree in 1918 from Johns Hopkins University in Baltimore. From there he spent a year interning in Boston, and then returned to Oxford to study neurosurgery. In 1921 he journeyed back across the Atlantic, then practiced neurosurgery in New York City for seven years. In 1928 he accepted an appointment as professor of neurology and neurosurgery at McGill University in Montreal, Canada. Eventually he became a naturalized Canadian citizen.

It was at McGill and in the neurosurgical wards in Montreal, beginning in the late 1920s and continuing through the 1950s, that Penfield carried out his pioneering work on mapping the human brain. His discoveries were a direct outgrowth of his interest in curing people suffering from focal epilepsies. As we saw earlier, focal epilepsies are caused by tiny scars in certain parts of the brain. People suffering from focal epileptic seizures often experience hallucinations, are overcome by feelings of elation, depression, or fear, perceive foul odors, and have muscle spasms. Penfield had devised innovative surgical techniques for removing from the brain lesions and other scar tissue causing epileptic seizures. An important part of his technique involved electrical stimulation of the exposed cerebral cortex using microelectrodes. This technique allowed Penfield to reduce the damage to the brain from the surgery itself. He soon discovered something fascinating: touching parts of the exposed cerebral cortex in his conscious patients with the microelectrodes had remarkable, even eerie, side effects. Penfield decided to follow up on this serendipitous discovery.

It is important to know at this point that though some of the brain's blood vessels have pain sensors, the nerves in the brain itself do not. If someone pokes your big toe with an electrically charged needle, you will feel pain and an electrical shock. If a neurosurgeon does essentially the same thing to your exposed brain, you will feel no pain sensation at all.

No one is sure why this is the case. Other nerves in the body do have pain sensors, at least in the sheaths that surround them. The pain you feel when you pinch a nerve in your arm or leg is caused by those sensors firing off pain signals to the brain. One answer, though without any hard scientific evidence and thus not entirely satisfying, is that the brain just cannot be bothered with feeling pain. It must concentrate on receiving, organizing, interpreting, and responding to all the sensory inputs from the rest of the body, including pain signals. If the brain also had to deal with pain messages from within itself, it might be too much to cope with. In any case, the human brain has evolved without internal pain sensors connected to its neurons.

Because the brain can feel no pain, it is possible to carry out brain surgery on patients who are conscious. The surgeon uses a local anesthetic during the initial portions of surgery, when the top of the skull is removed. The local anesthetic stops any pain signals that would come from the brain's blood vessels. However, a person can remain completely conscious and aware while his or her brain is operated upon.

Penfield would first obtain permission from the patient. Then, either before or after the actual neurosurgery, he would stimulate the person's temporal lobes with tiny electrical impulses delivered through a needle. The patient would suddenly undergo powerful recollections of past experiences: a melody from childhood; a smell; a visual memory. Whenever Penfield stimulated the same location in the temporal lobe, the patient would experience the same recollection. Stimulation of other areas of the brain caused different parts of the patient's body to twitch or otherwise move.

Penfield experimentally confirmed the suggestions first proposed by Jackson, Wernicke, Broca, Hitzig, and others decades earlier. His operating room experiments led to the construction of a map similar to the ones first devised by Fritsch, Hitzig, and Ferrier. Penfield's map of the human motor cortex is called the *motor homunculus*. *Homunculus* literally means "little man." The motor homunculus is a map of the brain's motor cortex. It pinpoints the location of areas controlling different parts of the body. It also shows the relative sensitivity and complexity of our body parts. For example, a larger part of the motor cortex is devoted to the control of the hands and fingers than to the control of the hips or neck. The homunculus in the cartoon map therefore has exaggerated hands and fingers, while the neck and hips are tiny.

Imaging the Brain

Like other realms of human behavior, scientific techniques can be subject to the whims of fashion and popularity. During the middle part of this century, the lesion approach for probing the brain fell from favor among neuroscientists, in large part because that method had become associated with "traditional" accounts of brain function. Also, other approaches, including Penfield's, had provided researchers with dramatic results. In the last several years, though, the lesion approach has made a comeback. In part, the return to this method has been inspired by newer theories of brain function made possible by other techniques.

Another major reason for the revival of the lesion method has been the new technology of computerized imaging, which makes it possible to actually peer into the living brain of a human being without opening up the skull. Doctors and researchers can now see the extent of brain lesions while the patients are still alive. They do not have to wait, as Paul Broca did, for their patients to die, so they can treat a dead human brain with chemicals and slice it up. Broca and Wernicke would no doubt have turned green with envy if they could have espied the future of neurological research.

These new imaging technologies are possible because of the development of powerful computers. They combine computer technology with X rays and radiomedicine, medical techniques using trace amounts of radioactive materials. Researchers can now go boldly into regions of the human body—the *living* human body—where no one had gone before. And they can do it without ever lifting a scalpel. The major high-tech brain-imaging techniques in use today are the *CT scanner, PET,* and *MRI*.

In 1973 American physicist Allan Cormack and English physicist Godfrey Hounsfield introduced a radically new way to make X-ray images: the *computerized axial tomography* scan imager. The word *tomography* comes from the Greek word *tomos*, meaning "section" or "slice." Originally known as the CAT scanner, today the device is called

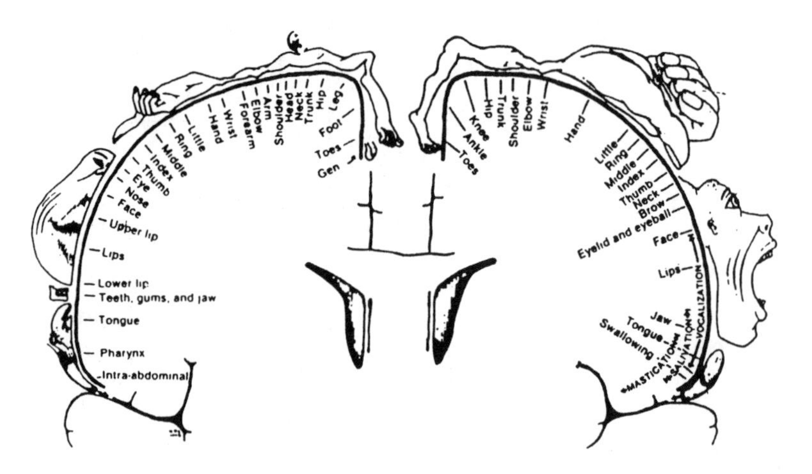

Research by Wilder Penfield led to the depiction of the "motor homunculus." This is a map of the motor cortex region, which runs from left to right across the top of the brain. It identifies the tiny areas in the motor cortex controlling the movement of different parts of the body with cartoon images of those parts and limbs. The size of the drawing indicates the amount of area in the brain dedicated to controlling it. Note how much brain area in the motor cortex is devoted to controlling the face, teeth, jaws, mouth, lips, tongue and other body parts associated with speaking. The hands also command a great deal of attention.
Reprinted with permission of Macmillan Publishing Company from *The Cerebral Cortex of Man* by Wilder Penfield and Theodore Rasmussen.

the CT scanner. Unlike an ordinary X-ray machine, it produces a three-dimensional image. It also allows doctors to distinguish between two internal structures with the same density, which is very difficult to do with regular X rays.

The CT scanner works by combining a sophisticated X-ray machine with the number-crunching power of a computer. For a brain scan, the patient lies on a narrow table called a gantry, with his or her head inside a structure that looks like a doughnut. The patient's head is kept completely still during the procedure, either by giving the patient a mild sedative or by immobilizing the head with straps or pillows. Inside the doughnut is the CT's rotating X-ray tube, moving along a circular path. As the scanner in the doughnut rotates, the tube sends a beam of X-rays through the patient's head to a set of sensitive detectors that also rotate in the doughnut, opposite the X-ray tube.

As the X rays pass through the patient's head, they also pass through brain tissue with different densities. Gray matter has a density differ-

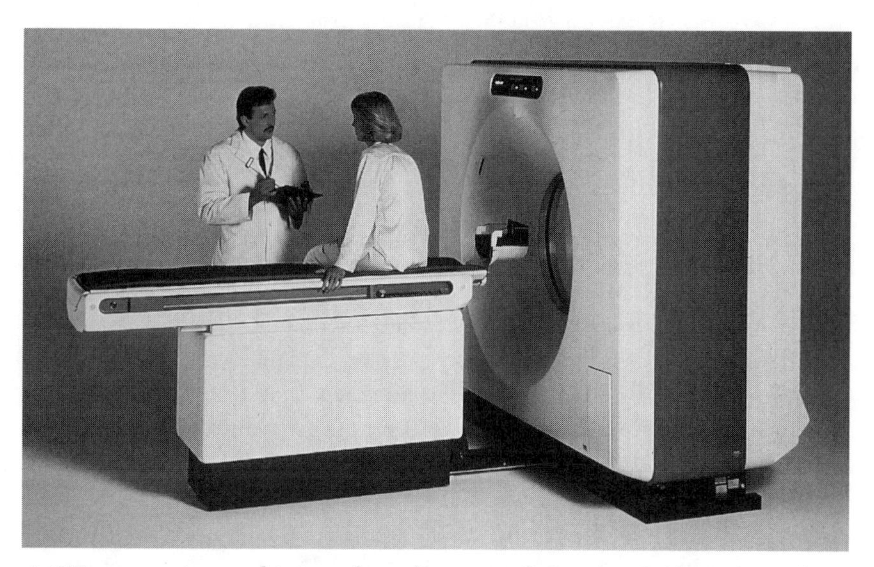

A CT scanner is a sophisticated combination of computer and X-ray machine that creates detailed three-dimensional X-ray "slices" of a body.
Illustration courtesy of GE Medical Systems.

ent from that of white matter, and damaged or diseased brain tissue has a density different from healthy tissue. Tissues with different densities absorb different amounts of X rays, and the detectors spot those changes. The detectors in turn convert the X rays into electronic signals and send them to the computer. Using an elaborate and powerful program, the computer notes the intensities of the electronic signals and records their precise location as the scanner was rotating. Then the computer software takes the intensity data and the location data and creates an image of the "slice" of brain the X rays pass through.

The CT scanner can scan a whole set of "slices" through the brain, simply by changing the angle at which the X rays enter the person's head. The computer can take the layers of X-ray images and turn them into a three-dimensional image of the brain inside the person's head. Moreover, using sophisticated mathematical formulas, the computer can rotate the three-dimensional image into almost any position. Doctors and researchers can therefore look at the living brain from angles that are normally impossible. For example, they can look from the inside of the brainstem upward.

In 1979 Cormack and Hounsfield won the Nobel Prize in Medicine for their development of the CT scanner. And for good reason. It is obviously a powerful improvement over two-dimensional X rays. However, the CT scan has its own drawback. Though it gives the researcher an astonishingly detailed look at brain structure, it provides little information about cerebral *function*. The CT scan is not a dynamic image, only a static one. This disadvantage is overcome by other new imaging techniques.

All the matter we see—the stuff that makes trees, cars, birds, water, air, stars, tigers, and people—is made of atoms. Atoms in turn are composed of subatomic particles called electrons, protons, and neutrons. All of these subatomic particles are "normal" matter. Positrons are a form of *antimatter*: subatomic particles that are mostly identical to "normal" subatomic particles but with an opposite electrical charge and spin. Antimatter, including positrons, is more than just fanciful "rubber science" on *Star Trek* or the fictional musings of the late Isaac Asimov for his robotic positronic brains. It actually exists in the universe, albeit in very tiny quantities. It is real. Positrons in particular are "antielectrons." They have the same structure and the same mass as electrons, but electrons have a negative electrical charge, while positrons have a positive charge.

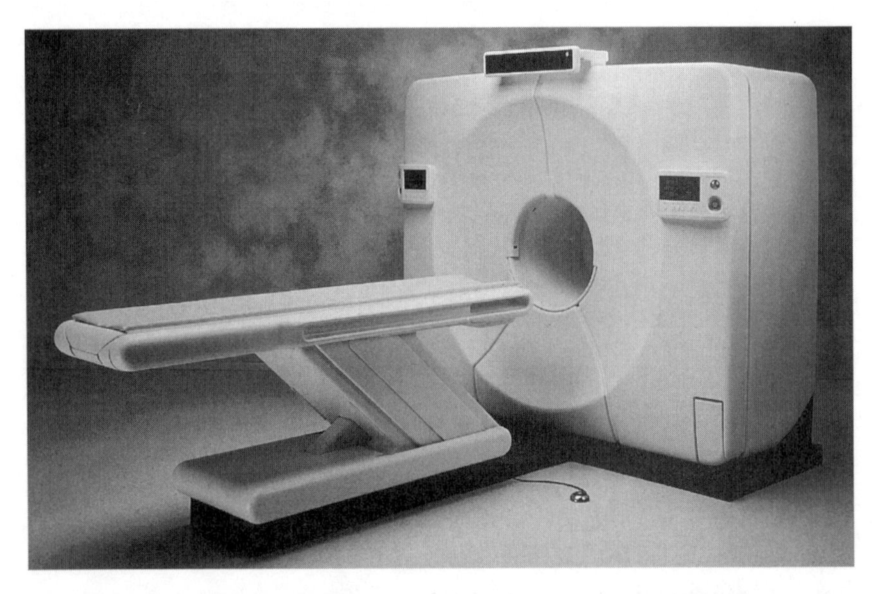

A PET scanner uses a special form of antimatter to create moving images of the inside of the brain and other parts of the body.
Illustration courtesy of GE Medical Systems.

The Positron Emission Tomography (PET) scanner is an example of a machine that would have been pure science fiction less than a century ago. It uses this form of antimatter to create an image of the brain as a living organ. It does this by measuring changes in the metabolism of the brain as it works.

First the patient receives an injection of a glucose-like compound. Glucose, a form of sugar, serves as food for the brain; however, this is a form of glucose the brain *cannot* metabolize. The compound is "tagged" with a radioactive isotope. A radioisotope is an element that is temporarily radioactive. The isotope emits positrons as it decays back into a nonradioactive form. Two common isotopes used for PET scans are oxygen-11 (which physicists abbreviate as O^{11}) and nitrogen-13 (N^{13}).

The brain's blood vessels carry the special glucose compound to whatever parts of the brain are currently active. The more active they are, the more blood and food they require and get. However, the radio-tagged compound cannot be used by the brain. So it begins to build up in those brain regions that are most active.

Meanwhile, the compound emits positrons from its radioactive isotopes. As those positrons hit the normal matter around them, they annihilate in a burst of pure energy in the form of gamma rays. The sophisticated detectors embedded in a doughnut-shaped structure, something like that of the CT scanner, catch and record the gamma rays being emitted from the active brain regions. They send that information to the PET's powerful computer. The computer in turn manipulates the data and creates a moving, changing, color-coded image of the brain's most active areas.

The lag-time between scan and final image is about an hour. But the PET imager can do something truly astonishing: it can create moving images. You can actually watch a PET-scan motion picture of your brain at work. The disadvantage to the PET scan is that the image is rather coarse; it is not as detailed as that of the CT scan.

MRI, or magnetic resonance imaging, used to be known as nuclear magnetic resonance imaging, or NMR. The name was changed because so many people are frightened by the word *nuclear*. They equate it with "radioactivity" and thus with danger. MRI (or NMR) does not use radioactive materials. Rather, it uses a very powerful magnet, radio-frequency signals, and a sophisticated computer to create images. Radio waves are a form of electromagnetic radiation like visible light, but they are not radioactive; that is, they are not forms of *ionizing radiation*, which can damage living tissue. In an MRI scan, the radio waves and magnets are used to shake a person's nuclear particles around a bit. Chemists and physicists had used MRI technology for many years to analyze samples of solids and liquids. It was adapted and improved for medical imaging and diagnostics in the early 1980s. MRI has proved to be a powerful new weapon against disease and a valuable tool for brain researchers.

For an MRI scan, a patient is placed inside still another doughnut-shaped machine. This one is not a fancy X-ray machine but an extremely powerful magnet. Its magnetic field can be up to thirty thousand times as powerful as that of the Earth. It is so powerful, in fact, that people cannot wear or have any metal objects on them and stand near the machine when it is in operation. The powerful magnetic field will rip them right off. (If you have a metal plate in your head,

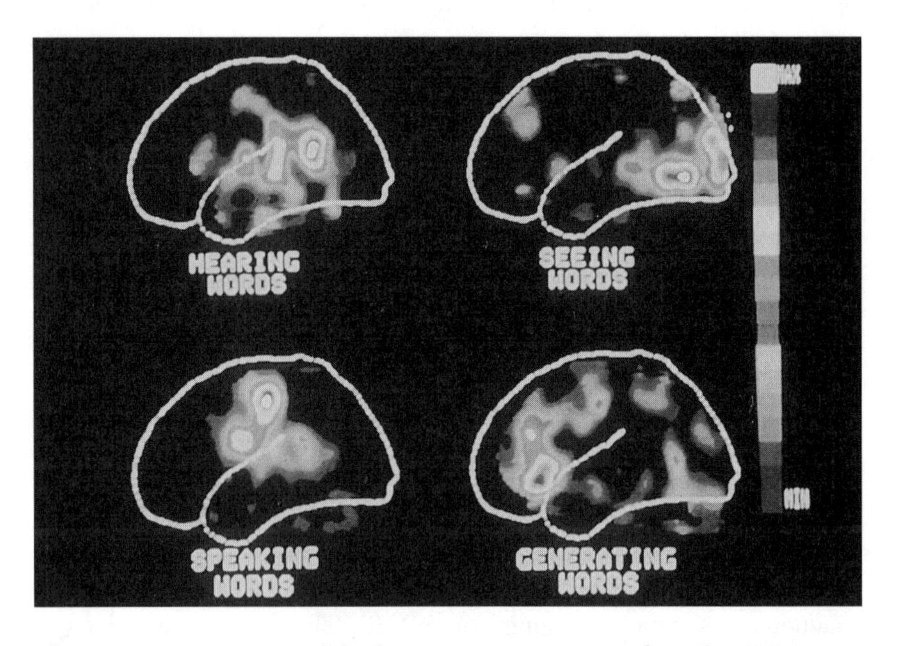

These computer images of the brain in action were made with a PET scanner. They show which parts of the brain are most active when a person is hearing words (top left), seeing words (top right), speaking words (bottom left), and mentally generating words (bottom right).
Illustrations courtesy of the U.S. National Institutes of Mental Health.

you are obviously not a candidate for MRI.) When the MRI machine is turned on, its intense magnetic field affects the nuclei of certain atoms in the body.

Atoms are basically made of two parts: a nucleus of protons and neutrons, and a "shell" of electrons. The nuclei within the atoms that make up the body's tissues are a bit like tiny magnets. They each have a "north" and "south pole" and "spin" on their axes. Under normal circumstances, the nuclei's poles point in many different angles, and they spin in many different directions. This is particularly true of the single protons that are the nuclei of hydrogen atoms, which in turn are a component of ordinary water.

When the MRI's powerful magnetic field turns on, it causes the poles of the nuclei in the affected area to align themselves in the same direction as the magnetic field. They act like tiny iron filings exposed to a simple bar magnet. Their north and south poles all point in the same direction, even though their spinning is still random in direction. The magnetic field also causes the atomic nuclei to vibrate at a specific frequency. This causes them to behave like tiny radios; under the right circumstances, they can both receive and transmit radio signals. Next, the MRI machine passes a powerful burst of radio-frequency signals through the patient's target area. This causes the nuclei to "flip" about and lose their alignment in the magnetic field. When the radio beam is turned off, the atomic nuclei "flip" back to their original position. As they do so, they emit radio waves of their own.

The MRI machine detects the emitted radio waves and converts them into electrical signals that are sent to the MRI's computer. The nuclei of different atoms in different body tissues emit radio waves that differ in duration and strength. They have different signal "signatures." As with the CT scanner, the MRI's computer reads and records these signals and their location, then turns them into an image of the inside of the body or brain.

MRI images of the brain can be astonishingly clear and detailed. They are often more precise than CT images. Like the CT scan images, they are static, not dynamic. But they give neuroscientists a clear look at parts of the brain the CT scanner and PET scanner see only dimly.

Each of these three imaging technologies—CT scanner, PET scanner, and MRI—has advantages and disadvantages. Together, however,

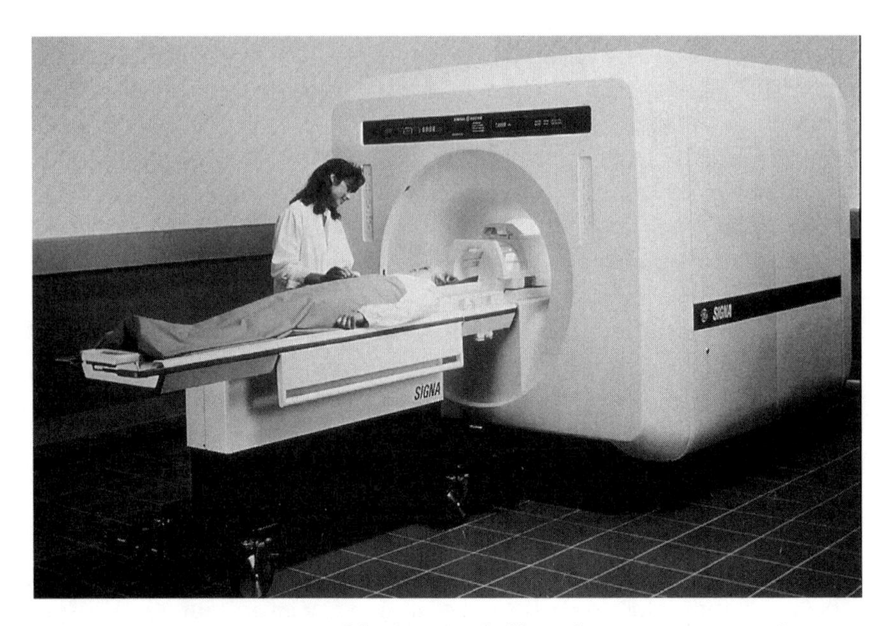

An MRI scanner uses powerful magnetic fields and a computer to make non-invasive images of the inside of the human body. MRI scanners are particularly good for imaging the living human brain.
Illustration courtesy of GE Medical Systems.

they give brain researchers wonderful new ways to peer into the brain. And they are revolutionizing our understanding of the brain and its role in language.

Our understanding of the interconnections between language and the brain has, for the most part, not come from experiments like those of Penfield. It has come rather from the kinds of observations first made by Fritsch, Hitzig, Broca, Wernicke, and Ferrier. Dr. Antonio Damasio calls this "the lesion method" of probing the brain. Damasio and his wife Hanna are on the faculty of the Department of Neurology at the University of Iowa College of Medicine in Iowa City. In the heart of middle America, the Damasios are forging a powerful and perhaps controversial new vision of the neural basis of memory, human behavior, and language. They are using as their tools both the latest tools of technology and the time-tested techniques of Broca and Wernicke.

If the Damasios are correct, their new paradigm for the brain and language is a curiously mixed vindication of Paul Broca's belief that specific regions of the brain control or modulate specific functions. Brain-based functions such as language are indeed localized, but the picture is more eerie than anyone previously imagined.

As young Ryan Patrick Nash begins creating and learning language, he is doing more than exercising that clump of brain tissue near his left ear called Broca's area. Much more.

CHAPTER 7

"BOSWELL," APHASIAS, AND MIND BLINDNESS

In 1976 Drs. Antonio and Hanna Damasio began studying a man they identify only as "Boswell" (not his real name). Boswell had suffered a disease called herpes simplex encephalitis, an inflammation of the brain caused by the herpes simplex virus. Many of us have frequently experienced the most common herpes simplex infection, cold sores on our lips or inside our mouths. The same virus also causes genital herpes. On rare occasions, though, the herpes virus can cause an inflammation of the brain. In Boswell's case the consequences were devastating. He suffered the near-total destruction of several important areas in his brain, including the hippocampus and the amygdala. As we saw in Chapter 5, both of these tiny structures deep in the brain are vitally important to memory. Boswell also suffered considerable damage to several areas of his temporal cortexes.

The Damasios and others have used detailed maps of these brain regions first developed in 1909 by the great German neuroanatomist Korbinian Brodmann. These special maps divide the brain into about four dozen different numbered regions or areas, each distinguished by the structure of its nerve cells and nerve fibers. Neuroscientists often use them as identifiers or "roadmarks" (as in, "It's easy to find my house; just turn left at the crooked pine tree, which is about a mile past the ruins of the old fort."). For example, Broca's area includes Brodmann areas 44 and 45. The damaged regions in Boswell's brain include Brodmann areas 20, 21, and 38, the frontal part of area 22, and portions of areas 35, 36, and 37.

The One-minute Man

Boswell has become a living experiment in brain function. The terrible brain damage he has suffered, while truly tragic, has given the Damasios and their colleagues a unique window into the brain. They can observe what different parts of the brain do by discovering what Boswell can no longer do and what he can still do.

The Damasios have uncovered some fascinating details about how the damage to Boswell's brain has affected his cognitive abilities. Boswell's sense perceptions remain nearly flawless. The only exception is his sense of smell, for the olfactory cortex is included in the areas of his brain destroyed by the infection. It is clear from his descriptions of what he sees, touches, and hears—and, to a lesser degree, tastes; olfaction influences our taste perception—that the sensory *content* of his perceptions does not differ in any way from Damasio's own sensory perceptions. Nor has Boswell suffered any diminishment in their *quality*. He reports no changes in his experience of texture, color, motion, sound, pitch, or other sense perceptions. He experiences the entire multileveled range of any specific perception, including the sensory and motor components. As Antonio Damasio has written, "In strictly perceptual terms, [Boswell] can bind features into an entity and entities into an event." An "entity," as Damasio defines it, is a person, object, or place.

That is the good news for Boswell. The rest is not such good news for him but a fascinating example of a "natural experiment" for Damasio and others. For one thing, Boswell is unable to retain knowledge of any new entity or event. Suppose you had never met Boswell before, and you walked into his room and introduced yourself to him. After less than a minute Boswell would not know who you are. His

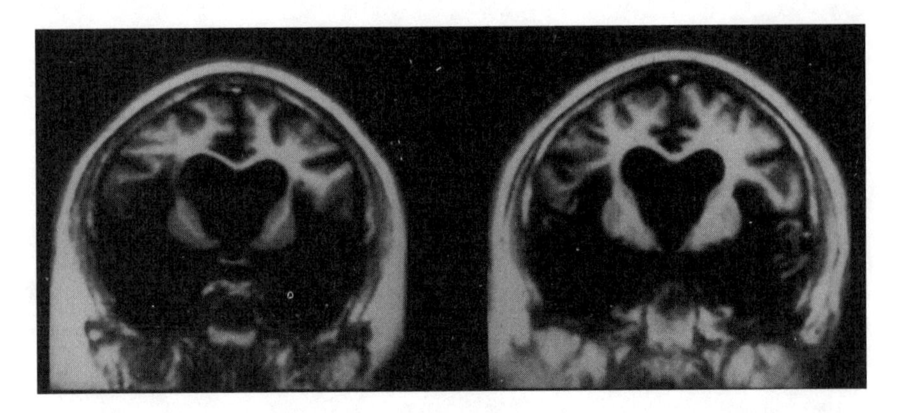

This MRI scan of the brain of "Boswell," a patient of Hanna and Antonio Damasio, shows how much damage (the black areas) his brain suffered, leading to bizarre effects on his memory and language ability.
Reprinted by permission of the *Seminars in the Neurosciences* (2; 279, 1990) and Harcourt, Brace & Co., Ltd.

experience of you would be that you are a total stranger. If you had known him for decades and had been visiting him every day since 1976, he would still not know who you are. Because of the damage to his brain, Boswell cannot access any new information about people, objects, or experiences for longer than forty seconds. His memory stretches back that far and no further. Boswell is "the one-minute man." He has lost all knowledge of every movie he might have seen since his illness. Many of us would like to forget some of the turkeys we've inflicted upon ourselves at an outrageous ticket price. Boswell has no choice. He cannot even experience *watching* a movie. After less than a minute, what he has seen is gone from his experience.

Boswell also cannot retrieve many of the memories acquired before his illness in 1976. For example, he cannot recognize or remember any unique event or entity. Most of us who have experienced the death of an important person in our lives can recall the moment we got the news. I can remember, with still-painful clarity, when and where I was and what I was doing when I learned of my former wife's sudden death from a cerebral hemorrhage. I can recall how I felt; I can still feel those feelings in my body and in my mind. I can recall the events of the days that followed, as I flew back to the city where she had lived to meet with her family and help settle her affairs. Most of us can recall and reconstruct in proper sequential fashion the events that comprise the "uniqueness" of such a unique experience. Boswell cannot. The same is true of specific, unique persons or objects. If he were to walk to a parking lot and look at his own car, Boswell would recognize it as a car, but not as *his car*, a specific and unique car. If shown a picture of an old friend's face, he can identify it as a face, but he cannot recognize it as a unique face, the face of his friend.

Lawnmowers and Eagles

Boswell has also lost much of his ability to recall entities and events at what Hanna and Antonio Damasio describe as "non-unique categorical levels." To understand this loss he has experienced, consider the concept of *taxonomic levels*. As we noted briefly in Chapter 1, taxonomy is the science that studies the theory, practice, and rules for classifying living and extinct organisms. Taxonomists place organisms in different categories by shape or anatomy, or by similarities in DNA structure, or by some mathematical procedure. In the case of living and extinct organisms, the smallest taxonomic unit is the species. The levels continue "upward" as species are grouped into genera, genera into families, and on through orders, classes, phyla (or divisions, for plants), and kingdoms. In somewhat the same fashion, we can group entities, events, and concepts into different "mental" taxonomic levels.

Suppose Antonio Damasio were to show me a picture of a lawnmower. I could easily tell him that it was a lawnmower. I could also tell him that it was a tool. "Tool" is the "broad category" level of taxonomic ranking; the genus category, to borrow from taxonomy. "Lawnmower" is what Antonio Damasio has called the "basic object" level, the "species" if you will. Boswell has lost much, though not all, of his ability to identify entities at the "species" level. Shown the appropriate pictures, he can identify a specific house as a "ranch-style house" and a specific tool as a "lawnmower." He recognizes the "species" as well as the "genus." Boswell can identify the "species" as well as "genus" of most human-made objects, and he can recall them when given their names. He has no problem identifying pieces of furniture, practically every kind of garden tool, or kitchen utensils. However, he has extreme difficulty in identifying musical instruments, even though they are plainly as human-made as any garden trowel.

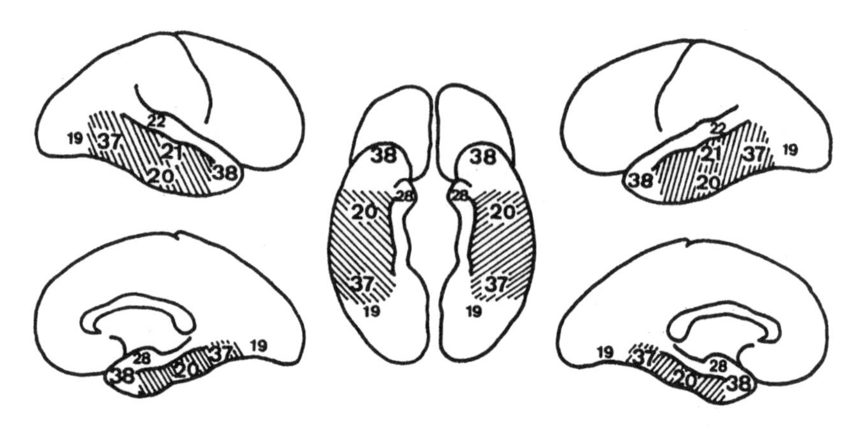

When the shaded areas in the brain are damaged by stroke or injury, a person can lose the ability to remember specific objects or persons. These kinds of impairments are caused by damage to either temporal lobe, or to both. The middle panel is a view of the brain from below; the front of the brain is at the top, and the left hemisphere is on the right. The two left panels show outer and inner views of the right hemisphere, while the two right panels show outer and inner views of the left hemisphere. The numbers refer to specific Brodmann areas in the brain, and are part of a map of the cerebral cortex first developed in 1909.
Reprinted by permission of the *Seminars in the Neurosciences* (2; 280, 1990) and Harcourt, Brace & Co., Ltd.

Shown a picture of a bald eagle, though, Boswell can only identify it as "a bird." "Eagle" is out, not to mention "bald eagle." The same lack of recognition applies to numerous entities from the natural world. He has no trouble perceiving them with his senses: remember, his sensory perception ability functions almost perfectly. Yet he cannot recognize most fruits and animals. He cannot identify at the "basic object" level fruits and vegetables with rounded shapes (apples, oranges, and plums are all "fruits"), members of the cat family (house cats and tigers are simply "animals"), or horse-like animals (forget about zebras and donkeys). Given a picture of a raccoon, Boswell will say, "It's an animal." He does not recall its behavior, its size, or where it lives. He does know that these entities are alive, a still broader taxonomic level than "animal" or "fruit." On the other hand, Boswell has no trouble identifying entities like elephant, giraffe, and banana. And even though they are just as "natural" and "living" as any eagle, he quickly and easily identifies human body parts.

Boswell can also retrieve the concepts having to do with the attri-

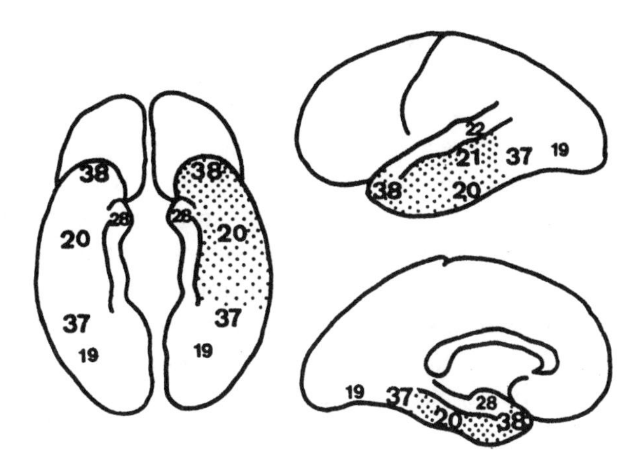

When the front part of the brain's left temporal lobe is damaged by stroke or injury, the person suffers losses in the ability to recall specific words. The middle panel is a view of the brain from below; the front of the brain is at the top, and the left temporal lobe is on the right. The two right panels show outer and inner views of the left hemisphere and temporal lobe. The numbers refer to specific Brodmann areas in the brain, and are part of a map of the cerebral cortex first developed in 1909.
Reprinted by permission of the *Seminars in the Neurosciences* (2; 281, 1990) and Harcourt, Brace & Co., Ltd.

butes of entities. He knows what "beautiful" is. He understands "above," "below," "during," "after," and "before." He grasps "jumping," "running," "swimming," "flying." He understands relationship concepts; he knows what "in love" means.

As the Damasios and their colleagues examined the kinds of impairments Boswell suffers, they discovered a pattern. Boswell has serious problems with many different kinds of entities—and they are all denoted by *proper and common nouns*. He has no impairment of concepts denoted by adjectives, conjunctions, prepositions, or verbs. These words deal with concepts having to do with attributes, states of being, and relationships. His syntax is perfect; Boswell has suffered no loss of access to the basic rules that govern language formation.

Antonio and Hanna Damasio believe that the losses of Boswell's cognitive abilities caused by his specific pattern of brain damage reveal some important clues to how we think and how the brain stores language. For example, the destruction of areas in the middle and frontal regions of Boswell's left and right temporal lobes impairs his brain's *conceptual* system. Boswell clearly has problems forming concepts and linking them to specific events and entities. Also, Boswell's disease damaged his brain's ability to form words and sentences. The Damasios have traced the cause of this loss to scars on Boswell's left perisylvian cortex. This area of the brain's left hemisphere encompasses regions known to be associated with language, such as Broca's and Wernicke's areas, but it is also broader than just those two regions. As we will soon discover, the Damasios are convinced that Boswell's peculiar problem with proper and common nouns is linked to damage in both these regions of his brain. Not only Broca's and Wernicke's areas play a role in language; the connection between those areas and the brain's frontal lobes is also essential.

Losing the Word Connection

Boswell's condition is a form of *aphasia*, which is the medical term for a difficulty in comprehending words that is caused by brain damage. The word itself, like so many scientific and medical terms, is based on Greek. *Phasis* means "speaking," and the prefix *a-* means "not." Broca and Wernicke in the mid-nineteenth century had discovered the approximate location of language areas in the brain's left hemisphere through their studies of people afflicted with various forms of aphasia.

They also discovered the phenomenon of *cerebral dominance*, which simply means that in the vast majority of cases one hemisphere of the brain is the predominant location for the language centers. For 99 percent of right-handed people and well over 60 percent of left-handers, the dominant hemisphere is the left. The vast majority of southpaws who do not have a dominant left hemisphere have their language centers equally distributed in both hemispheres. Only a very small percentage of people, either left- or right-handed, have dominant right brain hemispheres for language. In nearly all cases, these people suffered some kind of brain damage in infancy. Because the brain is still growing and developing in infants and young children, it is extremely plastic. It quickly adapts to such situations, and other structures in the undamaged hemisphere take over.

Nearly any injury or illness that affects the cerebral hemispheres can cause aphasia. The leading causes are head injury, stroke, brain

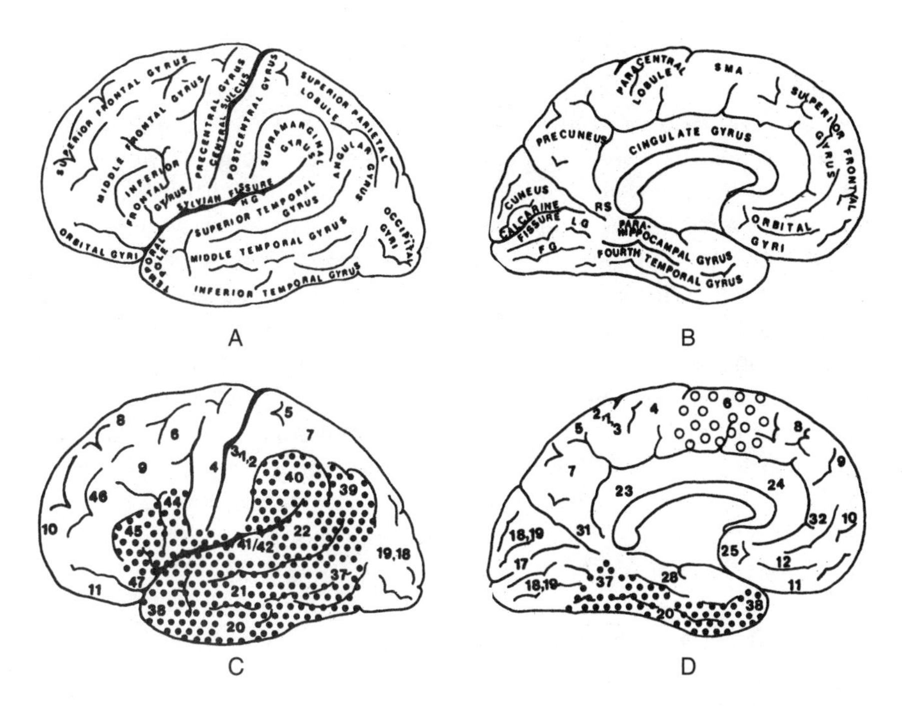

(A) and (B) in this four-part illustration show external and internal views of the brain's left hemisphere, with the main ridges (or gyri) and fissures (or sulci) of its surface and outer layers labeled. (C) and (D) are different drawings of the same areas. The numbers indicate specific Brodmann areas, using a brain map developed in 1909 by Korbinian Brodmann. The dark dots indicate brain areas in which damage from strokes or accidents leads to aphasia. The light dots indicate brain areas that when damaged cause a severe form of aphasia called mutism.
Reprinted by permission of the *New England Journal of Medicine* (326; 533, 1992)

tumors, and degenerative brain diseases like Alzheimer's disease. Head injuries alone cause more than two hundred thousand new cases of aphasia each year in the United States. Strokes cause another hundred thousand.

People with aphasia are no longer able to connect the grammar and symbols of language with the nonverbal knowledge, concepts, and representations that constitute thought. Damasio notes, "Nonverbal knowledge is knowledge in the true sense. It pertains to concepts and conceptual structure. You see," he points out, "you don't need language to *know* something. You don't need language, for example, to *know* what a dog is. A dog doesn't possess language—and a dog certainly knows what a dog is!" So people with aphasia, according to Damasio, have lost the ability to "translate," as it were, nonverbal thoughts and concepts into words and sentences. This is what has happened to Boswell. Shown a picture of a rake, for example, he cannot "translate" the nonverbal concept of "rake" into the word *rake*.

The converse is also true. Aphasiacs cannot translate a word or sentence into the appropriate concept or mental representation. For example, a researcher shows you and an aphasic patient the word *banana* written on a piece of paper and asks you to "describe it." You would probably say something like, "It's a fruit that is long and yellow and slightly curved. You peel off the skin, and the fruit inside is white and firm. They come from South and Central America, I think." But the aphasiac can offer nothing in the way of a description, being unable to connect the word *banana* to the nonverbal, mental concept of a "banana." It is as if the bridge that connects the two cities of language and thought has been dynamited into oblivion.

Obviously, aphasia is a devastating blow to the person who has suffered it. It not only wrecks the person's ability to communicate, it also can impair activities and abilities that rely on "internal speech." Internal speech is the internal monologue that frequently goes on inside our heads. Try mentally adding the numbers 27 and 41. If you are like most people, what you did was *mentally say*, "Hmmm; 7 plus 1 is 8, and—let's see—4 and 2 are 6; 68." You were speaking to yourself inside your mind. The ability to carry out arithmetical calculations, creativity, and decision-making can all be severely disrupted by aphasia. Needless to say, aphasia also has profound effects on a person's emotional and psychological state of being. And more than three hundred thousand new people are added to the tragic rolls, every year.

Doctors and researchers have identified several major types of aphasia. One is called *Broca's aphasia*, also known as *expressive*, *motor*, *nonfluent*, or *telegrammatic* aphasia. Broca's aphasia comes in two varieties. One, called *Broca's area aphasia*, occurs with brain damage only in Broca's area itself or in nearby white matter. This form of Broca's aphasia is mild and does not last long. A person may have a mild stroke, for example, and lose the ability to speak for a few days or weeks. But speech does return, and the person eventually regains all of his or her language ability. This mild disturbance of the person's speech is technically called *aphemia*; it is not permanent damage to the person's language ability.

The other variety of Broca's aphasia is called *true Broca's aphasia*. Patients with true Broca's aphasia suffer damage to an area of the brain that includes, but is much larger than, Broca's area. They have little problem understanding speech. If you speak to them about relatives or friends, or what you did on your vacation, or the President's response to some world crisis, they will understand what you are saying. They also usually select the correct words to use in speech, especially nouns. However, they have extreme difficulty in retrieving pronouns, verbs, prepositions, and conjunctions. Their speech is labored and slow; it is filled with numerous pauses and hesitations. It has a flat tone, unlike the modulation and melodic rhythm of normal speech. If normal speech is the Rocky Mountains, the speech of people with true Broca's aphasia is the Great Plains. It is also very difficult for these patients to repeat a sentence verbatim. If I have true Broca's aphasia and you say to me, "The apple tree has pretty blossoms," I will understand exactly what you said. But I will not be able to repeat that sentence. I may say something like, "Blossoms ... abble ... uh ... buh ... abble ... tree" I can get the nouns, but the rest of the sentence is a lost cause.

Another, even more basic, linguistic problem suffered by people with true Broca's aphasia is a significant loss in their ability to produce phonemes, or basic speech sounds, correctly. For example, they often pronounce a /p/ as a /b/, saying "abble" instead of *apple*. Patients also have difficulty telling the difference between these and other similar-sounding phonemes.

The key sign of true Broca's aphasia is a defect called *agrammatism*, the inability to organize the words in a sentence in proper grammatical fashion and the incorrect use of what linguists call *grammatical morphemes*. These include the conjunctions and prepositions that make up the grammatical "glue" of a sentence (such as *and, or, but, to*, and *from*) and suffixes like *-ed* and *-ing* added to verbs to indicate their tense (for example, in *loved* or *swimming*). Instead of saying "I will go home tomorrow," a person with agrammatism might say "Go I home tomorrow."

Another important type of aphasia is *Wernicke's aphasia*, also called *receptive, sensory, fluent*, or *jargon* aphasia. The brain regions damaged include Wernicke's area, which lies behind Broca's area in the left cerebral hemisphere along the Sylvian fissure. Patients with Wernicke's aphasia can speak fluently, but their speech sounds like nonsensical jargon. They can produce individual sounds with no problem. However, they often get the order of sounds and sound clusters mixed up. They may, for example, say "pymarid" instead of *pyramid*. Like those with Broca's aphasia, they cannot name things correctly, cannot properly assemble phonemes into syllables or proper words, and are unable to repeat sentences correctly. They appear to have lost the ability to create grammatical speech, language that follows rules of syntax. They also have great difficulty selecting the right words for their intended meanings. They may use *headman* when they want to say *president*. Wernicke's patients often choose generic terms, like *thing* or *stuff*, because they cannot come up with the precise word they're looking for. They cannot gain access to the brain's lexical storage area or areas.

People with Wernicke's aphasia have great difficulty understanding the speech of others. Their auditory comprehension has been damaged. However, neuroscientists no longer believe that Wernicke's area is the region where auditory comprehension takes place. It appears, instead, that this region processes speech sounds that are later used to identify concepts. This is a complex process involving many areas of the brain, and Wernicke's area plays only one part. Also, this region is probably not where word selection takes place. Again, Wernicke's area now appears to be just one part of a larger network of brain areas that connect speech sounds and words to the proper concept or meaning.

A third important kind of aphasia is called *conduction aphasia*. This aphasia involves damage to one of two regions in the brain: either Broadmann area 40 in the left cerebral hemisphere, lying above and behind both Broca's and Wernicke's areas; or Brodmann areas 41 and 42, which lie just above Wernicke's area in the left primary auditory cortexes. Also damaged or destroyed are the feedback and feed-forward neural projections or "highways" that connect the temporal, parietal, and frontal cortexes. The Damasios note that these connections are probably part of the neural network that makes it possible for us to combine phonemes, the basic sounds of words, into morphemes, the syllables and words themselves. Without this set of neural connections, it is very difficult, if not impossible, to internally vocalize or express a word.

People with conduction aphasia can understand essential sentences and can speak intelligibly. Other linguistic tasks are considerably more difficult. This form of aphasia shares some of the features of Broca's and Wernicke's aphasias. They include the inability to combine phonemes correctly and to repeat sentences. They might pronounce *banana* as "abana," for example. People with this form of aphasia cannot come up with the right words in specific naming tests. If shown a picture of an apple, a person with conduction aphasia would not be able to conjure up the word *apple* as the name of the object.

Finally, there is a form of aphasia called *global aphasia*. Global aphasia involves an almost total loss of the ability to speak and understand language. It combines all the worst features of Broca's and Wernicke's aphasias. What Damasio has called *deliberate speech*, the ability to consciously and deliberately speak about some aspect of reality or experience, is almost completely gone. However, people with global aphasia still have *nondeliberate* or *automatic* speech. For example, they can curse—quite well, in fact, with all the appropriate inflections and linguistic structures. They can hum tunes they learned before their brain damage; they can rattle off the names of the week and recite "Thirty days hath September . . . " without any problem. Recognizing grammatically elaborate sentences, though, is impossible for them. At best, they can comprehend only a few verbs or nouns they may hear. You might say to a person with global aphasia, "Jim, after I saw Jennie—who, as you recall, is my sister's neighbor, the one with the dog that had puppies last month?—right—well, after I saw her I headed back to work, and that's when Jack called me on the car phone." I could understand what you're saying and follow your train of thought; but Jim is lost. He catches "dog" and "puppies" and "neighbor," but that's it. The sentence is far too complex grammatically for him to follow.

Many people with global aphasia have suffered massive strokes that have damaged multiple brain areas. These often include Broca's area and Wernicke's area, as well as the frontal region or temporoparietal region of the brain. Patients with global aphasia thus usually suffer weakness on the right side of their faces and partial or total paralysis of the right side of their bodies. Remember what we know about cerebral bilateralization: the brain's right hemisphere controls the left side of the body, and vice versa. Paralysis of the body's right side means massive damage to the motor areas of the left cerebral hemiphere. Not only are many different language-related areas in the left hemisphere damaged in global aphasia, so are many motor areas.

Because of its importance in revealing how the brain works, the study of aphasia has come to occupy an honored place in medical research. A graphic summary of the main types of aphasia is found in the following table, adapted from one in Damasio's article on aphasia in a 1992 issue of the *New England Journal of Medicine*.

APHASIAS

Type	*Language Comprehension*	*Speech*	*Repetition Ability*	*Other Signs*
Broca's Aphasia	Intact, or largely preserved	Nonfluent; effortful	Impaired	Paralysis affecting right arm and leg; person is aware of defect; sometimes depression
Wernicke's Aphasia	Impaired	Fluent; abundant; well articulated; melodic	Impaired	No motor signs; person may be agitated, anxious, euphoric, or paranoid
Conduction Aphasia	Intact, or largely preserved	Fluent, but with some defects in articulation	Impaired	Often none; person may have cortical sensory loss, weakness in right arm, or weakness in right side of the face
Global Aphasia	Impaired	Scant and nonfluent	Impaired	Partial or total paralysis of the right side of the body

"Mind Blindness"

Aphasia is only one of several important "natural experiments" that have given neuroresearchers insights into language and the brain. Another is a medical condition called *agnosia* (from the Greek *gnosis*, "knowing"). Sometimes also called "mind blindness," agnosia is a neurological defect characterized by the inability to comprehend visual, auditory, or other sensations. The sensory apparatus is still intact—eyes, ears, taste buds, whatever—but the afflicted person has lost the ability to understand the sensations arriving from the sensory sphere. For example, auditory agnosia is the mental inability to interpret sounds. A person with auditory agnosia might not be able to associate the sound of a doorbell with the fact that someone is at the front door. Tactile agnosia is the mental inability to distinguish objects by touch. If I were blindfolded and had my hand placed on a sleeping cat, I would know that it was a cat I was touching. A person with tactile agnosia might be unable to make that same identification. Optic agnosia is the mental inability to interpret images that are seen.

One particular form of optic agnosia is *face agnosia*. It is not something new to brain science; the condition was first described more than a hundred years ago. However, it rarely received much attention from researchers; it is so bizarre that most doctors explained it away either as the result of some specific neurological malfunction or as some strange psychological aberration.

Antonio and Hanna Damasio and their colleague Daniel Tranel have given a riveting description of a typical case of face agnosia. They write of a sixty-five-year-old woman, identified as EH, who suddenly could no longer recognize the faces of her husband, daughter, other relatives, or friends. Even more bizarre, she could not recognize her own face in a mirror. Intellectually, she knew that the face in the mirror must be hers, but she experienced no sense of familiarity with it. It didn't *feel* like her face.

EH later reported that about two months before the onset of her face agnosia, she had noticed a change in her perception of colors. They suddenly appeared "washed out" or "dirty." in nature. She continued to have otherwise-normal visual perception. She had no history of mental disturbances or of any neurological problems.

When the Damasios and their colleagues began testing EH, they discovered some more intriguing facets to her face agnosia. All her difficulties seemed limited to the arena of visual perception. Even there, they were rather selective. For example:

- EH could not recognize the faces of any friends or relatives, either in person or from photographs. She did not even experience any feeling that they ought to be familiar to her.
- Similarly, she could not recognize the faces of celebrities, either from movies or still photos. The researchers gave her two tests involving photos of fifty people. In both tests, forty-two of the standardized photos were people she had never met, strangers. These were the "nontarget" faces. In one test the other eight, the

"target" faces, were of people she knew well before her face agnosia began. In the second test the eight target photos were of famous politicians and actors. EH was asked to identify them if she could. She was also asked to rank the faces on a scale of 1 to 6, with 1 representing "definite familiarity" and 6 representing "definite unfamiliarity." In both tests she rated all the target faces—relatives and celebrities alike—as unfamiliar. What's more, she ranked them all as 6s—"definitely unfamiliar."

- EH was unable to learn to recognize the faces of people she enountered after the onset of her condition. Their faces remained forever strange and unfamiliar to her.
- Though she could not identify their faces by visual inspection, EH was able to identify people by the sound of their voice. She never lost that ability. The face of her husband, for example, had become the face of a total stranger; but she could instantly tell who he was when he spoke. She could also learn to identify people she met after the beginning of her face agnosia by their voices.
- Her ability to speak was unaffected by her face agnosia, as were her intellect and her memory for most verbal and nonverbal material.
- EH's vision was practically perfect 20/20 in both eyes, and she performed normally on many different kinds of visual tests.

However, EH did have one very significant problem with her vision. She now suffered from *achromatopsia* (from the Greek words *achromata,* "without color," and *opsis,* "vision"). Achromatopsia is, essentially, complete color-blindness. People with this condition have lost more than the "mere" ability to perceive color in objects. They have lost the ability to even *imagine* colors. They see the world in shades of gray: roses, sports cars, fruits, people. More than that, they do not perceive the color of entities they recall from memory. If they think about a banana they ate before their brain damage, they do not perceive its yellowness. They can recall its taste, its smell, its shape, the texture of the banana fruit in their mouths, but not its color. It has no color but gray.

Though achromatopsia frequently accompanies cases of face agnosia, it is not the cause of this condition. In the case of EH, the Damasios and their colleagues were able to track down the immediate cause: two mild strokes in her visual association cortex. The first occured on the right side and caused her initial partial loss of color vision. The second, in the left visual association cortex, completed the damage and, along with the initial brain damage, led to her face agnosia.

Since the early 1970s a new generation of neuroscientists has started to pay close attention to cases of face agnosia. It is usually caused by damage in two specific areas of the brain. One is the underside of the occipital lobe, which lies at the back of the brain and processes visual data. The other is the temporal association cortex, which is on the upper surface of the temporal lobes on the sides of the brain and is vital to long- and short-term memory.

People with face agnosia are unable to recognize a person on the basis of a face. However, like EH, many can identify the person from the sound of the person's voice. Brain researchers have known about this aspect of face agnosia for many years. In 1982 the Damasios discovered face agnosia patients who could identify a person from the person's posture or gait. These are visual characteristics. The patients were looking at the people to be identified. They couldn't name them based on their faces. But if all they saw was the way the person walked, they knew who it was. They identified people on the basis of visual information other than faces. Like EH, they could also identify the person simply on the basis of *sound*—the sound of their voice, for example.

In fact, face agnosia comes in many variations. Some patients can identify faces from photographs or movies but not in person. These patients suffer a defect in their visual perception. Others cannot identify a person using *any* sensory channel—not just visual, but also auditory or tactile. Patients with this type of *amnesiac associative* face agnosia, as the Damasios have called it, can not even identify people by their voices, much less the image of their gait.

In many cases, people with face agnosia also suffer an impairment of their ability to visually recognize other kinds of unique stimuli. EH is one example. As the Damasios and their colleagues continued to work with her, they discovered she had great difficulty identifying her clothes, her car, her house, and other objects once special to her. She had no problem identifying her car as "a car," or her house as "a house." But the only way she could find her car in a crowded parking lot was to look for the license plate. Her memory for that kind of information had not been damaged by her strokes.

Other people suffering damage to these brain regions may experience different kinds of defects in their ability to recognize entities that are not faces. Unlike EH, they may recognize and name their dog as "Fido." But they cannot tell you that Fido is "a dog." They have access to identification of an entity as a *unique* entity ("Oh! That's Fido!"), in other words, but cannot recognize that same entity as a member of a larger category ("Fido is a dog.").

Another patient studied by the Damasios, known by the initials PSD, is very good at recognizing and naming human-made tools: shovels, saws, electric razors, screwdrivers. In repeated tests, his success rates at naming such objects range from 73 percent to 100 percent. But he has great difficulty recognizing and naming natural entities. Show PSD a rose and he will answer, hesistantly, "A plant?" Show him a picture of a dog named Fido and he will venture to call it "an animal." With these kinds of entities, PSD's identification success rate is less than 30 percent. In this way, PSD is much like Boswell. But even these distinctions of categories sometimes blur. PSD, for example, may do well at identifying and naming many human-made entities, but, like Boswell, he has trouble with musical instruments. Confronted with pictures of them, he makes correct identifications only 30 percent of the time. If he can hear the sounds the instruments make, though, PSD can nail down their identity perfectly.

Hanna and Antonio Damasio also worked with a patient they call AN. This man suffered damage to the front of his brain's left temporal lobe, an important language area. AN's difficulties with language were intriguingly limited. He could not come up with the verbal tags—the names—for entities, but he still recognized them. AN could describe objects in detail, but in repeated tests he could come up with names for only about half of them. Even this defect was not universal. For some linguistic categories, AN was all thumbs. His success rate at naming animals was 38 percent; for faces, 10 percent; for vegetables, 19 percent. But he could come up with the names for at least 70 percent of the tools and personal effects he was tested on. AN could give a detailed description of a lawnmower and explain its function. He was unable to describe anything about a raccoon when shown a picture of it; he could only name it as "an animal."

THE BRAIN'S STORAGE BINS

These fascinating discoveries about face agnosia have some intriguing implications. They strongly suggest that the information that comprises a visual record of a person or object is fragmented. The brain does not store all visual information about a person in one location. Rather, bits and pieces of the picture are stored away in different places. If the former were true, then a brain lesion that prevented you from identifying people from their faces would also render you unable to identify them from watching the way they walked. But this clearly does not happen to all people suffering from face agnosia.

People suffering from aphasia and various forms of agnosia have specific and fascinating problems with speech and naming, with understanding and using language. And these defects reveal a peculiar kind of mental "split" or "uncoupling." It is as if the brain stores certain kinds of nonverbal knowledge in one or more sets of "storage bins" or neural networks, while storing the verbal tags for this knowledge in other collections of storage bins.

One result is that a person may not be able to properly access the verbal tag—the name—when he or she receives the otherwise-correct nonverbal stimulus. If you are asphasic, when I show you a picture of your cat Isis, you cannot respond, "That's my cat Isis." You may be able to say, "That's a cat." Or you may only be able to respond, "Um, I'm pretty sure that's an animal, but I just can't think of what it is." Your husband tiptoes into the room, you look up and see his face, and you cannot identify him. He is a total stranger, as far as you are concerned. If he walks into the room wearing his work shoes, however, you might instantly identify him from the sound.

Another result of this apparent split in functions is the opposite face of the coin. Given the proper name or verbal tag, a person may not be able to access the nonverbal information normally attached to it. I say the word *cow* and you look at me blankly and shrug your shoulders. This is a remarkable response, given that you have been raising cattle for most of your adult life. I say, "Describe this to me," and show you a card with the word *lawnmower* written on it. You cannot do it. You cannot tell me what a *lawnmower* is, even though you have owned and used one for years.

Just as important to this emerging picture of brain function and language are the apparent exceptions these patients have to their defects. Some people who can easily name most human-made objects do poorly with musical instruments, which are manifestly objects made by humans. Other people cannot process the verbal tags of specific kinds of clothing but do well at naming items in other "inanimate" categories such as tools. We find these exceptions confusing. We tend to think of our knowledge of different entities or events in terms of their definitions, their verbal tags. We forget that in the "real world" of phenomena and immediate experiences, events and entities do not come with labels attached. Our experiences of events and entities are, in the beginning, nonverbal in nature.

Even in the absence of access to the verbal tags for entities or events, agnosics may still have access to the nonverbal knowledge. For example, some cannot recognize or describe a cup. However, if you give them a cup and say something like, "Show me what you do with this," they will take the cup in their hands and lift it to their lips. They *know* what the cup is, what it is for, and how to use it. So they definitely have access to the nonverbal knowledge of "cup." Nonetheless, they cannot *experience* knowing it. That knowledge never becomes conscious. The brain has the knowledge of "cup" stored away, including the bodily or *somatic* knowledge of what to do with it: raise it to your lips, since it is something you drink from. But that information never produces the experience of knowing, or even the feeling of knowing.

This general idea, that the brain stores representations in pieces rather than as a whole, is nothing new. Neuroscientists have long known this is true of how the brain deals with visual images themselves. There is no single place in the visual cortex that contains the image of, say, a book. When I look at a book, the brain's visual perception system breaks that image up into many different components. Those components include edges, lines, shadows, texture, and color. Specific regions of the visual cortex take care of processing and storing each of those components. More than that, specific areas store specific subsets of each component. The visual cortex, for example, has specific areas devoted to lines of specific angles.

There is at least one general truth we can generalize from decades of scientific study of the body and the brain: "If it ain't broke, don't fix it. Just use it again." It makes perfect sense, therefore, that the human brain uses the same "divide and recombine" strategy for storing and reconstructing *all* experiences as it does with visual images. And there is every reason to assume it does the same thing with language.

Their work with Boswell, EH, AN, and many other patients has led the Damasios and their associates to abandon the time-honored "commonsense" model for how the brain organizes knowledge. Their new paradigm for how we organize knowledge of all kinds, including that required for language, says that many different parts of the brain process, store, and release sets of shared features or interactions. In an article in *Trends in Neurosciences* Antonio Damasio listed eight specific "constraints" or organizational markers that provide the underpinning for this new structure:

1. *Features*: the different features that comprise the physical structure of the object or event that the brain is apprehending. These features are essentially the information provided the brain by the senses. They include the entitity's color, motion, shape, smell, sound, and texture. For example, here I am sitting at my desk, computer screen in front of me and a cup of steaming coffee off to my left near the office window. That cup of coffee has specific features. It is brown, with a curved handle on its right side from my point of view; the handmade cup has a dragon curling around it; the body of the cup has a glossy texture; steam rises from the coffee; the coffee has a rich aroma.
2. *Operations:* the movements, positions, or other operations of the entity in space. "Space" in this case includes the physical limits of the entity itself and the position the entity occupies in space relative to other objects. For example, the chair in front of my desk occupies a particular space in relation to the space where my desk sits. If I roll the chair over to the bookshelves, it has changed its location in space relative to the desk and the bookshelves.
3. *Motor interactions*: the body movements that the person uses when he or she is perceiving the object or person, especially eye and hand movements. Thus, as I sit in the chair at my desk, my brain perceives and stores all the motions of my hand, head, and upper body as I reach out to grab that steaming cup of coffee.
4. *Class size:* the size of the "taxonomic class" or "category" the

entity belongs to. In other words, the particular entity being experienced belongs to some larger set of objects or beings. Those entities taken together all share some common physical characteristics or operations. My dragon-decorated coffee mug belongs to a large class or category of entities called "coffee cup." Coffee cups, in turn, belong to a still-larger class of objects called "cups." They all share common features, such as their small bowl-like shape and their handles, that identify them as coffee mugs.

5. *Value:* the inherited or acquired *biological* value of the entity to the person perceiving it. Some entities trigger instinctive biological reactions; others cause the perceiver to experience biological responses he or she has learned in social settings, such as the family or at school. The coffee cup has no such value to me.
6. *Somatic responses:* the body's reactions to an entity, which are determined by the biological values the perceiver has for it. This constraint also includes the state of the person's body (sexually excited? fearful? relaxed?) when he or she was learning something. The coffee in the cup triggers a response from my body when I smell it: I want to drink the coffee and experience that caffeine "high." In fact, just seeing my favorite coffee mug may trigger that reaction.
7. *Frequency:* how often the entity or event occurs in the universe or interacts with the person perceiving it. My brain knows that "coffee cup" occurs frequently in my personal universe, especially when I am sitting at my desk and working.
8. *Complexity:* the complexity of the events of which the entity is a part. This helps define the entity's uniqueness. My coffee cup is not exactly unique, but it does occupy an important role in the complex events surrounding writing. Coffee often fuels my writing; sometimes getting up to get a cup gives me a chance to stretch and take a break; making coffee for myself while writing recalls memories of making coffee for Judy and me when we first woke up; then I remember an enjoyable conversation with a friend over a cup of coffee downtown. And so on.

When Antonio and Hanna Damasio assert that the brain deals with language in the same way and with the same neurological mechanisms that it does with any other entity or event, they are not whistling in the dark. They have decades of solid neurological research to back up their hypothesis. As we learn more about how the brain represents objects "out there," or events, or the relationships among objects and events, we will also come to a greater understanding of how the brain creates, stores, and manipulates language.

CHAPTER 8

CONVERGENCE ZONES AND HYPERCARD® STACKS

As we have seen from the studies of Boswell, EH, AN, and PSD, the question of how the brain stores information, and then turns that data into memories or uses it to identify immediate perceptions, is a central issue in brain research. Most of us, including brain researchers and psychologists, subscribe to a fairly intuitive explanation, one that makes a lot of "common sense." And it now looks as though it is completely wrong. By contrast, the new model for the way the brain stores and uses information is the biological version of what computer programmers call HyperCard®* stacks.

*HyperCard® is a registered trademark of the Apple Computer Co.

The Brain, Language, and Common Sense

The commonsense explanation of how the brain processes and stores information, including information associated with language, goes something like this:

The brain begins by receiving data from the senses about a particular object, or scene, or event happening in the environment. The data naturally arrive in somewhat fragmented form. An object visually detected, for example, consists of lines, edges, shades of light, different colors, and so on. It may be moving, or it may be at rest while the background moves. It may emit sounds (which the aural sense picks up), or smells (olfaction), or have texture (touch). Different regions in the brain receive all the various pieces of information about the object and process those data.

Next, the brain creates a complete representation of the object. It stores that representation at a single anatomical site, a specific collection of neurons. This specific neural network receives the information from the different brain regions that have processed the various components of the object, such as edges, lines, color, movement, and smell. Suppose we recognize the object ("Oh yes, that's a kangaroo hopping down Maple Street") or recall it in memory ("Oh yes, I recall the time the kangaroo escaped from Walk in the Wild and hopped down Maple Street"). According to this commonplace view, we are reactivating that particular ensemble of neurons. We essentally create an "internal image" of the object, stored in the brain at a particular location, and we mentally "inspect" it.

If this is in fact the way the brain creates and retrieves memories and perceptions, then it must do so in a fairly straightforward manner. The extraction and integration of the neural signals representing the perception must move in one direction and in sequence. The cascade will begin in the primary sensory cortexes. These regions of the brain lie just behind the Rolandic fissure, which runs across the top of your head from your left to right ear. The area just in front of the Rolandic fissure is the motor cortex, and it controls your body's movements. The sensory cortexes include areas of the parietal lobe, lying along the top of the brain; the occipital lobe, which is the rearmost part of the brain; and the temporal lobes along the sides of the brain. The sensory cortexes store the bits and pieces of sensory data. Then the signals will move forward from these regions at the back or *posterior* parts of the brain. They will pass through the so-called *association* or *integrative* cortexes. These are regions of the brain that lie just in front and to the side of the sensory cortexes. They include parts of the temporal lobes as well as the frontal lobe, which lies in front of the motor cortex. Then the signals will move along neuronal extensions to the forward or *anterior* regions of the temporal and frontal lobes. These are the *multimodal* cortexes of the brain, as many researchers call them.

This traditional, intuitive explanation for how the brain creates and retrieves memories has rarely been questioned. It is simply assumed to be correct. Even the great Russian psychologist Aleksandr Romanovich Luria (1902–1977) accepted it. Luria was one of the founders of neuropsychology, the field of science that has contributed greatly to our understanding of the human brain and its functions. In the 1920s and 1930s Luria carried out many important studies of the function of speech. He was particularly interested in how language might help control the emotional processes. Luria also explored the relationship between speech and the mental development of children and came to believe that the two were inextricably linked. His exploration of the relationship between language and thought led him to investigate different kinds of speech defects, including aphasia. His work on aphasia then led him to to study the brain in general, which in turn helped him during World War II to make important advances in the rehabilitation of soldiers with brain injuries. Luria published more than two hundred books and articles. Among them *Higher Cortical Functions in Man* offers this traditional view of how the brain creates and stores representations of reality.

These kinds of assumptions—the "obvious to anyone with any common sense" kinds of assumptions—can be deadly in science. The ultimate tests of any such assumption are observation and experimentation. It turns out that this commonsense, intuitive explanation of how the brain stores and activates memories fails these tests. Suppose this hypothesis is correct. We can predict, then, that the fragments comprising a concept, object, or scene will always be recalled in the same way and with the same characteristics. But our own real-life experience tells us this is not the case at all. Our memories of events, people, places, can become distorted. We can add new features to them or conveniently forget others. We can recall a scene from memory and "stand" in another location, seeing it from a different perspective. We can revise our memories of an event, "changing the ending" or the sequence of actions and reactions.

Then there are novelists, playwrights, screenwriters, and comedians, who create new events out of the fragments of old memories, experiences, and pure imagination. If the process of creating memories were purely linear, grounded in physical brain structures, book reviewers would not have Harold Robbins to kick around and Tom Robbins to praise. Creating new worlds, characters, events, and jokes out of thin air requires a different process, one in which the brain can recombine fragments of memories in a myriad different patterns that are not immutably tied to "reality."

There is also the matter of space, physical space in the brain. Where do we put it all? Are there enough neuronal interconnections in the brain to store *every* variation of *every* memory and *every* perception we experience? If the traditional hypothesis is correct, then the temporal and frontal lobes at the front and sides of your brain must have enough neurons and neuronal connections to house all of this stuff. After all, these are the regions of the "highest brain functions." Right? Where all the integrated and complex representations of our experiences are stored and recalled from? The simple fact, though, is that these very brain regions actually have *far fewer* neurons than the rearmost parts of the brain.

However, the most damaging objections to this traditional, commonsense view of the brain and perception come from the most important realm of all, the realm of scientific observation and experimentation. The Damasios' patient nicknamed "Boswell" is a good case in point. Boswell has suffered considerable damage to several anterior, "high-level" areas of his brain. If the traditional view of the brain's cognitive functions were correct, damage to the parts of his temporal lobes near the front would seriously impair not only Boswell's highest levels of perception but also nearly all his memory for practically everything. Yet despite just this kind of damage, this is not what has happened to him. Boswell suffers from bizarre and wide-ranging memory losses that are strangely selective, not "across the board" by any means. Nor has he suffered any impairment to his sensory perception.

Corroborative evidence comes from studies of people who have lesions or damaged areas in their prefrontal cortexes, the parts of the brain nearest the front of the head. The prefrontal cortexes are another of the end-points in the traditional view of the brain's neural architecture. Damage these regions, the traditional view implies, and you destroy a person's cognitive abilities. Yet that is not what seems to happen in real life. Lesions in these brain areas do not seem to be associated with damage to either perception or conventional memory. EVR, a patient of Hanna and Antonio Damasio, suffered damage to a part of the prefrontal cortex. Despite this injury, EVR continues to have normal perceptual processes, learning ability, and memory. Even the fabled frontal cortexes, the parts of the brain lying just behind the prefrontal cortexes that we often assume to be "the seat of consciousness" in humans, do not appear to function in accord with the traditional cognitive model of the brain. The Damasios think that the frontal cortexes, like the temporal cortex, are involved in "tying together" combinations of events. The records of those events are stored elsewhere in the brain. The temporal and frontal cortexes, they believe, are particularly concerned with special domains of knowledge. The frontal cortex, in particular, seems to deal with social and personal knowledge. But neither cortex has anything to do either with perceiving the features that make up these events or with storing memories of them.

The only brain damage that affects a person's perceptual quality is injury involving some areas of the sensory cortex strips along the top of the brain. And the effects are very selective, at that. For a good example, we look once again at our visual perceptive ability, including our perception of color. The occipital lobe at the rear of the brain contains the visual cortex, the areas of the brain that process visual information including color. Scars from strokes or head injuries in certain regions of the visual cortex can seriously disrupt our ability to perceive color, form, texture, and the physical placement of an object's components. But the type and extent of the disruption very much depends on the precise location of the lesion.

At the same time, this sort of injury to the visual cortex also affects our recall and recognition abilities. EH's achromatopsia, complete color-blindness, is an example of this kind of damage and its strange memory side effects. As we learned earlier, EH cannot perceive the color of any entity, that is, an object or person with a specific set of features, sitting in front of her right now. She also cannot even perceive color within the memory-entities she recalls. Why should her memory be affected by strokes that damaged a specific tiny region of her visual cortex? The traditional brain cognition model says that memory and recall is stored in other areas farther "upstream" in the brain. But the experience of EH and others clearly tells us something else. The same region of the brain that governs a particular type of perception, such as sight, probably supports our ability to *recall* that perception.

Once again, this makes sense from a purely biological perspective. It is a highly economical state of affairs. There is no point in reinscribing memories in some other brain region. This one works just fine.

According to the Damasios, then, all the evidence from scientific investigations of the brain's ability to perceive the outside world and to think about what it perceives point to a method of operation that does not fit the traditional model. They suggest that the brain ties together the different components of entities that are stored in many different areas of the brain. Each brain region can support the recall and recognition of most entities at the "category" level—the larger, general, "genus" level, as opposed to the specific, unique, "species" level. "That's an animal." "This is a tool." "It's a person." Meanwhile, the binding together of the knowledge we need to recognize the uniqueness of entities or events, which the Damasios define as being made of interacting objects or persons, requires the activity of regions in both the rear and the front of the brain. "That tool is a lawnmower." "That car is my car." "This is the face of John, the man I love."

The Convergence Zone Hypothesis

The evidence accumulated by researchers studying brain-damaged patients from around the world for more than a hundred years paints a considerably different picture of how the brain stores information. The Damasios and others now believe that the brain's different neural systems store, process, and recall information in a multilevel fashion. The data accumulated by our internal and external senses does not reside in a few specific locations in the brain. Instead, many different areas in the brain are devoted to processing specific characteristics of entities and events belonging to specific "knowledge domains." One such "knowledge domain" might be the entity we name as the color "blue." Another might be the event we call "being slapped."

There seems to be no evidence that specific neural subsystems in the brain are somehow dedicated to representing particular conceptual categories. There is no one place in the brain that stores "coffee cup," for example. Fragments that comprise that concept are stored in different locations; "white" is in one area of the brain, "cone shape" in another, "handle shape" in still another location, "coffee smell" somewhere else.

The same seems to be true of memories. I cannot point to a particular part of the brain and say, "This is where my brain stores the memory of my grandmother's Hungarian apple streudel and its odor wafting through her house in Culver City." Rather, the brain breaks up each sensory experience into many component parts, then stores different parts in different regions.

But the brain must also be able to combine back together all the pieces that constitute an entity (i.e., object or person) or event (entities interacting). The brain must do this not only for recall, for memory, but also for the process of immediate real-time recognition. We all know how quickly we can recognize some entities. We all know how we sometimes stumble about mentally, trying to recall that person's name. A car, a tree, the smell of a cup of steaming coffee, my father's face, the sound of a violin—to recognize any of these entities or events, our brain must be able to compare them to previously stored information.

As the bits and pieces of evidence accumulated, Hannah and Antonio Damasio began to see a picture emerge. It was a new view of how the brain retrieves information about events, the entities that compose events, and the features that make up entities. It is a picture with exciting implications for how the human brain creates, stores, and retrieves language. And it may offer some intriguing hints about other phenomena that baffle brain researchers, psychologists, and therapists.

To begin at the beginning, say the Damasios, the brain stores the different parts of an entity's image or representation—the pieces of a specific puzzle picture, if you will—in many different areas. Since this is so, a mechanism must exist that allows the brain to bind the pieces together to make a coherent picture. This is not a static picture, either, not merely a "still photograph." We perceive reality not as a series of color slides flashed upon a screen but as a continually flowing, seamless "motion picture" web of experiences, moving in time as well as space. This is true of our immediate sensory experiences, and it is also the case with many of our memory experiences. I can pause and remember, with great clarity, how it felt to hold my grandson when he and his mother were last visiting. I can recall his movements in my arms, how he smelled, the texture of the baby clothes he wore, and I can hear again the sounds he made.

We are also able to recognize, almost at once, a myriad of entities or events presented to us by our senses. When I look out my office window, I immediately recognize the tree I see as a mountain ash. I recognize our neighbor Barbara as she walks down to her car. I recognize grass, its color. I recognize that it is early afternoon. When I look up at the clock above the computer, I know *at once* that it is a clock. I know what time it is. If I am out on the front porch and I hear a phone ringing inside the house, I can tell at once that it is the house phone, and not my office phone. The sound of the bell is different for each, and I recognize the sound.

The brain thus has a mechanism by which it can immediately compare current sensory data to previously stored data and make an identification. It also has a mechanism to re-create, in vivid detail, previous experiences of events and entitites. And bound up in that mechanism, or those mechanisms, is some process by which I am conscious of recognizing or remembering an event or entity.

The Damasios believe that the mechanism in question is a set of regions within the brain that they call *convergence zones*. The entire process, they propose, goes something like this:

We begin with our sensory perception of an entity (a person or some other living being, a place, or some object) or of a complex event composed of various interacting entities. The data from our senses, both external and internal, travel to the brain as a series of neural impulses. The brain receives this neural activity in a fragmented fashion. It absorbs bits and pieces, various puzzle parts, and not a coherent, holistic image or series of images. The brain receives these fragmented neural impulses in geographically separated areas. These regions are located in the sensory and motor cortexes, and they are made of clusters of neurons. The brain associates these stored neural patterns with one another in some pertinent fashion. They could be associated on the basis of their similarity (for example, "categories of animals," or "human-made objects," or "cone-shaped," or "stippled texture"), temporal sequence ("First A happened, then B, then C . . ."), temporal *coincidence* ("Ring bell . . . food . . . ring bell . . . food . . ."), spatial placement ("The cooking spices are on the same shelf as the flour"), or various combinations ("Cone-shaped objects located on this particular shelf in the kitchen").

The same networks of neurons that receive and register the perception of sensory data about an entity's physical properties also store the neural patterns representing the physical property. This means that the brain stores the "memories," as it were, of each specific aspect or property of an entity or event as fragments. The fragments of one particular entity, for example, might be "dark brown," "bean shape," "smooth texture," and "*coffee odor.*" These fragments are scattered throughout the brain's sensory and motor cortexes.

We experience an experience, either immediately perceived or in memory, not as unconnected pieces but in a holistic fashion, all at once. The multiple pieces of that experience must fit together seamlessly. The integration must also take place nearly instantly. And it does, in mere milliseconds. The widely separated brain regions storing the neural patterns of an experience release those puzzle pieces almost simultaneously and in the correct order. According to the Damasios, a process of recurring feedback interactions takes place among the various sites storing the information about an event or entity. The interactions of the neural impulses take place over and over again in what the Damasios call a process of "phase-locked co-activation." The term *phase lock* essentially means that a series of events takes place in a specific sequence that never varies.

For this kind of "remembering" or "mental reconstruction" to take place, the brain must have some set of instructions or "triggers" to command the simultaneous release of these mental fragments. The instructions that trigger the co-activation of stored neural impulses do not reside in the same locations containing those neural traces or "memories" of the features that compose an object or person. The brain stores them in other, separate locations. It is these areas that the Damasios call convergence zones.

Convergence zones, then, are actual physical places in the brain. They are made of tiny bundles of neurons that act as intermediaries or "third parties" among the brain regions storing all the different pieces of "coffee cup" or "Freddy Freeloader" or "kissing Judy." The codes lodged in the convergence zones trigger *and synchronize* specific neural activity patterns stored in the sensory and motor cortexes. The patterns correspond to representations of an entity's physical structure ("cone shape," "white," "rough texture," and so on), or an event's sequence of actions ("Make the following sounds in this sequence in order to speak"). The patterns are associated with one another in some fashion. The neural codes for those associations are stored with them. The convergence zones thus trigger them in the correct sequence.

The convergence zones and the storage regions are linked by *projections*. These are thin loops of neurons that extend from storage areas to convergence zones, and from the convergence zones back to the storage areas in the sensory and motor cortexes. When the Damasios talk about "feedback loops," they are not simply creating a metaphor. They mean something literal. It is a process that depends on physical connections between a convergence zone and specific neural storage areas.

Suppose you want to have a brick wall along the side of your yard, but you don't have the materials. Shirley has the bricks, Devon has the cement, and April has the water. Is this a problem? Not at all. You hire Susan, who gets the bricks from Shirley, the cement from Devon, and the water from April. Then Susan mixes the mortar and lays the bricks in precisely the pattern you want and in the location you specified. "Shirley," "Devon," and "April" are regions in your brain that store specific fragments of the "brick wall." "Susan" is another part in your brain, a convergence zone. It holds the instructions that order "Shirley" and the others to release their fragments and that then combine them together to make a "brick wall." Susan may have to talk with "Shirley" several times in order to get all the bricks she needs, or call up Devon to get some more cement. But Susan gets the job done in a twinkling of an eye.

The Coffee Cup

One example that the Damasios like to use for the convergence zone process is a coffee cup. Suppose, they say, that someone asks you to think about a Styrofoam coffee cup. What happens in your brain when you get that request? What does *not* happen, first of all, is that you open up some neuronal "filing cabinet" in your brain that has a file labeled "Cups, Coffee—Picture" and pull out an image of a Styrofoam coffee cup filled with hot steaming coffee.

What *does* happen is that you tell one of your many neuronal assistants to *reconstruct the image of a coffee cup*. The "assistant" in this case is the set of stored codes that open up a whole bunch of very tiny filing cabinet drawers. Each drawer consists of a small cluster of neurons. One cluster stores your knowledge of cone shapes. Another stores the color white; another the concept "crushable objects"; another the texture of Styrofoam; another the concept of "objects that can be manipulated"; and another the concept of "objects that hold liquids." Still other regions store the associated somatic or "body" memories: the shape your hands take to hold a Styrofoam coffee cup; its temperature; how your entire hand moves to carry the cup to your lips; and on and on.

In less than the blink of an eye, so fast that it seems instantaneous to you, your brain finds all the right pieces, gathers them up, and fits them all together in the right pattern. The codes for that pattern reside in the convergence zones. Voila! You recall the shape, temperature, and texture of a Styrofoam coffee cup, and its weight in your hands, and the smell of the coffee, and the sight of the steam rising up, and how your hand carries the cup to your lips, and the taste, and what it sounds and feels like to crush the empty cup.

In the case of language, convergence zones are the link between brain areas dealing with nonverbal knowledge and areas handling language. Neural projections provide the physical links between convergence zones and storage areas. The convergence zones contain the codes that trigger appropriate associations that must be made between verbal and nonverbal information.

When a person sees an object, a convergence zone activates the brain region that contains the word for the object. It also makes possible the opposite kind of activity: given the word, the convergence zone will help call up the concept associated with it. So when I see an unusual Australian animal with a pouch, hopping about on two powerful hind legs, I can say, "Aha! There's a kangaroo hopping down Maple Street. That's not something you see every day in Spokane." Conversely, if Judy comes running into the house and says, "I just saw a kangaroo hopping down Maple Street," I will instantly form in my mind the image of a kangaroo . . . hopping . . . down Maple Street. All this is possible, if the Damasios are correct, because of convergence zones in my brain.

Let's take the Styrofoam coffee cup example again. Suppose Dr. Damasio comes to you, holds up the coffee cup, and asks you what it is. Once again, you do not go to the Rolodex in your brain and find the card that has the word *cup*. Rather, you put a convergence zone to work. This one contains the codes to open several different tiny card files and bring together their contents. One neuron cluster holds the phoneme /k/, another the phoneme /ə/, and a third the phoneme /p/. The convergence zone's codes recall and combine those phonemes in the correct order in response to the proper stimulus. In this case the stimulus is the Styrofoam coffee cup. One result: In your "mind's ear" you hear the word *cup*. Another result: additional connections via convergence zones activate the proper sets of muscles and you say, "That's a Styrofoam coffee cup."

WHERE ARE THEY?

But are convergence zones really real? Have they actually been found in the brain? Antonio Damasio says: well, not yet. "What we're talking about, it's important to keep in mind here, is a hypothetical construct. No one has yet actually found a convergence zone in the brain. They must exist, though, at the microscopic level. They are ensembles of neurons that could include many thousands of neurons, and they would exist within the areas of the brain that are traditionally described."

Damasio theorizes that many different convergence zones exist. They are located in the brain's basal ganglia, limbic nuclei, and limbic cortexes, which are special structures found deep inside the center of the brain that help govern our emotions and memory. The Damasios also think that convergence zones will probably be found in various regions of the association cortexes along the top and rear of the brain. The location of convergence zones for different entities varies from person to person, but it is not random.

The location depends, for example, on the subject matter of the recorded material. It also depends on the recorded matter's complexity. Some entities consist of only a few features; others of many. The same is true of events; some are fairly simple, while others are composed of many different entities interacting or related in a complex fashion. The convergence zones that bind features into entities tend to be located in regions closer to the posterior parts of the brain, the locations of the sensory and motor cortexes. Convergence zones binding complex sets of entities into still more complex events, on the other hand, lie closer to the anterior parts of the brain, the location of the cerebral cortex.

"The kind of neural architecture we're specificially hypothesizing in our papers, the convergence zones we're talking about, would be involved in the higher-order cortexes of the brain," Antonio Damasio says. "They have access to information that's generated in the primary cortex. What they do is 'broker' the information generated in these 'earlier' cortexes. Now, there's probably some architecture of convergence zones in the early cortexes, but we don't yet have sufficient evidence for them."

By means of this feedback process, the convergence zones send back to the earlier cortexes their processed versions of the released neural traces. Then the neural activity proceeds forward once again. The data are passed down the projections either to the same convergence zone or to others.

In this model of information storage and retrieval proposed by the Damasios, there is no final or central area in the brain that stores the various neural "pieces" that compose an event or entity. Nor is there some single area of the brain that integrates neural puzzle pieces that may be housed in different locations. Rather, the integration occurs when activations take place *within a specific window in time.*

Antonio Damasio explains, "When we talk about a temporal window, what we mean is that these different parts of a representation of a person, or object, or event, have to be pulled together and be in consciousness within a very short span of time. That's the only way they can *cohere*, stick together. So time helps bind them together.

"Just think about the opposite of what actually appears to happen. Imagine all the components of such a representation appearing *separately* in our consciousness. Were that to happen, they simply could not appear as some sort of holistic construct. So it is their proximity to one another *in time* that makes them cohere."

He pauses a moment, thinking. Then: "Here's a real-life example. I look out my window from where I'm sitting. I see a car coming down the street, and I hear the sound of the car. There is no one single place in the brain that contains a motion picture screen showing that image, and that has the sound track playing. And yet I have them together in my consciousness. Why is that? It is because of their coincidence in time. All the elements of that picture and sound track are evoked at the same time."

We must begin creating our linguistic convergence zones when we first begin learning language. The entire language acquision process involves the creation of new convergence zones. Some deal with different linguistic categories: sounds, rhythms, syllables, words, rules of grammar, and so on. Others are involved with memory, with movements of the vocal tract, or, for sign language, with hand movements. Convergence zones, says Damasio, are quite flexible. While we continually form new ones to deal with new categories, the old ones can also change and rearrange themselves throughout our lives.

Language, the Brain, and the HyperCard Stack

This is a fascinating and provocative new suggestion for how the brain stores information. What the Damasios are saying, in effect, is that the brain does not store representations of reality *in space*. The brain, rather, stores those representations *in time*. What is stored spatially, in different geographical locations within the brain, are merely the fragments of a representation. The entire representation of an entity or event does not exist anywhere in the brain. It comes into being only within a temporal window.

Some years ago, several brain researchers suggested that the brain was like a *hologram*. A hologram is a three-dimensional image of an object, created using laser beams. Basically, a laser beam is split into two separate beams. One falls directly onto a glass photographic plate and is called the reference beam. The other illuminates the object to be imaged, which then reflects the beam back onto the photographic plate. The two beams thus meet and form interference patterns on the plate. This is like dropping two pebbles close together into a puddle of water. Ripples move out from each pebble. When the ripples meet, some cancel each other out, while others reinforce one another to create even bigger ripples. The pattern they create is called an interference pattern. When the photographic plate is developed, the result is a hologram.

We cannot see any image simply by looking at the plate. All we see are blurs and blobs. To reproduce a three-dimensional image of the object, we shine a light on the photographic plate containing the hologram. Ideally, we use the original reference laser beam. What we see in front of us is not a flat two-dimensional image but a three-dimensional holographic image.

The intriguing thing about a hologram is that the entire image is located in every part of the plate. If we take an ordinary photographic negative and tear it in two, any positive image made from half of the negative is only half of the image. But suppose we break the holographic plate in two, then shine the laser beam through one piece. What we see is the entire image, not simply half of it. We could break the holographic plate into thirty pieces, and each piece would contain the entire image. The image gets more and more fuzzy as we use smaller and smaller pieces—but the entire image is still there.

The holographic model of the brain proposes that the brain stores data as a hologram stores an image. In other words, every piece of information in the brain is located everywhere in the brain. True, different parts of the brain do seem to specialize. There is no denying the reality of Broca's area, for example, or the existence of the visual cortex. But the holographic model suggests that all that data is also squirreled away in other locations.

At first blush, the Damasios' model of the brain seems a bit like a hologram, since memories are distributed throughout the brain and not in specific locations. However, the Damasios' model is really the holographic model turned inside out. The brain stores *fragments* of the representation of an object or person or event in many specific areas. It stores the entire representation *nowhere at all*. The whole image, the entire representation of an entity or event, exists only when the fragments are co-activated within a temporal window.

The Damasios' model for the way the brain stores and retrieves data is more like a popular form of computer software, HyperCard, originally developed by the Apple Computer Company and included with many of the computers the company makes. In its simplest form, it is a way of organizing and retrieving information by means of "stacks." Each stack consists of a series of "cards," like three-by-five-inch index cards on which you might write recipes. Indeed, the HyperCard software can even present the user with an image of an index card on the computer screen.

Each card has a "background" or general heading. All the cards can have a common background, but they do not have to. For your recipe cards, for example, you might use headings like "Main Dishes," "Desserts," "Salads," and "Soups." Each card in the stack contains some unique and specific piece of information. It can be a graphic image, or a name, or a description, or whatever. In somewhat the same way, your recipe cards each bear a unique recipe. Also, each card can contain one or more "buttons." The buttons are context-sensitive. When you push the button, using a key on the keyboard or the computer's mouse, you quickly jump to another card in the stack that is connected to the first one via the context-sensitive button. Now, that is something you cannot do with your recipe cards, but it would certainly be a nice feature.

Suppose I create a HyperCard stack to represent the house in which Judy and I live. The common background for every card in the stack is "Our House (Is a Very Very Very Fine House)." I represent each room in the house with a series of cards. I also create cards to represent the other components of the house, such as plumbing, wiring, and gas lines. One of the cards that represents the "upstairs bathroom" has an image of the toilet. Embedded in the image is a button connected to "plumbing." If I push that button, I immediately jump to one of the plumbing cards. A button in that card might jump me to a kitchen card.

That particular kitchen card, in turn, might include a description of the kitchen sink. If I push a particular button in that card, I am taken to a "kitchen countertop" card that lists everything on or in that part of the kitchen countertop. There I find the word *toaster*. I push a button connected to that word, and—whoa!—now I am looking at a card with a picture of our toaster. I started at the toilet in the upstairs bathroom. Now I'm at the toaster in the kitchen. The toaster card could then link me to bread, to the kitchen cabinets, to any of several cookbooks, or to the cards representing the house's electrical outlets.

I haven't even mentioned the separate HyperCard stacks representing the garage, the back yard, and the front yard. These HyperCard stacks in turn are all linked together to create a total representation of the property we own, and all that is on and in it.

Each card in the HyperCard stack represents just one fragment of the total representation of the house. Taken as a whole, they create a total image. However, the cards do not exist in any one pile in any particular location. They are part of an electronic file created by the HyperCard software. That file, in turn, does not sit in one specific place on the computer's hard disk. Like most files and programs on a hard disk, the file containing all the cards in the "Our House" HyperCard stack is fragmented. It exists as bits and pieces physically stored in different locations on the hard disk. It does not look fragmented, of course, when we run the program and call up the file. That is because the computer knows how to bind the different fragments together.

If the Damasios are correct, the human brain works the same way. Sitting between our ears, in other words, is the greatest HyperCard stack ever seen on Earth—and perhaps in the universe. It is a meta-stack, in fact, a whole stack of HyperCard stacks, all interconnected by convergence zones and neural projections. And one entire subset of neural HyperCard stacks deals with language.

"I like that," Damasio says, when the HyperCard stack comparison is explained to him. "I like it. That sounds like a reasonable metaphor, as long as you don't push it *too* far!"

CHAPTER 9

LANGUAGE, THE BRAIN, AND CONSCIOUSNESS

The work by Hanna and Antonio Damasio and their colleagues, as well as other brain researchers, has given us a vivid new picture of how the brain processes languages. These discoveries came about primarily through work with people who have suffered brain damage from strokes, accidents, or illnesses. As we have seen, this kind of scientific observation has a long and honorable past. It goes back to the work by Broca and Wernicke more than a century ago that revealed for the first time that specific regions of the brain seem to be involved with language.

Still more insights into how the brain processes language come from another area of scientific research and observation: brain surgery. One of the pioneers in this field was Wilder Penfield, the American-Canadian neurosurgeon. His explorations of living human brains during surgery using microelectrodes made possible some of the first detailed maps of the brain's different functional regions. Today, other researchers have picked up where Penfield left off. They include a brain surgeon in Seattle whose meticulous explorations of the living brains of epileptics are changing the maps of the brain's language areas.

One of the consequences of all this research into the brain and language, of course, has been a new and deeper understanding of how the brain creates, stores, and recalls the various components of our mother tongue. But another, even more remarkable consequence is a new understanding of consciousness itself and the very creation of our sense of self-awareness.

Language's Threefold Foundation

The brain seems to carry out the task of creating and storing language by using three different sets of neurological structures or neural networks. These three structures all interact with one another to produce what we identify as language.

First, many different systems in the left and right hemispheres of the brain process the wealth of data from the outside world. This is "nonlanguage" information that arrives through our different senses: smell, taste, touch, hearing, and especially sight. It also comes from special sensors inside our bodies called *somatosensory receptors*, which for example tell the brain about the position of our feet and body as we walk, or the movement of our hands as we reach out to catch the plummeting baseball. This flood of data represents the interactions between our body and the environment. The environment, of course, includes everything "out there."

The brain also deals with information about the body's "internal environment" and its interactions with itself. The brain collects this raw information and processes it by categorizing it. The categories include "shape," "color," "temporal sequence," "emotional state," "spatial position," "texture," and so on. The human brain also creates additional levels of representations for these initial classifications. These additional categories might include, for example, "natural objects," "human-made objects," "happy-feeling events," "fear-feeling events," and various categories of relationships among or between entities and events. Some of these additional levels of reality-representations are actually quite abstract. They form the basis for our ability to create symbols and metaphors.

A second set of neural systems, smaller than the first, lies mostly in the left cerebral hemisphere. These neural clusters contain the representations of phonemes (the basic sounds that are the building blocks of words), words themselves (which are, as we know, combinations of phonemes), and the rules for combining words (which we call syntax or grammar). These particular neural networks can receive stimulation from other areas within the brain or from outside the brain. When they receive internal stimulation they assemble phonemes into words and words into sentences, using the syntactic rules they contain. When the stimulation comes from the outside—from someone speaking, for example, or from reading a piece of text—these neural networks carry out the first steps in processing the visual or auditory signals into understood language.

Finally, a third set of neural structures acts to connect the two sets of neural systems that handle language and nonlanguage data. These mediators are, of course, the Damasios' convergence zones. The convergence zones for language, like the language centers themselves, are mostly located in the left cerebral hemisphere.

The Color Connection

Along with several other researchers, the Damasios have uncovered some fascinating lines of evidence for the way the brain handles language. One particularly striking set of observations has to do with our perception of color and with the way we communicate those perceptions with language.

Each year, during the first part of October, hot-air balloon aficionados from around the world gather at a park just north of Albuquerque for the annual Hot-air Balloon Festival. Hundreds of balloons take to the air, dotting the clear blue New Mexico sky with a riot of colors and shapes. When the balloons make night ascents, the flames from the gas burners light up the balloon bags like gargantuan lanterns. Other cities and towns may have similar festivals, but there is nothing quite like the sight of more than six-hundred color-daubed hot-air balloons hanging above the Southwestern landscape. Thousands of tourists join local residents to watch the spectacle. Perhaps you have been one of them. So, how exactly do you *see* this modern-day masterpiece of color painted on the New Mexico sky?

The processing of color signals begins in your retina, the complex layers of tissue at the back of the eye. A set of cells called *cones* detects the differences in the wavelengths of light that constitute color. Some cone cells are sensitive to red light, others to green, and still a third set to blue light. These are the three primary colors of light, which combine in various ways to produce all the colors of the palette. The cone cells respond to the light striking them by firing off electrochemical signals along their axons, different signals for different colors. Those signals travel on to the brain through the optic nerve. The signals go to the primary visual cortex at the back of the brain. Several other parts of the brain are also specifically dedicated to detecting and processing color information. They include two areas buried deep in the center of the brain and two regions lying near the edge of the occipital lobe at the rear of the brain. Taken together, these brain structures work with the visual cortex at the rearmost part of the brain to create the representations we know as colors.

The concepts for color and different ranges of color or hue are generally universal among humans. Some researchers have suggested this is not true, that some cultures not only do not have names for certain hues but actually do not perceive the differences among or between some colors. More recent evidence from psychology and anthropology contradicts this position. It does appear that, even if people of a particular culture do not have a name for a specific hue or color, they do recognize differences among hues. Even people born with different forms of color-blindness know that certain ranges of hue are different from other ranges.

However, the representations of the "entity" called color, or a specific color like blue, are not the same as the *words* for colors like *blue*. Color concepts are nonlinguistic in nature, and our ability to perceive the concept we call color depends on a specific location in the brain. Along with researcher Matthew Rizzo, the Damasios have found that when the tiny color-coordinating regions inside two fissures of brain tissue at the rear of the brain are damaged or destroyed, the result is achromatopsia, the defect suffered by EH, Damasio's patient with face agnosia.

As we saw in Chapter 7, achromatopsics, people with achromatopsia, may know that they once could imagine color, but they cannot now. They cannot even imagine what that imagining was like, because they have lost the ability to access the basic category called "color." So this defect is like an amnesia. A person suffering from some kinds of amnesia may not remember the identities of people she has otherwise known all her life. She may know that she once knew them. People will assure her, and she will believe them and incorporate that understanding into her worldview. But her experience is that she does not know them. Some forms of amnesia are permanent. The woman may never again have the experience of knowing this person is her mother, that person her daughter, another person her closest friend.

The same is true of achromatopsia. The damage to those special color-processing areas permanently destroys any ability of the person to experience the concept of color. So this kind of "natural experiment," as unfortunate as it is, has revealed to us something important about our brains and our ability to experience certain concepts. The concept of color, to be specific, depends on specific regions deep in the brain, areas that we know about and can point to. The information that codes for this experience, that represents it in the brain, is somehow contained in the neural networks hidden within two folds of brain tissue at the back of the brain.

But what about the words for colors? Do people lose access to that data when their color-processing regions are destroyed? Not at all. Achromatopsics are perfectly capable of using the words *blue, green, red, yellow*, and other names for colors. They can read them, write them, and speak them aloud. They can speak them in grammatically correct sentences, too, so they do not lose access to the syntactic rules for using color words. However, damage to other parts of the brain does destroy a person's ability to use color words.

One is the left posterior temporal cortex. As its name suggests, this is part of the brain that lies to the rear of the brain's left temporal lobe. (Recall that the temporal lobes lie to the brain's left and right sides, about where our ears are.) Another part of the brain that handles words for colors is the left inferior parietal cortex. This is the region of the brain that lies on the underside, which *inferior* means in medical jargon, of the left parietal lobe. (The parietal lobes are situated above the temporal lobes and behind the frontal lobes, arching from left to right across the top of the brain.) People with damage to these areas lose much of their ability to produce the proper word "shapes." When they try to say a word, it comes out phonemically distorted. This defect covers a wide range of categories, including the category of "color." For example, they will know that the sweater I am wearing is blue. If asked to name the color, though, they might say *buh* instead of *blue*.

Another brain region important for words denoting color lies close to, but is not a part of, the color-processing region at the back of the brain. People with brain lesions in this specific region suffer from a defect called *color anomia*. An *anomia* (from the Greek word *onoma*, meaning "name") is the inability to remember names. People with color anomia cannot match the words for colors with the colors themselves. Color anomics have not lost the ability to experience color in a normal fashion. If they are given a set of paint chips, for example, they can correctly arrange them by their different hues. If I have color anomia and someone gives me a black-and-white photo of a banana, and a set of paint chips, I will have no trouble picking the right chip for the banana in the picture. What's more, I could say aloud, "Bananas are yellow," or, "The banana was once a bright yellow. But after sitting for days on the blue kitchen counter top, it had begun turning black." I know the words for colors and can use them correctly in sentences.

What color anomics lack is the ability to hook the words to the colors. Suppose you say to me, "Yellow," and spread out a set of paint chips in front of me. I am just as likely to pick the green one as the yellow one. Or the chartreuse one. Or the blue one. The defect works in the opposite direction, as well. If you hand me the yellow paint chip, I may say, "Blue." Or, "Green." Or, "Um, orange?" Yet I will not hesitate to place the red paint chip next to the black-and-white photo of a children's Radio Flyer wagon.

Color anomics know color concepts; they experience colors. Their visual system works fine, including their retinas, color-processing areas, and their visual cortex at the very rear of the brain. The brain systems for forming words also function perfectly. So do the regions that contain the syntactical rules for sentence formation in whatever language they speak. Researchers know these parts of the brain are functioning well in color anomics. Nevertheless, people with color anomia cannot match the words for colors with the colors. It is clear that what does *not* work is some set of neurons that links together the concept and language regions. The convergence zones are damaged, say the Damasios. Without their connecting role between the brain's language-storage regions and color-processing regions, you and I and everyone else could not speak about the brilliant hues of the hot-air balloons in the azure New Mexico sky.

George Ojemann and the Brain's Language Regions

More than a century after the pioneering discoveries about the brain and language made by Paul Broca and Karl Wernicke, we are beginning to learn that the standard model of language processing in the brain, the model based in large part on Broca and Wernicke's work, is wrong. The brain creates, stores, and manipulates language in areas far removed from Broca's and Wernicke's. We now are beginning to have access to new, highly detailed maps of language function in the brain. One of the people who has pioneered the creation of these new maps is a neurosurgeon at the University of Washington in Seattle named George Ojemann. He has done it in large part by following in the footsteps of the other famous neurosurgeon originally from Washington State, Wilder Penfield.

What Ojemann and several colleagues have revealed is a picture of cortical brain function that meshes well with Antonio and Hanna Damasio's hypothesis of convergence zones. The resulting map is a blend of the old and the new. Broca's and Wernicke's areas, the old standbys of cortical language function, are still there. But there is also a mosaic of new language sites, many but not all of them in the left cerebral hemisphere, that resemble a pointillist painting or a "cerebral fingerprint."

Ojemann's work at mapping language centers in the brain is not his primary vocation. Like Wilder Penfield's before him, his ground-breaking work arises from what he does for a living: neurosurgery. He explains, "My clinical interest is in the surgical treatment of epilepsy. A fair number of these patients are awake when we operate on them. As you know, the brain has no pain sensors. So these [experiments] are all done during operations [to cure people with several and otherwise untreatable cases of epilepsy]."

Language and language functions are only a part of the brain mapping that Ojemann has done. "My main interest," he says, "is in using this particular clinical opportunity to investigate how the brain works. Actually, we've done a moderate number of studies, not just on language, but also on nondominant functions, in the nondominant hemisphere, spatial functions, for example. And we've also done a fair number of studies on memory changes."

Ojemann and other researchers today have at their disposal a variety of tools to create the new maps of cortical language function. "We use several different techniques," Ojemann explains. "First, there's electrical stimulation mapping. This is a technique for blocking functions in local areas of the brain, and then seeing if that piece or area has a function."

We have already seen how the Damasios, among others, use data that comes from "natural experiments" to explore the brain's language functions. These often change when specific areas of the brain are damaged, resulting in aphasias, for example. The losses of language ability that take place establish a link between the damaged brain area and the linguistic function that has been disrupted or lost.

Another source of this type of data is electrical stimulation of a cortical region during a brain operation. This is the kind of work first made famous by Wilder Penfield beginning in the 1930s. What Penfield did, in essence, was create temporary changes in specific brain areas. He then noted the motor, sensory, or mental function that seemed to be associated with that particular brain area. During operations to cure people of epilepsy, Penfield often used a microelectrode probe to stimulate different parts of the patient's exposed brain. He discovered that specific parts of the brain's motor cortex, for example, controlled very specific regions of the body: fingers, toes, eyelids, and so on. Penfield also uncovered areas that seemed to store different sensory memories: the smell of mom's apple pie, or the sound of a piano concerto.

Ojemann's "electrical stimulation mapping" uses the latest high-tech versions of this venerable technique. But it is not the only tool in his belt, as it were. Researchers like Ojemann also rely on physiological studies made with different types of brain-imaging technologies and electrical recording techniques. The studies are then matched with a person's language behavior and performance, or lack thereof, while he or she was being tested. The brain-imaging technologies being used include MRI and PET scans. The electrical techniques include *electroencephalography, electrocorticography,* and microelectrode recordings made during brain surgery. Ojemann has employed different versions of all three. He explains, "We use an imaging technique that involves recording electrical activity directly from the surface of the brain during surgery, as well as microelectrical recording of activity in certain brain regions. We use [this last technique] in areas we're going to take out of the brain," Ojemann says. "Obviously, we consider these brain areas nonessential, or we wouldn't be removing them [to cure epilepsy]."

Electroencephalography literally means "electrical writing in the head." The technique records the infinitesimal changes in the electrical signals emitted by the brain as it functions. As we have already seen, the brain is a kind of electrochemical supercomputer. Its neurons pass information among themselves by means of electrical signals that are triggered and maintained by chemical reactions. The hundred-trillion-plus synapses of the human brain, all firing off in an unbelievably complex pattern instant by instant, produce a myriad of subtle electrical signals that ripple across the brain.

The development of the first *galvanometers*, devices that can detect electrical currents, made it possible for researchers to detect weak electrical currents in the brain as far back as the 1820s. It was not until 1929, however, that a German psychiatrist named Hans Berger (1873–1941) invented a machine sensitive enough to track and measure these electrical signals, or "brain waves" as we commonly call them. That machine is called an electroencephalograph.

An electroencephalograph consists of a series of electrodes or electrical sensors that detect the brain's electrical activity, a machine that receives the signals and amplifies them, and a device to record the signals in some permanent form. This has long been a rotating paper-covered drum and a series of colored pens that chart the signals onto the paper. These days, though, it is more common to display the brain wave traces on a computer screen and store the data permanently on computer disk.

The electrode wires—the number employed varies, depending on the type of data being gathered—are first attached with glue or tape to various locations on the person's head. The other ends of the wires connect to the amplifier. The electrical impulses produced by the brain's activity are very small, in the range of one hundred microvolts (one ten-thousandth of a volt) or less. The amplifier detects the differences in electrical potential between pairs of electrodes and amplifies it a millionfold. The electroencephalograph then displays the results, either on paper with the colored pens or on a computer screen, as a series of oscillating, jiggling lines. This record is called an electroencephalogram, or EEG.

With this information a skilled doctor can determine the frequency of brain waves being detected. Researchers today classify brain waves into four major types. *Beta waves*, with a frequency greater than thirteen cycles per second, occur mainly in adults and are usually associated with the brain's sensory-motor areas. *Alpha waves*, from eight to thirteen cycles per second, occur usually in adults resting with their eyes closed and mind at rest. Both beta and alpha waves are most common in healthy, awake adults. *Theta waves*, from four to seven cycles per second, are most common in children aged two to five and in psychopaths. *Delta waves*, from one to three cycles per second, are commonly found in sleep states, in very young infants, and associated with some brain tumors. Some brain waves detected by an electroencephalograph reflect electrical activity happening in the brain's deep centers. Others are caused by activities as simple as eye movements.

In recent years computer technology has greatly enhanced the amount and quality of data researchers can acquire using EEGs. In particular, computerized EEGs can detect *evoked potentials*. These are the infinitesimal changes in voltage that occur as the brain responds to specific stimuli. The computer essentially "filters out" the "background noise" that otherwise obscures a researcher's detection of these minute changes in brain waves. Neuroscientists have used evoked potential EEGs to study stroke victims, people with brain tumors and multiple sclerosis, newborns, and the effect of language use on the brain's electrical activity.

Electrical stimulation of brain areas is not the same as an EEG. An EEG reading is a passive recording of the brain's ongoing electrical activity, often in response to specific tasks or actions. For example, a researcher taking EEG readings may first ask a subject to sit quietly with his eyes closed. The researcher takes her readings. Then she may ask the subject to open his eyes; she takes EEG readings. Then the subject may be asked to move his left forefinger, his right forefinger, and so on, all while the researcher takes readings. She might ask him to read silently a series of words flashed on a screen; or read the words out loud, or repeat a sequence of words from memory. The EEGs record the brain's electrical responses to these activities and sensory inputs.

By contrast, electrical stimulation is an active process. The researcher stimulates specific regions of the brain with tiny electrical impulses. Then the researcher notes the person's responses to these stimuli, perhaps with EEGs, perhaps with other techniques such as PET scans.

Ojemann in particular has used a variation of the EEG technique called electrocorticography, or ECoG. ECoG is a highly sophisticated technique for recording the electrical activity of individual neurons in the brain's various cortexes. Ojemann works with people suffering from epileptic seizures occurring in their temporal lobes, the two areas lying on the left and right sides of the brain. Standard drug treatments have not been able to control the seizures, and surgery is the next option for treatment. By using ECoG to map the different areas of the brain, Ojemann is able to find the precise area in the person's temporal lobe that is malfunctioning and causing the epileptic seizures. He then removes that tiny portion of brain tissue.

Following standard legal and ethical requirements, Ojemann first meets with a patient before the operation. He explains his additional goals, pointing out the scientific nature of the microelectrode recordings he wishes to do. Only when a patient gives informed, signed consent does Ojemann proceed. During the operation, he again asks the patient, who is conscious, for consent, letting the patient know when he is about to begin the microelectrode recordings. If a patient changes his or her mind at this point, and a few have, Ojemann abandons the scientific mapping portion of the operation and continues with the anti-seizure surgery.

The procedure itself begins with Ojemann, using local anesthesia so the patient remains conscious, opening a hole in the skull over the temporal lobe. He then uses ECoG to explore and map the temporal lobe's speech and memory functions. The entire process takes from two to three hours. His tools are highly sharpened and specially insulated tungsten microelectrodes. Their tips have a diameter of less than five microns (one micron, or millionth of a meter, is 0.00003937 of an inch!). A rod clamped to the patient's skull holds the electrode firm, and the electrode is remotely controlled using a hydraulic micromanipulator. The micromanipulator is essentially a special clamp that can raise and lower the electrode very tiny distances. With several patients Ojemann has used two electrodes at once, mounted together in the micromanipulator with their tips about two to four millimeters apart, about one-eighth of an inch or the thickness of a book of matches.

The rod-clamping device, of course, keeps the electrodes rock-steady in relationship to the skull. However, the brain tissue itself is in motion, too. It is alive and pulsates slightly with the movement of blood and fluids through it. So Ojemann and his colleagues came up with an ingenious device they call a "pressure foot." This is a piece of Plexiglas about one and a half centimeters in diameter, attached to the micromanipulator and lowered onto the surface of the brain. It places a very slight pressure on the cerebral surface, enough to reduce any wiggling while the electrode is in place, but not enough to restrict circulation of fluids through the area. Then the electrode or electrodes are lowered through a one-millimeter hole in the center of the pressure foot. A silver electrode is attached to the pressure foot, close to the central hole, and records the surface ECoG near the tungsten microelectrodes. Other more standard-sized electrodes are also placed directly on other areas of the cortex to record ECoGs and evoked potentials.

Once Ojemann has located a neuron or small neuron cluster whose electrical output has remained stable for several minutes, he begins the testing process. These recordings from "single units," as Ojemann has called them, each take from fifteen to thirty minutes. During this time the fully conscious patient is lying on one side (the right side if the brain's left hemisphere is being operated upon, or vice versa), his or her head on a padded head rest. Surgical drapes screen the area being operated on from the rest of the face and body. The patient is looking at the anesthetist and those carrying out the tests and can talk with them but cannot see the surgeon, the operating nurse, or the operation itself.

Using this rigorous, controlled scientific protocol, Ojemann and his colleagues have uncovered some exciting new information about how the brain stores language—and languages.

Fingerprints for Language

What Ojemann, the Damasios, and other neuroscientists have learned since the 1970s about the cortical organization of language is fascinating, to say the least. These discoveries not only dovetail with research involving people with brain damage; they also appear to substantiate the convergence zone HyperCard theory of Hanna and Antonio Damasio.

To understand what George Ojemann has found, we need to have some context. For more than a hundred years neuroscientists have clung to a standard model of language organization in the brain. As we noted earlier, Paul Broca and Karl Wernicke laid the groundwork for the model in the nineteenth century with their discoveries of the areas in the brain's left hemisphere that bear their names. To borrow a metaphor from the computer world, this model says that language processing in the brain takes place in a serial or linear fashion, moving in a line from one point to the next. It begins in Wernicke's area in the posterior temporal cortex, where the decoding of language concepts occurs. It then proceeds, says this standard model, to Broca's area on the left rear edge of the brain's frontal lobe, which governs the motor expression of spoken language.

But in recent years, research has revealed that the brain does not conform to this relatively simple model of language processing. For one thing, it is clear that the brain processes almost nothing in linear fashion. We now know, for example, that the visual cortex at the rear of the brain deals with images in a piecemeal way. It breaks down a visual image into its many different components, stores representational traces of those components in different neural regions, and then somehow recombines them as part of the recognition and memory processes.

In many ways, it now appears that the organization of language in the brain is similar to that of visual images. Language function is compartmentalized, and there are many more compartments than neuroscientists previously assumed. The compartments or clumps of neurons are each about the size of a grape. The cells in each grape-sized language area, says Ojemann, appear to be connected to other distant areas of the brain. Each patch of cells appears to specialize in one particular language-related function. One clump may recall verbs, while another recalls pronouns. One patch of language cells may deal with a specific grammatical rule, while another processes the words from a foreign language. The accompanying illustration shows the distribution in the brain of its many tiny language patches, as mapped by Ojemann.

Brain researchers have long known of one significant difference between language organization in the brain and other functions. Language functions are *lateralized*. That is, they are concentrated in one hemisphere of the brain and not spread equally through both of them, or *bilateralized*, as brain researchers would say. Most other sensory and motor functions are not concentrated in one hemisphere but are

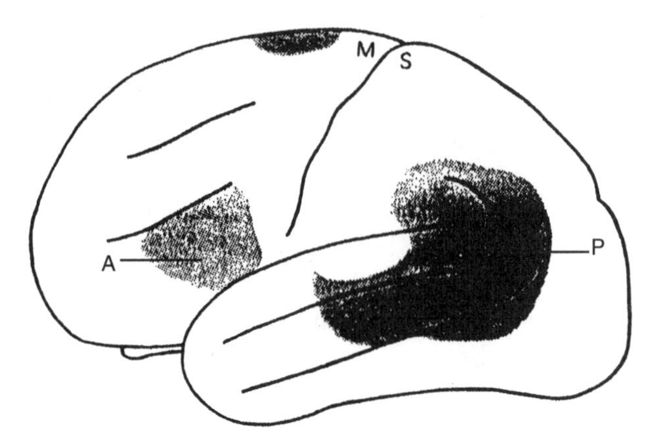

Location of essential cortical areas for language in the traditional textbook model, here as presented in Penfield and Roberts (1959), are indicated by shading. *A*, frontal (Broca's) language area; *P*, posterior (Wernicke's language area); *M* and *S*, motor and sensory cortex. Compare to language localization in an individual subject and variance in that localization across a population.
From Ojemann, George A. Cortical Organization of Language. *The Journal of Neuroscience* 11 (August 1991), p. 2284.

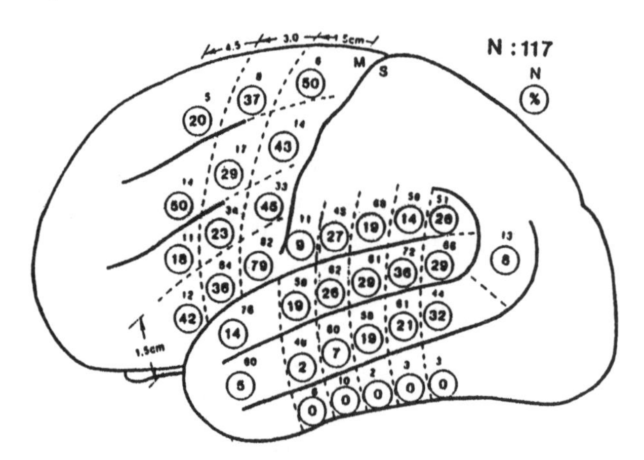

Variability in localization of sites essential for naming, based on electrical stimulation mapping in left, language-dominant hemisphere of 117 patients. Individual maps were aligned with reference to Rolandic cortex and end of Sylvian fissure. The cortex was then divided into zones represented by intersecting *solid* and *broken lines*. The *upper number* in each zone indicates the number of subjects in whom a site was tested in that zone; the *lower circled number* indicates the percentage of those subjects in whom naming errors were evoked at sites in that zone. *M* and *S* indicate motor and sensory cortex, respectively. From G. Ojemann et al. (1989).
From Ojemann, George A. Cortical Organization of Language. *The Journal of Neuroscience* 11 (August 1991), p. 2284.

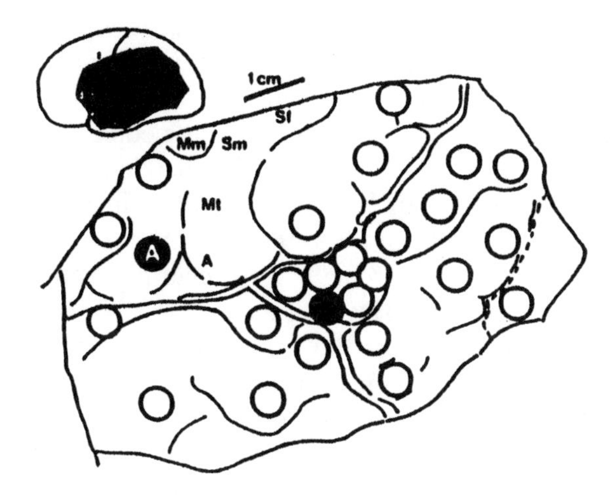

Location of two sites at which stimulation altered naming in left, dominant hemisphere of a 36-yr-old female subject. *Circles* are sites of bipolar stimulation through electrodes separated by 5 mm, using trains of biphasic square-wave pulses at 60 Hz, of 2.5 msec total duration, and 4 mA between pulse peaks. *Solid circles*, sites of repeated naming errors; *open circles*, no errors. *Solid circle* labeled *A*, naming errors, predominantly arrest of speech; *other solid circle*, anomia. *Letters* outside of the circles indicate evoked motor (*Mm, Mt, A*) and sensory (*Sm, Sf*) responses identifying Rolandic cortex. The *shaded area* in the *inset* indicates the location of intraoperative cortical exposure. Note site of repeated naming errors in superior temporal gyrus and lack of errors at immediately surrounding sites [from Ojemann, 1988; additional examples of localized essential areas for naming with sharp boundaries are presented in Ojemann (1983, 1991) and in G. Ojemann et al. (1989)]
From Ojemann, George A. Cortical Organization of Language. *The Journal of Neuroscience* 11 (August 1991), p. 2283.

bilateral in distribution, spread around through both the left and right cerebral hemispheres. However, the left cerebral hemisphere is the language hemisphere. This was one of Broca's great discoveries, as we saw earlier. A century of brain research has essentially confirmed it, and so does Ojemann's, but with some modifications.

Ojemann says, "The first issue is, 'Why lateralization?' Why is language function in humans concentrated in the left cerebral hemisphere instead of the right? Well, what we've found is that this lateralization of language is true in most people—but not everybody." The common belief has been that nearly all people have their language functions located in the left cerebral hemisphere, where Broca's and

Wernicke's areas are located. Broca's area, as we have seen, lies in the left frontal lobe, while Wernicke's area includes parts of the left temporal and parietal lobes, a region often called the temperoparietal cortex. It was assumed that most of the people who did not have lateralized language functions were left-handed. The percentage of right-handed people with language functions in the left hemisphere was thought to range from 60 to 90 percent.

The reality is a bit different. A very small percentage of people are left-handed because of early brain damage to their left frontal or parietal cortexes, the regions at the front and along the top of the brain. The developing infant brain is an incredibly plastic organ. When this kind of damage happens in early infancy, the brain will simply develop its language functions in the undamaged right hemisphere. When these people are excluded from surveys, it appears that there is no relationship between left-handedness and language lateralization. In other words, despite my left-handedness, I am just as likely to have my language functions located in my left hemisphere as is my right-handed wife.

It also seems that the percentage of people with "normal" lateralization of language in the brain is higher than most previous estimates. Fully 95 percent of all people have their language functions located in their brain's left hemispheres. But the rest of you . . . now, *you* are somewhat fascinating. Work by Ojemann carried out in 1988 shows that only 5 percent of people may have bilateral language functions, language regions in both sides of the brain. In most such cases, the language regions were mostly in the right hemisphere; the rest had some language functions in the right hemisphere, with most in the left.

For most people the vast majority of the grape-sized language compartments Ojemann has discovered in his electrical probes of human brains are in the temporal and parietal lobe regions of their brain's left hemisphere. But this is not a universal situation. A small but significant number of the grape-sized language areas are also found in the brain's right hemisphere. This does not invalidate the work of Broca, Wernicke, and many other brain scientists. There is no doubt that language is, for the most part, a lateralized brain function. Ojemann's work has simply given us a better picture of how other parts of the brain are also involved in creating and processing language.

One of Ojemann's most surprising findings from electrical stimulation studies is that the language areas are *individually* localized in the dominant language hemisphere. The physical arrangement of language functions in the brain differs from person to person. Even more interesting, says Ojemann, "the locations seem to be unique. We've related that variation not only to differences between males and females but also to differences in patients' verbal abilities." These patterns are as unique as fingerprints; call them "language brainprints," if you will, or a "language-print." We each have our own special pattern for language ability.

Ojemann is not sure why this great variability in language location exists, but he has offered some possible reasons. For one thing, each of us has a brain that is slightly different in form from any other. The folds in the cortex of my left temporal lobe, for example, will be different in shape and location from those of my brother, or my wife, or the man who lives down the street. That kind of variation is caused by small but well-understood variations in each person's genetic code. Our brains, like every other part of our body, develop according to a pattern that is guided by our genetic code. Each brain has the same overall structure that we explored in Chapter 5. But these tiny variations in each person's genetic code, called *polymorphisms* by geneticists, are what give each of us a brain with unique patterns of fissures and ridges.

But these genetic differences, says Ojemann, are not enough to account for the unique distribution patterns for the brain's multiple language patches. Though no one has yet been able to determine the extent to which they do, it is quite possible that our environment and experiences also play a role. From the moment of our birth, each of us lives through a unique set of experiences, and our brains process each and every one of them. Each sensory experience, each person we see, each sound we hear, each pain or pleasure we feel, the brain processes and stores. As it does so, it builds up its network of interconnected cells and neuron clusters. Our brains are very plastic during our infancy and early childhood. There is plenty of room for improvisation on the basic structure, as it were. As it responds to its particular set of experiences, different from every other person's set of experiences, each brain creates a network that is slightly different in structure and connections from every other. Ojemann has found as much variability in the distribution of language areas in children from ages four to ten as in adults. So it is clear that whatever causes our unique "brainprints" for language happens early in our lives.

Language Compartments

Hanna and Antonio Damasio and others have found that the front part of the left temporal cortex is dedicated to language. The particular language region Damasio has uncovered lies along the front and bottom of the left temporal lobe. It includes Brodmann areas 38, 21, 20, and 37. Research done by the Damasios has uncovered some fascinating facts about this language area.

For example, damage to these four parts of the temporal lobe makes it nearly impossible for a person to name *concrete entities*. (As a reminder, the Damasios define an "entity" as a person or thing.) People with lesions in this area of their brains cannot "get to" the names for unique entities (*Bill Clinton*), nor can they gain access to the common nouns for either natural or human-made varied entities at the level of categories (*kangaroo* or *skyscraper*). It is as if they cannot tap into their brain's "reference lexicon," the collection of words that denote concrete entities and actions.

This particular kind of brain damage is strictly a linguistic defect. It does not affect the person's knowledge of the entities. People with damage to these brain areas can describe the entity; they just cannot name it. The patients cannot say *kangaroo*; but if you ask them, "What's a kangaroo?" they can tell you that it's an unusual animal that lives in Australia, hops about, and has a pouch. They cannot name President Bill Clinton; but if you show them a picture of the man, they can tell you that he is young, handsome, the President, and from Arkansas. Still more interesting, they can give this description in a fashion that is completely grammatically correct. So the brain defect is linguistically selective: it does not affect syntax.

When the part of the left temporal lobe called Brodmann area 38 is damaged, another language deficiency occurs. The person's language defect is limited to the *retrieval of proper nouns only*, such as the names of people or places (*Jeffrey Wights; Lafayette, California; Mount St. Helens*). People with brain lesions in this specific area can still use common nouns in a perfectly normal fashion, and they have complete access to all the nonverbal knowledge associated with the entities behind the proper and common nouns. "That's a kangaroo," they will say when you show them a picture of the animal.

Brain lesions have these specific effects on language only when they occur in the left temporal lobe. Damage to the same regions in the right temporal lobe has no effect at all on this kind of "lexical access."

When George Ojemann carried out his mapping studies of living human brains using electrical stimulation, he found the same kind of "modular" organization. The brain stores different bits and pieces of language in different "filing cabinets." Ojemann calls them "essential areas" for specific language functions. His technique was fairly straightforward and effective. Ojemann would carry out tests on patients to gauge their ability to name objects, or to read words, or to determine the extent of their verbal memory.

At the same time he would be recording the activity of clusters of neurons at specific areas of their brains. Sometimes he would even be able to record the activity of single brain cells. Two-thirds of the neurons or neuron clusters he recorded changed their electrical activity *only during one test*. Conclusion? Those specific neurons or neuron clusters were dedicated to handling particular tasks. They were essential areas for specific linguistic functions. The brain contains essential areas for the specific task of naming objects in a specific language, as well. That includes a specific area for naming objects in American Sign Language. Thus, says Ojemann, the neurological system for specific languages includes both essential areas and widely scattered neurons and neuron clusters. Some of the latter are found in the brain's non-language-dominant hemisphere as well as in the dominant one.

The conclusion, says Ojemann, is almost inescapable: the brain organizes language into specific "modules" or tiny regions. Our language ability is not concentrated in Broca's area or Wernicke's area in the left hemisphere of the brain. Regions in the left side of the brain are indeed particularly rich in these centers of different language nodes. But neuron clusters for language exist elsewhere in the brain, as well.

Ojemann has also found some puzzling new features to the way the brain processes language. He says, "We have some brand new data that have not yet been published. We analyzed a series of microelectrical recordings of neuronal activity in each hemisphere during measures of language functions. We found that neurons in either hemisphere are active during language, but the ones in the dominant hemisphere are *active earlier*. They also show more *inhibition* in the places where we were recording."

Even when language regions on both sides of the brain became active, the language regions in the dominant, left hemisphere took the lead. First they would fire off, and then the other language patches in the brain followed suit. Meanwhile, some language centers actually decreased their activity while the patients were speaking or otherwise using their language abilities.

"Now, that's a little unexpected," says Ojemann, amused. "It's hard to imagine that the brain runs by decreasing activity rather than increasing it. But that's actually what we found, in the language-dominant hemisphere." When we think of the brain operating, processing data arriving from the senses or combining thoughts and memories into new creations, we naturally assume that the neurons are madly firing off electrical impulses. Those impulses in turn activate other neurons and continue to weave the complex tapestry of electrochemical events that constitute thought and memory. It is hard to imagine that the activity of some regions of the brain is actually suppressed rather than juiced up. In fact, the inhibition or suppression of neural activity is not at all uncommon in the brain.

One of the best-known brain chemicals, known as GABA, suppresses the activity of certain kinds of brain cells. When a person gets drunk, the excessive alcohol acts to suppress the release of GABA. That in turn means that brain areas ordinarily slowed down are not. This is why drunks act loudly, aggressively and in a generally offensive fashion. A drunk person passes out when the alcohol level in the brain gets so high that other brain regions shut down. What Ojemann has found is that some language regions in the brain are also naturally suppressed during language functioning. No one yet knows why.

Finally, Ojemann's microelectrical probes of the brain have revealed some intriguing supporting evidence for the Damasios' convergence zone theory. As we discovered in the last chapter, in this theory the brain stores different bits and pieces of a sensory experience or concept in different parts of the brain, and separate "coordinating" regions or convergence zones contain the "codes" that bring the pieces together in our consciousness.

According to Ojemann, the different parts of the brain's language systems seem to operate in parallel, rather than in a linear fashion. This is similar in some ways to the new supercomputers that use parallel processing of problems, rather than the standard serial or linear processing of most computers. A standard computer, like the one on my desk, basically handles its activities one step at a time. It moves from one step to the next, like a Buddhist fingering prayer beads strung on a piece of twine.

Parallel processing computers work in a very different fashion. They first break a problem down into all its specific pieces. The computer then works on all the different parts simultaneously, combining the results together for the final conclusion. It appears, says Ojemann, that the brain works the same way to create, store, and use language. He has found very little experimental or observational evidence for the textbook model of linear language processing we encountered earlier. As we recall, this model supposes that the brain processes language one step at a time, moving from rearmost to frontal regions of the brain. Ojemann's microelectrode recordings of brain activity during naming and other language tasks clearly reveal a parallel processing kind of activity, not a linear back-to-front procedure in the brain.

This appears to be clear observational support for the existence of convergence zones. Different areas of the brain are dedicated to handing specific components of language ability: naming, verbal memory, grammar rules, storage of specific phonemes like /k/, /ə/, and /p/ (but not the word *cup*), and even different storage areas for these components in different languages. Given the right stimulus, the brain activates all the necessary regions, nearly simultaneously, in order for us to understand spoken or signed speech, and then to speak ourselves. The only logical way that this can take place is for convergence zones to coordinate the activity.

When it comes to language, our brains therefore operate like parallel computers, or like a software stack of HyperCards.

Language and Consciousness

The HyperCard stack or convergence zone model of brain function offers an elegant explanation for how our brain creates and uses language. An increasing amount of hard scientific data appears to support this hypothesis. But an even more exciting—and controversial—conclusion can be drawn from the work by Ojemann, the Damasios, and others. It appears that there is a deep and powerful connection between our conscious awareness of events or entities and our ability to create and use language. Consciousness and language may well be linked.

Consciousness, in its most basic sense, is awareness: awareness of yourself and of the world outside yourself. Untold numbers of philosophical papers and books have been written about the nature of consciousness. Most of us nonphilosophers would find most of them boring. Some of these studies and speculations about consciousness are crackpot at best. But others are exciting and thought-provoking explorations of this state we all possess but few of us ever stop to think about.

Antonio Damasio has thought about it. Damasio thinks we become *conscious* of an event or entity, either in real time or in memory, when we *attend to* the set of co-activated sequences. That is, the sequence of neural activity representing an experience becomes enhanced. It stands out against the rest of the brain's ongoing background activity. It is a bit like noticing the moving and flashing lights of an airplane against the star-speckled darkness of the night sky. Or, think of yourself sitting in your apartment's living room. You've lived there for quite some time, and the smells of your surroundings have faded from your consciousness. Suddenly, you smell smoke! A set of neural patterns becomes enhanced and stands out from the brain's background activity. You attend to it. You are conscious of an experience.

Now, think about driving across town. Are you vividly conscious of every stoplight you stop at, every time you tap the brake or the accelerator, every lane change you make? You stop, you tap, you change lanes, but rarely are you fully conscious of these actions. We all drive "unconsciously," of course. Most of the time, we do fine. We are not conscious of those events because they do not stand out from the brain's background activity. Until, of course, someone in a pickup truck runs the red light ... and smashes the Volkswagen that just entered the intersection ... and the truck becomes airborne and, as you stare out your windshield, it seems to be bearing right down on your suddenly vulnerable nose ...!

However, language is not necessarily a requirement for consciousness, says Damasio. "We don't need language in order to have some kind of *basic* consciousness," he asserts. "I'm convinced that some animals have consciousness—and I don't just mean our pets, either. However, they do not have the consciousness at the same level that humans do. Language plays a role in the level or sophistication of consciousness. That's because language provides one more level of *distancing*, if you will, of the person from the object. It distances something we call *self* from objects 'out there.' "

We will explore this question of animals, consciousness, and language in more detail a little later. What Antonio Damasio says about *human* consciousness and *human* language, though, is worth noting. "I believe there is a kind of nonverbal sense of self," he says, and "language creates the *I* of that sense of self."

If Antonio Damasio is right, then infants, in the process of acquiring language, also create their *I*.

Part Three

The Birth of Language

Chapter 10

From Cries to Words

We adults do not remember how as infants we learned language. As we grew from infants to children to teenagers to adults, we somehow lost the memories of those early efforts. The reason has to do with the way we learn to perceive the world around us. Adults do not think in the same way children do, much less infants. More to the point, adults do not perceive the world the way infants do. What we learn changes the way we perceive reality. Our brains develop "filters" that screen out sensory and other inputs that we have learned are not important. These filters are not literal screens, blocking certain sensory information. Rather, the brain somehow learns to ignore certain data. This kind of negative learning, like all learning, is a still-mysterious process taking place within and among clusters of brain cells.

Our memory and social filters are analogous to the perceptual filters animals use in their natural environments. A deer may pay little attention to the buzzing of bees or the flickering sight of a butterfly. But it will certainly pay attention to the odor of a cougar. A cougar is an immediate threat to the deer's survival. It makes eminent sense for the deer's brain to know that smell and have specific reactions developed to respond to it. Butterflies and bees do not have the same meaning to a deer.

In a somewhat similar sense, humans have also developed perceptual and sensory filters. In a deer or cougar such filters are mostly "hard-wired" into the brain. That is, the animals' genetic codes carry information that "programs" the brain's neurons and neuron connections to detect or ignore certain stimuli. Humans also have hard-wired filters. Like all animals with eyes, for example, we have certain clusters of neurons in the visual cortex at the back of our brains that detect specific types of lines and edges in a visual scene. The human genetic code contains instructions that build those filters right into the brain.

Our social filters, on the other hand, are learned. For example, in American society men learn to "see" women in a way that differs from the way they "see" men. Sometimes that means not seeing a woman or women at all. They become "invisible" to men because women are judged not as important as men. Sometimes men see women primarily, or even exclusively, in a sexual context. Again, this is a cultural filter, which the brain uses to determine what is important and what is not.

Our individual loss of memory of how we learn to speak probably falls somewhere between hard-wired and learned filters. We have no particular survival reason to remember how we learned language. Therefore we have no strong biological imperative to do so. Furthermore, as we move from infancy to young childhood, the way we perceive the world inexorably begins to change.

Those social filters start to develop early in our lives. We quickly begin learning what our parents believe we ought to know, and feel, and think. Then we discover what our young friends say we ought to know, feel, and think. When we reach grade school, we learn about society's do's and don't's. By the time we reach adulthood, whatever memories we may have of how we learned language are long gone, along with our memories of our first steps and our birth. And even if those memories do still exist in some neuronal circuit in our brain, we do not have a way to get to them. It is a bit like having a computer whose basic operating system or program has been erased or changed. Billions of bytes of data may be sitting on the computer's hard disk, but there is no way to get at it.

And so I watch and listen, with utter fascination, as my young grandson makes his first halting attempts at language. For several months he has been babbling, creating vowel and consonant sounds, stringing them together in meaningless syllables. Soon his attempts will become more confident, more meaningful. But exactly how is he doing this? What process takes place in his brain? What role does genetic hardwiring play, and what is the role of his environment, the society in which he moves like a fish through water?

If only I could remember . . . but I can't.

Early Research

We have been fascinated and puzzled by this process for untold centuries. The first serious scientific attempts to explain the birth of language go back more than two hundred years. Even before that, at least one remarkable man offered some startlingly sophisticated suggestions about how infants create language.

His name was Akbar the Great, and he was the Mogul Emperor of India. He was born in 1542 and became emperor when he was only fourteen years old. Over the next six decades his armies swept across India and the neighboring lands. By the time of his death in 1605 his empire stretched from the eastern reaches of modern-day India and the Bay of Bengal to the country today known as Afghanistan, and from northern India to its southern tip. Akbar was more than a military genius, however. He was a learned man. His reign was marked by religious tolerance, administrative reform, and a blossoming of the arts and sciences in India.

One of the subjects that fascinated Akbar the Great was language. He believed that infants learned language by listening to others, and that children who were isolated from other humans would not be able to speak. A contemporary account asserts that he went so far as to carry out a human experiment to prove his hypothesis. The *Akbarnama* relates that:

> some who heard this [hypothesis] appeared to deny it. . . . [Akbar the Great] had a *serai* [or mansion] built in a place which civi-

> lized sounds did not reach. The newly born were put into that place of experience, and honest and active guards were put over them. For a time, tongue-tied wet-nurses were admitted there. As they had closed the door of speech, the place was commonly called the Gang Mahai [the dumb-house]. [Four years later] he went with a few special attendants to the house of experiment. No cry came from that house of silence, nor was any speech heard there. In spite of their four years, they had no part of the talisman of speech, and nothing came out except the noise of the dumb.

Anyone attempting that kind of experiment today would be arrested for child abuse, and rightly so.

In Europe the first systematic attempts to gather information about the development of language in infants date back to the late eighteenth century. These early approaches to the study of child language used parents' written diaries of observations about their children. The earliest known such diary was composed by the philosopher Dietrich Tiedemann (1748–1803). Tiedemann kept a written record of his son Friedrich's first two years, including his earliest attempts at speech. The diary spans dates from 1782 to 1784. In one of the first entries, when Friedrich was about six months old, Tiedemann noted his son's earliest emotional expressions:

> On February 10th [1782] he showed the first signs of surprise and approval; so far his only expressions of pain, anger, impatience, and pleasure had been crying, writhing, laughing. Now, when he saw something new and delightful, he greeted it with the exclamation "ach!"—the natural sign of admiration.

A month later, when his son was seven months old, Tiedemann wrote that young Friedrich began "to articulate consciously and to repeat sounds. His mother said to him the syllable 'Ma'; he gazed attentively at her mouth, and attempted to imitate the syllable."

By November 1782, according to Tiedemann's diary, his son was saying "Mama" and "Papa" and knew to whom the words referred. Friedrich was now about fifteen months old. When he was nineteen months old Tiedemann wrote: "At the sight of an object, he would repeat its name if he had frequently heard it, but he still found it hard to pronounce words of several syllables."

On the 30th of July Friedrich finally succeeded in uttering complete, though short, sentences, for example: "There he stands"; "There he lies." At this point the boy was not quite two years old.

On February 14, 1784, Tiedemann stopped writing his observations of his son's linguistic advances. "Other business [prevents] me from their continuation," he wrote. "I greatly desire that others may make similar ones."

Others did. And still do.

Learning How Children Learn to Speak

It has not been easy. Linguists regularly use several standard techniques to gather linguistic information from adults. They include carefully structured interviews; compiling a representative sampling of words (called a *corpus*) from a language; historical or linguistic reconstructions of languages; and carrying out various kinds of experiments and tests with native speakers. However, many of these methods will not succeed with children, much less infants. For example, many kinds of experimental testing routines simply do not work. The abilities of young children to pay attention or remember instructions are not well developed. Neither can youngsters below the age of three make clear judgments about their own language abilities. Then there's the common but frustrating problem often encountered by linguists, psychologists, and parents. Children will often stop talking as soon as you turn on a tape recorder, point a camera at them, or offer the phone ("Here's Grandpa—say hello!").

What is a linguist to do? Quite a bit, in fact, in the last several decades. The tape recorder, despite some children's aversion to them, was one of the first such breakthroughs. In 1930 German researchers developed the first practical tape recorder, using magnetized plastic tape. As these new devices became available to scientists, linguists and psychologists began to use them to gather a wealth of raw data on infant language acquisition. Today audio tapes and recorders are relatively cheap, reliable, and unobtrusive. Researchers may attach small radio-microphones to children's clothing or place them in strategic places in a room. The recording equipment can then be kept out of sight in a separate room or a closed closet.

Audio recorders have their drawbacks, though. One is the aforementioned "recorder shyness syndrome." A more important difficulty is a lack of context for the child's utterances. What exactly is going on when a child says, "Fell down"? Did the child fall down? Did the research assistant fall down? Perhaps it was a pile of building blocks, or a jacket hanging on a wall-hook. If all the researcher has is the tape and the transcript, who knows?

The increasingly common use of video cameras helps solve these puzzles. Having videotapes of what the child is doing or seeing makes it possible to interpret more accurately what he or she is saying. Videotapes also can reveal small nonverbal gestures and other body language cues. Of course, video also has its drawbacks. It can be obtrusive. Faulty lighting or camera placement can mean the loss of helpful information. And high-quality video equipment can be expensive.

The single most important advance in language acquisition research, though, will undoubtedly be the personal computer. Child-language researchers face one huge and daunting problem. Collecting and transcribing data samples uses up enormous amounts of time. It can take ten hours or more to transcribe and edit just one hour's worth of audiotaped conversation. And if the researchers or their graduate assistants are working with videotapes and have to note all the visual cues—well, that is enough to make a linguistics or psychology graduate student want to switch fields and become a medical doctor.

The computer is changing all that. It is now possible, for example, to transcribe tape-recorded information directly into a computer file. The computer files can then be analyzed and edited with sophisticated software. Researchers can also easily copy the files and pass on the data to their colleagues.

Moreover, linguistic researchers can now use computers to carry out the same kinds of analysis on video images. Some of today's desktop computers far surpass the mini and mainframe computers of the 1960s and 1970s in raw processing power and memory capacity. Scientists can now digitize still and moving images, store them as computer files, and then analyze them in great detail.

Another computer advance that is helping researchers is CHILDES, the Child Language Data Exchange System. This is an international computer data network for people studying language acquisition in children and infants. Researchers around the world can store copies of their data in this central database. They can get copies of other researchers' data, study it for their own purposes, apply it to their own research, and then pass their new finding back into CHILDES. The result, hopefully, will be a great savings in time and money, easy access to new and relevant information, and higher standards of data analysis.

Linguistic researchers studying language acquisition in children usually make use of two main techniques to obtain their data. The first is called *naturalistic sampling*. In this technique the researchers gather samples of a child's spontaneous use of language or prelinguistic vocalizations. The child may be in familiar surroundings, such as the family living room or a playground. On the other hand, researchers may bring the child and his or her parents to a specialized room filled with toys. This allows the researchers to make fully effective use of recording equipment. The room may have windows with one-way glass. Researchers can watch and film without the child's knowledge—and, more important, without their presence affecting the child's natural language use.

Naturalistic sampling can provide the researchers with plenty of information about how the child produces speech and vocalizations. It does have drawbacks, though. For example, samples never contain everything, so researchers can miss some important piece of information about the child's language development. Also sampling gives researchers little, if any, information about how children understand what they are hearing.

The other main technique researchers use is *experimentation*. Many researchers now apply the techniques of experimental psychology to the study of infant language acquisition. The researcher formulates a hypothesis about some aspect of children's ability to understand or use language. Then the researcher sets up a task for the subjects to carry out that will presumably shed light on the truth or falsity of the hypothesis. The researcher recruits subjects who perform the task, he makes the observations, then carries out a statistical analysis and comes up with some conclusions.

The main problem with the experimentation approach is that humans in the lab do not necessarily respond to stimuli as they would outside the lab. It is extremely difficult to control all the variables that might arise. This makes it just as difficult as it is with sampling to extrapolate from specific data gained in a laboratory setting to how children acquire and use language in the hustle and bustle of the real world. For example, researchers must constantly be on the lookout for *observer effects*. To what degree, in other words, does their very presence affect the responses of their young subjects?

One way to factor out observer effect is to stay out of the picture. Researchers often observe their subjects from a distance, using video cameras or one-way glass, as the youngsters' parents or caregivers help the children carry out the actual task at hand. Linguists studying language acquisition have to be cautious in their conclusions. Their work can take many years to reach fruition. And if they are good scientists, they constantly look for new experimental and observational methods that can tightly control as many variables as possible.

Despite all these difficulties, many researchers have had considerable success in learning more about what happens during the first few months and years of life, as a child enters the realm of true language.

The First Twelve Months

With his first cries at birth, Ryan Patrick Nash, like all infants, began the journey into the universe of verbal language. The journey is not one of random steps. The process of human language acquisition follows an ordered sequence of specific stages that lead to a child's first words, phrases, and sentences. This may seem self-evident, but the scientific evidence for the precise sequence did not surface until the late 1970s. What is particularly fascinating about the sequence for human language acquisition is its overall similarity. No matter what language community the infant lives in—English, Russian, Urdu, or Polynesian—the sequence is the same.

This is especially true during the infant's first twelve months or so of life. Different researchers who study language acquisition in infants tend to come up with their own specific timetables. The accompanying chart illustrates three fairly typical examples. The differences that appear in the chart are the result of how the researchers organized and categorized their data. And the data they gather come from real infants, each of whom has his or her own particular "timetable" for learning how to speak the mother tongue. Each child is unique and develops language abilities at an individual pace. Overall, though, the process seems to be much the same everywhere.

Timetables for Talking

Month	Crystal	Oller	Dworkin
0-1	I: Basic Biological Stage	Phonation Stage	Crying Stage
1-2			Crying and Cooing
2-3	II: Cooing and Laughing	Cooing Stage	
3-4			
4-5		Expansion Stage	Laughing and Gurgling
5-6	III: Vocal Play		
6-7		Canonical Babbling Stage	Repeating Sounds
7-8	IV: Babbling		
8-9			
9-10			Repeating Words/First Words
10-11	V: Melodic Utterance		
11-12			
12-13			True Speech Begins
13-14			
14-15			
15-16			
16-17			
17-18			

In *The Cambridge Encyclopedia of Language*, David Crystal presents a timetable for language acquisition that divides the process into five major stages: *basic biological sounds; cooing and laughing; vocal play; babbling*; and *melodic utterances*.

Another timetable comes from D. Kimbrough Oller and colleagues at the Mailman Center for Child Development at the University of Miami in Miami, Florida. Since the early 1980s they have examined the way hearing and deaf babies babble, compared babbling of infants from different languages, and explored the similarities and differences between human infant babbling and the vocalizations made by non-human species. The result has been a wealth of new understanding about the first few months of language creation by human beings.

This research has led Oller to propose a somewhat different sequence of events for the development of language. His timetable focuses specifically on the rise of babbling, of course, and it includes four stages: the *phonation* stage, similar to Crystal's *biological sounds* stage; the *cooing* stage; the *expansion* stage; and the *canonical* ("official" or "authentic") *babbling* stage.

Still another variation on the stages of language acquisition comes from Dr. Paul Dworkin. Dworkin is chair of pediatrics at St. Francis Hospital and Medical Center in Hartford, Connecticut, and head of the division of general pediatrics at the University of Connecticut. In a 1992 article in *American Baby* magazine he offers a timetable for infant language acquisition that includes nine stages during a child's first four years. These stages of development cover considerably more time than do the first two timetables, which go no further than eighteen months. The first six stages in Dworkin's timetable include *undifferentiated crying; differentiated crying and cooing; laughing, chuckling, and babbling; imitating sounds; imitating words and speaking first words;* and *the beginning of true speech*.

Despite the different timetables offered by different researchers, nearly all of them agree on this point: infants learn their mother tongue in a fairly predicable pattern. Even when we take into account the individual variability of each child's journey into language, it tends to go like this:

1. First, we cry. Crying begins by being undifferentiated, then becomes more specific (hunger, fear, sleepy, dirty diaper, and so on). We are only a few weeks old. We are not yet able to make any kind of truly linguistic sound. The sounds we make are purely biological.
2. By the time we are one to two months old, we begin making sounds that sound a little like vowels. At first these are formed at the front of the vocal tract (sounds like /u/). By the time we are two to three months old, we begin cooing.
3. We begin making vowel-like sounds further back in the mouth (like /ə/, /a/, and /ɑ/) and start gurgling, laughing, and chuckling. We are about four to six months old now, able to imitate the sounds made by our parents and to change pitch and inflection.
4. Simple vowel-consonant combinations follow, such as /mɒ/ (*ma ma ma ma*), /bɒ/ (*ba ba*), and /dɒ/ (*dada*). We sound as though we are starting to babble. We are about six to eight months old now, and our language facilities are rapidly developing.
5. Around this time we begin to take up serious babbling, what Oller calls canonical babbling. We string vowel-consonant combinations together and repeat them over and over. We probably understand what some words mean. Our brain's cognitive, memory, and linguistic regions have developed to the point where a word now becomes associated with an entity. We may understand that *bottle* means the bottle with the

milk, for example, and that *mama* is asssociated with the mother-person.
6. Between about nine months to a year, we speak our first words. We are beginning to master true speech.

Then language ability begins to explode. By our eighteenth month we have a vocabulary of about twenty to fifty words and can understand probably five times as many. By the time we are two our vocabulary probably exceeds two hundred words; by age three it has reached a thousand. Why the explosive increase in vocabulary? Throughout our first two to three years, the brain is undergoing tremendous growth. This certainly plays a part. At the same time, the more words we learn and the more mature our grammatical ability to combine words into phrases and sentences becomes, the more words we are *able* to learn and comprehend. We are lifting up our language ability by our bootstraps.

In the Beginning

The infants of many animal species are born fully prepared to take on the world. Their motor and muscular systems are well developed; they begin walking within hours after birth. Their senses of smell, sight, hearing, and taste are already mature. Their brains, as we noted earlier, are already "hard-wired" with the ability to make the sounds of communication needed for survival.

Not so with human infants. After nine months in the womb a human baby is still not "mature" enough to make a go of it in the world. Even its skull is not fully formed. That is why newborns have that "soft spot" in the middle of their heads; the bones have not completely grown together there yet. The nervous system of a newborn infant is unable to provide any semblance of fine motor control, and the muscle system is undeveloped in many ways. Newborns cannot lift their heads, or crawl (much less stand up and walk), or talk.

Other things they can do well. For example, they can grab a bar or our fingers and hold on with a death grip. This is a handy survival reflex for a primate whose parents spend much of their lives in trees, and the reflex lives on. Infant humans also have well-developed sensory systems, at least for stimuli that mean staying alive. They can smell the difference between mom and some other human. They can see much better than researchers once thought: for example, they can identify their mother's face and distinguish between faces of different people. They also taste the difference between sweet and bitter, clearly prefering sweet and hating bitter. That, too, makes, survival sense; many poisonous plants have a bitter taste.

Infants can also hear sounds, and some sounds they hear better than others. They seem to have a particularly sensitive capacity to hear speech sounds. One way researchers have uncovered this sensitivity to speech is by means of head-movement tests to observe those sounds that regain a child's interest. They begin by exposing an infant to a particular sound, repeated over and over again, such as /bɑ/ /bɑ/ /bɑ/ and so on. After a few moments the infant, clearly becoming bored, looks away or begins doing something else. The researchers then alter the sound a bit, replacing the /bɑ/ with a /pɑ/, for example. At once the infant looks up again with renewed interest. This is a different sound, and the child can clearly distinguish it.

Babies are also particularly attuned to high-pitched sounds. They clearly prefer such sounds to those of a lower pitch; they like them and quickly respond to them. Not surprisingly, parents almost instinctively talk to their infants in high-pitched sounds. Perhaps we are genetically programmed to do so, just as infants appear to be genetically predisposed to prefer such sounds. Or perhaps we quickly but unconsciously learn that the baby responds to us much more quickly when we talk like Mickey Mouse rather than Lou Rawls. In any case, "baby talk" the world over uses high-pitched sounds.

The noises made during the first few weeks of life are directly related to the infant's biological state and activities. Researchers usually categorize these sounds as either *reflexive noises* or *vegetative noises*. Reflexive noises signal that the infant is experiencing certain physiological or emotional states. The sounds an infant makes when it is hungry, in pain, or feeling some other discomfort are reflexive noises. Sounds that signal eating, excreting, breathing, and other bodily actions concerned with physical survival are vegetative noises. They include burping, swallowing, sucking, and coughing. Researchers have studied these biological sounds in considerable detail.

During the first two or three weeks of a child's life, parents often find it difficult to interpret the meaning of their infant's cries. That is because this crying is *undifferentiated*. The infant does not yet have enough motor control of the vocal tract to vary the pitch or intensity of its cries.

By about four weeks of age, infants have gained enough motor control in the vocal tract to create different cries for different stimuli. Infants of this age typically have a wide range of cries, indicating fear, boredom, hunger, pain, loneliness, dirty diapers, and other discomfiting situations. An infant's typical basic cry is a series of pulses, each about a second long, separated by short pauses. The sounds are very similar to the vowel [a]. Cries of pain have a shorter rhythm than those of hunger. Discomfort cries are about one-half second long and grouped in very short sequences. Vegetative sounds are even more brief, about one-quarter of a second in duration, and tend to contain more consonant-like sounds.

The infant is not making sounds that are even close to the building blocks of language. However, even these basic biological noises have something important in common with the sounds of language. These pulsing cries of hunger, fear, or pain have a rhythm. This is not surprising. A rhythmic sequence is a natural by-product of the way the sounds are produced. The infant uses his or her vocal cords, more properly called vocal folds, to modulate a stream of air passing through them. The pulsating opening and closing of the vocal folds of the larynx produces a rhythmic quality to the sounds. It also makes the pitch vary in a regular pattern. All of these—rhythm, pitch patterns, and modulation of exhaled breath by the vocal folds—are basic characteristics of verbal speech.

THE COOING BABY

Somewhere between the fourth and eighth weeks of life, newborn infants begin making other sounds besides crying. During the first month or so, infants produce sounds by moving air through the front part of the mouth. These tend to sound like /u/, as in *boot* or *coo*, which is why Oller and other researchers call this the cooing stage. Cooing consists of consonant-like sounds made toward the back of the mouth, sometimes with a nasal quality, followed by short vowel-like sounds. Infants now begin performing the initial activities needed to create verbal language: moving the tongue, vertically and horizontally, and the lips. They begin responding to the smiles and speech of their mother and father, other adult caregivers, and siblings.

By about eight weeks infants begin making other vowel-like sounds. As they gain more and more motor control of the vocal apparatus, they can make vowel-like sounds from the middle and back of the mouth—sounds similar to /ə/, /a/, and /ɑ/. They may create these sounds by accident at first, as they breathe in and out. Oller has labeled this period the phonation stage and calls such noises "comfort sounds." Other researchers have called them "quasi-resonant nuclei" or "quasi-vowels," and they are probably the precursors to the production of vowels. Infants at this early age still do not have control of their lips and cannot make plosive consonant-like sounds, so it is rare for them to produce syllables with consonants and vowels combined. But that is about to change.

Infants next begin to string cooing sounds together into sequences that sound a little like syllables, especially in sound sequences like [ga] and [gu] and [da]. By the age of about four months, most babies have begun laughing and gurgling. These are still basically biological and not language sounds. Clearly, though, the infant is gaining muscle control of the different parts of the vocal tract.

And what is taking place with infants born deaf? If their parents are also deaf, and speak in sign language, many deaf infants by now are beginning to carry out motions with their hands and arms that are analogous to what hearing infants do with their vocal tracts. This parallel development of signing skills in deaf infants is one of the more remarkable and exciting discoveries in recent years. We will explore this discovery in more detail in the next chapter.

Baby Begins Babbling

During this period the infant's cooing sounds begin to evolve into something new. The sounds of vocal play are longer and steadier than those of cooing. Simple observation reveals that the infant is having fun making these new and more complex sounds. These new sound segments are longer than cooing, lasting more than a second. They consist of a wide variety of frequently repeated vowel and consonant sounds, starting at a high pitch with glides from high to low. Some are nasal, like the /m/ in /mamama/, created when the mouth's soft palate at the back of the mouth lowers so that air vibrates in the infant's nose. Others are fricative sounds, such as the /f/ in fafafa; this is the kind of sound produced when the tongue is held close to the teeth or top of the mouth and creates audible friction. Other sounds are uvular, made with the back of the tongue pressed against the uvula, which hangs down at the front of the throat, like the /ʀ/ sound in the French word *rue*; or labial sounds made with both lips, such as the /b/ in /baba/. The variety of sounds the infant makes changes from day to day. As time goes on, the infant begins combining sounds into longer and longer sequences.

According to Oller, who has called this period in the infant's life the expansion stage, babies now begin creating a wide variety of new sounds. Squeals, growls, whispers, yells, labial trills and vibrants—more commonly known as "raspberries!"—all begin appearing in their sound repertoire. They also begin using sounds that are more like vowels than are the comfort sounds of the phonation stage. At this point they are still not creating full syllables, but they are getting closer. Some of the sounds infants make at this point are what Oller calls *marginal babbling*. By that he means that the noises appear to sound like babbling, but they are not quite to that stage. For as we will soon discover, babbling is not a stage in speaking that has fuzzy boundaries. Both Oller and other researchers have discovered that true babbling has specific characteristics.

Infants now begin to imitate and repeat sounds their parents make. Mom says *mama* and baby Ryan will repeat it. Delighted, of course, mom says it again, with a big encouraging smile. And yes! Ryan repeats it! *Mama! Mama!* With a big smile in return. Ryan doesn't understand what *mama* means, but he knows that that he is getting great feedback from the mother-figure. Over the next several weeks, he will learn how to change vocal inflection and pitch as he repeats various sounds and words. In this phase infants appear to be talking, but they are not. They have not yet made the immense cognitive leap that connects the word with the object, person, or event. But it will happen soon.

By the sixth month of life, infants have begun accumulating a rather large sound repertoire. At two months they could make vowel-like sounds. At about six months they are beginning to add consonant-like sounds such as [b], [d], [m], [n], and [p]. And then, sometime between the sixth and seventh months, the expansion or verbal play stage segues into babbling.

The change is clear and dramatic. Parents can tell the difference almost at once. Basically, babbling is the production of sequences of identifiable vowel and consonant sounds. The difference between verbal play and babbling is one of content and repetition. Oller calls this the canonical babbling stage. Unlike the expansion stage's marginal babbling or the sounds the infant makes in the phonation and cooing stages, canonical babbling is full-fledged. It involves consonants as well as vowel sounds, strung together in sequences such as /mɒmɒmɒmɒ/ (*mamamama*) and /dɒdɒdɒdɒ/ (*dadada*). Babbling infants use a smaller set of sounds than in verbal play, but they use them over and over. Sound sequences that use the same consonant sound over and over, such as /mɒmɒmɒmɒ/, /dɒdɒdɒdɒ/, and /bɒbɒbɒ/ (*bababa*) are examples of *reduplicated babbling*. *Variegated babbling* is the production of sound sequences in which the consonants and vowels change from syllable to syllable, such as sequences /mɒnɒmɒnɒ/ (*manamana*), /dɒbɒdɒbɒ/ (*dabadaba*), and (*dabadaba*), and lɪpu/(*lipu*).

One of the most important aspects of babbling is its rhythm. As we just discovered, babies create rhythmic sounds from the moment they are born. The very construction of the vocal folds leads infants to make rhythmic, pulsating little cries. The rhythm of babbling and of speech grows from our natural ability to make rhythmic sounds. Babbling itself has the rhythmic texture of genuine language. That is a large part of its charm and importance. The babbling child not only creates sounds that resemble syllables, the basic building blocks of words, but uses them in the same rhythmic patterns as real language.

Another important characteristic of babbling is the selection of sounds the child is using. Babbling is not random use of a random selection of sounds. The sounds the infant uses in babbling turn out to be the ones he or she will use in her first words and phrases. By this early point in life, the child has already started screening and selecting sounds. During the first few weeks and months, the sounds this particular baby made were the sounds that *all* babies make, assuming they are normal in their physiological and mental development. The basic biological noises are the same, whether the infant is born in Bangladesh or Bolivia. Infants make the same cooing and laughing sounds, and to a certain degree the same sounds of vocal play, no matter where they are born or what culture they live in or what language their parents speak. But by the time they have progressed to canonical babbling, infants are already becoming selective about the sounds they make.

By this point, the infant's mother and father may be delighted. They likely believe their child is speaking his or her first words. However, closer and more objective observation will show that the child still does not associate these syllables with anyone or anything in particular. That comes later, sometime between the ninth month and the end of the first year, or shortly after.

At this stage utterances begin taking on more and more of the melodic, rhythmic intonations of real language. Instead of merely making vowel and consonant sounds and syllables, young children are now putting them together to make words. And they are associating the words with concrete objects in the world around them. My grandson Ryan, for example, has started to say *mama* when he looks at mom, *dada* when he sees his father, and *fa* when he spots a bunch of flowers. These children are beginning to make the cognitive leap into that mysterious land we call true language. They *know what some words mean*.

Dr. Elizabeth Bates of the University of California at San Diego, an expert in infant language acquisition, has noted the remarkable changes that are happening during this period in the infant human brain. Between birth and age two, she has said, the infant brain undergoes an extraordinary growth spurt in synaptic connections. Synapses are, as we recall, the connections between neurons. Chemicals called neurotransmitters carry the electrical "message" from one neuron to another. The more synapses a brain has, the more sophisticated and complex is its ability to store, process, and interpret information about the world. It is presumably during these first twelve to twenty-four months that each of us begins developing the unique pattern of tiny language neuron clusters that George Ojemann has found in his surgeries. As we saw in Chapter 9, most are in the left hemisphere, but some are in the top of the brain's cortex and others are in the right hemisphere.

This explosive growth in synapses would also be part of the rapid creation of the convergence zones hypothesized by Hanna and Antonio Damasio. Just as a computer neural network "learns" by repeated enforcement or encouragement of particular connections, so the brain creates and reinforces particular synaptic pathways through repeated practice. And during the first two years of life, learning proceeds at a gargantuan rate. The child gobbles up experiences, "drinks life to the lees," as Lord Tennyson said in his poem "Ulysses." Every waking moment provides a new experience, a fresh input for the young brain to acquire, store, massage, and fit into a picture of the world.

When we sing to our children or grandchildren, read to them, talk to them, and merely talk in front of them, we provide them with the raw material from which they create language. The infant's language capability is like a primed pump waiting for someone to begin pumping water from the well. We, the parents and grandparents and caregivers of these infants, give the infant's pump its first few pushes. We provide the positive feedback. It is our encouragement, our smiles, our hugs, our *mama* and *dada* and *car* and *chair* and *hot*—all the songs and stories and words and phrases we offer and repeat with our children—that enable the young child to get the water moving. Once it begins flowing, only catastrophe or death will stop it.

Some time around the end of her first year, the infant speaks his or her first word, taking the step into the realm of true language. The infant may still continue to babble as well as construct definite syllables and words. But the babbling decreases as true language takes over, and it eventually disappears around twenty months of age. The child has begun to create and use words in his or her mother tongue.

Climbing the Tower of Babbling

The only way to understand how infant humans create language is to get "up close and personal" with infants who are doing it. And it is not enough to start that process when they have already begun using words. By then they have already made an astonishing journey. Language is an incredibly complex process of communication, a process with layers beneath layers beneath layers. Yet we do it almost effortlessly. Even youngsters of one or two years of age, still struggling to string words together into decent sentences, and sentences into discourse, have clearly mastered the basics of language.

In order to understand how that happens, linguists and psychologists realized, they would have to study infants *from the beginning*, from birth onward. The process of language acquisition begins at birth, as we have seen. Each stage is vital. But probably the most fascinating of them, and in some ways the most important, is the babbling stage. It is at this point that children begin "practicing" language with its basic units, combining the right sounds in the correct rhythm and intonation.

A handful of scientists have been studying this process. They include Kimbrough Oller and his colleagues and graduate students at the University of Miami in Miami, Florida. In 1982 Oller reported on a study of babbling in English-learning and Spanish-learning infants. The purpose was to determine whether infants learning different languages had similar or differing babbling patterns. Difference in babbling among infants learning different language would suggest that babbling was strongly influenced by the infant's environment. A high degree of similarity, on the other hand, would strongly suggest a powerful innate tendency for babbling to occur in a specific pattern.

Oller and his associates found that, despite the large phonetic differences between Spanish and English, the infants babbled in almost exactly the same fashion. Both English- and Spanish-learning infants created syllables consisting of a consonant followed by a vowel, and the consonants tended to be voiceless unaspirated plosives like [p] and [t]. Their production of vowel-like sounds was also very similar. Even sophisticated listeners would find it hard to tell the difference between the babbling of Spanish-learning infants and that of English-learning infants.

In another study published in 1988, Oller and his colleagues took on the long-held belief that deaf infants during the first year of their lives babble vocally in the same way as do hearing infants. This notion in turn was long used to support the assumption that hearing ability plays only a minor role in the development of babbling in infants. The problem with these beliefs was that—as with many assumptions about infants and language before the 1980s—little scientific evidence existed to support them. They were part of the "everybody knows" collection of knowledge.

Oller's research team carried out a careful longitudinal study with two groups of infants. A longitudinal study is one that stretches out over a long period of time. One group consisted of infants who were deaf, and the other of infants with normal hearing ability. All twenty-one of the hearing infants, it turned out, began canonical babbling between six and ten months of age. However, by age ten months, none of the nine deaf infants had begun verbal canonical babbling. This was despite the fact that the deaf infants got intensive stimulation and assistance with auditory amplification of various sounds.

The two researchers found themselves compelled to ask whether *any* deaf infant might be able to babble verbally. Some apparently do; the researchers concluded that this must happen only in those cases where the infant either had some small hearing ability or was able to incorporate some visual understanding of sounds by lip reading. In any case, their work clearly established that hearing sounds made by others is profoundly important to developing normal verbal babbling.

Second Languages and the Brain

Most of us, of course, learned one language as infants, our mother tongue. It may have been American Sign Language (ASL) or English, Langue des Signes Québécoises (LSQ) or Chinese, Russian or Tlingit, Vietnamese or Xhosa. No matter: our young brains were like dry sponges ready to soak up the rain of language falling upon us. They were tiny computers, prewired and loaded with a universal operating system, prepared to run whatever "language program" our parents and community popped into our little ears or eyes. We learned one language because that was the one language spoken by our parents and by the community into which we were born.

Some of us, though, were born into bilingual families, with parents who spoke more than one language; or we began our lives in a community where two or more languages were well established and frequently spoken. We learned from infancy to be fluent in two languages at once. Others of us first learned our mother tongue but as young children picked up a second language. Perhaps we showed an early facility for languages or had the opportunity to attend schools that stressed the excitement and intellectual adventure of learning a second tongue. We, too, came to learn a second or third language before we were adults.

And some of us, to our regret, managed to miss the language boat. Perhaps we had parents fluent in two languages, but for some reason they did not teach us both. Or perhaps we had the opportunity to learn a second language as youngsters, but we decided that was about as exciting as learning the piano or the accordion. And now, as adults, we find that learning Spanish, or Italian, or Russian is about as easy as bicycling around Mount Rainier in a winter blizzard. What happened to our brains? And what happens in the brains of youngsters that makes it possible for them to learn new languages with ease?

In the last chapter we learned about some of the remarkable work being done by University of Washington neurosurgeon George Ojemann. As we recall, Ojemann has been electrically probing the brains of people afflicted with epilepsy. His purpose has been to map the brain. For many areas in the cortex, the brain's outer wrinkled layer of neurons, Ojemann has identified particular functions, including language functions. Ojemann's electrical stimulation studies of living human brains have also uncovered the same kind of language organization discovered by researchers who study people suffering from brain damage. Some of these support Antonio and Hanna Damasio's convergence zone theory of language, which we encountered in Chapter 8. For example, studies by different researchers of people with damaged brains have provided evidence that there is no single area of the brain dedicated to language. As Ojemann's work has shown, these studies of brain-damaged people reveal that language in the brain is compartmentalized into many different areas.

In one study of fifty-five people, for example, Ojemann examined the way electrical stimulation of specific brain areas interfered with patients' ability to either read words or to name objects in their mother tongue. He electrically stimulated a total of 111 different sites in the brains of his subjects. Ojemann found that at seventy-seven percent of the sites at which the stimulation interfered with either language function, only one of the two functions was affected. In another study of fourteen subjects, Ojemann tested their sentence-reading ability, their recent verbal memory, their ability to mimic facial movements associated with speaking, and their ability to identify specific phonemes. Ninety-one different sites in their brains showed some disturbance when Ojemann applied electrical stimulation to the cortex. Fifty-seven percent of those sites showed changes in only one of the four abilities tested. Once again, it is clear that the brain stores the various bits and pieces of language in entirely separate "filing cabinets."

This separation of areas appears to go beyond just different language-related activities. These studies of people with brain damage caused by stroke or accidents have also revealed that *different areas of the brain handle different languages*. If you speak both English and

Spanish, for example, one set of brain regions takes care of English while an entirely different set of areas handles Spanish. Ojemann's electrical probes of the brain have confirmed these findings. The essential areas for naming objects in a second or third language in which the person is less fluent than in his or her mother tongue are actually larger than those for the primary language. The neurons in the areas that deal with your mother tongue, such as English, are tightly wired together and take up a small amount of space in the brain.

However, when you learn a second or third language, such as French or Italian, other tiny areas in your brain take up the various tasks of recalling nouns, processing verbs, handling French or Italian grammar, and so forth. Those areas, says Ojemann, are larger in size than the ones that handle your primary language. It is as if the brain starts over again when you begin learning a new language, following the same pattern of dedicating specific tiny parts of the brain to handling specific language tasks. Because these new language areas have to compete for space in existing areas, they tend to be larger and more diffuse, grabbing whatever nondedicated neurons are in the vicinity.

Nevertheless, the general distribution of the areas that handle second or third languages is the same as that for the areas of the mother tongue. Some of the language patches are in the brain's right hemisphere, but most are on the left side of the brain. In fact, nearly all languages are lateralized in the brain's left hemisphere, including pictographic languages like Chinese and manual languages like American Sign Language.

The flexibility of the child's brain, and the competition for needed neurons in the more "rigid" brains of adolescents and adults, may help explain a well-known fact about learning second or third languages. Basically, our ability to learn secondary languages starts to decrease with age. Research has revealed that youngsters under the age of two can learn new languages about as easily as they learn their mother tongue. From birth to about age twelve or thirteen we can learn a new language without too much difficulty.

Once we hit our teen years, though, our ability to learn new languages drops like a stone thrown into a well. We can certainly learn additional languages when we are older, and some people seem to have the remarkable ability to pick up new languages effortlessly throughout their lives. For most of us, though, it is a struggle.

My own attempts to learn Spanish as a teenager were mediocre at best. In my early twenties an old girlfriend—she is one of those people gifted in language, and went on to become a Russian translator for the U.S. Army—tried to teach me French. I failed miserably. One of my great regrets in life, in fact, is that I did not pester my mother or grandmother into teaching me Hungarian. I probably could have picked it up well enough as a child. But now, of course, it is out of the question.

Why do I and millions of others have this difficulty as adults? Why did my mother, by contrast, have relatively little trouble learning English as a second language when at age 11 she came to America from her native Hungary just before World War II? And why can young children learn additional languages with as much fluency and ease as their mother tongues? The answer may well relate to the brain's growth rate. As noted earlier in this chapter, Elizabeth Bates of the University of California at San Diego has pointed out the tremendous increase, in young children, in the number of synapses and the complexity of their interconnections throughout the brain. Synaptic connections are where the action is when it comes to perceiving, remembering, thinking, and communicating. It is this incredible spurt in growth and complexity during the first two years of life that gives the infant human brain its incredible plasticity and flexibility. It is primed to learn language—any language, or any languages.

A particularly fascinating research report published in 1977 dealt with *polyglots*, people who can speak and understand several different languages. The researchers studied several polyglots suffering from aphasias caused by strokes or other brain damage. These patients had lesions in their brains that affected most, but not all, of the languages they knew. Specific tests for specific linguistic abilities, such as naming, grammar, and ability to pronounce word-sounds (phomemes), revealed that they had lost abilities for some languages but remained fully fluent in others. Nor was the remaining language necessarily their mother tongue.

This kind of language damage to polyglots reinforces the findings by Ojemann, the Damasios, and other researchers. If only one or two areas of the brain control our linguistic abilities, this kind of language loss could not happen. Only if the brain's language functions are scattered about in many different areas, with each language having its own set of "command and control" areas, could polyglots lose some languages but not others.

What is particularly intriguing about this pattern of brain damage is that it resembles the kinds of linguistic losses suffered by some of Damasio's patients, such as Boswell. These people, we recall, lost access to words in specific classes or categories. They could not, for example, name unique animals, but they could easily identify specific tools. Only if language storage and retrieval were distributed in numerous areas could this kind of effect occur.

One interesting finding by Ojemann from his electrical stimulation studies reveals the same kind of distributed pattern to language processes in the brain. By electrically stimulating one or the other of two specific language sites, Ojemann created disturbances in patients' abilities to name the same object in one or another of two different languages. Suppose you are fluent in both English and Spanish. Ojemann is operating on you to cure you of an otherwise intractable case of epilepsy, and you have agreed to take part in his electrical stimulation mapping of the brain. He holds up a picture of a dog, stimulates one area of your brain, and asks you to name the entity in English and then in Spanish. Next, he stimulates another brain region, and again asks you to name it first in English and then in Spanish. When the one brain area is electrically stimulated, you have no problem saying *dog*, but you cannot find the word *perro*. When the other brain area is stimulated, the opposite effect occurs: you can immediately say *perro*, but not for the life of you can you come up with *dog*.

Another finding by Ojemann is just as intriguing: the same pattern of disturbance in naming ability—this separation by language—occurs in naming an entity in either a spoken or a signed language. It is still another piece of concrete evidence that signed languages, languages "on the hands," are fully functional and mature languages on a par with any language "on the tongue."

Many of these findings about multiple language fluency, and the loss of it in stroke patients, were made in adults, of course. But all of these abilities are intimately tied to children and infants. Polyglots, for example, usually reveal their remarkable language ability early in childhood. Researchers, teachers, and parents have long known that children have a much easier time of learning second or third languages than do teenagers and adults. As noted earlier, this easy fluency in multiple languages is probably linked to the rapid growth of the young child's brain and the incredible multiplication of its interconnections and neural networks.

George Ojemann has even found concrete evidence for the presence of many language mini-centers in the young human brain. He has mapped the brains of several epilepsy patients between four and ten years of age and found specific tiny areas that deal with naming objects or persons. The locations of the language areas in children are apparently as unique and individual as those in adults.

Dr. Fabio Franco, a researcher at the University of Trieste in Italy, has offered a striking example of brain changes in an adult who from childhood was fluent in two languages. Franco did a study of people who do simultaneous translation. His subjects worked for the United Nations General Assembly and Security Council or as personal translators for heads of state. One of them was a twenty-two-year-old woman named Carla. Born and raised in Italy, Carla learned both Italian and English as a child and was fluent in both. Then she began training as a simultaneous translator. As she proceeded through her translator training, Franco periodically monitored her brain's language activity using advanced brain imaging techniques. These sophisticated machines, such as the MRI and PET scanners we encountered in Chapter 5, can take "snapshots" of the brain's activity as it carries out certain tasks like speaking, reading, writing, or hearing words spoken by others. The images reveal which areas of the brain are active and which are not.

The images of Carla's brain in action revealed a remarkable transformation. At the beginning of her translator training, most of the language processing in Carla's brain took place in the left cerebral hemisphere. This was the case for both Italian, her mother tongue, and English, her second language. As she became more adept at simultaneous translation, though, a change took place. The right side of her brain took over more and more of the processing of English, while the left side continued to deal with speaking Italian. Franco thinks this happened because essential language areas in Carla's left cerebral hemisphere were already dedicated to language.

In order for Carla to be able to simultaneously translate from English to Italian, and vice versa, other areas of her brain had to take over the work of understanding and speaking English. The brain found a series of tiny areas in its right hemisphere—an area usually not associated with language—that could take over. The result was that Carla not only remained fluent in both languages, as she had been from childhood, but was also able to shift instantly from Italian to English and back again.

Your children may not be multilingual or bilingual, but in fact being monolingual is wonder enough. Language is the greatest and most powerful tool your youngsters will ever have. With it, the world and its limitless possibilities opens to them. And the greatest wonder is that the tool of language is theirs by nature as well as nurture. Their ability to speak or sign is woven into the fabric of their genes and their brain. It is literally their birthright.

CHAPTER 11

BREAKTHROUGHS

Our understanding of the brain and language has undergone tremendous growth in the last few years. So has our knowledge of how human infants begin acquiring and using language. Much of the most exciting work has to do with processes that occur during a child's first year of life. Other researchers have looked at linguistic abilities that develop a little later. Still others are peering into the living brains of adults and "watching" language in action. The researchers making these breakthroughs include a Canadian psychologist in British Columbia, a researcher in California, and a team of scientists in Connecticut.

THE DIFFERENCE BETWEEN /Pa/ AND /Ba/

We learned at the beginning of this journey into linguistics that all spoken languages use a combination of language sounds called phones. As we learned earlier, a phone is the smallest perceptible discrete segment of speech sound, a sound segment a listener can clearly identify as a vowel or consonant.

The number of possible phones we can make with our mouths is huge. No one language uses all of them, though some use more than others. Each language uses only a relatively small selection of the nearly infinite number of phones available. Those particular sounds used in a particular language are called phonemes. The phoneme /b/, for example, is common to nearly all languages. The phonemes ʕ and ħ, which represent glottal sounds, are used in Arabic but almost never in English.

We adults have no trouble, for the most part, in forming the phonemes of our mother tongue. We have fully developed vocal tracts, mature nervous systems, and a lifetime of practice at speaking. Infants and young children do not. It takes a long time, several years in fact, before young children can create all the sounds needed to speak their mother tongue. The motor control needed to shape the lips, move the tongue, and open and close the glottis is considerable. It is not surprising that baby talk sounds the way it does.

What is surprising is that infants can *discriminate nearly every possible phonetic contrast*. We adults cannot. We can only distinguish between the phones we use in our language. A phoneme, as we recall, is formally defined as the smallest contrastive unit in the sound system of a particular language. That is, phonemes are the particular phones we use to distinguish meaning in our mother tongue. [f] and [b] are phones, or sounds, that the normal human mouth can make. Those two sounds are also phonemes in many languages, because they create a difference in meaning. For example, in English the word *feet* (/fit/) has a different meaning from the word *beet* (/bit/). The only difference between the two words is the phones [f] and [b]. In English, therefore, those phones are phonemes, and linguists write them as /f/ and /b/.

However, there is also quite a bit of variation in the way we actually speak these sounds in real life, in real speech. The phoneme /b/ in *beet* does not have quite the same sound as the phoneme /b/ in *boot*. We do not hear the difference. We have learned that the difference, in this case, does not matter. The subtle sound difference between the /b/ in *beet* and the /b/ in *boot* does not create a difference in meaning. We long ago categorized both /b/'s as members of the same phoneme. We have labeled the /b/ in *beet* and the /b/ in *boot* as equivalent. In contrast, we have learned to distinguish between /bɑ/ and /pɑ/. They are labeled as different phonemes, so that is how we hear them. Psychologists and linguists call this process by which labeling limits our ability to discriminate among phonemes and phones *categorical perception*. Some of the early ground-breaking work on categorical perception was done in the late 1960s by Alvin Liberman and his colleagues.

All available evidence says that we stop using our ability to discriminate between nearly all phones very early in life. Two big questions in linguistics and the study of infant language acquisition are (1) Why does this happen? and (2) How does this come about? The answer to "why" is straightforward. Infants stop using their ability to distinguish between a myriad of different speech sounds because their brains quickly learn to "filter out" the speech sounds not used in their mother tongue.

But that still leaves the question of "how." How does that process happen? And when exactly does it occur? When does an infant's brain, like that of my grandson Ryan, begin developing the "perceptual filters" that start blocking our ability to hear the difference between phones we will not use in our mother tongue? A researcher at the University of British Columbia (UBC) in Vancouver has begun uncovering the answers to some of these questions. In the process of doing so, she is helping us all learn just how astonishing are the innate language abilities of even the youngest infants.

Janet Werker is an associate professor of developmental psychology at UBC, where since 1985 she has taught and done research into the linguistic abilities of infants and young children. The research carried out by Werker and others has a striking scientific elegance. As Werker explains, it all has to do with our ability to perceive subtle differences between and among phones based on their pitch and voicing.

Werker offers an example of how adults can—and cannot—distinguish between different kinds of minimal pairs of consonants. "A pair of consonant sounds like /bɑ/ and /pɑ/," she explains, "are identical in all respects except one. They both are 'stop' consonants produced with the two lips, so they're called bilabials. The way in which they differ is in *voicing*. When you say /pɑ/ you can feel a puff of air. With /bɑ/, what happens is that at the same time your vocal chords start vibrating, you 'release' the consonant. When you say /pɑ/, though, you're releasing the consonant even *before* your vocal chords start vibrating. That's why there's that puff of air."

It is possible for researchers to manipulate these particular dimensions of specific sounds. Today researchers use computers to generate exactly the sounds they want, with the precise timing needed for a controlled scientific study. One acoustic cue that signals either the simultaneous release of the consonant or a delay in its release is called *voice onset time*. By using a properly programmed computer connected to a sound generator, Werker and others manipulate that cue by producing a sequence of sounds that simulates when the voicing starts before the release of the consonant.

"If you do an acoustic analysis of speech patterns you have a fundamental frequency, the pitch," Werker explains. "Then you have overtones from that, overtones of the fundamental frequency that are exaggerated due to the shape of the vocal tract. So one way to do these kinds of experiments is to assume that 20 milliseconds is the particular timing for the start of one cue as opposed to the next one." A millisecond is a thousandth of a second, a pretty tiny slice of time in the everyday scheme of things.

"Then we program the computer to have the voice onset time take place 60 milliseconds before the consonant's release, 40 milliseconds before, 20 milliseconds before, at the same time as, 20 milliseconds after, 40 milliseconds after, 60 milliseconds after, and so on."

This computerized generation of specific sounds then creates what Werker calls a continuum of sounds that goes from /pɑ/ to /bɑ/. Everything about the sound is the same *except* for this one acoustic dimension, this one variable. It is very controlled, and control of variables is the key to getting clean scientific data.

Suppose, Werker continues, she wants to investigate scientifically this whole process of categorical perception. She wants to get a baseline of data for adults, of course, but she also wants to do the same kinds of tests on young children, infants, and—if possible—even newborns. With today's sophisticated computers, software, and sound generators, she can do just that.

Werker presents the subject with a set of eight sounds along a continuum of sounds. Each sound differs from the other in its voice release time, and the changes in voice release time proceed in equal steps. When we change this variable in our real-life speaking, we change the phone or basic speech sound. The computer does the same thing.

"Let's suppose," Werker says, "that I have the sound /bɑ/, with the voicing starting 40 milliseconds before the release of the consonant. Then I follow that with the same sound, but the voice release time of the consonant starts 20 milliseconds before I release it; then at the same time as the release of the consonant; then 20 milliseconds after.

You, an adult, will hear all those phones as /bɑ/. But with longer delays—say, 40, 60, 80, 100 milliseconds after—you'd report it as /pɑ/. You'd label the first four as /bɑ/, the next four as /pɑ/."

Now Werker changes the experiment a bit. Suppose, she says, that she presented you with these sounds *in pairs*. One pair of phones may consist of voicing 40 milliseconds before and voicing 20 milliseconds before. "You will not be able to hear the difference between pairs of sounds that were equally different—say, two pairs of sounds that were each 20 milliseconds apart in voice onset time—if you have learned to label them as the same sound," Werker says. "You'd only be able to discriminate between phones you hear in pairs if one had been a plus-20 millisecond pair and the other a plus-40 millisecond pair." There is a break point where that discrimination happens, in other words, and that is the essence of what Liberman first identified as categorical perception. The working definition of categorical perception is that our ability to label *predicts our ability to discriminate*. "If you give two sound stimuli the same label—you call them both /bɑ/—then you would not be able to discriminate them," Werker says. "But if you called one /bɑ/ and the other /pɑ/, then you would be able to discriminate them."

What is particularly intriguing about categorical perception of sounds, Werker adds, is that we can actually *perceive* differences between basic speech sounds or phones that are much finer than we label. One good example is—once again—our perception of color and the words we use for colors. We only have a specific set of names for colors in our vocabulary. But suppose you hand me some paint chips in two different variations of the "same color." Even though I can *see* the difference between them, I will still have labeled them with the same term (*red*, or *green*, or *blue*). Although there are some exceptions, speech is basically perceived much more categorically.

Werker's interest in categorical perception, human infants, and their developing linguistic abilities began blossoming in the late 1970s, when she was in graduate school. She recalls, "At the time I became interested in this kind of work there was a lot of research that had been done by Liberman of Haskins Laboratories, and other people. This was the work that indicated that adults perceived speech categorically.

"I was coming across a lot of research that claimed that speech perception is special. Now, that may or not be true. But it interested me. Even in 1971, and certainly over the next several years, research was cropping up that suggested that even young infants show something like categorical perception. That is, these people were suggesting that infants as young as four months can discriminate differences *across* phoneme boundaries, such as a /bɑ/ versus a /pɑ/, better than *within* phoneme categories—that is, one form of /bɑ/ versus another /bɑ/. There was even a hypothesis floating around, stated by Peter Eimas, that infants are born with the ability to discriminate the universal set of phonetic contrasts, and that this ability changes as a function of language experience."

What particularly intrigued the young Janet Werker were several studies in the mid-1970s suggesting that infants can discriminate nonnative phone contrasts just as well as they can native contrasts. In 1976, for example, Dr. Sandra Trehub, in a paper published in *Child Development*, showed that English-learning infants could discriminate a phonetic contrast found in Czech that is not used in English. Trehub also tested English adults in a completely different procedure and concluded that English-speaking adults could not discriminate the Czech contrasts.

That same year Dr. Lynn Streeter published a paper in *Nature* that suggested that Kikuyu-speaking African infants can discriminate /bɑ/ from /pɑ/. "This is rather interesting," Werker says, "because this contrast is used in the English language, but not in Kikuyu." As we learned earlier, Czech is an Indo-European language, like English. But Kikuyu belongs to an entirely different and unrelated African language family. Other researchers in other labs were coming up with similar results. The pattern of results seemed to suggest that we are born with an ability to discriminate phones from what Werker has called "the universal phonetic inventory" upon which all languages draw.

One might assume, at this point, that adults should also to be able to discriminate a wide range of phonetic contrasts. But that did not seem to be the case at all. Werker was also finding research suggesting that adults have difficulty discriminating sounds or phonetic contrasts that they do not use in their native language. It is well known, for example, that Japanese speakers are not able to discriminate between /lɑ/ and /rɑ/. The Japanese language uses a single phoneme that lies midway between /lɑ/ and /rɑ/. There are other examples, as well, of speech sounds that nonnative speakers fail to discriminate.

The Thai language, for example, discriminates between two specific /p/ phonemes; but English-speaking adults cannot tell them apart.

For Werker, it was all utterly fascinating and irresistible. "It looked like this categorical perception ability was something we're born with," she explained, "something that we bring to the language acquisition process." Furthermore, the early evidence suggested that we lose this innate ability to perceive all possible phonemes by the time we are adults and committed to a mother tongue. Werker decided to explore "this intriguing possibility," as she has called it. She began her work on categorical perception in infants in graduate school. Her first paper was published in 1981.

What Werker has specifically done in the years since then is try to trace how speech perception changes during children's first few months and years of development. Can infants really discriminate between some phone pairs better than adults? If so, when do they stop using this universal phonetic discrimination ability, and why?

To Hear It All

The problem with most of the research done in the 1970s, Werker soon realized, was that no one had properly tested any of these supposed abilities. At that time no scientist had carried out the same set of rigorous scientific tests for both infants and adults. The suspicion among many, including Werker, was that the procedures used to test infants were in fact more sensitive than those used to test adults. As a result, researchers might be seeing a difference in procedures rather than a real age-related difference in sensitivity.

Werker knew that she and her colleagues would have to develop a set of rigorous testing procedures that could be successfully used with both adults and infants. It would be the only way to get solid data from both groups, and data that could be honestly compared. She settled on a variation of the well-known "head-turning" procedure.

The researcher presents the subjects with several slightly different versions of the same phoneme, repeating them continuously at about two-second intervals. Every four to twenty repetitions, on a random basis, the researcher changes the phoneme. So the subject may hear /bɑ/ repeated five times, and then suddenly the researcher changes it to /pɑ/. Then /pɑ/ might repeat seventeen times, once every two seconds, until the researcher suddenly changes it to /bɑ/. Babies are conditioned to turn their heads toward the sound every time they hear it change from one phoneme (/bɑ/) to another (/pɑ/). The testers use positive reinforcement, such as activating a cute toy animal or giving the infant smiles and verbal praise each time he or she correctly turns the head when the phoneme changes.

Werker and her colleagues used the same procedure with adults. The only difference was that, instead of turning their heads, adults pushed a button when they detected a phoneme change.

Werker began publishing the results of her investigations in 1983. To say the least, they have proved illuminating. In one of her early series of experiments, for example, she compared Hindi-speaking adults, English-speaking adults, and infants from English-speaking families. She looked at the ability of these three groups to distinguish between the /bɑ/ and /dɑ/ phonemes—a distinction made in both Hindi and English—and also between two pairs of syllables used in Hindi but not in English. One pair consisted of two *t* sounds, a dental *t* or /t/ and a retroflex *t* or /ʈ/, creating a contrast not found in English. The other Hindi syllable pair involved the kind of voice release that we looked at earlier, using two Hindi phonemes written as /t^h/ and /d^h/.

Werker discovered, first of all, that everyone in all three groups, both adults and infants, could discriminate between /bɑ/ and /dɑ/. What was particularly fascinating, though, was that non-Hindi infants aged six to eight months—the infants learning English as their mother tongue—performed like Hindi adults. They could discriminate between both pairs of Hindi syllables, just as the Hindi adults could. The English-speaking adults, on the other hand, had great difficulty hearing the difference between the Hindi syllables.

The results of this experiment, as well as others Werker has conducted, support the hypothesis: All human infants appear to be born with the ability to distinguish every possible phoneme. And by the time we are adults, we can hear the phonemes of other languages only with extreme difficulty. When does this radical reduction in our universal phoneme-hearing ability begin setting in? In a series of experiments with twelve-year-old English-speaking children, Werker found they were no better able to hear the differences between non-English phonemes than were English-speaking adults.

Then she carried out the same sets of experiments with eight-year-olds, and then with four-year-old English-speaking children. Much to her surprise, not even the four-year-olds could easily discriminate between Hindi phonemes. Hindi-speaking four-year-old children could, but not their English-speaking counterparts. Clearly, the children were losing their universal phonetic-hearing ability by the time they are four.

This phenomenon was not limited to speakers of English and Hindi. Werker carried out similar experiments with speakers of a Native American language in the Interior Salish family, called Nthlakapmx by the native speakers and Thompson by English-speaking Canadians. The same loss of phonetic discrimination cropped up. Nthlakapmx-speaking infants and adults could discriminate the Nthlakapmx phonemes; English speakers apparently could not.

Werker then looked at even younger children, between four months and two years old, and tested their ability to make these kinds of phonetic discriminations. The results were even more interesting. No more than 20 percent of English-learning or -speaking infants between ten and twelve months old could discriminate between non-English phonemes. This was similar to the pattern of older children. About half of the infants eight to ten months old could make the discrimination. And nearly all of the four- to eight-month-olds could do it. Werker later retested infants from the youngest group, when they were about a year old. English-learning youngsters who had once been able to tell the difference between Hindi phonemes and Nthlakapmx phonemes now could not.

Werker has not tested infants younger than about four months old, but she is confident of the outcome. "Infants younger than that probably do perform the same way," she says. "However, the procedure that I settled on couldn't be used with infants younger than four months. As it was, that turned out to be early enough. In any case," she continues, "my prediction from other studies I've done, and am doing, is that younger infants will perform equally well."

Werker's research does not show adults *totally* losing all ability to hear the phonemes of other languages. Though the task becomes much more difficult, the universal phoneme-hearing ability does not completely vanish, even in adulthood. "In some of our tests," says Werker, "it's clear that adults can hear these differences. They may think they are just guessing at the answers, but they are actually doing much better than mere chance would dictate. So unconsciously, anyway, they can discriminate between different speech sounds." This unconscious ability to still hear those "alien sounds" may play a role in our ability to learn second and third languages.

NATURE, NURTURE, AND SECOND LANGUAGES

At first glance, Werker's findings seem to contradict what we know of children's abilities to learn second or third languages. As we saw in the last chapter, youngsters have a fairly easy time of learning new languages until they reach puberty. Teenagers and adults, of course, can also learn new languages, but almost always with considerably more difficulty. If children stop using their universal phone-hearing ability before they are a year old, though, how can they learn new languages so easily? The answer seems to lie in the role of experience, in our practice in creating and using language.

This is a variation on the old controversy about "nature versus nurture." The simplest statement of this contention is that either our genetic code totally preprograms us for certain abilities, or our environment and upbringing instill certain abilities in us. Substitute words like *diseases*, *sexual orientation*, or *addictions* for *abilities* and you get a good sense of the current argument about nature versus nurture. The reality, of course, is considerably more subtle than these simplistic statements assert. Both nature and nurture play a role in determining our abilities, our predisposition to certain diseases, and our addictive weakness. The jury is still out on sexual orientation, though increasing evidence points to a deeply ingrained genetic influence. In any case, the real puzzle has always been about the balance of influence between nature and nurture.

Researchers exploring infant language acquisition have always known the importance of an infant's early experience in creating and using his or her mother tongue. Janet Werker's research has shed some light on the role of early language experience in the development of a child's perceptions of his or her world. This process is called *perceptual development*. As we will soon see, it plays an important role in the ability to learn second or third languages.

Werker's observations also strongly suggest—perhaps *suggest* is not an even strong enough word—the existence of a powerful genetic predisposition in humans for language. The infant human brain has a powerful potential to create language. It is a large stone balanced at the top of a hill, waiting only for someone to give it a good shove. The shove comes from the environment the newborn infant enters: parents at first, along with other family members, and later friends and schoolmates. Experience and genetic predisposition work together. The result is language.

The question that arises, though, is exactly how the infant's experience interacts with the steady development of his or her innate perceptual abilities to create language.

Several different models exist for how experience affects perceptual development. One model is called *induction*. This model says that a particular capability, like learning a first or even second language, depends entirely on experience. Infants cannot distinguish between speech sounds without some previous experience. They have no innate ability to do so; they start from zero and must learn it all.

The model called *attunement* asserts that experience makes possible the *development* of a capability. Babies are born with the ability to distinguish among speech sounds, but experience makes the "boundaries" between the sounds a bit sharper and easier for them to hear. Experience primes the pump, as it were.

The *facilitation* model says that experience only affects the *rate* at which a child acquires a capability. This model asserts that a child's speech perception will improve even without any practical experience. Practice at hearing specific sounds will only increase the rate at which the child learns to distinguish among them. Thus, hearing specific sounds might improve an infant's ability to discriminate among them. Even without that kind of experience, though, speech perception will still improve over time.

Maintenance/loss is the "use it or lose it" model. It holds that a perceptual ability is fully developed at the very beginning, and experience serves only to maintain it and keep it from being lost. If this model is correct, a child fully acquires a capability such as language acquisition *before* he or she develops much experience, but experience is necessary to maintain the capability. Infants' exposure to the particular phonemes of their mother tongue means they will continue to distinguish among those speech sounds. Speech sounds they do not continue to hear or experience, they will eventually stop using. "Practice, practice, practice," as my piano teachers used to say.

Finally, the *maturation* model says that a child develops and maintains a capability totally independent of experience; that is, experience plays no role at all. According to this model, a perceptual ability like phoneme discrimination unfolds totally independent of any input from the environment. The infant's ability to discriminate among speech sounds will grow and mature no matter what kinds of experience the child has hearing different speech sounds or being exposed to new languages.

These five models for how experience affects the development of a capability like learning languages can be put on a line that runs from "total experience" to "no experience." The following graphic illustrates this:

MATURATION	↑	Experience is totally **unimportant**.
MAINTENANCE/LOSS	↑	Experience only keeps ability alive.
FACILITATION	↑	Experience only affects rate of change.
ATTUNEMENT	↑	Experience is influential.
INDUCTION	↑	Experience is totally **important**.

Now when we look at the evidence, the picture becomes clearer. First of all, the cumulative weight of Werker's experiments says that all human infants—Indian or American, Russian or African, native Australian or native German—are born with the remarkable ability to perceive and discriminate all possible speech sounds. Werker has also identified the approximate time in their young lives when babies begin "losing" this ability: sometime between four and ten months of age. It is during this time that infants continue to be able to distinguish among phonemes in their mother tongue but begin ignoring the ability to "hear" phonemes used in other languages. By the time we are a year or so old, we can no longer discriminate phonemes that are not used in our mother tongue.

At the same time, generations of children have learned second or third languages with considerable ease. That is, youngsters can regain their ability to easily distinguish among speech sounds or phonemes that are not used in their mother tongue, and thus learn to speak new languages fluently.

Werker believes these seemingly contradictory facts indicate that the maintenance/loss model for the effects of experience applies to language acquisition. Humans are born with the ability to hear all speech sounds. However, they only maintain the ability to distinguish among those phonemes they have experience hearing and using. Those are usually the ones of their mother tongue. But if young children also learn a second language, and practice distinguishing among and using speech sounds in that language, they will regain the abilities other babies stop using.

To test this model, Werker conducted another study in 1984. She tested a group of English-speaking adults who as very young children had also learned to speak some Hindi. After their second year they had no further exposure to this second language. They grew up speaking English as their mother tongue. Werker discovered that these adults had a much better ability to distinguish among Hindi speech sounds and syllables than did a control group of English-speaking adults who had never been exposed to Hindi. They also did nearly as well as a group of adults who were native Hindi speakers. This group of English-speaking adults who had learned some Hindi before they were two had retained some of their ability to "hear" Hindi sounds even as adults. Werker's study thus supports the maintenance/loss model for learning languages. It is clearly a case of "use it or lose it."

Of course, this work by Werker has some obvious implications for parents and educators. If we want our children to be bilingual, to have a working knowledge and understanding of languages other than their mother tongue, then our children must start learning new languages early in life. Most of us do not live in bilingual families, so most of our children will not begin speaking second or third languages before they are two. However, the maintenance/loss model for learning new languages still applies. If they begin learning a second language in grammar school, children can still regain their ability to distinguish among the sounds of other languages, an ability they apparently lost years earlier. Practice is the key, practice and use. Even if the language is one that is very different from their mother tongue, as Chinese or Japanese or Hindi is from English, children will again be able to "hear" the sounds and learn the tongue.

And is it worth learning a new language? Of course. To know another tongue is to have a leg up on every "monolingual" in the business and political worlds of the twenty-first century. To know another language is to enter a new universe of literature, poetry, and song. To know another tongue is to know a new culture.

"Our work is opening up a thousand new questions," says Werker happily. "It allows us to start making predictions based on a specific scientific theory, and then test those questions to see if they're false or not." That, of course, is what science is all about. Take a theory and test it to destruction, to see where it breaks down.

And more than that, as Werker noted with a smile: "Also, this work is fun!"

Neural Nets and The Past Tense

Janet Werker's research has focused on language processes happening in the first few months after birth. Laura Ann Petitto, whose work is described in Chapter 12, has studied babbling in deaf and hearing children, which also occurs in the first year of life. Other researchers are giving us new insights into language abilities that develop in children who are further along in mastering their mother tongue.

Our own experience tells us that English is a fairly idiosyncratic language. We usually do not pay much attention to that. By the time we are adolescents we speak our mother tongue fluently. When was the last time we thought about how to pluralize a noun? We don't; we just do it. We have learned the grammatical rules, the exceptions to the rules, and the exceptions to the exceptions.

Children are in a somewhat different situation. They are not yet fluent in their mother tongue; they are still learning it, at least until their teen years. For them, it would seem, every new grammatical exception would be a stumbling block.

Consider, for example, the process of changing a verb's *tense* to mark the time at which an action takes place, such as the past, present, or future. In English, putting a verb into past tense usually means adding the suffix *-ed* to the verb's present tense form. Thus the past tense of *add* is *added*. That of *drip* is *dripped*. The past tense of *talk* is *talked*, and so on. However, English has many exceptions to this fairly broad form-changing rule. *Go* becomes *went*. *Make* becomes *made*. *Has* becomes *had*.

If tense in English were a perfectly regular process, learning it would be easy. Young Ryan Nash would simply determine from experience that the way to change a verb from present to past tense is "add an *-ed*." A small cluster of neurons in his brain would soon learn this rule and commit it to memory. Each time Ryan needed to switch from present to past tense, the language convergence zones in his brain would call up that piece of stored grammatical information and *voila!*

However, the actual rules of grammatical tense are much more difficult. In spite of these complexities, children like Ryan master the exceptions and irregularities of even a language as idiosyncratic as English.

The process seems to take about three to five years before it is complete, though with some grammatical constructions it can take longer. When children are around two years of age, they are probably beginning to create intelligible two- and three-word sentences. The grammar may not always be correct. The sentences are often "telegraphic" in character—*Mommy comed home! Kitty here! Where fowers?*—but we can understand what they mean.

At about age three, the child begins to string clauses together using *and, when, if, so, what, after*, and other connecting words. The grammar is still imperfect much of the time, and tense may be incorrectly formulated. Parents are treated to expositions like *Daddy and me goed to the store and we got cookies and cake and peanuts and hangaber and then we saw Jeannie but she was sad because her kitty died so she buwwied her kitty and pwanted fowers!* At about four years of age, children begin the process of mastering the idiosyncrasies of the language's grammar. It takes time. The child is still likely to say sentences like *Mommy goed to work and I stayed home* or *My toy just got brokened.*

By the time they are about seven years old, children are well on the way to mastering the grammatical irregularities of English. They understand the similarity in meaning of two sentences that may look different, such as those with active and passive forms. *The dog followed the cat*, they know, has the same meaning as *The cat was followed by the dog*. They are also doing much better with tense and all its exceptions, and are likely to be using more sophisticated connecting words in their sentences. *My mom went to work when I stayed at home since I was sick*, the kind of sentence they are likely to use, is much more "adult-sounding" than their earlier efforts.

Many linguists and psychologists have long sought to uncover the process by which children learn the various forms for tense. The most commonly accepted theory has been that children go through a series of learning stages. The first stage involves memorizing the most common verbs they encounter and the ones that go together. *Play* goes with *played*, *go* with *went*, *see* with *saw*, *want* with *wanted*, and so on. In the next stage they learns the basic grammatical rule of *-ed*: whenever you encounter a new verb, add *-ed* to it to make it past tense. (Of course, children are not consciously thinking about it in this fashion; they are just *learning* it.) During this period they make many grammatical mistakes. *Go* becomes *goed*, *make* becomes *maked*, *see* becomes *seed*. Finally, children enter the third stage. They discover that they should not apply the *-ed* rule in every case, and they begin learning the various exceptions and memorizing each of them.

But is this really the way children learn the rules of tense? Psychologist David Rumelhart and his colleagues at Stanford University have developed a computer model that suggests children do not learn in stages by adopting a progressive set of new rules. If their model is correct, then the process is more one of generalizing than memorizing and rule-making.

Rumelhart and his associates developed a computer *neural network*. A biological neural network is a web of neurons intricately connected to one another by various synaptic pathways. As we saw earlier, the brain itself is not a homogeneous agglomeration of neurons, connected willy-nilly to one another. It has an incredibly intricate architecture composed of myriad smaller neural structures or networks, all connected to one another at a variety of different levels. Synapses, as we saw in Chapter 5, are the connections between neurons, and the brain has many trillions of them.

A computer neural network is a simple human-made model of the real-life networks inside our skulls. It consists of a number of "elements" that correspond to neurons and are connected in various ways. The elements—indeed, the entire neural network—is usually a piece of software running on a computer. Some neural nets, though, are actually pieces of hardware, custom-built computers meant to mimic on a small scale the actual functions of real-life biological neural nets in our brain that link together to create our mind.

Dr. John Cramer, a physicist at the University of Washington in Seattle, explains computer neural nets this way. A neural network, he says, is "a set of 'nodes' which accept one or more inputs and generate one or more outputs. Each node or simulated nerve cell has a 'weight' assigned to it, and by *weight* I mean a numerical value of importance for each node. The weights in the nodes determine linear relations between inputs and outputs." Each node or element is like a tiny neuron. It receives information from outside of itself (one or more inputs), and from that information it generates some kind of response (one or more outputs). A neural network has at least three layers of nodes: the input layer, an output layer, and a layer between that computer scientists call the intermediate layer. It can have more than three, Cramer adds, but "there is a [mathematical] theorem showing that a net with more than three layers is equivalent to one with just three."

Suppose, then, that we imagine a neural network that has three layers. Layer 1, the input layer, is the topmost one. Below it is Layer 2, the intermediate layer, and below that is Layer 3, the output layer. "At each layer," explains Cramer, "the *inputs* to all nodes come from the *outputs* from all nodes above it. That's why it is called a network."

As Cramer has explained, the weights of each node are basically a set of numerical values of importance. 1.0 is one value of importance for a node; 0.5 is another; 2.5 is still another; and so on. In some neural networks the weights may initially be set in a random pattern, while other neural networks start out with all the nodes having one initial value, such as 0.0 or 1.0. Then the researcher begins "training" the network. First, both a set of inputs and the desired outputs are selected. Next, the inputs are applied one at a time to the neural net and its nodes, and the network is allowed to generate its outputs. The outputs change the weights for the nodes in the next layer up. Then the actual output is compared with the desired one.

"If they match," says Cramer, "the weights along the path leading from input to output nodes are increased—a 'pleasure' signal. If input and output do not match, then the weights along the path leading from input to output nodes are decreased—a 'pain' signal. The researcher adds the weights to do this, with large weights having bigger effects on the next layer's nodes than small weights. This process proceeds until the system gets it right every time."

One example, says Cramer, is the use of neural nets in experiments with computer visual perception. Both scientists and business people would like to develop a computer that can "read"—that is, that can actually learn how to identify written, printed, or scripted letters and words. In neural networks that have actually been built and tested, the input layers are *pixels* or "picture elements," as on a computer screen or the dots of gray in a newspaper photograph. The pixels in the input layer are arranged in a square matrix, say 32 x 32 pixels. "This layer is then 'shown' letters of the alphabet in various type fonts or in handwritten text," he notes. "The outputs are all the possible characters that are to be recognized. In principle, such a system can be trained to 'see' and recognize all letters in any configuration."

Rumelhart's neural net did not deal with seeing and identifying letters but with "learning" how to recognize and create the correct past tenses of verbs. The "learning" consisted of changes in the strengths of the connections—the "weights," as Cramer calls them—between and among the different elements. The changes occurred as the computer neural network responded to different inputs or learning opportunities. In this particular experiment, Rumelhart and his colleagues began by giving the network a series of verbs in both their present and past tenses. This had the effect of strengthening the network connections activated by verbs occurring on a frequent basis. Then came the interesting part of the experiment: the researchers gave the computer examples of new, previously unseen verbs and asked it to predict the verbs' past tense forms.

The results were intriguing, according to Rumelhart. The computer neural network began by tending to add *-ed* to the new verbs, just as young children often do. Then, as it continued to learn new examples, the network began grouping its knowledge into "clusters of exceptions." For example, *sing* and *sang* went into the same cluster as *ring* and *rang*. As it continued to gather knowledge, the neural network became able to identify the past tense of more and more verbs whose past tenses are exceptions to the general *-ed* rule.

Rumelhart's findings suggest a process for learning tense that differs somewhat from the standard assumptions of stages. In this model, children do indeed begin by adding *-ed* to verbs in order to create their past tense. More than that, though, it appears young children also begin generalizing from one example of an exception to another, and another, and another. They learn to detect *patterns* of exceptions. They then create mental groups or clusters of exceptions that follow the same patterns. An example of such pattern might be *ring/rang/rung* instead of the "logical" *ring/ringed/ringed*. Another member of this cluster would be *sing/sang/sung.*

What is particularly fascinating about this process—if it is correct—is that it dovetails with the Damasios' convergence zone theory of infant language acquisition and speech. It also matches with Ojemann's discovery of numerous tiny language-related neuron clusters in the brain. The Damasios' theory and Ojemann's neurological observations both fit with a "neural network" model for language in the brain. Indeed, the HyperCard analogy for the Damasios' convergence zones is in some ways like a neural network.

It appears that children learn about tense both by applying a set of rules and by generalizing from numerous examples. Both forms of learning would involve small clusters of brain cells storing the learned information. Some of the knowledge, such as that dealing with grammatical rules, might be stored in brain regions genetically set aside for that purpose. Other clusters of neurons might store groups of exceptions, such as *ring* and *rang*. The information on when to use the standard grammatical rule and when to access an exception would be stored in convergence zones.

Rumelhart himself has been quoted as saying that this model is far from perfect. It is mainly meant to function as a hypothesis rather than an answer to the question of how young children learn to create past tenses. But it is a very suggestive hypothesis, especially in light of the neurological work of Ojemann and the Damasios.

Seeing Language in the Brain

In Chapter 6 we encountered several high-tech machines that are giving scientists the opportunity to look at the living brain in action. They include the CT scanner, the PET scanner, and MRI machines. Computerized tomography (CT) scanners are computerized X-ray machines that produce highly detailed X-ray slices of whatever body part they image, including the brain. Positron emission tomography (PET) scanners use the radiation emitted by a simple form of antimatter called positrons to create images of the brain and other soft-tissue organs in the body. Magnetic resonance imaging (MRI) machines use radio waves and super-strong magnets to make images of a slice of a body part such as the brain.

Recently researchers in England and the United States developed a new "souped-up" version of the standard medical MRI machine. The first work was done in the late 1980s by Sir Peter Mansfield of Nottingham, England. Following up on his work were Dr. Seiji Ogawa of the Bell Laboratories in New Jersey and Dr. Kenneth Kwong of Massachusetts General Hospital in Boston. Kwong demonstrated the first working "Fast MRI" machine in August 1991. These scientists basically took the kind of MRI scanner used in hospitals and modified it to speed the imaging process. They also developed new computer programs that can turn the nonmoving images made by a typical MRI machine into movies.

With these new Fast MRI imagers, researchers are now watching the living brains of people as they speak. They are creating movies of the brain at work, as it dreams, fantasizes, thinks, listens, and talks.

Every cell in the body needs oxygen to survive. The blood hemoglobin molecules in red blood cells pick up the oxygen from our lungs and carry it to the cells. The cells take the oxygen from the blood, use it to run their various cellular activities, and in the process release waste products like carbon dioxide. The blood carries the carbon dioxide back to the lungs, and we exhale it. MRI works because active brain cells use more oxygen than neurons that are not firing.

As the brain cells work away at some task—like ordering another cluster of neurons to release the pattern for a phoneme, or recalling the memory of a coffee cup's conical shape—they release a specialized chemical. That chemical calls forth oxygenated blood from the tiny blood vessels in the brain. The oxygen travels into working cells, while the blood swirls past them to enter the tiny veins that eventually carry it back to the lungs. Both oxygen-rich and oxygen-depleted blood have faint but distinct magnetic signals. Each is different from the other, like magnetic fingerprints, and the MRI machine charts the flow of oxygen-rich blood by detecting its faint magnetic fingerprint. The computer connected to the MRI scanner then takes the magnetic signals and "massages" them into movies of the brain's working neural networks.

One of the first published reports on the use of the new Fast MRI machines to image the brain at work was published in June 1993. The research was conducted by a team of scientists that included Dr. Robert G. Shulman, a professor of biochemistry and molecular biophysics at Yale University in New Haven, Connecticut. Shulman and his colleagues created MRI motion pictures showing tiny areas of the brain "lighting up" as they processed spoken language.

According to Shulman, the researchers began by getting a "baseline image" of the brain at rest. The subject would lie quietly with his or her head in the MRI scanner, neither talking nor reading. Then the researchers had the subject carry out simple language tasks, such as speaking the first verb that came to mind when the researcher spoke a particular noun. If I were to say *dog*, for example, the first verb you think of might be *bark*, and you would say "bark." I might say *book* and you might reply with *read*. I might then say *clock*, and you would say *tick*. As you speak the verbs, the Fast MRI machine is busy making detailed images of your brain and turning them into motion pictures.

In a similar test, the subjects were asked to merely repeat aloud a word spoken to them. I say *potato*, you say *potato*. I say *tree*, and you repeat it. The Fast MRI machine again created moving images of the subjects' brains as they repeated the words given to them.

In the first example, said Shulman, the Fast MRI scanner created vivid images that pinpointed particular regions of the brain that generate spoken verbs. Those regions glow in vivid computer-generated color in the MRI images. In the second example, the Fast MRI scanner showed a second, different cluster of tiny brain areas lighting up as the subject repeated words. Both clusters of language areas are located behind the left eyeball, deep in the outer convoluted layer of brain tissue called the left frontal cortex. These particular language regions are about the size of a pencil eraser or the head of a carpenter's nail.

In Chapter 9 we met Dr. George Ojemann of the University of Washington, who has been mapping the location of language areas. As we learned, Ojemann has mapped the location of many tiny language regions in the brains of epileptic patients undergoing surgery. The language regions Ojemann has found appear to be about the size of grapes and scattered throughout various regions of the brain. Most are in the brain's left hemisphere, with some in the right. Many, according to Ojemann's findings, are located in the front part of the brain, the frontal lobe or cortex. The MRI movies of the Yale University group provide dramatic confirmation of Ojemann's language area maps, including both the size of the tiny language regions and their location.

Other research teams have also been using the new Fast MRI technology to explore the brain and language. At the National Institutes of Health near Washington, D.C., for example, scientists have studied the activity of the brain as people silently speak words in their mind. Once again, the researchers would watch as still other tiny brain regions glowed in false computerized color. Different regions would light up in the brains of different people, according to visiting researcher Dr.

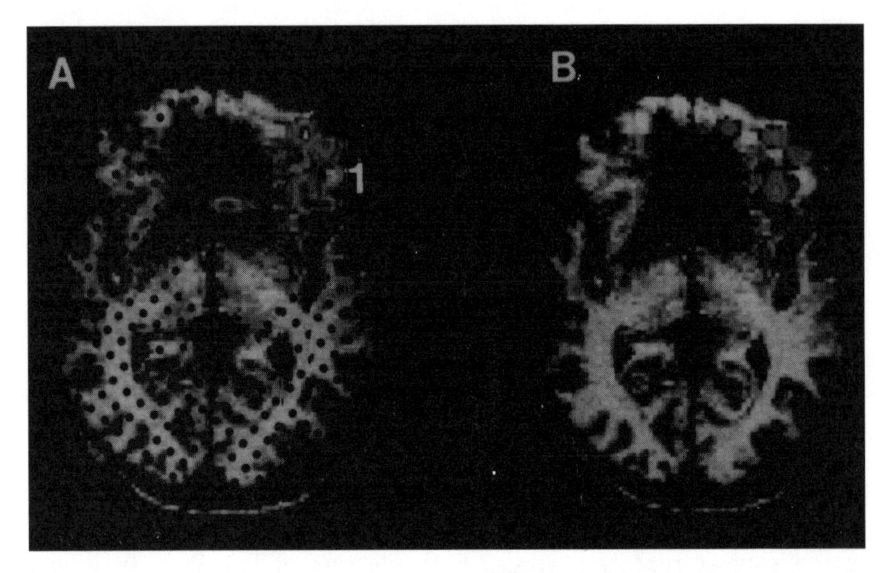

These two images of the human brain were made by Dr. Robert Shulman of Yale University and his colleagues. They show areas of the brain in action as a person uses language. Image (A) reveals particular areas in the brain that generate spoken verbs. Image (B) shows that different regions of the brain "light up" when a person verbally repeats words spoken to him. Both clusters of language regions are located in the brain's left frontal cortex, in an area right behind the left eyeball.

Reprinted by permission from McCarthy et al., *Proceedings of the National Academy of Sciences (USA)* 90: 4952-4956 (1993).

Robert Turner of London. Some of the regions were in known language areas of the brain, but other brain areas also lit up.

As we saw in Chapter 8, Hanna and Antonio Damasio believe that many different areas of the brain are simultaneously involved in the creation and production of language. Specialized regions they call convergence zones act to coordinate the simultaneous activation of different brain regions. These convergence zones thus help bring together at the same time all the different "pieces" of a word: the right choice of words, the particular speech sounds or phonemes to create the words, the appropriate grammatical rules, and so on. All of this happens in less than a split second, continuously, creating the seamless garments of consciousness and language.

The Fast MRI movies being created by the NIH researchers provide powerful support for the Damasios' convergence zone proposal. They reveal in dramatic and undeniable fashion that many different regions of the brain, both language and nonlanguage, simultaneously activate when we simply *think* a word silently in our minds.

There is something almost mystical about the idea of watching parts of the brain "light up" as a person speaks aloud, or reads, or silently repeats words. The idea would certainly make for a vivid movie or television special effect. Of course, in real life our children's brains do not sparkle as they begin learning to master language. But their eyes often do, and we frequently hear a "sparkle" in their voices as our children and grandchildren excitedly tumble down the road of language. The discoveries being made by people like Janet Werker, and David Rumelhart, by Hanna and Antonio Damasio and George Ojemann, by Robert Shulman and so many others, are exciting for what they tell us about how we create language, use language, and sometimes lose language.

But none of these is as profound as the breakthrough made by one fifteen-month-old boy in Colorado who for the first time says *Mama!* and knows what it means.

CHAPTER 12

FROM CHIMPSKY TO CHOMSKY

The research of Canadian psychologist Janet Werker has given us new insights into some of the earliest processes in an infant's journey from cries to mother tongue. We now know something about how infants go from being able to distinguish among all possible speech sounds to "hearing" just those unique to their mother tongue. Meanwhile, more than three thousand miles to the east, in more than thirteen years of pioneering research, another Canadian psychologist has uncovered still more new information about another important milepost in this journey. She has proposed a new and exciting theory of just how human infants acquire that most special of all human capabilities: language.

FROM CHIMPSKY TO SIGN

Laura Ann Petitto is a professor of psychology at McGill University in Montreal. Her field of expertise is the acquisition and use of language by humans. She has been studying it since the early 1970s. Petitto first became interested in the development of language in infants in 1972 when she began living with not a child but a chimpanzee. For three and a half years she was the primary teacher at Columbia University of Nim Chimpsky. That's *Chimpsky*, not *Chomsky*. Nim Chimpsky was a chimpanzee, the object of a detailed scientific exploration of whether nonhuman primates could or do possess language.

"I began working with Chimpsky in 1972," Petitto recalls, "and left the project in 1976. I wasn't a student at Columbia for the whole time. I was also at a small college in New Jersey. I commuted to Columbia and took courses there." Petitto's work with the Chimpsky project ignited her interest in the development of language in humans. "I left the Nim Chimpsky Project having a very clear sense that something about this capacity that our species has in regard to human language was unique. I wanted to find out what it was. So I began my investigations."

Petitto obtained her undergraduate degree, then worked with Dr. Ursula Bellugi at the Salk Institute for Biological Studies near San Diego, California. At the same time she enrolled as a graduate student in theoretical linguistics at the University of California, Los Angeles. Bellugi is a leading researcher on the structure and grammar of American Sign Language. ASL is the naturally evolved signed language of most deaf people in the United States and parts of Canada.

Petitto then began working at Gallaudet University, the world-famous university founded by and dedicated to the education of the deaf and hearing-impaired. Her mentor there was another pioneer in sign language research, Dr. William Stokoe. He was the first person to unravel the "code" for the phonological structure of a natural signed language. Petitto explains, "For many years people simply assumed that signed languages like ASL were basically 'pictures on the hand,' nothing more than a loose collection of hand movements that convey concrete information." No one really believed that the hand movements of signed languages were anything like the phonemes, morphemes, or words of "real" spoken languages, conveying abstract meanings.

According to Petitto, Stokoe and Bellugi proved otherwise. "In fact, intensive research on the structure and grammars of different signed languages proves that they all have the full expressive and grammatical complexity of any spoken languages."

After her work with Stokoe at Gallaudet, Petitto returned to graduate-student life, this time at Harvard University. There she became the student of Dr. Roger Brown. Although her doctoral degree comes from Harvard, where Brown was her advisor, she adds, "I was at MIT most of the time of my first year in graduate school. It was there I came into contact with Noam Chomsky." Chomsky has followed her progress ever since and has remarked on "the dramatic discoveries" produced by her recent research.

By the time she accepted a position at McGill University in 1983, Petitto had laid the groundwork for her professional journey. She had explored the possibility of another species possessing language, had learned a great deal about sign language, and had gone on to study cognition and linguistics. At McGill she began to hone in on the beginnings of language.

The questions that interest Petitto all converge on the notion of whether our capacity for language is biologically controlled. "Is there anything about language that is genetically transmitted?" she asks. "What are the key aspects of the environment that interface with the genetic predisposition? And notice," she adds, "that the way the word *genetic* is used nowadays is not the way it's been used in the past."

This is a good point, and one that most of us do not understand. As Petitto notes, *genetic* no longer means a blueprint. As presently understood by molecular genetics, the word *genetics* implies more of a biological *suggestion*. You *could* be more likely to come down with Type I diabetes than most other people. You *might* stand a good chance of getting colon cancer. You *could* very well develop schizophrenic behaviors, if ... It is not a lead-pipe cinch but rather a biological possibility. That possibility may or may not become an actuality. It all depends on what Petitto calls the "contextuals," environmental or other nongenetic forces and influences. Researchers studying AIDS, for example, are looking for so-called co-factors, environmental or biological factors that may increase the likelihood that someone who is HIV positive will develop full-blown AIDS.

Petitto's suggestion is that our ability to create and use language may be genetic *in this sense*, as a biological suggestion or strong predisposition. "That is literally how I mean it. Not in the old-fashioned sense. The questions we're asking are, What is language at the neurological level? What is the nature of the patterned ensembles of neurons that might exist? What might they be specifically sensitive to? How might they interact with perceptual and motoric constraints? And how might they interact with aspects of the environment that are setting its switches?

"And if you want to understand the biological foundations of behavior, you have to look at its genesis, its ontogeny. That's why I began to study the very early processes of language acquisition."

Babbling in Sign and Sound

One such process that has fascinated her, and that she has explored for several years now, is the same one that has intrigued Kimbrough Oller: babbling. Oller and his colleagues have examined babbling in infants from several different cultures, using several different languages. But they have all been speaking infants who babble verbally. And that makes sense. The assumption has long been that babbling is a speech-based mechanism. It reflects the maturing ability of an infant to use his or her vocal apparatus to create speech sounds. Oller himself convincingly proved that deaf infants do not learn verbal babbling. They do not get the requisite aural input.

This apparently serves to reinforce the prevailing view about the innate connection between babbling and spoken speech. Human language, this view states, has a unique link to the mechanisms for producing verbal speech. Only if the human vocal apparatus matures properly, and if the neural pathways that govern the motor control of the vocal apparatus are working, do infants babble. If this view is true, says Petitto, "then the very structure of language results from the literal constraints imposed on the mechanisms for producing speech. Language's grammatical regularities and other aspects of its structure, according to this view, reflect evolutionary developments of our vocal mechanisms."

If we cannot speak verbally, then we cannot create language. Even deaf people who used signed languages would have to have functioning vocal speech mechanisms, this view suggested.

Petitto wondered if this position was in fact true. It was an assumption, but was it correct? It seemed to her that this early process of language acquisition could stand some close scientific scrutiny. Moreover, it was just the kind of question that, when answered, would reveal new understanding of the biological foundations of language behavior. Suppose babbling was indeed tied to the maturation of our capacity for language, and specifically to the development of the mechanisms responsible for speech production. Then babbling would likely be specific only to spoken language.

However, suppose babbling was actually tied to the maturation of some *brain-based* language capacity. And suppose this capacity was sensitive not to sound but to particular *kinds of patterns* in the "input," the information the brain receives through the senses. The input could be sound, such as the happy "gootchie-goo" baby talk that parents direct at their infants, or the ordinary conversation babies hear, or the television, or songs, or poetry, or music. The input could be visual, such as body and hand movements. If this theory were true, then babbling would *not* be limited to verbally speaking infants. Deaf infants learning sign languages would babble, too. They would babble "on their hands," as Petitto puts it.

Petitto began her first explorations of this theory more than a decade ago. Her initial publication of her discoveries in this field appeared in a 1981 Salk Institute Technical Report. She described her work in more detail in her 1983 doctoral dissertation. The research was difficult, Petitto says, because of both its theoretical implications and the difficulty of finding the right subjects to study. Says Petitto, "These included deaf infants of deaf parents who had no exposure whatever to spoken language." She also ran into considerable skepticism in the linguistic and psychological community.

"After I presented some of my findings in 1985, I was basically told that I had better be able to 'stake my life on the findings,' that my colleagues were 'watching me.' Because if my findings were true, a lot of people might be 'wrong.' Of course," she adds, "that's a little silly. Previous research is *not* 'wrong.' It has taught us an amazing amount about the acquisition of spoken language."

But Petitto was after bigger game. She sought to discover the neurological, genetic, and environmental foundations for our ability to acquire language, *period*, whether the input to our brains comes from sound, for spoken language, or from vision, for signed language.

To this end Petitto personally conducted three follow-up studies to confirm the findings of her earlier research. The results of those studies were published in 1985, 1986, and 1987. She then began her most recent, ongoing study, working with Paula Marentette, at that time her graduate student. She used naturalistic and experimental techniques to gather data from five infants. She videotaped each of them at three different ages—ten, twelve, and fourteen months. Two of the infants were profoundly deaf. They had deaf parents and were learning American Sign Language as their mother tongue. The other three infants had normal hearing, as did their parents. They were learning a spoken language as their mother tongue and had no exposure at all to any signed language.

Petitto and Marentette applied the same criteria to possible signed or manual babbling as they did to vocal babbling. They used a highly precise transcription system that made it possible to carry out direct comparisons of vocal babbling with hand movements that could be manual babbling. They also analyzed the data from the two sets of infants using the same methods.

The results were astounding. In brief: normally developing babies babble. Period. If they are deaf, and their parents are deaf, and they are learning a signed language as their mother tongue, they *still* babble. They babble on their hands and not with their tongues. They do not babble in some particular signed language, of course, any more than speaking infants babble in English or Spanish or Tagalog. Babbling is still not language. Like verbal babbling, manual babbling consists of a small number of manually created "phonemes" of a signed language. It has a simple syllabic organization, as does verbal babbling. The infants create it without it having any meaning or any reference to some real entity, the same as verbal babbling.

The manual babbling by deaf infants discovered by Petitto included frequent examples of reduplication of signed syllables. But it was more than that. Verbally babbling infants combine the speech sounds they hear and learn into new combinations of babble. Manually babbling deaf infants do the same. They take different signed units and combine them in novel ways. Says Petitto, "This supports the observation that infants must be born with a sensitivity to certain patterns in their language-input. It's not the method, sound or sight, that's important, but the patterns they contain."

On the Same Track

Petitto's research on deaf and hearing infants uncovered other fascinating parallels. Both groups of infants—deaf infants of deaf parents learning a signed language and hearing infants learning a spoken language—followed the same babbling "timeline." Both deaf infants and hearing infants moved through the same stages of babbling, manual and vocal, at the same time. Petitto also discovered that the overall timeline for acquiring signed languages is the same as the timeline for a spoken language, which we explored in Chapter 10. Infants learning a signed language like ASL pass through the same stages of language development that infants learning a spoken language pass through. Furthermore, they pass through all those stages, from crying to cooing to babbling to true language, on the *exact same timetable* as hearing and speaking infants. Petitto has found that all young children also talk and sign about the same topics as they journey into the world of language.

Finally, Petitto discovered that hearing infants do not necessarily *favor speech* as their chosen mode of language. She studied hearing infants who lived in bilingual or, as she calls them, "bimodal" homes. The mother was deaf and signed, while the father was hearing and spoke, or vice versa. Says Petitto, "Infants learning language in these situations did not prefer speech to signing. Indeed, such bilingual children show no preference for speech at all! Instead, they acquire each and every language milestone for *both speech and signing*, and they do it on the identical time course. That is, they manually babble and vocally babble at the same time. They produce their first words and first signs at the same time, and so on, all the way up the line."

This finding in particular is amazing. As Petitto points out, it "fundamentally challenges all the . . . explanations of language that focus on the supremacy of speech and speech production in our species." If speech-making and the vocal mechanisms were the key to language, then these babies from speaking/signing bimodal homes would invariably prefer speaking over signing. That they emphatically do not is a body blow to the "speaking with the mouth is fundamental" camp of language acquisition.

The Foundations of Language Acquisition

Petitto's discoveries have led her to propose a new theory of how humans acquire language. Her theory has three major points.

First, our brains must contain at birth some kind of pattern recognition mechanism. This mechanism, or "hard-wired filter," to use computer jargon, is sensitive to specific patterns that appear in the "input" the brain receives from the outside world. That input may be visual or verbal. What matters are the patterns. In particular, Petitto proposes that our children possess an innate and unique sensitivity to the rhythmic and distributional patterns of prosody. We rarely speak in a monotone; our speech has a natural rhythm, caused by the rise and fall of the pitch, stress, and tone we give to sounds, syllables, and words. Signed languages also have a natural rhythm. That is what prosody is, and babies are born with the ingrained ability to detect those rhythms. Petitto proposes that this pattern recognition mechanism in infants' brains is therefore sensitive to syllables, which are the basic units of rhythm in both spoken and signed languages.

"It appears," says Petitto, "that the brain has a dedicated architecture, specific clusters of neurons that are especially sensitive to specific aspects of language structure. In particular, they're sensitive to these rhythmic *patterns* carried by the input," and not to the particular delivery system. This inborn, genetically coded sensitivity to "units of rhythm" in either sound or movement makes it possible for infants to recognize the basic "boundaries" or building blocks of a language. They can now begin to acquire those basic building blocks, either signed or spoken, as the brain recognizes them and stores them for later use. They then begin using those building blocks to create new and larger language structures. First and foremost, they can find the rhythmic boundaries of words. Then, slowly at first but then in a rush, will come more words, followed by phrases, clauses, and sentences.

Petitto points out a particularly intriguing implication to this pattern recognition ability of infants and its connection to language. It allows infants to begin acquiring language without yet knowing what language is. "This has been the classic conundrum in child language," says Petitto. "How can a child learn language without knowing language, or without knowing what the 'target state' looks like"—that is, without knowing what he or she is supposed to be saying and knowing what it means. However, possessing an innate ability to detect language-like patterns allows babies to quickly detect the basic sounds that compose words, and then to create words themselves without ever having any previous understanding of the meaning of the words.

Petitto offers an example: "Suppose you are in Russia and you don't speak Russian. A man is speaking emphatically to you about a pencil. You can't even begin to hope to understand the meaning of his words if you don't know where the words begin and end, or even understand the syllables from which the words are made. This is the same problem an infant faces" when exposed to language, says Petitto. The pattern recognition mechanism contained in the brain's neural networks solves this problem. The baby begins life with the inborn ability to detect the patterns of language.

The second major point to Petitto's theory of child language acquisition is that the pattern recognition mechanism in an infant's brain interacts with other brain processes. Petitto says that one such connection exists between the brain mechanism that detects language-like patterns in sound or movement and those parts of the brain that govern different kinds of body movements. The different physical mechanisms for producing language, such as the vocal system in speech or the hands in signing, are restricted in the kinds of movements they can make. The "motor production" regions in our brain act to constrain the production of language-like structure. The result is a fine-tuned connection between a language's structure—including its grammar and prosody or rhythms—and the motor production of these structures, the body's ability to create the structures of language. This is not the same as a link between a language's structure and the specific mechanism for speech, for example, or for the fine hand movements of signed language. It is a more basic connection.

These motor constraints on the development of any type of language are not limited to language, either. Petitto suggests that they are reflections of more fundamental constraints on movements of the entire body. We cannot move our arms or hands or legs or heads in any direction we wish. We are not "gumbies," but animals. The general construction of our bodies, and the nature of the muscles and bones and ligaments, put limits on the movements of our body parts.

Evidence for this kind of connection flows directly from Petitto's discovery of manual babbling. When deaf babies babble on their hands, they use rhythmic movements of their hands that sign language researchers call "movement/opening" and "hold/closing" movements. The foundation of the basic sign-syllable is the vowel-like "movement" and consonant-like "hold" alternation of hand movements. This is an exact parallel to the consonant-vowel foundation of voiced syllables. My grandson Ryan babbled in the vocal mode, making simple consonant-vowel combinations and stringing them together in more and more creative combinations. If he had been babbling in the manual mode, he would have been making the opening/closing hand-babbling movements typical of any sign-learning infant.

Another connection exists between the brain's mechanism for detecting language-like patterns and the parts of the brain that detect and process sensory information. Petitto says that the infant has constraints on general perception, as well, and that these constraints also interact with the pattern detection mechanism. Babies acquiring a signed language as their mother tongue, for example, can tell the difference between a simple gesture of the hand or arm that has no linguistic meaning and a sign. Dad sits at the kitchen table doing a crossword puzzle. His left hand taps absently on the table. That is not a manual sign, and baby Sharon ignores it. But Sharon has already started repeating the sign-syllables she has seen in the signed words for *father, mother, flowers, cat, baby, Alison,* and *love*. She is already stringing them together and manually babbling the sign equivalents of *fafafafafa, babababa,* and *labalabalaba*. It is clear, then, that there are limitations on the general perceptual mechanism of infants, and that these constraints are connected in a deep fashion to the "language filters" in their brains.

The third major component of Petitto's theory of infant language acquisition is the environment. The sensory input from the outside world carries the information that the infant's brain uses as raw material to fashion the child's mother tongue. According to Petitto, though, the exact nature of that environmental input is largely irrelevant. "As long as the input [entering the brain] contains the relevant patterns, the infant will try to learn it." The form of the input, be it sounds or hand signs, is unimportant. Says Petitto, "The crucial factor is that the input must contain those key structural features in order for language acquisition to begin and be maintained." It does not matter how that input gets to the brain's potential language regions. It can come through the eyes or through the ears. What matters is the pattern that the input carries with it. "We have found no evidence that the brains of children are sensitive to *how* the input gets in, to the particular 'modality,' as we say. That's why a child could entertain structure if it's on the hands or the mouth."

One lesson for parents of infants that arises from Petitto's work is the importance of exposing infants from their first days to lots of language input. The form of the input is not particularly important. It can be music, poetry, baby talk (which we all love to bathe babies in, whether we are parents, grandparents or strangers on the street), reading stories, casual signing, baby-talk signing, signing stories—it does not matter. The important thing is to create rhythm and inflection. Every human language rests on a foundation of rhythm, either spoken or signed. Experts in early child development have long stressed the importance of talking to our infants, singing to them, reading to them even when they are still in the cradle. Petitto has provided the biological and neurological affirmation for these practices. They work, and the reason they work is that we are genetically primed for them to work.

"Many previous theories of infant language acquisition wanted to just say, 'Well, this is just a general perceptual thing and the child over time learns the form of language,' or 'Forms of language are just an epiphenomenon of speech, of the ability to produce speech, to produce the mouth movements. It sounds like it's structural, but it's structural because the mouth has a structure.' So the structure of language has traditionally been looked upon as some artifact or epiphenomenon of the mechanism for producing speech," Petitto says. "I pulled apart those two things, speech and language. What has never been integrated into the equation is that we absolutely have to postulate something in the brain with a sensitivity to basic aspects of language's structure."

More than three decades ago linguist Noam Chomsky first proposed that the human brain must have some unique "language organ" within it that makes it possible for our species to create and use language. He rejected the idea that other animals might be capable of language. Humans, he asserted, are unique in this regard. And the root of this unique capability, our ability to create a nearly infinite number of languages from a small set of basic grammar rules, must lie in the rapidly growing ball of neural tissue within the skull of every newborn human child. Chomsky was still a fairly new and certainly controversial figure in linguistics when he first offered his remarkable hypothesis. More than two decades later, he would meet a young psycholinguist named Laura Ann Petitto. He would teach some of the classes she took and would talk with her about her work. And now her work appears to dramatically confirm Chomsky's original hypothesis. It is a classic example of how science works best, moving from hypothesis to test, from idea to reality, from "what if" to "what is."

CHAPTER 13

BEYOND THE MOTHER TONGUE

We have taken an extended journey through the worlds of language and languages. First came our initial examination of how to define language. Then we explored the many language families, paying close attention to our own. Indo-European has a rich and complex history, rooted as it is in Proto-Indo-European and the prehistoric rise of humans in Europe and Turkey. English, the mother tongue of most of us reading this book, is itself a language with an exciting, bloody, patchwork history. It has come a long way from being nothing more than the language of the "Angles" living on a large island at the edge of the Atlantic.

From there we plunged into the realms of speech sounds and syllables, phonemes and phones, morphemes and grammar, prosody and discourse. These are the building blocks of any spoken language. We learned, too, that signed languages are indeed true languages, with their own fully developed equivalents for phonemes and words, their own mature grammars and dialects and differences. When an infant begins learning his or her mother tongue, be it spoken or signed, these are some of the bits and pieces acquired within months of birth.

We discovered the wonders of the human brain. It is in the brain, we found, that language has its genetic and biological roots. The brain's complex organization may at times seem somewhat baffling, but it is beautiful and awesome as well. Our journey into the brain led us into encounters with several brilliant researchers who are exploring this neurological frontier within our skulls. Here we discovered how the brain may work like a special computer program as it puts together the bits and pieces of language and thought, perception and imagination, memory and consciousness itself. We found the brain is primed to detect the patterns of sound or movement that make up a language. The brain is also like a parallel computer in the way it processes information that turns into language. And we discovered that language and its parts are stored in many places in the brain besides the traditionally known locations. Indeed, each of us carries within our brain a unique "fingerprint" pattern of language storage locations.

Next we entered the realm of the very young, the infant child, the baby who is beginning his or her own journey into the worlds of language. Here, too, we found exciting new discoveries. We learned of the timetable of language acquisition that all babies, deaf or hearing, follow during their first months and years of life. We discovered that all babies can at first distinguish among all possible speech-sounds; that they begin forgetting that ability before they are a year old; and that "use it or lose it" is the rule for becoming fluent in additional languages. In addition, it turns out that all babies babble, either with their mouths if they are learning a spoken language or on the hands if they are learning sign. Babies have no preference for speech over sign, or vice versa. And babies learn language aspects such as tense in a fashion few of us suspected.

Finally, a psycholinguist in Montreal gave us a glimpse at a new and exciting theory about how all human infants are capable of acquiring language. Her theory is based on more than a decade of pioneering research. And it gives concrete support to a controversial hypothesis first advanced more than thirty years ago by the most famous linguist of our time.

It has been "a long strange trip," as the Grateful Dead's Jerry Garcia once sang. But that is only appropriate. Language itself is a strange trip, and one that hopefully lasts our lifetime. It is a journey we all take. It is a wondrous one.

But do we take it alone?

Animals and Language

For as long as we have been humans, it appears we have yearned to communicate with others not our kind. Most other cultures in human history have believed that we can and do communicate with other animals. The myths and folk tales of many societies abound with stories of animals speaking to humans, and humans and animals speaking with one another. Some myths tell of animals turned into humans, and of humans changed into animals. In some myths the animals are the guides or protectors of the humans. Most such stories, though, hasten to point out that "this was all long ago," and that animals and humans do not speak to one another any more.

Our desire to "talk to the animals," as the fictional Dr. Doolittle did, remains with us still. We even couch our questions and attempts in terms remarkably similar to those of the ancient myths. We just camouflage it in scientific terms. Instead of suggesting that some animals were once humans, we wonder if some animals have brains as complex as ours. Most of us in Western society do not speak of animals as being "spirit guides," but we do speculate that they "might have something to teach us."

In the myths of Native American peoples, it was Crow and Coyote, Eagle and Bear who spoke to us. Today, we wonder if we might be able to communicate with chimpanzees and dolphins.

It is a powerful longing, this desire to speak with the animals. I wish we could do it. I would love to converse with a dolphin or whale, or exchange folk tales with a chimp. But can I? Can any of us? Do whales or chimpanzees possess the gift of language? The modern controversy has raged for decades now. The answer, I fear, will disappoint many of us.

One researcher with a particularly clear view of the issue of language and animals is Laura Ann Petitto, whom we met in the last chapter. Petitto, as we saw, began her career in language studies by living with Nim Chimpsky, the chimpanzee who was the subject of a pioneering study of language and animals. That experience has given Petitto a unique perspective and some definite opinions.

"I was Nim Chimpsky's primary teacher and lived with him for three and a half years," Petitto recalls. "That project raised some important theoretical questions. One of the biggest was, Is language part of our biological endowment? When these studies began, the hypothesis had already been offered by Noam Chomsky and others that language *was* part of our biological heritage."

Language, as we have found, is a very complex human capacity. So researchers must be somewhat cautious when they say that language is "part of our biological endowment," that is, biologically based or genetically linked. How exactly do they define their terms? What exactly do we mean by *language*? Petitto, too, asks these questions. She says, "Whenever you have some kind of complex behavior that you suspect could be part of a species' biological endowment, then there are proofs you must go through to determine if this is true or not. These kinds of biologically based traits work in several specific ways. They are species-specific, for example. They are typically tightly maturationally controlled, developing on a specific timetable. If there is some kind of brain trauma, you can alter the function. Those kinds of proofs."

In terms of language, scientists must begin by laying to rest the issue of species specificity. Is language really species-specific, unique to humans? The research with Nim Chimpsky, to which Petitto dedicated more than three years of her then-young life, was an attempt to answer this question. Specifically, the researchers wanted to determine if language was, in principle, entirely learnable from environmental input.

According to Petitto, the results were very straightforward. "That research pretty conclusively showed that apes are very complex cognitively and communicatively. They can be referential and intentional, and they can demonstrate a variety of cognitive capacities. But there were key aspects of human language that they failed to master."

Despite what we read in the papers or in popular books, the Nim Chimpsky findings are not controversial. Says Petitto flatly, "No ape project or primate project, including quite extreme ones that aren't in the realm of science, such as Koko, claims that these apes master all the aspects of human language. *Everybody* shows some humility about this!"

But what about the most famous chimp language experiments of all, carried out by Dr. Roger Fouts of Central Washington University, which appear to show chimps learning and using sign languages? Petitto vigorously disagrees. "No. No. Fouts will not tell you that his apes are reciting Shakespeare, writing poetry, or writing great novels."

But are they communicating with sign language? Petitto chuckles. "It is undeniable that other species communicate. We are not alone on this planet as far as communication. That's clearly true. No one is arguing that these animals do not communicate. But remember: communication and language are not the same thing."

Antonio Damasio has made the same point about language, consciousness, and the brain: "We do not need language in order to have some kind of *basic* consciousness. I'm convinced that some animals have consciousness, but they do not have consciousness at the same level that humans do." Damasio believes that language plays an important, even essential, role in how sophisticated a level of consciousness or awareness a being has. Language, he says, is another level of what he calls *distancing* between the person and the outer world.

As we saw earlier, the Damasios suggest that consciousness is a result of the brain "attending" to some specific input from the world out there, piped in through the senses and reconstructed by the brain's many convergence zones. "Attending" is basically paying intense attention to something: that bird call, the taste of the cherry pie, the memory of an old lover's death, that pickup truck flying through the air and heading right for me.

Petitto, too, is quite familiar with the psychological mechanism called attending. And it applies directly to Nim Chimpsky and the question of animals and language. Petitto explains, "Nim Chimpsky did not attend to the relevant aspects of the signing he was seeing. And not just Nim, but all these apes in these sign language studies. One of the most striking things you notice when you're around these signing apes or the ones who work at a keyboard is that language is almost superfluous. The researcher is one place to the right, the board is to the left, the hands are waving wildly in the middle. The animals are simply not *attending* to the relevant aspects of the communicative interaction. Most of these apes, when they do produce a kind of communicative act, are overlapping with the experimenter. It's almost to the point of 'talking at the same time.' What is being exchanged?"

Because Nim was not attending to the stream of symbolic communication that is language, adds Petitto, he actually never extracted the essential information flowing out and through the language stream. "These apes do not have lexical knowledge, vocabulary knowledge.

They don't have the phonemic inventory, the collection of basic speech-sounds or speech-forms, from which all human language is formed. If you don't know the basic building blocks of English, you cannot *make* English! You cannot engage in complex grammatical forms, with nested embeddings, about what you did yesterday, or what you're going to do tomorrow or next year.

"And that is exactly what we see in the apes," she continues. "It's predicted from their lack of attention and their inability to put together the basic collection of speech-form building blocks of a language. From that you can predict the very things they never achieve. They don't achieve complex syntax. They don't achieve referencing to abstract things that aren't physically present. The ape doesn't do that, and it's probably because it doesn't have the relevant brain tissue."

Petitto's final point is perhaps the most damning. For it is true, all modern examinations of primate brains reveal the same essential fact. As complex as their brains are, they simply do not have the amount of complexity characteristic of the brain itself or of the language regions found in the human brain. It simply is not there.

The jury is still out on dolphin and whale brains. Whale brains, in particular, are considerably larger than human brains. Superficially, at least, they appear as convoluted and complex. But to date no one has done the kind of detailed microscopic examination of whale or dolphin brains that has been done with human and ape brains. We do not know if they possess the requisite complexity of structure essential for language.

We do know that whales and dolphins communicate with a complex system of whistles, clicks, and other sounds. But as Petitto notes, communication and language are not the same thing. Whales do sing; and, unlike the songs of birds, whale songs do change over time. However, there is still no way to say for certain that whale songs are language. Sophisticated communication? Almost certainly. Language? No one knows. And to say that whale songs are of the same level of sophistication, emotional content, and self-aware creativity as human songs is simply the worst kind of anthropomorphising, of projecting our own self-portrait on another creature of the earth. That is not fair to the whale, and it is certainly not fair to us.

It is wishful thinking, and wishful thinking and science are not the same thing.

PHONING ET

Perhaps the greatest challenge to both our use and understanding of the nature of language would be what science fiction writers call "First Contact." Should we ever encounter an intelligent alien species, our ability to communicate using arbitrary symbols representing abstract ideas and concrete entities will be stretched as never before. Such an encounter would also test every theory ever proposed about the origins and nature of language. The reason is simple. Everything we know about language, from its evolutionary origins to its acquisition by every newborn baby, from its structural roots in our brains to its incredible breadth of different variations, floats like a flimsy coracle on an unspoken sea of basic "givens."

The only species with whom we communicate using language is our own. Though we can communicate with other animals, like cats, dogs, chimps, and dolphins, we do not communicate with them using language. As best we can tell, other animals do not have the requisite brain complexity or fine motor control of either hand or mouth to create and use language. We use language with one another, then, but with members of no other species.

We can use language to communicate with one another because of all that we share. We share the same basic ecological setting: "Biosphere 1," the planet Earth, in all its glory and pollution. We share the same basic environmental influences: water, air, earth; wind and sun and rain; stars and moon above at night, the sun in the day; cold and heat. We all share the same basic bodily needs: food and shelter, air and water. We all share the same psychological and emotional needs: love and caring, companionship and self-confidence, security and challenge. And we all share the same genetic heritage: the human genome, or genetic code, that carries the instructions to make us physically what we are. We are *Homo sapiens sapiens*, "the thinking human." Our brains are uniquely tuned to the language frequency, endowed with an innate ability to detect the basic rhythms and structures in sound or movement that can become the building blocks of symbolic communication.

Suppose, though, we someday meet Others. Perhaps we will only encounter alien intelligence remotely. It could be we will detect their electromagnetic signals through our various SETI programs (SETI stands for Search for Extra-Terrestrial Intelligence). These projects are using radiotelescopes to listen for radio signals from alien civilizations on other planets circling other stars. If we detected such signals, we might decide to reply. That could lead to a radio conversation across the gulfs of space.

Of course, such conversations would also stretch across hundreds if not thousands of centuries. The distances between the stars are huge beyond comprehension. A beam of light or of radio waves (just another form of light), which travels faster than anything else, takes more than four years just to get to the nearest star. Such a radio beam would take twenty-nine thousand years to reach the center of our galaxy and more than a million years to reach the nearest large galaxy.

When American astronauts explored the moon in the late 1960s and early 1970s, it took a second and a half for the radio broadcasts from Earth to reach them and for their radioed replies to get back to NASA. We could all hear the awkward delay in the conversations between Mission Control and Neil Armstrong. When space scientists talk about communicating with the computers aboard distant space probes like Pioneer 10 or Voyager 2, they speak of "round-trip light times." The round-trip light time to Voyager 2, now heading down and out of the solar system, is already more than eleven hours. When we have a conversation with another person, we hear and respond nearly instantly. The colloquy proceeds in a continuous flow of words. Not so with an interstellar conversation! The pauses between replies would be measured in human lifetimes.

Speaking with ET face to face, we would not encounter these kinds of difficulties. But any attempt to communicate with aliens from other worlds will run up against three fundamental problems: (1) *Can* we talk? (2) How *will* we talk? (3) What will we talk *about*?

First and most important: Will it even be possible to communicate with ET in any fashion resembling language? At the beginning of this book we looked at several criteria for language as proposed by linguist Charles Hockett. Human languages naturally possess all thirteen of Hockett's criteria, while monkey calls do not meet several of them. We can confidently assume that alien communication systems will be true languages in Hockett's sense. For example, the aliens will no doubt use small collections of "elements" like sounds or movements that are imbued with an arbitrary set of meanings. Their language signals will have stable associations with their real-world experiences. They will pass on their language systems to succeeding generations by the process of teaching and learning, but their infants will also be born with some innate ability to learn their alien mother tongues. Their languages will bind both time and space, conveying information about their pasts and possible futures.

Will an *alien* language have any points of connection with any *human* language? Probably not, if the alien language uses some sort of "modality" or delivery system unknown to earthlings. We can imagine, for example, an alien language based on smells. Such a language probably cannot exist on Earth; pheromones, the chemical compounds our noses detect and our brains interpret as odors, do not travel fast enough or far enough to be a good medium for language. On some alien planet, though, they might be the perfect transmission carrier for linguistic information. But an alien who "speaks" using smells will not communicate much of anything on Earth; and humans making auditory noises on Planet Z will not get very far, either.

However, if we ever meet aliens who communicate using sounds or movements, we may stand a chance of finding a way to translate their language into ours, and vice versa. At least we will share the same delivery systems. That will make solving the second problem, how we will talk, considerably easier than it would be otherwise. We will first figure out the respective language-symbols for the most basic things we have in common. We will begin with numbers and mathematics.

We will not start with "words" for *head, hand, eye, me,* or *you*. If I point to my chest and say *me*, will you the Alien know I mean *me*? Or do I mean *chest*, or *stomach*? Or did I just make the language-gesture that means *I feel sexually aroused*? Numbers and basic mathematical concepts, though, are truly universal. *One* is always *one*. *Ten* is always *ten*, no matter what planet you come from. It will not be difficult, for example, to figure out the comparative symbols for 10^0 (or 1), 10^1 (10), 10^2 (100), 10^3 (1000), and so on. The gravitational constant is the same everywhere. So is the Pythagorean theorem.

We will begin to communicate in mathematics. Of course, communication and language are not the same thing. And I cannot talk to you about the bicycle ride I took yesterday in Manito Park using the Pythagorean theorem. Eventually you and I will have to figure out our mutual language symbols for *me, you, head,* and *run*. We will have to decipher each other's grammatical structures. It will take a long time. But I suspect that with enough commonalities, we will make a start.

One result will probably be some kind of *pidgin* tongue. Sometimes called makeshift or marginal languages, pidgins are systems of communication used by people who do not share a common language but who need to talk with one another. Pidgins have limited vocabulary and simplified grammar. They are not anyone's native tongue, but pidgins are spoken today by millions of people around the world and play a very important role in politics and commerce. They are not the crude "Me Tarzan, you Jane" stereotype of movies and novels but creative variations on natural languages, with their own structures and rules. Most pidgins used today reflect the colonial patterns of Western exploration and exploitation of the Third World, and are based on English, Dutch, French, Portuguese, and Spanish. But many other pidgins exist as well. One of the most famous non-European pidgins is found where I live, the Pacific Northwest. It is Chinook Jargon, once used by Northwest Indians as a trading language with European trappers, explorers, and settlers.

Pidgins do not last very long. They tend to disappear when one or another of the languages becomes dominant, or when the reason for the pidgin's existence disappears. The pidgin English used in Vietnam, for example, disappeared as soon as the last Americans left in 1975. It is possible that a human/alien pidgin language might last for many centuries, as we struggled to understand one another more and more clearly. If we no longer needed or wanted to understand one another, though, the pidgin would disappear. We might not have anything to trade with them, for example, or the aliens might be offended by our eating habits and leave.

On the other hand, a human/alien pidgin could evolve into a *creole*. A creole language is a pidgin that eventually becomes the mother tongue of a community or society. This is simply part of the process by which languages change and new languages come into existence. It has happened many times in the past. It is happening today in places like the Caribbean and Africa. As more people use the pidgin, it becomes the main method of communication. Within one or two generations, the formerly native language or languages become absorbed into the creole. The study of pidgins and creoles is an exciting and fruitful area of linguistics today. It is opening many new insights into how languages come into existence and change over time.

We can imagine circumstances in which a human/alien pidgin tongue could metamorphose into a creole language. The aliens arrive;

nothing horrible happens, like nuclear war or massive stock market crashes. We give them a long-term lease on the moon's far side and begin the slow process of learning one another's languages. Over a period of a few years a pidgin develops, based first on words for mathematical terms and equations and later on simple understandings of each other's grammar and vocabulary. The pidgin is a mixture of English, Russian, French, Tagalog (the Philippine Islands are by now a major spacefaring nation) and <<>>!@^+*|/>, the alien language. The aliens stick around and begin massive mining operations on the lunar farside, where they have found extensive deposits of a metal their culture considers sacred. We set up a simple but lucrative long-term trading deal: lunar metal in exchange for controlled fusion technology. The "Mr. Fusion"–powered cars of *Back to the Future* become a reality.

The pidgin becomes popular, a fad. It sweeps the planet. Mick Jagger/clone3 hits the top of the charts with a rock song in Pidgin. Then the newsnets start a channel in Pidgin. Pidgin As a Second Language (PASL) classes become the rage in grammar school. "PASL's No Hassle!" shows up on bumper stickers everywhere.

Fifty years later the aliens are still mining the moon, we are driving Mr. Fusion–powered flying cars, and the human/alien pidgin has become the mother tongue of a new generation of humans. It has become a creole, and it is well on the way to becoming standardized in pronunciation, grammar, and vocabulary. Soon it will be a full-fledged language.

Our great-great-grandchildren and the aliens will long ago have solved the third problem, what we will talk about. They will be talking about politics, religion, economics, physics, cosmology, biology, art, dance, rock 'n' roll, and language.

As I finish writing the manuscript for this book, my grandson is entering his second year of life. Ryan Patrick Nash has not yet said his first clear, unambiguous word, but his parents assure us he is so close it could happen any day. Soon young Ryan will begin sampling the wonders of language. It is the most sophisticated form of communication on our planet.

It is an ocean. Ryan begins by running along the seashore, dipping his toes into the foaming surf and testing the temperature. Then he will venture in farther and farther: ankle-high, then calf-high, and then he will plunge in up to his knees. Ryan's brain, like that of your child or grandchild, is a powerful engine. We cannot see it, for a safety cage of bone hides it from our eyes, but his brain has shifted from third gear into fourth, and then into overdrive. Neuron connections are multiplying at an awesome pace. Dime-sized clusters of brain cells are learning and storing sound-shapes, nouns, verbs, modifiers, grammatical rules. Other tiny regions are storing nonlinguistic impressions and concepts: *mama, dada, cat, hot, green, yummy!, ouch!, milk, sweet, grass, car, tree, ear, toe*, and so much more.

Young Ryan Nash soon will move from one word to two, from simple phrases to full sentences, from stumbling grammar to a command of "could have" and "what if." Later the door of the written word will open, and it will reveal to him universes that once existed, may exist in the future, may never come into being except in his imagination. Ryan will begin to read aloud; he will also read silently, forming the words and sentences in his mind. Isaac Asimov and Emile Zola; Miguel de Cervantes and Gary Snyder; Ernest Hemingway and Robert Heinlein; Niccolo Machiavelli and Thomas Merton; Thales and Tolstoi; all will come to life, all will speak in his mind and to his spirit. The worlds of poetry, drama, fiction, philosophy, politics, and religion will open up.

All the while, from this moment until the day he dies, Ryan will speak in his mother tongue. With language he will bridge the enormous gulf between person and person, universe without and world within, perception and concept, reality and imagination.

Caged in flesh, bound by the walls of space and time, walking the path between the gulfs of birth and death, Ryan Nash will still possess language.

And language will set him free.

APPENDIX 1

LANGUAGES OF THE WORLD

Between three thousand and six thousand languages exist in the world today. The precise number is not known; what is known is that fewer languages are alive today than fifty to a hundred years ago. The inexorable march of English and French as major global languages, the ravages of colonization and exploitation of Third World cultures by First World countries, and the rise of world-girdling electronic media have taken their toll.

The following list of one hundred languages is based on two larger tables. One, a list of three hundred languages, appears in *The ABC's of Languages and Linguistics*. The other, a list of about a thousand languages, can be found in *The Cambridge Encyclopedia of Language*. This particular list is admittedly culturally biased: it includes languages in which Americans might have some interest for social, political, religious, or other reasons. The list presented on the following pages includes the name of the language, where it is spoken, the language family to which it belongs, and the approximate number of speakers.

Some comments on these headings:

- *Name of Language:* Many languages have more than one name. This list includes the most common or best-known name. In the case of Bantu languages, the name includes a prefix that begins with a small letter; the name is listed alphabetically by the capital letter at the beginning of the word's stem.

- *Language Family:* Twenty-nine language families are listed in *The Cambridge Encyclopedia of Language*. However, linguists know much less about some families than others. The classifications for language families in Africa and the Americas tend to be considerably more abstract than for families in Europe and Asia.
- *Where Spoken:* Locations are denoted by countries, regions, and—in some cases—provinces or states where the language is mainly spoken. Though languages rarely honor political boundaries, at least not voluntarily, it is often the most easily understandable method at hand for identifying the geographical locations of most languages. Also, some languages are widely dispersed in location. For them, the list provides only a few locations.
- *Number of Speakers:* These numbers, listed in millions, can only be approximate. Estimates vary widely in different parts of the world. Some are extrapolations based on shaky estimates made many years ago. The numbers do *not* include those who may speak a language (e.g., English or French) as a second language.

Language Name	*Language Family*	*Where Spoken*	*Number of speakers (millions)*
Afrikaans	Indo-European	South Africa	4.0–5.0
Albanian	Indo-European	Albania, Yugoslavia, Italy, Greece	3.0–4.5
Amharic	Afro-Asiatic	Ethiopia	8.0–13.0
Arabic	Afro-Asiatic	Northern Africa, Middle East	120.0–150.0
Armenian	Indo-European	Armenia, Middle East	4.0–5.0
Balinese	Austronesian	Bali, Lombok	2.0–3.0
Bari	Nilo-Saharan	Sudan	0.25–0.5
Basque	Isolate	Spain, France, Western U.S.	0.5–0.7
Bemba	Niger-Congo	Zambia, Zaire	0.17–2.5
Bengali	Indo-European	Bangladesh, West Bengal (India)	80.0–150.0
Breton	Indo-European	NW France	0.6–1.0
Bulgarian	Indo-European	Bulgaria, Yugoslavia, Greece	8.0–8.5
Burmese	Sino-Tibetan	Burma, Bangladesh	20.0–27.0
Byelorussian	Indo-European	Byelorus	9.0–10.0
Catalan	Indo-European	NE Spain, Balearic Islands, Sardinia, France, Andorra, Argentina	5.0–7.0
Chamorro	Austronesian	Guam	0.05

Language Name	*Language Family*	*Where Spoken*	*Number of speakers (millions)*
Cherokee	Macro-Siouan	Oklahoma, South Carolina	0.02–0.05
Chinese	Sino-Tibetan	China, Taiwan, U.S.	1000.0
Chocktaw	Macro-Algonquian	Oklahoma, Mississippi	0.01
Cree	Macro-Algonquian	Canada, U.S.	0.03–0.06
Créole French	Indo-European	Haiti, Lesser Antilles, Mauritius, other Indian Ocean islands	6.5
Czech	Indo-European	Czech Republic, Slovakia	9.0–10.0
Dakota	Macro-Siouan	N. and S. Dakota, Manitoba	0.01–0.02
Dan	Niger-Congo	Ivory Coast, Liberia, Guinea	0.1
Danish	Indo-European	Denmark, Germany	5.0–5.25
Dinka	Nilo-Saharan	Sudan	0.5–2.0
English	Indo-European	North America, British Isles, Australia, New Zealand, South Africa	300.0–350.0
Inuit	Esquimo-Aleut	Greenland, Canada, Alaska	0.06–0.09
Estonian	Uralic	Estonia	1.0
Fijian	Austronesian	Fiji	0.2–0.3
Finnish	Uralic	Finland, Russia, Sweden	4.5–5.0
French	Indo-European	France, Belgium, Canada, United States, Switzerland	60.0–70.0
Frisian	Indo-European	Netherlands, Germany	0.25–0.35
Ganda	Niger-Congo	Uganda	1.5–3.5
Georgian	Caucasian	Georgia (Eurasia)	3.0–4.0
German	Indo-European	Germany, Austria, Switzerland, U.S., Russia	95.0–100.0
Greek	Indo-European	Greece, Cyprus, Turkey	10.0–10.5
Hebrew	Afro-Asiatic	Israel, U.S., Europe	3.0–4.0
Hindi	Indo-European	India, Pakistan, Trinidad, Guyana, Fiji, Mauritius	130.0–200.0
Hungarian	Uralic	Hungary, Romania, other Balkan countries	13.5–14.0
Icelandic	Indo-European	Iceland	0.23–0.25
Indonesian-Malay	Austronesian	Indonesia, Malaysia, Singapore, Thailand, Brunei	30.0
Irish Gaelic	Indo-European	Ireland, Scotland	0.03–0.1
Iroquois	Macro-Siouan	Ontario, New York, Wisconsin, Quebec	0.01
Italian	Indo-European	Italy, U.S., France, Argentina, Switzerland, Canada, Brazil	56.0–60.0
Japanese	Isolate (Altaic?)	Japan, Brazil, California, Hawaii	120.0
Javanese	Austronesian	Java, Malaysia, Suriname	45.0–65.0
Juang	Afro-Asiatic	India	0.13–0.16
Kashmiri	Indo-European	Kashmir (India-Pakistan)	2.0–3.0
Khmer	Mon-Khmer	Cambodia, Thailand, Vietnam	5.0–8.0
Kikuyu	Niger-Congo	Kenya	1.0–4.0
Korean	Isolate (Altaic?)	Korea, NE China, Japan, Siberia, Hawaii	50.0–60.0

Language Name	Language Family	Where Spoken	Number of speakers (millions)
Kurdish	Indo-European	Turkey, Iran, Iraq, Syria, Russia	5.0–10.0
Latvian	Indo-European	Latvia	1.5–2.0
Lithuanian	Indo-European	Lithuania	2.5–3.0
Macedonian	Indo-European	Macedonia, Bulgaria, Greece	1.0–1.5
Malagasy	Austronesian	Madagascar	9.0
Maldivian	Indo-European	Maldive Islands	0.1–0.15
Maori	Austronesian	New Zealand	0.1
Masai	Nilo-Saharan	Kenya, Tanzania	0.19–0.4
Mixtec	Oto-Manguean	Mexico	0.25–0.4
Nahuatl (Aztec)	Uto-Aztecan	Mexico, El Salvador	1.0
Navajo	Na-Dené	Southwestern U.S.	0.12–0.14
Nepali	Indo-European	Nepal, Uttar Pradesh (India)	5.0–10.0
Netherlandic	Indo-European	Netherlands, Belguim, Canada, France	15.0–20.0
Nubian	Nilo-Saharan	Sudan, Egypt	1.0
Ojibwa	Macro-Algonquian	Canada, Northern U.S.	0.04–0.05
Persian (Farsi)	Indo-European	Iran, Afghanistan, Tadzhikistan, Iraq	20.0–30.0
Polish	Indo-European	Poland, U.S.	37.0–40.0
Portuguese	Indo-European	Brazil, Portugal, Spain, Uruguay, Argentina, Azores, Goa, Madeira	120.0–135.0
Provençal	Indo-European	S. France	9.5–12.0
Punjabi	Indo-European	Punjab (India), Pakistan	40.0–70.0
Puôc	Mon-Khmer	Northern Vietnam	0.005
Quechua	Andean-Equatorial	Colombia, Peru, Ecuador, Bolivia, Argentina, Chile	6.0–10.0
Romany	Indo-European	S. Asia, Near East, Europe, U.S.	0.45–0.9
Russian	Indo-European	Russia	130.0–150.0
Serbo-Croat	Indo-European	Serbia, Croatia, Bosnia, Herzegovina	17.0–17.5
Sinhalese	Indo-European	Sri Lanka	9.0–12.0
Slovak	Indo-European	Slovakia	4.0–5.0
Somali	Afro-Asiatic	Somalia, Ethiopia, Djibouti, Kenya	2.0–5.0
Spanish	Indo-European	Latin America, Spain, U.S.	150.0–250.0
Swedish	Indo-European	Sweden, Finland	8.0–8.5
Tagalog	Austronesian	Philippines	12.0
Tamil	Dravidian	Tamil Nadu (India), Sri Lanka, Malaysia, Singapore	35.0–55.0
Tatar	Altaic	Kazakhstan, Tadzhikistan, Kirghizia, China, Bulgaria, Turkey, Romania	5.5–6.0
Thai	Tai	Thailand, Laos, China, Vietnam	20.0–30.0
Tibetan	Sino-Tibetan	Tibet, Bhutan, Nepal, India, Sikkim	3.0–4.0
Tlingit	Na-Dené	Alaska, NW U.S., NW Canada	0.002
Tuareg	Afro-Asiatic	Niger, Mali, Algeria	0.05–0.85
Turkish	Altaic	Turkey, Bulgaria, other Balkan states, Cyprus, Greece	27.0–35.0
Tzeltal	Pentuian	Mexico	0.05–0.8

Language Name	*Language Family*	*Where Spoken*	*Number of speakers (millions)*
Ukrainian	Indo-European	Ukraine, Canada, U.S.	40.0–45.0
Uzbek	Altaic	Uzbekistan, Tadzhikistan, Afghanistan	10.0–14.0
Vietnamese	Mon-Khmer?	Vietnam, Thailand, Cambodia, Laos, New Caledonia, France, Dakar, U.S.	35.0–50.0
Warlpiri	Australian	N. Australia	0.2–0.3
Welsh	Indo-European	Wales	0.5
Xhosa	Niger-Congo	South Africa	3.0–5.0
Yiddish	Indo-European	U.S., Israel, Russia, Latin America, Canada, E. Europe	0.2–0.5
Yoruba	Niger-Congo	Nigeria, Benin	17.0
Zuni	Penutian	New Mexico	0.003

APPENDIX 2

The Indo-European Family of Languages

Many different arrangements exist for the Indo-European family of languages. The main text mentions several. This chart of the Indo-European languages is adapted from one that appears in *Webster's Ninth New Collegiate Dictionary*. It includes ten major branches of the Indo-European family tree (including Germanic, which includes English) and 128 languages both living and extinct. Extinct languages are in italics. Some "living" languages listed in the Ancient and Medieval Columns—such as Sanskrit, Greek, and Latin—are actually used only in written literature or religious rituals.

Indo-European Languages

Branch	*Group*	*Languages and Major Dialects*			*Area of Origin*
		Ancient	*Medieval*	*Modern*	
GERMANIC	East		*Gothic*		eastern Europe
	North		*Old Norse*	Danish	Denmark
				Faeroese	Faeroe Islands
				Icelandic	Iceland
				Norwegian	Norway
				Swedish	Sweden
	West		*Middle Dutch*	Afrikaans	South Africa

Branch	*Group*	*Languages and Major Dialects*			*Area of Origin*
		Ancient	*Medieval*	*Modern*	
				Dutch	Netherlands
			Old English	English	England
			Middle English		
			Middle Flemish	Flemish	Belgium
			Old Frisian	Frisian	Netherlands, Germany
			Old High German	German	Germany
			Middle High German		
				Yiddish	Germany, eastern Europe
			Old Saxon	Low German	northern Germany
			MIddle Old German		
CELTIC	Continental	*Gaulish*			Gaul
	Goidelic		*Old Irish*	Irish Gaelic	Ireland
			Middle Irish		Isle of Man
				Manx	Scotland
				Scottish Gaelic	
	Brythonic		*Middle Breton*	Breton	Brittany
			Old Cornish	*Cornish*	Cornwall
			Old Welsh	Welsh	Wales
			Middle Welsh		
ITALIC	Osco-Umbrian	Oscan, Sabellian, Umbrian			ancient Italy
	Romance	*Venetic, Faliscan, Lanuvian, Praenestine*			ancient Italy
		Latin		Catalan	Spain
				Dalmatian	Adriatic Coast
			Old French	French	France, Belgium, Switzerland
			Middle French		
				Haitian Creole	Haiti
				Italian	Italy, Switzerland
				Judeo-Spanish	Mediterranean area
				Portuguese	Portugal
			Old Provencal	Provencial	southern France
				Rhaeto-Romanic	Italy, Switzerland
				Romanian	Romania, Balkans
				Sardinian	Sardinia
				Spanish	Spain
ALBANIAN	Albanian			Albanian	Albania, southern Italy
GREEK	Greek	Greek	Greek	Greek	Greece, eastern Mediterranean
BALTO-SLAVIC	Baltic		*Old Prussian*		East Prussia
				Latvian	Latvia
				Lithuanian	Lithuania
	Slavic: South		Old Church Slavonic		
				Bulgarian	Bulgaria
				Macedonian	Macedonia
				Serbo-Croatian	Bosnia, Croatia, Serbia, Yugoslavia
				Slovene	Bosnia, Croatia, Serbia, Yugoslavia
	Slavic: West		*Old Czech*	Czech, Slovak	Czech Rebublic, Slovakia
				Kashubian, Polish	Poland
				Polabian, Wendish	Germany
	Slavic: East		*Old Russian*	Belorussian	Belorus
				Russian	Russia
				Ukrainian	Ukraine

Branch	*Group*	*Languages and Major Dialects*			*Area of Origin*
		Ancient	*Medieval*	*Modern*	
ARMENIAN	Armenian		Armenian	Armenian	Asia Minor, Caucasus
ANATOLIAN	*Anatolian*	*Hittite, Lycian, Lydian*			ancient Asia Minor
		Luwian			
		Palaic			
		Hieroglyphic Hittite			
INDO-IRANIAN	Iranian: West	*Old Persian*	*Pahlavi*		Persia
			Persian	Baluchi	Pakistan
				Kurdish	Iran, Iraq, Turkey
				Persian	Iran
				Tajiki	central Asia
	Iranian: East	Avestan			ancient Persia
			Sogdian		central Asia
			Khotanese		central Asia
				Ossetic	Caucasus
				Passhto	Afghanistan, Pakistan
	Indic: Dard			Kafiri, Khowar,	upper Indus valley
				Shina	Kashmir
				Kashmiri	
	Indic: Sanskritic	Sanskrit, Pali			India
		Prakrits	*Prakrits*		
				Assamese	Assam
				Bengali	Bengal
				Bihari	Bihar
				Gujarati	Gujarat
				Hindi	northern India
				Konkani	western India
				Lahnda	western Punjab
				Marathi	western India
				Nepali	Nepal
				Oriya	Orissa
				Panjabi	Punjab
				Rajasthani	Rajasthan
				Romany	[uncertain]
				Sindhi	Sind
				Sinhalese	Sri Lanka
				Urdu	Pakistan, India
TOCHARIAN		*Tocharian A*			central Asia
		Tocharian B			
[UNCERTAIN]		*Ligurian, Messapian,*			ancient Italy
		Illyrian, Thracian,			Balkans
		Phrygian			Asia Minor

INDO-EUROPEAN LANGUAGES: BRIEF HISTORIES

Depending on which scholar you talk with, the Indo-European language family includes ten or eleven branches. The one of most immediate importance to English speakers is the Germanic branch, for English is at its roots a Germanic language. The history of English, including its origins as a Germanic tongue, appears in Chapter 2. However, the other branches of Indo-European are also interesting in their own right. Many have obscure histories, while others have well-documented origins. Two, and perhaps three, Indo-European language groups are now extinct; they are no longer spoken by any group of people living today. Several have played an important role in the development of English.

In the discussion that follows, asterisks (*) indicate extinct languages.

About three million people living in Albania and parts of Greece, Italy, and the former Yugoslavia speak *Albanian*. The two main dialects are *Gheg* in the north and *Tosk* in the south. Each in turn consists of many other subdialects. Linguists who reconstruct the pedigrees of languages work with written records as well as living speakers. Old written records give them a "window" into the past. This makes it possible for them to reconstruct both the pronunciation of words and their possible antecedents and origins. In the case of Albanian, no written records of the language exist before the fifteenth century. The Albanian alphabet, which is based on the Roman one most Westerners use, did not exist until 1909. Albanian is therefore a language whose origins are cloaked in obscurity.

Colin Renfrew suggests that Albanian may be the living remnant of the ancient and now-extinct **Illyrian* language group. Ancient Greek writings do refer to the "Illyrians" who lived in what is now Yugoslavia and Albania. Renfrew sees these references as supportive of an Illyrian-Albanian link. There are no surviving written records of the *Illyrian language. However, in *Archaeology and Language* Renfrew suggests that *Illyrian arose from *Anatolian (see below) and in turn gave rise to now-extinct languages in northern Europe that might have been ancestral to Celtic and Germanic. Renfrew also suggests that Albanian might alternatively be related to either *Thracian or its antecedent *Dacian. This now-extinct language once flourished in the region now known as Romania, as well as the eastern region of Greece, Bulgaria, and small parts of Turkey. However, records of only about two dozen written words in all survive from the *Thracian tongue. That is a rather thin thread for a possible Albanian connection.

**Anatolian* is an extinct group of languages once spoken by people who lived in several parts of modern-day Turkey and Syria. The language dates back to at least 2000 B.C.E. The oldest known texts in an Indo-European tongue are written in *Hittite, an Anatolian language. They date to the seventeenth century B.C.E. Other Anatolian languages, all now dead and gone, included *Lycian, *Lydian, *Luwian, and *Palaic. *Phrygian may also have been an *Anatolian language, but many linguists still dispute that relationship.

The Anatolian *Hittite language has an interesting history. For many years scholars considered the Hittites as merely one of several obscure tribes living in what is now northern Syria. The Bible mentions them in two places. One is Genesis 15:18–21, in the story of the great covenant forged between Yahweh and Abram:

> That day Yahweh made a covenant with Abram in these terms: "To your descendants I give this country, from the River of Egypt to the Great River, the River Euphrates, the Kenites, the Kenizzites, the Kadmonites, the Hittites, the Perizzites, the Rephaim, the Amorites, the Canaanites, the Girgashites, and the Jebusites.

The other biblical reference occurs in I Kings 10:29. King Solomon's assistants bought chariots and horses from Egypt, and "also supplied the Hittite and Aramaean kings."

These two references long represented most of our knowledge of the Hittites. The major players at the time, it seemed, were the Syrians and the Israelites. In the late ninteenth century, however, archaeologists working in northern Syria and in central Turkey (Anatolia) uncovered a series of mysterious inscriptions carved in an unknown hieroglyphic script. In 1880 the British scholar Archibald Sayce boldly predicted that these strange tablets were the remains of the hitherto-undiscovered empire of the biblical Hittites, located in Anatolia. His colleagues scoffed.

Eleven years later British archaeologist Sir Flinders Petrie uncovered new evidence of the mysterious "Hatti" in his excavations of the capital city of the heretic Egyptian pharaoh Akhnaton. The tablets Petrie found clearly showed that Sayce had been right: the Hittites had indeed been a major force in Anatolia. Two years later more evidence of the Hittites came to light in the ancient city of Boghazköy in central Anatolia. Hugo Winckler, a German archaeologist, heard of the discovery and began an extensive excavation of the site in 1906. He soon uncovered a tremendous treasure trove: some ten thousand clay tablets. Some were written in Babylonian, an ancient script that scholars had already deciphered. Others were written in the still-mysterious language that researchers now identified as *Hittite. Nine years later a Czech scholar, Friedrich Hrozný, finally deciphered the *Hittite script and opened the door on that ancient language.

Because of Hrozný's great accomplishment, and the work of others after him, we now have a picture of the Hittites much different from that of barely a century ago. The Hittites were an ancient people with a culture that flourished from about 1600 to 1200 B.C.E. They apparently entered the region of east-central Turkey, once known as Cappadocia, around 1800 B.C.E. Their empire, actually more of a loose confederation, reached its height of power and influence in western Asia during a two-hundred-year period from 1400 to 1200 B.C.E. It broke up under the onslaught of the Assyrians, Phrygians, and Thracians around 1200 B.C.E. Linguists did not determine the language's Indo-European connection until 1915.

The archive of clay tablets at Boghazköy also revealed the existence of *Palaic, another ancient Anatolian language. The script first used by Sayce to make his prescient proposal, however, did not appear in the clay tablets. It was not until 1947 that linguists finally identified it as a dialect of Hittite now called *Luwian.

The *Armenian* branch of the Indo-European family includes just one language, Armenian. Most of the five million people who speak Armenian live in Armenia, which lies to the east of Turkey and was once part of the Soviet Union, and parts of eastern Turkey. *Grabar,* the older and classical form of Armenian, is used in older literature and in the religious ceremonies of the contemporary Armenian Church. Spoken Armenian dates to around 1000 B.C.E. The earliest written form did not appear until after the advent of Christianity, in about the fifth century C.E.

Some scholars think that Armenian might be related to the ancient *Thracian or *Phrygian tongues, which were once spoken in the Balkan region. They refer to the two as part of a single major branch of Indo-European, the *Thraco-Phrygian* branch, and to Armenian as a Thraco-Phrygian language. All we know of *Phrygian comes from about two dozen inscriptions from the sixth century B.C.E and another hundred from the first three centuries C.E. However, the connection between ancient *Phrygian and *Thracian does not seem to exist under closer scrutiny. *Phrygian, for one thing, seems more closely related to Greek than to anything else. Moreover, any relationship between Armenian and these ancient tongues is probably obscure at best.

The *Baltic* languages include *Old Prussian, Latvian, and Lithuanian. Old Prussian is extinct. Very little is known about the origins of these languages. For example, the earliest document in Lithuanian is less than five hundred years old. Some linguists include the Baltic and Slavonic languages in a single Balto-Slavic branch because of their several similarities. However, there is still some dispute about this. The similarities may result from mutual influence rather than a common origin.

Celtic languages once were spoken by people living throughout large areas of prehistoric Europe. Renfrew suggests that they had their most immediate origin in central Europe and that ancestral *Celtic may have sprung from *Illyrian. Certainly by the end of the first millenium B.C.E. and the beginning of the Current Era, Celtic languages were spoken by people from central Europe westwards through France and Spain, and north of the Alps to Germany. The main continental Celtic languages included *Hispano-Celtic (in present-day Spain and Portugal), *Gallic (in France), and *Lepontic (in northern Italy).

By the middle of the third century B.C.E. Celtic peoples were living in the British Isles and Ireland. The *Goidelic Celtic language was spoken by people living in Ireland, Scotland, and on the Isle of Man. It eventually evolved into Irish, Scottish, and *Manx. The early inhabitants of England and Wales spoke a Celtic language that scholars today call *Brythonic. It eventually evolved into Welsh, *Cornish, and Breton, which is still spoken by some people living in Brittany, in France.

In the middle of the fifth century C.E., a series of invasions by Germanic-speaking people from Europe pushed the Celtic-speaking inhabitants of the British Isles into small enclaves in Wales, Ireland, and a few other locations. As English evolved and became the language of the politically dominant inhabitants of England, the Celtic languages declined in influence. Most became extinct. Today the only surviving Celtic languages are Irish, Welsh, and Scottish, though attempts are being made to revive *Manx and Cornish.

The *Greek* or *Hellenic* branch consists only of Greek. But it holds a very important place in Western history. The thoughts of ancient Greeks, preserved for posterity in this ancient but still-living language, have had a profound influence on our civilization. No direct connection exists between Greek and English, which was originally a Germanic language. However, borrowing and coinages based on Greek permeate scientific and technical English. The earliest evidence of the existence of Greek itself goes back to the fourteenth century B.C.E. Inscriptions found in Crete and known for many years as *Linear B* were finally shown in 1952 to be an early form of Greek. Classical Greek dates from the eighth century B.C.E., and is the language in which the *Iliad* and *Odyssey* were written. The other great works of Greek literature and philosophy—the plays, the poetry, the works of Plato and Aristotle—all were composed by the end of the fourth century B.C.E. At that point a different version of spoken and written Greek had emerged called *koine* or "common" Greek. This was the dominant language of the eastern Mediterranean region for more than a thousand years. Much of the Christian New Testament was composed in the written form of *koine.* Contemporary spoken and written Greek derives from *koine*.

Two large groups of languages, Indo-Aryan and Iranian, compose the Indo-European branch called *Indo-Iranian*. The Iranian languages go back at least three thousand years, first appearing in the regions known today as Afghanistan and Iran. *Avestan, a now-extinct Iranian language, was the sacred language of the Zoroastrians. Today's Iranian languages include Kurdish, Ossetic, Pashto, Persian (or Farsi), and Tadzhik. Many hundreds of languages reside in the Indo-Aryan group, including Hindi, Assamese, Bengali, Sinhalese, and Panjabi. Romany, the language of the Rom or Gypsies, is also an Indo-Aryan language. The Rom are descendants of people who left India at least a thousand years ago.

However, the most famous Indo-Aryan language, Sanskrit, is no longer in common use. Sanskrit was the sacred language of the *Vedas*, the holy writings of the Hindu religion. It was being used at least three thousand years ago, when the Vedas were composed. The discovery of a powerful connection between Sanskrit and languages like Greek and Latin led to the creation of modern-day linguistics. Without that discovery, and the rise of linguistics and its many branches, we would probably not have learned as much as we have today about how infants acquire language and how the brain creates and stores our mother tongues.

Latin, one of the best known of the *Italic* languages, dates to at least the sixth century B.C.E. As the city of Rome grew in power and conquered Italy, Latin displaced other languages on the Italian peninsula. *Oscan, *Venetic, and *Umbrian became extinct. Possibly Latin superseded *Etruscan, too. The Roman Empire grew to embrace all of the Mediterranean and more, pushing north into Switzerland and Germany and west to Great Britain. As Latin spread, it spun off its own "daughter" languages. These are the so-called *Romance languages* and include Catalan, *Dalmatian (which became extinct in 1898), French, Italian, Occitan (spoken in southern France), Portuguese, Rhaetian (spoken in northern Italy and Switzerland), Romanian, Sardinian, and Spanish.

As with the Baltic branch to which it may be related, we know very little about the origins and evolution of the *Slavic* languages. No records of *Slavic, the ancestral tongue, exist. The earliest written records are of Old Church Slavic and date to the ninth century C.E. Three main branches grew from Old Church Slavic: West, East, and South Slavonic. West Slavonic includes Polish, Czech, Slovak, and Sorbinian. The East Slavic group includes Ukrainian, Russian, and Belorussian. South Slavic includes Bulgarian, Macedonian, Serbo-Croatian, and Slovene.

**Tocharian* is an extinct Indo-European language that no one even knew existed until the late 1800s. In 1886 Aurel Stein, a Hungarian linguist and scholar employed by the British Museum, was sent to work at the Oriental College in Lahore, India. He launched a series of exploratory expeditions into Chinese Turkestan, now the Chinese province of Sinkiang. This desolate region of deserts and oases once supported a series of thriving civilizations. Now they were all but forgotten, the true archetypes of the romantic Indiana Jones–type visions of lost cities half-buried in the shifting sands. In fact, there were lost cities half-buried in the shifting sands. And those lost cities in the arid desert contained the well-preserved remains of some remarkable written records. Other European researchers knew that some of these archeological treasures existed, but they had not found what Stein uncovered.

In 1906, on an expedition to the small oasis town of Tun-Huang, he uncovered "The Cave of the Thousand Buddhas." There, hidden behind a plaster wall, a Buddhist monk showed Stein a huge library of ancient religious and commercial documents dating to the seventh century C.E. They were written in a north Indian alphabet that the scholars already understood. Some of the documents were translations of Sanskrit originals. Others were bilingual documents. All turned out to be in a previously unknown language, unequivocably Indo-European, that was named *Tocharian. We now know that *Tocharian was spoken in the northern part of Chinese Turkestan (though not by the Tochari people!) at least through the first few centuries of the Current Era. At least two dialects existed, called *Tocharian A and B.

APPENDIX 3

PHONETIC SYMBOLS AND THEIR CLASSIFICATION

The International Phonetic Alphabet (IPA) uses a special set of phonetic symbols. Linguists use them in phonetics to represent phones, the distinguishable sounds in any language, by placing them between brackets []. The same symbols are used in phonology to represent phonemes, the basic contrastive units in a specific language's sound system, by placing them between virgules //. The descriptions following the symbols refer to the articulatory characteristics of the speech-sound itself, as explained in Chapter 3. A more graphic arrangement of these phonetic symbols is found in the IPA grids in Chapter 3. Following the list of IPA phonetic symbols are explanations of the six factors of spoken language and of how linguists actually classify the symbols for the sounds.

THE IPA SYMBOLS

Phonetic Symbol	*Description*
Consonants:	
Plosives—	
p	voiceless bilabial plosive
b	voiced bilabial plosive
t	voiceless alveolar plosive
d	voiced alveolar plosive
ʈ	voiceless retroflex plosive
ɖ	voiced retroflex plosive
c	voiceless palatal plosive
ɟ	voiced palatal plosive
k	voiceless velar plosive
ɡ	voiced velar plosive
q	voiceless uvular plosive
ɢ	voiced uvular plosive
ʔ	glottal plosive
Nasals—	
m	voiced bilabial nasal
ɱ	voiced labiodental nasal
n	voiced alveolar nasal
ɳ	voiced retroflex nasal
ɲ	voiced palatal nasal
ŋ	voiced velar nasal
ɴ	voiced uvular nasal
Fricatives—	
ɸ	voiceless bilabial fricative
β	voiced bilabial fricative
f	voiceless labiodental fricative
v	voiced labiodental fricative
θ	voiceless dental fricative
ð	voiced dental fricative
s	voiceless alveolar fricative
z	voiced alveolar fricative
ʃ	voiceless post-alveolar fricative
ʒ	voiced post-alveolar fricative
ʂ	voiceless retroflex fricative
ʐ	voiced retroflex fricative
ç	voiceless palatal fricative
ʝ	voiced palatal fricative
x	voiceless velar fricative
ɣ	voiced velar fricative
χ	voiceless uvular fricative
ʁ	voiced uvular fricative

Phonetic Symbol	Description
ħ	voiceless pharyngeal fricative
ʕ	voiced pharyngeal fricative
h	voiceless glottal fricative
ɦ	voiced glottal fricative
Lateral Fricatives—	
ɬ	voiceless lateral fricative
ɮ	voiced lateral fricative
Approximants—	
ʋ	voiced labiodental approximant
ɹ	voiced alveolar approximant
ɻ	voiced retroflex approximant
j	voiced palatal approximant (or fricative)
ɰ	voiced velar approximant
Lateral Approximants—	
l	voiced lateral approximant
ɭ	voiced retroflex lateral approximant
ʎ	voiced palatal lateral approximant
ʟ	voiced velar lateral approximant
Trills—	
ʙ	voiced bilabial trill
r	voiced alveolar trill
ʀ	voiced uvular trill
Flaps—	
ɾ	voiced alveolar flap
ɽ	voiced retroflex flap
Ejective Stops—	
p’	bilabial ejective stop
t’	alveolar ejective stop
ʈ’	retroflex ejective stop
c’	palatal ejective stop
k’	velar ejective stop
q’	uvular ejective stop
Implosives—	
ƥ	voiceless bilabial implosive
ɓ	voiced bilabial implosive
ƭ	dental implosive
ɗ	alveolar implosive
ƈ	voiceless palatal implosive
ʄ	voiced palatal implosive
ƙ	voiceless velar implosive
ɠ	voiced velar implosive
ʠ	voiceless uvular implosive
ʛ	voiced uvular implosive

Phonetic Symbol	*Description*
Vowels:	
Closed—	
i	close front unrounded vowel
y	close front rounded vowel
ɨ	close central unrounded vowel
ʉ	close central rounded vowel
ɯ	close back unrounded vowel
u	close back rounded vowel
ɪ or ɩ	central-front unrounded vowel between close and mid-close
ʏ	central-front rounded vowel, between close and mid-close
ʊ	central-back rounded vowel between close and mid-close
Mid-Close—	
e	mid-close front unrounded vowel
ø	mid-close front rounded vowel
ɤ	mid-close back unrounded vowel
o	mid-close back rounded vowel
ə	central unrounded vowel, between mid-close and mid-open
ɵ	central rounded vowel between mid-close and mid-open
Mid-Open—	
ɛ	mid-open front unrounded vowel
œ	mid-open front rounded vowel
ʌ	mid-open back unrounded vowel
ɔ	mid-open back rounded vowel
æ	front unrounded vowel between mid-open and open
ɐ	central unrounded vowel between mid-open and open
Open—	
a	open front unrounded vowel
ɶ	open front rounded vowel
ɑ	open back unrounded vowel
ɒ	open back rounded vowel

Some other phonetic sound symbols:

ɚ	r-colored central vowel
ɕ	voiceless alveolo-palatal fricative
ʑ	voiced alveolo-palatal fricative
ʍ	voiceless labio-velar fricative
w	voiced labio-velar fricative
ɧ	simultaneous ɧ and x (fricative)
tʃ	voiceless palato-alveolar affricate
dʒ	voiced palato-alveolar affricate
ɥ	voiced labio-palatal approximant
bbb	voiced biabial trill
ppp	voiceless bilabial trill
ʘ	bilabial click
ʇ	dental click

Phonetic Symbol	Description
Vowels:	
ʗ	post-alveolar click
ʖ	lateral click
Diacritic markings (samples):	
ʼ	A diacritic mark indicating "ejective"
ʷ	A diacritic mark indicating "rounding"
ː	A diacritic mark indicating "long"
ˑ	A diacritic mark indicating "half-long"

THE SIX FACTORS OF SPOKEN LANGUAGE

Any description of the sounds we use to create language will have to deal with six physical factors: the *air stream*, the *vocal folds*, the *soft palate*, the *place of articulation*, the *manner of articulation*, and the *lips*.

The *air stream*—the flow of air coming out of or going into the mouth—is where it all begins. Most, but not all, speech sounds are created using air that is breathed out of the lungs. These sounds are classified as *egressive pulmonic* sounds (from the word *pulmonary*, which has to do with the lungs). We can also create vocal sounds using *ingressive pulmonic* air, air we breathe into our lungs. We may occasionally say *yes* or *no* in this fashion, or talk "under our breath," but this is an uncommon way of speaking. It sounds muffled and garbled and is unpleasant to listen to.

However, many languages incorporate sounds not made using the lungs. These *nonpulmonic* sounds include *clicks*, *implosives*, and *ejectives*. Clicks are sharp suction-like noises made with the lips or tongue. Click sounds do exist in English, but not as the components of words. The sound your mother made when she caught you looking at that forbidden magazine (*Playboy*? *Playgirl*? *The National Review*? *The Realist*?)—that *tsk tsk* or *tut tut* you remember so well—is a click. These are meaningful noises but not words. However, other languages do use clicks as consonants. The languages of the Hottentot and San (which many of us know as "bushman") tribes in Africa have extremely complex sets of clicks. The !Xu language has nearly four dozen different click consonants. Some historial linguists and paleolinguists think these click sounds are characteristic of languages most closely related to the earliest languages of the earliest humans.

Implosives and ejectives are made using the glottis, the space behind the Adam's apple between the vocal folds. It is possible to use the glottis to start an air stream flowing into or out of the mouth. Implosives occur when the glottis starts an air stream moving inward. Ejectives take place when the glottis creates an air stream moving outward from the mouth. Implosives and ejective sounds are called *glottalic*, not surprisingly. The former are glottalic ingressive sounds; the latter are glottalic egressive sounds. Many languages use implosive and ejective sounds, including English. For example, people in the north of England use ejectives at the ends of words in place of the more "standard" pulmonic [t], [k], and [p]. Implosives are rare in English but rather common in African and Native American languages.

Obviously, the *vocal folds* themselves contribute to the quality of the speech sound. When the vocal folds vibrate, the resulting sounds are called *voiced* sounds. When the vocal folds remain open, the result is *voiceless* sounds. The *h* sound in *honey* is a voiceless sound. Close the vocal folds entirely, thus closing the glottis, and the result is a glottal stop. A coughing sound is a glottal stop.

The *soft palate* or velum also contributes to the quality of speech sound. The velum's position affects speech sounds in three ways:

1. When the velum rises against the upper part of the pharynx, called the *nasopharyngeal wall*, it blocks air from moving out through the nose. This blockage is called a *velopharyngeal closure*. Air can then only escape through the open mouth, creating a set of oral sounds. It is a huge set: all the vowels and nearly all the consonants in spoken English.
2. When the soft palate is lowered, air can escape through both the mouth and nose and create *nasalized vowels*. Many languages use them, most notably French. Say *bon* ("good") the way French speakers do, with your nose wrinkled and your mouth pursed. The sound of the *o* in the word is a nasalized vowel.
3. When the velum is lowered with the mouth closed, all the air passes out through the nose. This formation in the vocal tract

creates speech sounds called *nasal consonants*. [m] and [n] are examples of nasal consonants.

The *place of articulation* refers to the point in the vocal tract at which a narrowing or closure takes place. It could be the lips, for example, or the hard palate.

The *manner of articulation* refers to the type of constriction or movement occurring at any articulation location.

Finally, the *lips* play a major role in the quality of speech sounds, and thus in their phonetic description. Is a vowel spread or rounded? Is a consonant closed or open? It all depends on the lips.

The Classification Game

As we saw in Chapter 3, part of the job of linguistics and linguists is to classify the sounds used to create language. The classification game can be complex, using arcane jargon and symbols as difficult to decipher as those of higher mathematics. In the end, though, the purpose of linguistic classification is to make the study of language and languages as standardized and as simple as possible.

One of the most commonly used classification schemes for vowels is the Cardinal Vowel Diagram, invented by a British phonetician named Daniel Jones (1881–1967). The Cardinal Vowel Diagram classifies vowels on a V-shaped grid. It is based on the three tongue positions (front, center, and back) and four tongue heights. The result is a set of standard reference points for vowels. The vowel points have numbers, and vowels are grouped into two main sets: a primary series (numbers 1–8) and a secondary series (9–16). The Cardinal Vowel Diagram also includes two additional points (numbers 17 and 18). A modifed form of this diagram appears as part of the IPA phonetic symbol grid in Chapter 3.

Phoneticians usually describe consonants according to six different criteria:

- The source of the air stream (pulmonic or nonpulmonic)
- The air stream's direction (egressive or ingressive)
- Whether the vocal folds are vibrating (voiced) or not (voiceless)
- Whether the soft palate is lowered (nasal) or raised (oral)

- The consonant's place of articulation
- The consonant's manner of articulation

In order to define the consonant's place of articulation, we need to know two reference points in the vocal tract. The first is which part of the vocal tract is moving—the active articulator. The second is the passive articulator—the part with which the active articulator makes contact. The active articulator *articulates with* the passive articulator. The various combinations of these two locations—passive and active articulators—in the vocal tract result in eleven different places of articulation. Each helps articulate different consonants.

1. *Bilabial*: Both lips are involved in creating the consonant. Examples are [b], [m], and [p].
2. *Labio-dental:* The lower lip articulates with the upper teeth. [f] and [v] are labio-dental consonants.
3. *Dental*: The tip, or *apex*, and edges of the tongue articulate with the upper teeth. The [θ] as the *th* in *thin*, and [ð] as the *th* in *breathe*, are examples of dental consonants.
4. *Alveolar*: The tongue's blade—the part just behind the tip—and sometimes the tip articulate with the alveolar ridge. [s] and [t] are examples.
5. *Retroflex*: The tip of the tongue curls back to articulate with the area between the back of the alveolar ridge and the front part of the hard palate. The sounds represented by the phones [ɖ] and [ʈ], which occur in many Indian English accents, are examples.
6. *Palato-alveolar*: The blade, and sometimes the tip, of the tongue articulate with the alveolar ridge, while the front of the tongue simulataneously rises toward the hard palate. The result is the *sh* sound [ʃ] in *shoe*.
7. *Palatal*: The front of the tongue articulates with the hard palate. Two examples are the [ç] sound in the German word *ich* and the [j] in the English *you* or the German *ja*.
8. *Velar*: The back of the tongue articulates with the soft palate, as in the [k] sound.
9. *Uvular*: The back of the tongue articulates with the uvula. One example is the [R] in the French word *rue*.

10. *Pharyngeal*: The pharynx's front wall articulates with its back wall. These sounds, such as the two phones represented by [ʕ] and [ħ], are common in Arabic.
11. *Glottal*: The vocal folds close up to cause a friction or closure of the glottis—the glottal stop, as heard in [h] or [ʔ].

Four different kinds of constriction by the articulators help define the precise manner of articulation of a consonant. They are *total closure, intermittent closure, partial closure*, and *narrowing*.

1. Three types of total closure can occur, creating *plosive* consonants, such as [p] or [b]; *affricate* consonants, such as the initial *ch* [tʃ] in *church*, or the *j* [dʒ] in *judge*; or *nasal* consonants, including [n] and [m]. When a nasal consonant is voiceless instead of voiced, linguists denote it by using a diacritic mark underneath the [m] and [n], creating [m̥] or [n̥].
2. Intermittant closures include the *roll*, or *trill*, and the *flap*. Rolls and trills are common in many German, French, and English dialects. Consider, for example, what Scottish speakers do with an *r*. A flap is a single tap made by one articulator on another. An example is the [ɾ] in the Spanish *pero* [pero] ("but")—which is not the same as the trill [r] in *perro* [pero] ("dog").
3. Partial closure gives a *lateral* quality to the consonant. The result are various kinds of [l] sounds.
4. Narrowing causes two kinds of consonantal sounds. *Fricatives* occur when two articulators come so close together that they create an audible friction to the speech sound. Examples include [f] and [h]. Fricatives with very high sound frequencies—such as [ʃ] and [z], and the initial [ʒ] sound in the French word *je*—are called *sibilants*.

As we noted earlier, a few consonants have some vowel-like qualities. They include the palatal [j], the bilabial [w], and two alveolars, [l] and [ɹ]. These consonants are usually referred to as *approximants*, since they are "approximately" consonants.

APPENDIX 4

Pronunciation Guides for Some IPA Symbols

The following list gives examples of the pronunciation in typical English words of several IPA phonetic symbols. It is based on information from *The ABCs of Languages and Linguistics*, *The Cambridge Encyclopedia of Language*, and *The Oxford Companion to the English Language*. It does not include all the IPA phonetic symbols. English uses only a small subset of the sounds represented in the IPA.

This list is meant only to serve as a useful guide. It is by no means authoritative. In fact, for living languages no authoritative "rules" of pronunciation can possibly exist. Pronunciation of words can and does vary. Speakers of different English dialects, for example, will pronounce the same phone differently. Also, we often pronounce a word one way when speaking it in isolation and another way when using it in sentences in daily conversation.

Consonants

Symbol	Letter(s)	Example
Plosives		
p	p	*s*p*y*
b	b	*b*uy
t	t	s*t*y
d	d	*d*ie
k	k	s*k*y
g	g	*g*irl
Fricatives		
f	f	*f*ree
v	v	*v*ise
θ	th	*th*in
ð	th	*th*is
s	s	*s*ite
z	z	*z*oo
ʃ	sh	*sh*oe
ʒ	s	A*s*ia
h	h	*h*igh
Nasals		
m	m	*m*y
n	n	*n*ear
ŋ	ng	you*ng*
Trill		
r	r	*r*ye
Approximant		
j	y	*y*et
Lateral approximant		
l	l	*l*ip

Vowels

Symbol	Letter(s)	Example
Close		
i	ee	m*ee*t
u	oo	b*oo*t
Close/Mid-close		
I	i	m*i*tt, h*i*d
ʊ	oo	f*oo*t
Mid-close		
ẹ	e	p*e*t
o	o	h*o*pe

Vowels

Symbol	*Letter(s)*	*Example*
Mid-close/Mid-open		
ə	a, u	sof*a*, h*u*b
Mid-open		
ʌ	u	m*u*tt, b*u*s
ɔ	au	c*au*ght
Open		
a	a	c*a*t
ɑ	a	h*a*rd
ɒ	o	n*o*t

Some Other Phonetic Sound Symbols

Symbol	*Letter(s)*	*Example*
Diphthongs		
aɪ	i	m*i*ght
aʊ	ou	h*ou*se
ɔɪ	oy	b*oy*
Voiceless labio-velar fricative		
ʍ	wh	*wh*ich
Affricates		
tʃ	ch	*ch*urch
dʒ	j	*j*ump
Voiced labio-velar approximant		
w	w	*w*itch

APPENDIX 5

Common Dictionary Symbols and Their Pronunciation

The following are some common pronunciation symbols, often used in dictionaries, and examples of words in which they appear. Most of these particular symbols come from *Webster's Ninth New Collegiate Dictionary*. Some are IPA symbols adapted for use in the dictionary, while others are Americanized equivalents or substitutes. They appear between reversed virgules (\\) to indicate that this is pronunciation information, and that they are neither phonetic symbols (which are placed between brackets []) or phonemic symbols (placed between normal virgules //).

Consonants

Symbol	*Examples*
\b\	*b*a*b*y, cup*b*oard
\ch\	*c*ello, *ch*ill, ten*si*on, ma*tch*
\d\	*d*ream, la*dd*er, seem*ed*, wou*ld*
\f\	sa*f*e, o*ff*er, lau*gh*, ca*lf*, tele*ph*one
\g\	*g*o, e*gg*, *gh*ost, pla*gue*
\h\	*G*ila monster, *h*ello, *j*ai alai, *wh*o
\hw\	mari*ju*ana
\j\	*g*em, *j*oy, bu*dg*et, sol*di*er, a*dj*ective, exa*gg*erate, re*gi*on
\k\	*c*atch, *k*id, *q*uit, a*cc*ount, *ch*aos, tri*ck*, a*cq*uire, bis*cu*it, *kh*aki, ta*lk*, li*qu*or
\k̲\	*H*anukkah, lo*ch*
\l\	sai*l*, fi*ll*ing
\m\	co*m*e, phle*gm*, co*mb*, du*mm*y, autu*mn*
\n\	*n*o, *gn*at, *kn*ot, ba*nn*er
\ŋ\	fi*n*ger, ha*nd*kerchief
\p\	tra*p*, she*ph*erd, su*pp*er
\r\	*r*ed, *rh*yme, me*rr*y, *wr*ite, dia*rrh*ea
\s\	ra*c*e, *s*ay, pret*z*el, *ps*alm, *sc*issors, ma*ss*, lis*t*en, is*th*mus
\sh\	o*c*ean, *s*ure, ma*ch*ine, spe*ci*al, *sh*y, ti*ss*ue, na*ti*on, cons*ci*ous, mis*si*on, fu*chs*ia
\t\	la*t*e, de*bt*, walk*ed*, recei*pt*, *Th*omas, bu*tt*on, ya*cht*, ni*ght*
\th\	*th*in
\t̲h̲\	brea*the*
\v\	o*f*, *v*ery, Ste*ph*en, sa*vv*y
\w\	q*u*it, *w*ay
\y\	opin*i*on, *y*ard
\z\	wa*s*, *x*ylophone, *z*one, *cz*ar, scis*s*ors, bu*zz*

Vowels

Symbol	*Examples*
\ə\	b*a*n*a*n*a*, sil*e*nt, mar*i*time, c*o*nnect, circ*u*s, verand*ah*, oc*ea*n, lunch*eo*n, fash*io*n, fam*ou*s
\'ə\ or \,ə\	w*a*s, ab*o*ve, h*u*mdr*u*m, d*oe*s, fl*oo*d, r*ou*gh
\ər\	li*ar*, batt*er*, hon*or*, mart*yr*, glam*our*
\'ər\	f*er*n, b*ir*d, f*ur*, *ear*th, h*urr*y
\a\	c*a*t, m*a*t, mer*i*ngue, pl*ai*d
\ā\	f*a*de, m*ai*n, g*au*ge, d*ay*, st*ea*k, v*ei*n, pr*ey*
\ä\	gu*a*rd, c*o*t, baz*aa*r, sh*ah*, h*ea*rt, bur*eau*cracy
\a\	c*ar*t and baz*aar* (in the speech of so-called r-droppers)
\au\	s*au*erkraut, l*ou*d, n*ow*
\e\	*a*ny, p*e*t, b*u*ry, *ae*sthetic, s*ai*d, s*ay*s, br*ea*d, l*eo*pard, fr*ie*nd
\ē\	m*e*, sk*i*, prett*y*, eas*y*, s*ee*, rec*ei*ve, p*eo*ple, k*ey*, gr*ie*f, h*ea*r, b*ee*r, w*ei*rd
\i\	hom*a*ge, *E*ngland, sl*i*p, w*o*men, b*u*sy, m*y*th, s*ie*ve, b*ui*lding
\ī\	f*i*ne, sl*y*, *ai*sle, papa*y*a, h*ei*ght, l*ie*, b*uy*, d*ye*, *eye*
\ō\	teleph*o*ne, s*ew*, c*oa*t, d*oe*, kn*ow*
\o\	t*a*lk, s*o*ft, c*au*ght, s*aw*, br*oa*d, c*ou*gh
\oi\	c*oi*n, destr*oy*
\ü\	tw*o*, fl*u*, man*eu*ver, cr*ew*, sh*oe*, thr*ough*, cl*ue*, cru*i*se
\u\	w*o*man, p*u*ll, w*oo*d

APPENDIX 6

A CHRONOLOGY OF THE ENGLISH LANGUAGE

This book has focused on spoken rather than written language. Thousands of languages exist that do not have written forms. Indeed, language first evolved as a spoken rather than written form of communication; writing appeared only tens of thousands—and perhaps hundreds of thousands—of years after the appearance of spoken language.

However, in the case of English and many other contemporary languages, the written and spoken forms evolved and changed together and influenced each other's growth. For that reason, the following chronology of the English language includes references to written as well as spoken English. This chronology is based in large part on the one appearing in *The Oxford Companion to the English Language*. It also includes data from numerous other sources.

1500 B.C.E.: People speaking early forms of a Celtic language cross the English Channel and the Irish Sea to settle in Great Britain, the Channel Islands, the Faeroe Islands, the Hebrides, the Isle of Man, Ireland, and the Orkney Islands.

500 B.C.E.–500 C.E.: The continental Celtic languages, unwritten and now extinct, are spoken throughout much of Europe and Asia Minor from Anatolia to Spain. Insular Celtic, the language spoken by the Celtic settlers of the British Isles, subdivides into British and Irish groups. The British Celtic group of languages later includes Cornish, Cumbric and Pictish (now extinct), and Welsh and Breton. The Irish Celtic group later includes Irish and Scottish Gaelic, and Manx Gaelic (extinct).

55 B.C.E.: Julius Caesar leads the first Roman military expedition into Britain.

43 C.E.: The Roman invasion of Britain begins in earnest. It will lead to nearly four centuries of Roman control over much of the island. This occupation marks a small beginning to the Latin influence on English.

122–127: Under orders of Emperor Hadrian, the Roman occupiers build a wall (Hadrian's Wall) stretching from Tyne to Solway, to prevent raids into the south of Britain by the Pictish occupants of northern Great Britain (today's Scotland).

150: Small bands of settlers from the German and Dutch coastlands begin arriving in Britain, with the permission of the Roman overseers.

180: Defeated in their attempts to subdue the Picts, the Romans retreat permanently to the south of Hadrian's Wall.

360: Picts and Scots cross Hadrian's Wall and begin attacking Britain.

370: Theodosius drives the Picts and Scots north out of Britain. He later becomes emperor of Rome.

436: The last Roman troops leave Britain, ending a long period of withdrawal in response to invasions and upheavals in Italy and elsewhere in the Roman Empire. Picts and Scots from Ireland begin invading Britain. Angles, Saxons, Jutes, and other settlers from the European continent soon begin arriving as mercenaries to help the Britons, then become invaders themselves.

450–480: Approximate dates of the oldest surviving written Old English inscriptions, in runic script.

495–550: Saxon and Angle kingdoms established in Argyll, East Anglia, Essex, Mercia, Middlesex, Northumbria, and Wessex.

c. 540: Creative period of the earliest known Welsh poets, including Aneirin, Llywarch Hên, and Taliesin.

557–638: Battles rage among the various Angle and Saxon kingdoms.

597: St. Augustine baptizes Æthelberht, the king of Kent, and the conversion to Christianity of the Anglo-Saxons begins. One result is that the Latin alphabet begins replacing the Celtic runic alphabet.

c. 658–680: Known creative period of Caedmon, the earliest known English-Christian poet.

c. 680: Aldhelm is the first known Anglo-Saxon writer of both prose and verse.

700: Approximate date of the earliest manuscript records in Old English.

730: St. Bede writes *A History of the English Church and People*, calling the people and the land *anglorum*, "English."

c. 760: *The Book of Kells*, an Irish translation of the Latin Gospels, is completed.

792–886: A series of raids and invasions of Britain by Scandinavians and Danes occur. The Danish language begins to exert significant influence on English.

c. early ninth century: The Anglo-Saxon poet Cynewulf writes "Christ," "Elena," "Fates of the Apostles," and "Juliania." All are later found preserved in a tenth-century manuscript.

828: Egbert of Wesseg unites the Seven Kingdoms of the Anglo-Saxons and is proclaimed *bretwalda* or Lord of Britain.

843: Kenneth MacAlpin unites the kingdoms of the Scots and the Picts.

871: Alfred, king of Wessex, translates Latin works into Old English, establishing Old English prose writing.

965: English armies invade the northern Welsh kingdom of Gwynedd.

970: Appearance of *The Exeter Book*, a collection of Old English poetry.

973: Scotland is a multilingual society, with Gaelic dominant, Norse in the north, Cumbric in the southwest, and Old English in the southeast. Latin is the official legal and ecclesiastical language.

c. 1000: Approximate date of the creation of the only surviving Old English manuscript of the epic poem *Beowulf*.

1007: Danish invaders defeat Æthelred the Unready and take over England.

1016–1042: Canute and his sons reign over Denmark, Norway, and England.

1042: St. Edward the Confessor, son of Æthelred the Unready, succeeds Canute's son Hardicanute as king of England.

1050: Appearance of *The Mabinogion*, a collection of Welsh mythological tales.

1051: Impressed by the Normans and their French-speaking counselors at his court, Edward names William of Normandy as his successor, but later reneges on the deal.

1066: Edward the Confessor dies, and his son Harold II is crowned king. William of Normandy, outraged by Edward's broken promise, raises an army and invades England (the last time England will be invaded). Harold II defeats him on September 25 at Stamford Bridge. William presses on, however, and Harold II rashly engages him on October 14 at Hastings. William defeats and kills Harold and is crowned William I (the Conqueror) of England on Christmas Day. The massive French influence of the English language begins, and French will be the official language in England for the next two and a half centuries.

1100–1183: The life of Wace, the Anglo-Norman poet.

1110: Earliest record of a miracle play, performed at Dunstable, England.

1140–1209: Life of Walter Map, Anglo-Latin poet.

1150: Middle English begins to clearly emerge from Old English. This is the date of the earliest surviving texts in Middle English.

1166: Appearance of "The Song of Canute," an English ballad written by a monk of Ely.

1167: Oxford University founded in response to the closure of the University of Paris to students from England.

1170: Chrétien de Troyes writes "Lancelot," a French ballad of courtly love that will later become incorporated into the English legend of King Arthur.

1171: Henry II invades Ireland and proclaims himself king, introducing Norman French and English to the island.

1176: Walter Map organizes the various Arthurian legends into their present form. First Welsh bardic competition, called the *eisteddfod*, held at Cardigan Castle.

1209: Cambridge University founded.

1272–1307: Edward I consolidates his rule over all of England, including Wales and, for a time, Scotland.

1284: The Statute of Ruddlan establishes English law in Wales but retains the legal use of the Welsh language.

1295: Appearance of *The Harrowing of Hell*, an early English miracle play.

1340?–1400: The life of Geoffrey Chaucer.

1348: English replaces French as the official language of instruction in most schools in England, except Cambridge and Oxford Universities.

1362: The Statute of Pleading replaces French with English as the official legal language in England. Written records continue to be kept in Latin. English is used for the first time in Parliament. Appearance of *Piers Plowman*, a Middle English poem ascribed to William Langland of Malvern.

1369: Chaucer writes *The Book of the Duchesse*.

1375: John Barbour writes *The Bruce*, about Scottish leader Robert Bruce. Robin Hood stories and legends begin appearing in popular Middle English literature.

1381: Chaucer writes *The House of Fame*.

1384: Publication of John Wycliffe's English translation of the Holy Bible. Publication of Chaucer's *The Parlemant of Fowles*.

1385: Chaucer writes his Middle English version of *Troilus and Cryseide*.

1387: Chaucer begins writing *The Canterbury Tales*, his epic Middle English poem, which at seventeen thousand lines is unfinished at his death in 1400.

c. late fourteenth century: Approximate date of composition of the *Ordinalia*, an 8,734-line trilogy of verse dramas written in Cornish, the ancient Celtic language of Cornwall.

c. 1400: The Great Vowel Shift in the English language has begun. It will change the sound of many vowels from Middle English pronunciations to sounds similar to those in contemporary English. Appearance of the earliest known literature in written Cornish.

1420–1485: Life of the great Welsh bard Dafydd [David] Nanmor.

1430: Early Modern English begins to emerge from Middle English.

1476: William Caxton produces the first English book printed in movable type, at Bruges in Belgium. Later this year he sets up the first printing press in England, at Westminster.

1477: Caxton publishes Chaucer's *Canterbury Tales*.

1483: Edward IV dies and is succeeded by his young son Edward V. Richard of Gloucester later kills Edward and his brother and takes the throne as Richard III.

1485: The part-Welsh Henry Tudor, Earl of Richmond, defeats and kills Richard III at the Battle of Bosworth. He ascends the English throne as Henry VII. The resulting increase in national pride brings a greater confidence in using vernacular English for original writing.

1490: William Caxton notes the changes in English that have occurred during his lifetime.

1497–1580: The life of the English dramatist John Heywood.

1499: Geoffry the Grammarian publishes the first English-to-Latin wordbook.

1500: The first black lead pencils are used in England.

1501: Publication of "The Palice of Honour," a dream allegory by Scottish poet and bishop Gawin Douglas.

1503–1542: The life of English poet Thomas Wyatt.

1508: *The Maying or Disport of Chaucer* is the first book printed in Scotland.

1510: First performances of *Everyman*, an English morality play.

1532: Most of Chaucer's works are finally published.

1536 and 1542: The Statute of Wales (Acts of Union) unites England and Wales and excludes the Welsh language from any official use.

1547: English poet Henry Howard is executed for high treason.

1551: Ralph Robinson translates Thomas More's *Utopia* into English from the original Latin.

1556: The Stationers' Company of London is granted a monopoly on printing in England.

1558–1594: The life of English dramatist Thomas Kyd.

1560–1620: The settlement of Ireland by English and Scottish immigrants introduces the English language to Ireland on a massive scale. It also sets the stage for nearly four hundred years of "the Troubles," the ongoing strife between Irish patriots and various English governments.

1564–1593: The life of English dramatist Christopher Marlowe.

1564–1616: The life of English dramatist and poet William Shakespeare, born April 23.

1567: Queen Elizabeth I recognizes the Welsh eisteddfod, or annual bardic competition.

1568: First modern eisteddfod held at Caerwys.

1572–1631: The life of English poet John Donne.

1572–1637: The life of English dramatist Ben Jonson.

1583: Sir Edmund Tilney forms the Queen's Company of Players, in London.

1585: Shakespeare moves from Stratford-on-Avon to London.

1587: First performance of Marlowe's blank-verse drama *Tamburlaine*.

1588: First performance of Marlowe's tragedy *Doctor Faustus*. William Morgan translates the Holy Bible into Welsh, creating a focus for the revival of the Welsh language.

1590: Publication of the first three books of Edmund Spenser's epic poem *The Faerie Queene*. William Shakespeare completes *Henry VI*, parts 2 and 3. Marlowe's *The Jew of Malta* is finished.

1591–92: Shakespeare completes *Henry VI*, part 1.

1592: Thomas Kyd's *The Spanish Tragedy* is performed for the first time. Shakespeare: *Richard III* and *Comedy of Errors*.

1593: Christopher Marlowe is murdered in a tavern brawl. Shakespeare: *The Taming of the Shrew* and *Titus Andronicus*. London theatres close because of the plague.

1594: London's theatres reopen. Shakespeare: *Love's Labors Lost, Romeo and Juliet, The Two Gentlemen of Verona*.

1595: English poet Robert Southwell, a Jesuit, is hanged. Shakespeare: *A Midsummer Night's Dream, Richard II*.

1596: Publication of Spenser's *The Faerie Queen*, books 4–6. Shakespeare: *King John, The Merchant of Venice*.

1597: Shakespeare: *Henry IV*, parts 1 and 2.

1598: Shakespeare: *Henry V, Much Ado About Nothing*.

1599: Shakespeare: *As You Like It, Julius Caesar, Twelfth Night*. The Globe Theatre is built in London.

c. 1600: The Great Vowel Shift is largely completed.

1600: Shakespeare: *Hamlet, The Merry Wives of Windsor*.

1601: Shakespeare: *Troilus and Cressida*.

1602: Thomas Campion writes "Observations in the Art of English Poesie." Shakespeare: *All's Well That Ends Well*.

1603: James VI, king of the Scots, ascends the English throne as James I of England. The development of a standard English language becomes possible, uniting the King's English and the King's Scots.

1604: Shakespeare: *Measure for Measure.*

1605: Sir Francis Bacon writes *The Advancement of Learning.* Shakespeare: *King Lear, Macbeth.*

1606: Ben Jonson's play *Volpone* is finished. Shakespeare: *Antony and Cleopatra.*

1607: The first permanent settlement of English-speaking people is established in North America, the Jamestown colony in Virginia. Shakespeare: *Coriolanus, Timon of Athens.*

1608–1674: The life of John Milton.

1608: Shakespeare: *Pericles.*

1609: Shakespeare: *Cymbeline.*

1610: Shakespeare: *A Winter's Tale.* The Stationers' Company of England begins sending a copy of every book printed to the Bodleian Library at Oxford.

1611: Shakespeare: *The Tempest.* John Donne writes "An Anatomy of the World." The Authorized or King James Version of the Bible is published, having a profound influence on the written English language.

1612: Shakespeare: *Henry VIII.*

1622: Appearance of the first English newspaper, the *Weekly News.*

1623: The First Folio of Shakespeare's plays is published in London.

1660: English poet John Dryden notes his admiration of the Académie Française and its goal of "fixing" the French language. He suggests a similar organization be set up to do the same thing for English.

1664: The Royal Academy of London appoints a committee to consider ways of improving English as a language of science.

1688: Aphra Behn's *Oronooko, or the History of the Royal Slave,* is published. It is one of the first novels written in English, and the first English novel written by a woman.

1700: By the beginning of the eighteenth century English privateers, explorers, and settlers have introduced the English language in North America (United States and Canada), Bermuda, Barbados, Jamaica, China, and India. As Early Modern English comes into contact with other languages and dialects, it begins emerging as Modern English.

1704: Sir Isaac Newton prints his second major scientific work, *Opticks*, in English.

1707: The Act of Union unites England and Scotland into the United Kingdom but keeps separate the respective state educational systems, legal systems, and religions.

1712: Following Dryden's footsteps, Irish writer Jonathan Swift proposes an English Academy to "fix" the English language.

1731: The Law French is finally abolished in England.

1755: Publication of Samuel Johnson's *Dictionary of the English Language*. For the first time, a written book exists that purports to represent "real" English.

1759–1796: The life of Scottish poet Robert Burns, who kindles a romantic resurgence of interest in the "old" Scottish dialect.

1768–1771: Initial publication of the first parts of the *Encyclopedia Britannica*.

1770–1850: The life of poet William Wordsworth.

1771–1832: The life of Sir Walter Scott.

1776: The English colonies in America revolt and declare their independence. The United States becomes the first country outside of England to have English as its principal language.

1777: Dolly Pentreath, the last native speaker of Cornish, dies.

1800: At the beginning of the nineteenth century, English explorers, colonists, and convicts have introduced the English language in Australia and New Zealand, and the island of Gibraltar has been ceded to Great Britain.

1803: The Act of Union incorporates Ireland into the United Kingdom.

1828: Noah Webster publishes his *American Dictionary of the English Language*, marking the emergence of American English as a dialect distinct from the English spoken in Great Britain.

1835: English becomes the official language of education for Indians in India.

1835–1910: The life of Samuel Langhorne Clemens, a.k.a. Mark Twain.

1839: Dutch settlers in southern Africa establish the first Boer Republic.

1842: The Philological Society is founded in London, dedicated to the study of comparative and historical philology. The Society will later sponsor the writing of the *Oxford English Dictionary*.

1856–1950: The life of Irish playwright George Bernard Shaw.

1858: The Philological Society calls for the creation of a new and accurate English dictionary.

1868: American inventor Christopher Latham Sholes and his associates patent the first typewriter.

1873: Formation of the English Dialect Society.

1876: Alexander Graham Bell invents the telephone.

1879: James A. H. Murray begins editing the Philological Society's *New English Dictionary on Historical Principles*, later renamed the *Oxford English Dictionary of the English Language*.

1882–1941: The life of James Joyce.

1887–1949: The life of American linguist Leonard Bloomfield.

1889: Formation of the American Dialect Society.

1900: By the beginning of the twentieth century, the English language has been introduced by explorers and settlers into Ceylon (Sri Lanka), Trinidad, southern Africa (now South Africa), Sierra Leone, Gambia, and Singapore.

1901: Guglielmo Marconi broadcasts the first radio message across the Atlantic Ocean, from Cornwall to Newfoundland.

1903–1950: The life of George Orwell.

1904: Cornish nationalist Henry Jenner publishes *A Handbook of the Cornish Language*, beginning a revival of interest in Cornish.

1906: The English Association is formed. The Fowler brothers publish *The King's English.*

1907: Lee De Forest's De Forest Radio Telephone Company broadcasts the first regular studio-based radio show in the United States. A powerful new media influence on spoken English is born.

1916: The Easter Uprising in Ireland takes place, a climax to centuries of partly language-inspired rebellion against England.

1919: Publication of H. L. Mencken's *The American Language*.

1921: A treaty is signed between the United Kingdom and the Irish Free State, which accepts dominion within the British Empire. *Dream Street*, produced by United Artists, is the first full-length "talkie" motion picture; and another powerful new media influence on spoken English begins to emerge. Publication of anthropologist Edward Sapir's book *Language*.

1922: James Joyce's *Ulysses* is published. Publication of Otto Jesperson's book *Language: Its Nature, Development, and Origin.*

1923: *Time* magazine begins publication.

1925: Afrikaans gains official status as a language in South Africa. Scottish inventor John Baird transmits recognizable human features by radio—the first effective television broadcast.

1926: Publication of Fowler's *Dictionary of Modern English Usage.*

1928: Birth of American linguist Avram Noam Chomsky.

1928: Publication of the *Oxford English Dictionary* is completed seventy years after it was first proposed. James Baird demonstrates a form of color television.

1933: Philo Farnsworth develops electronic television. Linguist Leonard Bloomfield's book *Language* is published.

1936: BBC London begins regular television broadcast service, launching the electronic medium that will have the most profound influence on the spread of the English language of any twentieth-century development.

1937: In Wales, a new constitution for the National Eisteddfod makes Welsh its official language.

1938: The invention of the first photocopying process.

1939: The Lakeland Dialect Society is established to sustain interest in and use of the regional Cumbrian English dialect. Publication of James Joyce's *Finnegans Wake.*

1945: World War II comes to an end. Modern English is well on its way to becoming the first true global language, World English.

1946: Chester Carlson invents the Xerox process of photocopying.

1951: The UNIVAC business computer begins operation in the United States.

1961: South Africa leaves the British Commonwealth and adopts Afrikaans and English as its two official languages. *Webster's Third International Dictionary* is published.

1962: The Welsh Language Society is established to promote the Welsh language. The Society soon launches its first activist protests aimed at gaining wider use of Welsh.

1965: *Aspects of the Theory of Syntax*, by American linguist Noam Chomsky, is published, creating a revolution in modern linguistics.

1967: The *Kesva Tavas Kernewek*, or Cornish Language Board, is established to revive and re-create the ancient Celtic Cornish language. The Welsh Language Act gives Welsh equal standing with English in Wales; Wales is no longer deemed part of England.

1969: Canada officially becomes bilingual, with French and English established as co-equal official languages.

1974: Ned Maddrell, the last native speaker of Manx Gaelic, dies.

1977: The Voyager 1 and 2 spacecraft are launched to the outer planets and beyond; each carries a record containing recordings of greetings in English (and many other languages) to any extraterrestrials who may someday find the spacecraft. Steven Jobs and Stephen Wozniak introduce the Apple II computer, the first modern desktop or personal computer. Personal computers will utterly change the storage and dissemination of the written English language.

1981: IBM introduces their personal computer.

APPENDIX 7

SCIENTIFIC NOMENCLATURE, WEIGHTS AND MEASURES

Whenever this book refers to scientific measurements it uses the SI (Systeme Internationale) or so-called metric system. Rather than slow you down with pauses to convert meters into feet or kilometers into miles, I have chosen to use metric system nomenclature throughout the book as if it were the accepted measurement system everywhere in the world, rather than everywhere except the United States and Great Britain. For those of us who would still like to "translate" centimeters into inches, though, here is a conversion table and an explanation of the more common SI abbreviations and prefixes.

Abbreviations and Prefixes for Numbers

a	atto-	=quintillionth	=0.000000000000000001	$=10^{-18}$
f	femto-	=quadrillionth	=0.000000000000001	$=10^{-15}$
p	pico-	=million millionth (trillionth)	=0.000000000001	$=10^{-12}$
n	nano-	=thousand millionth (billionth)	=0.000000001	$=10^{-9}$
u	micro-	=millionth	=0.000001	$=10^{-6}$
m	milli-	=thousandth	=0.001	$=10^{-3}$
c	centi-	=hundredth	=0.01	$=10^{-2}$
k	kilo-	=thousand	=1,000.0	$=10^{3}$
M	mega-	=million	=1,000,000.0	$=10^{6}$
G	giga-	=thousand million (billion)	=1,000,000,000.0	$=10^{9}$
T	tera-	=million million (trillion)	=1,000,000,000,000.0	$=10^{12}$
P	peta-	=thousand million million	=1,000,000,000,000,000.0	$=10^{15}$
E	exa-	=million million million	=1,000,000,000,000,000,000.0	$=10^{18}$

Metric Abbreviations

micrometer	= um
millimeter	= mm
centimeter	= cm
kilometer	= km
gram	= g
second	= s

Conversion Factors

Length			
1 cm	= 0.39 in	1 in	= 2.54 cm
1 m	= 3.28 ft or 1.09 yd	1 ft	= 30.5 cm or 0.305 m
1 km	= 0.62 mi	1 yd	= 91.44 cm or 0.9144 m
		1 mi	= 1.6 km
Mass			
1 g	= 0.04 oz	1 oz	= 28.3 g
1 kg	= 35 oz or 2.2 lb	1 lb	= 0.45 kg or 454 g

List of Sources

Allman, William F. The Clues in Idle Chatter. *U.S. News and World Report* (Aug. 19, 1991): 61–62.

———. The Mother Tongue. *U.S. News and World Report* (Nov. 5, 1990): 60–70.

Ambrus, Katherine. A Sense of Scents. *The Conservationist* (July 1987): 42–47.

Austerlitz, Robert. Alternatives in Long-range Comparison. In *Sprung From Some Common Source*, ed. Sydney M. Lamb and E. Douglas Mitchell, 353–64. Stanford, CA: Stanford University Press, 1991.

Bach, Emmon, and Roger Harms, eds. *Universals in Linguistic Theory*. New York: Holt, Rinehart & Winston, 1968.

Barinaga, Marcia. Priming the Brain's Language Pump. *Science* (Jan. 31, 1992): 535.

Beveridge, H., transl. *The Akbarnama.* 3 vols. Society of Bengal: Bibliotheca Indica, 1897–1910.

Black, Max. *The Labyrinth of Language*. New York: New American Library, 1968.

Blakeslee, Sandra. Brain Yields New Clues on Its Organization for Language. *New York Times*, Sept. 10, 1992.

———. Scanner Pinpoints Site of Thought as Brain Sees or Speaks. *New York Times*, June 1, 1993.

Bloomfield, Leonard. *Language*. New York: Holt, Rinehart & Winston, 1933.

Bower, Bruce. Babies Sound Off: The Power of Babble. *Science News* (June 21, 1986): 390.

———. Brain Images Reveal Key Language Areas. *Science News* (Sept. 1, 1990): 134.

———. Left Brain May Serve as Language Director. *Science News* (March 7, 1992): 149.

Burchfield, Robert. *Unlocking the English Language*. New York: Hill & Wang, 1991.

Campbell, Jeremy. *Grammatical Man: Information, Entropy, Language, and Life*. New York: Simon & Schuster, 1982.

Cannon, Garland. Jones's "Sprung From Some Common Source": 1786–1986. In *Sprung From Some Common Source*, ed. Sydney M. Lamb and E. Douglas Mitchell, 22–47. Stanford, CA: Stanford University Press, 1991.

Castaldo, Nancy. Animal Communication. *The Conservationist* (Sept. 1992): 16–23.

Chapman, Robert L. Language. In *Encyclopedia Americana*, vol. 16, 727–30. Danbury, CT: Grolier, 1988.

Chomsky, Noam. *Language and Problems of Knowledge: The Managua Lectures*. Cambridge, MA: MIT Press, 1988.

———. *Language and Mind*. New York: Harcourt Brace Jovanovich, 1972.

———. *Syntactic Structures*. The Hague: Mouton, 1957.

Creutzfeldt, O., et al. Neuronal Activity in the Human Lateral Temporal Lobe. I. Responses to Speech. *Experimental Brain Research* 77 (1989): 451–75.

———. Neuronal Activity in the Human Lateral Temporal Lobe. II. Responses to the Subject's Own Voice. *Experimental Brain Research* 77 (1989): 476–89.

Creutzfeldt, O., and G. Ojemann. Neuronal Activity in the Human Lateral Temporal Lobe. III. Activity Changes During Music. *Experimental Brain Research* 77 (1989): 490–98.

Crichton, Ian. Hybrid World of Pidgin and Creole. *Geographical Magazine* (May 1991): 12–13.

Crystal, David, ed. *The Cambridge Encyclopedia of Language*. New York: Cambridge University Press, 1987.

Damasio, Antonio R. Aphasia. *New England Journal of Medicine* (Feb. 20, 1992): 531–39.

———. The Brain Binds Entities and Events by Multiregional Activation From Convergence Zones. *Neural Computation* 1 (1989): 123–32.

———. Category-related Recognition Defects as a Clue to the Neural Substrates of Knowledge. *Trends in Neuroscience* (March 1990): 95–98.

———. Concepts in the Brain. *Mind and Language* (Spring/Summer 1989): 24–28.

———. Synchronous Activation in Multiple Cortical Regions: A Mechanism for Recall. *Neurosciences* 2 (1990): 287–96.

———. Time-locked Multiregional Retroactivation: A Systems-level Proposal for the Neural Substrates of Recall and Recognition. *Cognition* 33 (1989): 25–62.

Damasio, Antonio R., and Hanna Damasio. Brain and Language. *Scientific American* (Sept. 1992): 89–95.

Damasio, Antonio R., Daniel Tranel, and Hanna Damasio. Face Agnosia and the Neural Substrates of Memory. *Annual Review of Neuroscience* 13 (1990): 89–109.

Damasio, Antonio R., et al. Neural Regionalization of Knowledge Access: Preliminary Evidence. *Cold Spring Harbor Symposia on Quantitative Biology* 15 (1990): 1039–47.

Damasio, Hanna, and Antonio R. Damasio. The Neural Basis of Memory, Language, and Behavioral Guidance: Advances With the Lesion Method in Humans. *Neurosciences* 2 (1990): 277–86.

Davis, Joel. *Endorphins: New Waves in Brain Chemistry*. New York: Dial Press/Doubleday, 1984.

Diamond, Jared. Reinventions of Human Language. *Natural History* (May 1991): 22–28.

Dickerman, Edmund H. Languages of the World. In *Encyclopedia Americana*, vol. 16, 731–39. Danbury, CT: Grolier, 1988.

Dworkin, Paul. I'm Talkin'. *American Baby* (Oct. 1992): 96–122.

Egerod, Søren. Far Eastern Languages. In *Sprung From Some Common Source*, ed. Sydney M. Lamb and E. Douglas Mitchell, 205–32. Stanford, CA: Stanford University Press, 1991.

Eilers, Rebecca E., et al. The Role of Prematurity and Socioeconomic Status in the Onset of Canonical Babbling in Infants. In *Infant Behavior and Development*. In press.

Forward, Robert L., and Joel Davis. *Mirror Matter: Pioneering Antimatter Physics*. New York: John Wiley & Sons, 1988.

Gamkrelidze, Thomas V., and V. V. Ivanov. Early History of Indo-European Languages. *Scientific American* (March 1990): 110–16.

Garvey, Catherine. *Children's Talk: The Developing Child*. Cambridge, MA: Harvard University Press, 1984.

Gazzaniga, Michael S. *Nature's Mind: The Biological Roots of Thinking, Emotions, Sexuality, Language, and Intelligence*. New York: Basic Books, 1992.

Gelernter, Carey Quan. Baby Talk: Look Who's Listening. *Seattle Times*, March 9, 1992).

Geschwind, N. Aphasia. *New England Journal of Medicine* 284 (1971): 654–56.

———. Disconnexion Syndromes in Animals and Man. *Brain* 88 (1965): 237–94.

Gibbons, Ann. Déjà Vu All Over Again: Chimp-language Wars. *Science* (March 29, 1991): 1561–62.

Goodglass, H., and J. Berko. Agrammatism and Inflectional Morphology. *Journal of Speech and Hearing Research* 3 (1960): 257–67.

Goodglass, H., and E. Kaplan. *The Assessment of Aphasia and Related Disorders*. Philadelphia: Lea & Febinger, 1983.

Gould, Stephen Jay. Grimm's Greatest Tale. *Natural History* (Feb. 1989): 20–28.

———. *The Mismeasure of Man*. New York: Norton, 1981.

———. Hands-on Babbling. *Science News* (March 30, 1991): 205.
Hayes, Curtis W., Jacob Ornstein, and William W. Gage. *The ABCs of Languages and Linguistics*. Lincolnwood, IL: National Textbook, 1989.
Henson, Robert. Ugly Human at Two O'clock. *Discover* (June 1992): 18.
Horgan, John. Early Arrivals: Scientists Argue Over How Old the New World Is. *Scientific American* (Feb. 1992): 17–18.
Horgan, John. Free Radical: A Word (or Two) About Linguist Noam Chomsky. *Scientific American* (May 1990): 40–44.
Jakobson, R., and M. Halle. *Fundamentals of Language*. The Hague: Mouton, 1956.
James, Sharon L. *Normal Language Acquisition*. Boston: Little, Brown, 1989.
Kaiser, M., and V. Shervoroshkin. Nostratic. *Annual Review of Anthropology* 17 (1988): 309–29.
Kempler, Daniel, and Daina Van Lancker. The Right Turn of Phrase. *Psychology Today* (April 1987): 20, 22.
Koch, Christof. When Looking Is Not Seeing: Towards a Neurobiological View of Awareness. *Engineering and Science* 61 (Spring 1993): 2–13.
Kosellcek, Reinhart. Linguistic Change and the History of Events. *Journal of Modern History* (Dec. 1989): 649–66.
Kuebelbeck, Amy. Babies 'Talk': UW Decodes Their Body Language. *Seattle Times*, Aug. 14, 1990.
Kuhl, Patricia, et al. Linguistic Experience Alters Phonetic Perception in Infants by Six Months of Age. *Science* 255 (Jan. 31, 1992): 606–8.
Lamb, Sydney M., and E. Douglas Mitchell, eds. *Sprung From Some Common Source*. Stanford, CA: Stanford University Press, 1991.
Lewin, Roger. Linguists Search for the Mother Tongue. *Science* 242 (Nov. 25, 1988): 1128–29.
———. Trees From Genes and Tongue. *Science* 242 (Oct. 28, 1988): 514.
Luria, A. R. *Higher Cortical Functions in Man*. New York: Basic Books, 1966.
McArthur, Tom, ed. *The Oxford Companion to the English Language*. New York: Oxford University Press, 1992.
McCrum, Robert, et al. *The Story of English*. New York: Viking Penguin, 1986.
McNeill, David. *Psycholinguistics: A New Approach*. New York: Harper & Row, 1987.
Medvescek, Chris Ravashiere. Toddler Talk. *Parents Magazine* (Dec. 1992): 72–77.
Mish, Frederick C., editor in chief. *Webster's Ninth New Collegiate Dictionary*. Springfield, MA: Merriam-Webster, 1988.
Morell, Virginia. The Big Picture. *Science* 248 (April 27, 1990): 440.
———. Confusion in Early America. *Science* 248 (April 27, 1990): 439–41.
Murchison, C., and S. K. Langer. Tiedemann's Observations on the Development of the Mental Faculties of Children. *Pedagogical Seminary and Journal of Genetic Psychology* 34 (1927): 205–30.
Ojemann, George A. Cortical Organization of Language. *Journal of Neuroscience* 11, no. 8 (Aug. 1991): 2281–87.

Oller, D. Kimbrough. Description of Infant Vocalizations and Young Child Speech: Theoretical and Practical Tools. *Seminars in Speech and Language* 13, no. 3 (Aug. 1992): 178–93.

———. Development of Vocalizations in Infants. In *Human Communications and Its Disorders*, ed. H. Winitz. In press.

Oller, D. Kimbrough, and Rebecca E. Eilers. Development of Vocal Signaling in Human Infants: Toward a Methodology For Cross-species Vocalization Comparisons. In *Nonverbal Vocal Communications*, ed. Hanuš Papovšek, Uwe Jürgens, and Mechthild Papovšek, New York: Cambridge University Press, 1992.

———. The Role of Audition in Infant Babbling. *Child Development* 59 (1988): 441–49.

———. Similarity of Babbling in Spanish- and English-learning Babies. *Journal of Child Language* 9 (1982): 565–77.

Peters, Robert A. *A Linguistic History of English*. Boston: Houghton Mifflin, 1968.

Peterson, Ivars. Neural Networks for Learning Verbs. *Science News* (Feb. 27, 1993): 141.

Petitto, Laura Ann. On the Ontogenetic Requirements for Early Language Acquisition. In *Developmental Neurocognition: Speech and Face Processing in the First Year of Life*, ed. de Boysson-Bardies, et al., 365–83. New York: Kluwer Academic Press, 1993.

Pettito, Laura Ann, and Paula F. Marentette. Babbling in the Manual Mode: Evidence for the Ontogeny of Language. *Science* 251 (March 22, 1991): 1493–96.

Pinker, Steven. Rules of Language. *Science* 253 (Aug. 2, 1991): 530–35.

Pulgram, Ernst. Linguistics. In *Encyclopedia Americana*, vol. 17, 525–32. Danbury, CT: Grolier, 1988.

Renfrew, Colin. *Archaeology and Language: The Puzzle of Indo-European Origins*. New York: Cambridge University Press, 1987.

———. Origins of Indo-European Languages. *Scientific American* (Oct. 1989): 106–14.

Restak, Richard M. *The Brain*. New York: Bantam Books, 1984.

Rice, Mabel R., and Susan Kemper. *Child Language and Acquisition*. Baltimore: University Park Press, 1984.

Ross, Philip E. Are Humans Born to Speak? *Scientific American* 264 (April 1991): 146–47.

———. A Discipline Where Caution Prevails. *Scientific American* 264 (April 1991): 144.

———. Dueling Linguists. *Scientific American* 264 (April 1991): 142–43.

———. Hard Words. *Scientific American* 264 (April 1991): 138–47.

———. New Whoof in Whorf: An Old Language Theory Regains Its Authority. *Scientific American* (Feb. 1992): 24, 26.

Shevoroshkin, Vitaly, and Alexis Manaster Ramer. Some Recent Work on the Remote Relations of Languages. In *Sprung From Some Common*

Source, ed. Sydney M. Lamb and E. Douglas Mitchell, 178–99. Stanford, CA: Stanford University Press, 1991.

Stevenson, Victor, ed. *Words: The Evolution of Western Languages*. New York: Van Nostrand Reinhold, 1983.

The New Jerusalem Bible. Garden City, NY: Doubleday, 1985.

Theivenin, Deborah M., et al. Where's the Drift in Babbling Drift? A Cross-linguistic Study. *Applied Psycholinguistics* 6: (1985): 3–15.

Thomas, Clayton L., ed. *Taber's Cyclopedic Medical Dictionary*. 14th ed. Philadelphia: F. A. Davis, 1981.

Tyler, Charles. Speaking in Tongues. *Geographical Magazine* (May 1991): 10–14.

Watkins, Calvert. New Parameters in Historical Linguistics, Philology, and Culture History. *Language* 65 (1989): 783–99.

Werker, Janet F. Becoming a Native Listener. *American Scientist* 77 (Jan. 1989): 54–59.

Wilford, John Noble. In a Publishing Coup, Books in 'Unwritten' Languages. *New York Times*, Dec. 31, 1991.

Winner, Ellen. *The Point of Words: Children's Understanding of Metaphor and Irony*. Cambridge, MA: Harvard University Press, 1988.

Yarrow, Leah. Babbles, Coos, and Gurgles: How Babies Learn to Talk. *Parents Magazine* 65 (Sept. 1990): 69–75.

Young, Charles M. and Noam Chomsky: Anarchy in the U.S.A. *Rolling Stone* (May 28, 1992): 42–47, 70–73.

Zuckerman, Lord. Apes R Not Us. *New York Review of Books* (May 30, 1991): 43–49.

INDEX